TWENTIETH CENTURY WAR MACHINES

LAND

TWENTIETH CENTURY WAR MACHINES

CHRISTOPHER CHANT

ILLUSTRATIONS BY
JOHN BATCHELOR

LAND

CHANCELLOR
PRESS

This edition published by Chancellor Press
an imprint of Bounty Books, a Division of the
Octopus Publishing Group Ltd,
2-4 Heron Quays, London, E14 4JP

Printed in 1999
by Tat Wei Printing Packaging Singapore Pte Ltd

Contents

Portentous Beginnings

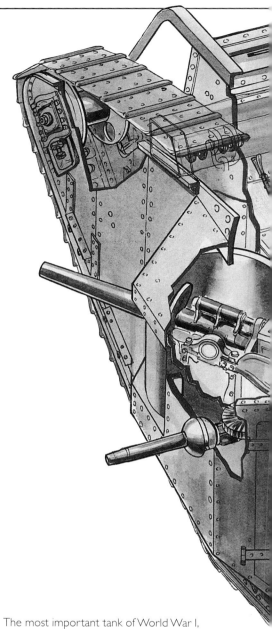

By November 1914, the mobile phase of World War I (1914-18) had ended, and a system of parallel trench lines, protected by barbed wire entanglements and machine-gun positions, extended between the North Sea and the Swiss frontier to end all chance of mobile warfare until a key could be found to unlock the trench system. In these trench lines German soldiers faced a coalition of Belgian, British and French soldiers, and the tactical method that evolved as each side sought to break the stalemate of this system was the infantry attack supported by artillery bombardment. The preliminary artillery bombardment always failed to cut all the barbed wire and destroy all the machine-gun positions, and thus the infantry assault that followed the artillery bombardment inevitably stalled on the defences or, in the event of an incipient breakthrough, ran out of momentum on ground churned into a quagmire by incessant artillery fire.

What was needed was a new tactical concept, one that would allow a penetration through barbed wire and past machine-gun posts, and would thus obviate the need for a massive and sustained artillery bombardment. The result was the tank, which was the concept of a number of British officers in 1915 and first emerged during December of that year as the Little Willie, which immediately demonstrated its superiority over the original No.1 Lincoln Machine conceptual prototype.

Little Willie was obsolescent even as it appeared, however, for even before the No.1 Lincoln Machine had started its trials, problems were emerging over the basic design's lack of stability when surmounting an obstacle. A new machine was therefore planned as the rhomboidal- or lozenge-shaped tank that became standard in World War I, combining the parapet-climbing superiority of the original but impractical 'bigwheel' concept with the trench-crossing, stability and silhouette advantages of the tracked chassis. The specification for the vehicle, to be called Big Willie, was settled in September.

The building of the new machine was seriously hampered by labour problems at Foster's of Lincoln, where the secrecy of the work was such that the employees could not be given war worker badges, and began to leave when they were accused of cowardice for not having volunteered for the services. During construction the machine was variously called the Wilson Machine, the Centipede, and Big Willie, but finally emerged at the end of 1915 as Mother, which weighed 28.45 tonnes and was powered by a 105hp (78.3kW) Foster-Daimler engine. Built of boiler plate rather than the lightweight pressed steel proposed for the production version, the machine had two lateral sponsons each carrying in its front a naval 6pdr (57mm) quick-firing gun; there were also four machine-guns disposed one in the rear of each sponson, one in the bow and one at the rear. Naval guns were used as the army's Master General of the Ordnance was opposed to the tank concept and therefore refused to release any weapons for use in the new machines.

Mother first ran in December 1915, at about the time that the cover name 'water carrier' (soon amended to 'tank') was ordained at Colonel Ernest Swinton's instigation in preference to the revealing name of 'landship'. After

The most important tank of World War I, the Tank Mk IV was a British type whose development was started in October 1916 for a first run in March 1917 and initial commitment to combat in the Battles of Messines, 3rd Ypres and Cambrai in the second half of 1917. The Mk IV was a development of the original Mk I incorporating a number of lessons learned from the production and combat employment of that type. This cutaway view illustrates the layout of the rhomboidal tank that proved successful in the trench warfare conditions of World War I. The tank had a crew of eight, and its two primary production models were the Tank Mk IV (Male) with a primary armament of two 6pdr (57mm) guns in the forward parts of the sponsons and a secondary armament of four 0.303in (7.7mm) Lewis or 0.315in (8mm) Hotchkiss machine guns, and the Tank Mk IV (Female) with an armament of six machine guns.

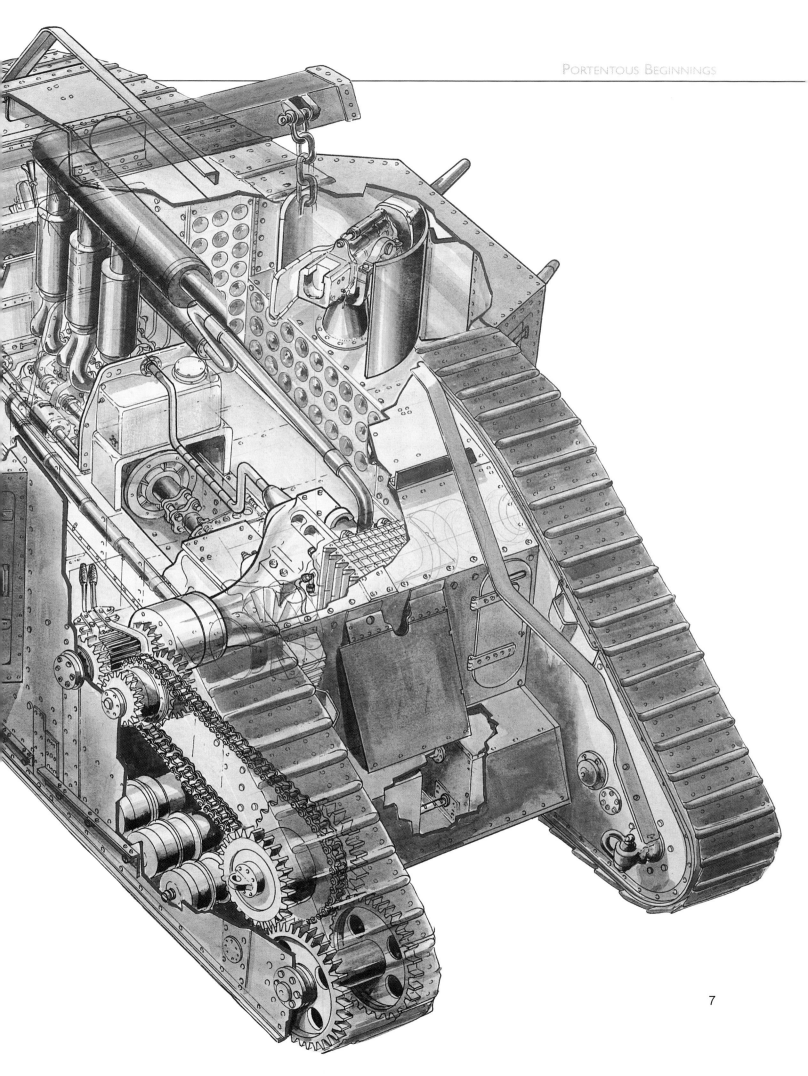

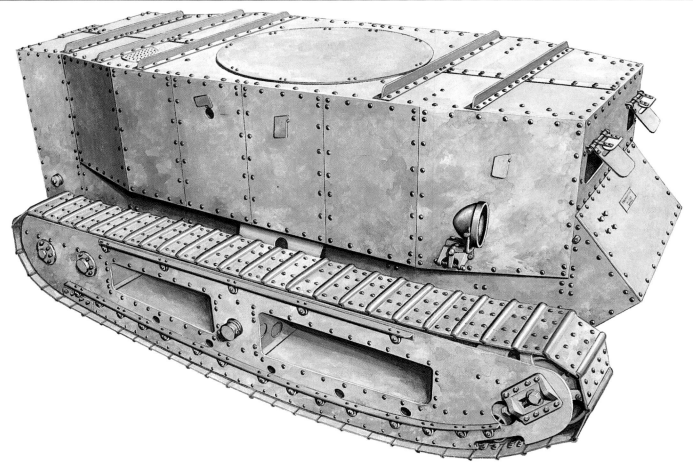

initial and successful running trials, Mother was fully completed in January 1916 and moved, together with Little Willie, to Hatfield Park for two official trials and demonstrations. Both tanks were put through trials in terrain very similar to that of the Western Front (complete with British and German trench layouts), and Mother was judged worthy of production. The Ministry of Munitions had refused to allow tank production in December, but in February the ministry relented, and ordered the production of 100 tanks based on Mother (25 by Foster's and the other 75 by the Metropolitan Carriage, Wagon and Finance Co.).

Winston Churchill, First Lord of the Admiralty and an early advocate of the tank, was now in France, having been forced to resign in May 1915 when a coalition government took over from the Liberal administration after the failure of the Dardanelles campaign. Though now only a regimental officer, Churchill sent to Field Marshal Sir Douglas Haig, the British commander-in-chief in France, a paper entitled 'Variants of the Offensive' which exaggerated the state of tank development and persuaded Haig to despatch Major Hugh Elles to report personally on the new weapon. It was Elles's approval that persuaded Haig to think in terms of an order for 40 tanks that led to the initial plan for 100 vehicles, later increased to 150.

In March 1916 the new tank arm was formed under Swinton, the conceptual father of the tank, initially as the Armoured Car Section, Motor Machine-gun Service, and then from May as the less revealing Heavy Section, Machine-gun Corps. (After the tank had been used in action the name was changed in November 1916 to the Heavy Branch, Machine-gun Corps and in July 1917 to the Tank Corps.) As the men for the new branch were being recruited and trained, production of the service version of Mother, the Tank Mk I, was being undertaken for the first deliveries to be made in June. At first it was planned

The Little Willie was the second tank prototype to be built, and was a development of the No.1 Lincoln Machine with revised trackwork to allow it to cross a 5ft (1.52m) trench and climb a 4ft 6in (1.27m) parapet. The simulated turret of the No.1 Lincoln Machine was removed and the resulting hole in the upper surface plated over, and the machine was generally operated with a pair of rear-mounted steering wheels (not illustrated).

that the production model should be all but identical with Mother, other than construction in mild steel rather than boiler plate and the installation of a frame of wood and chicken wire over the roof to prevent 'bombs' (grenades) from detonating on it.

However, in April 1916 Swinton decided that a proportion of the tanks (ultimately fixed at half of the production run) should be completed with the Hotchkiss 6pdr (57mm) guns replaced by two machine-guns. The more powerful variant was designated Tank Mk I Male, and at a combat weight of 28.45 tonnes carried an armament of two Hotchkiss L/40 guns in limited-movement mountings plus three or four Hotchkiss machine-guns: the role of this variant was to tackle guns, emplacements and other fixed defences. The lighter variant, with a combat weight of 27.43 tonnes, was designated Tank Mk I Female and carried an armament of one or two Hotchkiss air-cooled machine-guns plus four water-cooled Vickers machine-guns (in place of the Male's guns and sponson-mounted machine-guns): the role of this variant was protection of the heavier Males from infantry attack, and pursuit of enemy infantry.

The men of the new army branch were soon coming to grips with their extraordinary new machines, which offered great things but were extremely uncomfortable. The Tank Mk I lacked any form of sprung suspension, vision of the outside world was limited by the small size of the few vision slits, the engine was unsilenced (internal communication had to be undertaken mostly by hand signalling) and ventilation was virtually nonexistent. And, as operations were shortly to confirm, while the tank's construction (soft steel that was cut and drilled and then hardened before being bolted together) may have provided protection from small-arms fire, it was prone to spall and splash when struck on the outside. The crew had to wear thick clothing and face protection to avoid being pierced and cut by shards flying off the inside of the armour when it was struck on the outside (spall), or hit by the molten metal that penetrated the tank's ill-fitting plates when bullets melted upon hitting the tank (splash).

Seen on trials with the rear-mounted pair of steering wheels, the Little Willie was decidedly superior to the No.1 Lincoln Machine from which it was developed, but was already obsolescentin concept by the time it appeared as the immediate future lay with the rhomboidal tank with tracks running round considerably larger track frames on each side of the vehicle.

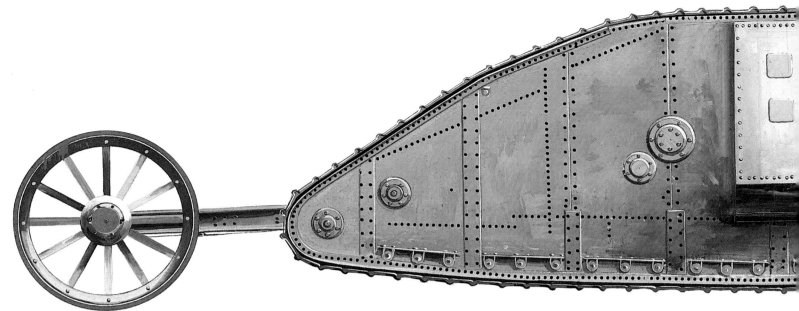

The tank went into action for the first time in September 1916 in one of the subsidiary components of the Battle of the Somme, namely the Battle of Flers-Courcelette: here the British Reserve and 4th Armies were to punch a 4 mile (6.4km) hole in the German line at Flers and Courcelette in the sector between Thiépval and Combles, the 10 assault divisions being supported by a proposed 50 tanks. Yet such was the technical infancy of the new weapon that some 18 Mk I tanks had broken down before the assault started, and the surviving 32 machines were allocated in penny packets (the largest number being seven tanks) to lead the infantry into battle with the totally dumbfounded German troops. In the event the tanks did well, but their role was hopelessly misjudged and their effect was minimal.

Although the tanks' actual successes had been poor, their use had finally persuaded the sceptical officers in France that the tank was a potentially decisive weapon. Tank orders were stepped up and tank arm personnel was increased to 9,000 by February 1917 and to 20,000 by the time of the Armistice in November 1918. After Flers-Courcelette, Haig requested the production of another 1,000 tanks. Stern moved swiftly to order the required armour and powerplants, although the limited power of the Foster-Daimler petrol engine led this astute pioneer to consider alternatives to this weakest feature of the Tank Mk I. That the army as a whole was still uncommitted to the tank found expression in the Army Council's October cancellation of Haig's order; however, the order was reinstated by Lloyd George, who was a keen advocate of any device that could reduce the horrific toll of head-on infantry battles. Lloyd George was to become prime minister on 6 December 1916, and Stern persuaded him of the need not only for more tanks but for better tanks. An improved machine was now under development as the Tank Mk IV, but to maintain the production of existing designs, Lloyd George sanctioned the assembly of 100 examples of Tanks Mk II and Mk III, essentially the Mk I with detail modifications. The Mk II (50 built) had a revised roof hatch with raised coaming and wider track shoes at every sixth link for greater traction, while the Mk III (50 built) was the Mk II armoured to the standard of the Mk IV. The Mks II and III complemented the Mk I machines in the trench battles of early 1917, but these first three models were rapidly superseded by the Mk IV during the second half of the year. Once discarded as first-line tanks, the Mks I, II and III were used as training tanks or as wireless tanks (one sponson fitted out as a 'wireless office' and the other carrying the

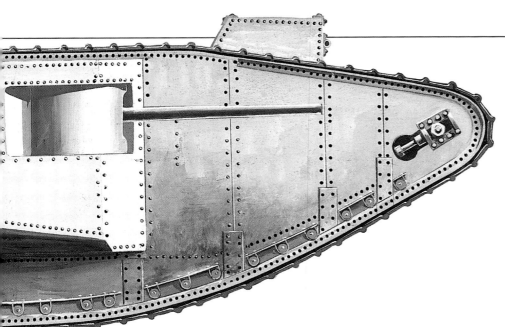

Mother was the true prototype of the basic design concept that became standard for British tanks in World War I. The nature of the tracks running right round rhomboidal frames gave the lower part of the trackwork approximatly the shape and radius of a 60ft (18.3 m) wheel for good trench-crossing and parapet-climbing capability. The revisionof the tracks meant, however, that a superimposed turret would have created centre of gravity problems, and it is this factor that led to the decision to use sponsons located on the outside of the plating that supported the track on each side.

wireless equipment) or, with their sponsons removed and the resultant openings plated over, as supply tanks.

The Tank Mk IV introduced sponsons with upward-swept lower sides, but this more practical design was not carried forward to the supply tenders' panniers. Each supply tank could tow three sleds each carrying 22.40 tonnes of stores, and in the case of Mk IV conversions an uprated 125hp (93.2kW) engine was often fitted to provide greater tractive power. These supply tanks were generally used to ferry forward ammunition and fuel, and to carry back the most seriously wounded.

By February 1917, the Tank Mk IV was ready for production. The type still relied on the indifferent Foster-Daimler engine and its associated gear system, but was otherwise a much improved vehicle incorporating the lessons of Flers-Courcelette. Several of the earlier tanks had suffered because of the gravity feed system from their internal fuel tank, which leaked petrol over the inside of the tank if it was punctured, and failed to work if the tank was ascending or descending a steep parapet. In the Mk IV, the fuel tank was moved to the outside of the vehicle between the rear horns, increased in capacity, provided with armour, and fitted with a pump to ensure an uninterrupted flow of petrol. Other major improvements included the use of thicker armour to defeat the Germans' new anti-tank rifle bullets; steel 'spuds' bolted to every third, fifth or ninth track shoe to increase traction; smaller sponsons that could be shifted inboard rather than removed for transport; an exhaust and external silencer for the engine; improved internal stowage, ventilation and cooling; shorter 6pdr (57mm) L/23 guns to prevent the muzzles digging into the ground; an unditching beam carried above the vehicle on special rails; and 0.303in (7.7mm) Lewis machine-guns in place of the original Hotchkiss weapons in ball-and-socket mountings. Experience soon confirmed that the Lewis gun was unsuitable for tank use as its air-cooling system filled the tank with fumes, the gun itself was vulnerable to enemy fire, and the need for a large opening in the sponson to accommodate the gun's air-cooling jacket increased the problem of splash (a revised Hotchkiss was then substituted, although without the original form of very limited-movement trunnion mounting).

Delivery of Mk IV tanks began in April 1917, and the production of 1,015 tanks was undertaken in the ratio of three female to two male tanks. The Tank Mk IV Female was somewhat different to the earlier females, for the sponsons

were shallower (allowing the incorporation of a pair of hatches on each side in the area previously covered by the sponson) and narrower. The lighter weight of these sponsons contributed significantly to the reduction in combat weight to 26.418 tonnes.

The growing sophistication of the tank is attested by the development of several Mk IV variants as dictated by the nature of combat experience. Possibly the most important of these was the Mk IV Fascine Tank. In its original form this could carry wooden fascines on its unditching beam rails, these chain-bound bundles of brushwood being dropped over the nose under control of the driver; later versions carried hexagonal wood or steel cribs for the same purpose of filling a trench and providing a roadway for the tank's further progress.

The key moment for the Tank Mk IV, and indeed for the tank in general, came in November 1917 with the beginning of the Battle of Cambrai. This was the first occasion in which tanks were used in a homogeneous mass, and the practice nearly proved decisive. The British 3rd Army was entrusted with a surprise offensive against the German 2nd Army: in ideal terrain conditions to the south of Cambrai, the British army was to attack without the protracted artillery bombardment that had previously been standard. This novel concept was designed to give the Germans no forewarning of the offensive, and also to prevent the ground from being churned up, which ensured excellent progress for the 400 tanks that spearheaded the offensive behind a sharp creeping barrage that forced the Germans to keep their heads down. Tactical surprise was achieved by this novel approach, and the tanks were instrumental in opening a 6 mile (9.7km) gap in the German line, through which the British advanced to a depth of 5 miles (8km). Two cavalry divisions were poised to exploit any advantage, but the extent of this success caught the British so unexpectedly that there were insufficient infantry and tanks in reserve to allow any rational exploitation. The Germans recovered with remarkable speed, and their counterattacks from the end of the month forced the British to fall back most of the way to their start line. The Battle of Cambrai was thus a draw,

The order for 100 (later 150) operational tanks based on the design of Mother was placed in February 1916, and resulted in the Tank Mk I that differed from Mother in being fabricated from armour rather than boiler plate, in having a raised frontal cupola for the commander and driver, and in possessing lateral sponsons that could be removed to facilitate rail transport. A problem with this last facility lay in the fact that the tank lacked sufficient torsional rigidity to resist the 'wringing' that could result from this practice, which often made it difficult to re-install the sponsons. The vehicle illustrated here is a Tank Mk I (Male) with a primary armament of two 6pdr (57mm) guns and a secondary armament of four Vickers or Hotchkiss machine-guns. Other details of the eight-man Tank Mk I (Male) included a weight of 28 tons, length of 32ft 6in (9.91m), width of 13ft 9in (4.19m), height of 8ft (2.44m), and speed of 3.7mph (5.95 km/h) on its 105 hp (78.3kW) Daimler-Foster petrol engine.

The tank of World War I was vulnerable to a number of factors including high-velocity bullets fired by special rifles, artillery fire on the rare occasions that such guns could be brought to bear, mechanical breakdown, and the conditions typical of the northern part of the Western Front, where churned ground, mud, shell holes, and the very size of the trench network could bring such vehicles to a halt.

but this cannot disguise the fact that the first mass use of tanks had in general secured unprecedented results.

As usual, however, a large number of tanks had suffered mechanical breakdown, and many tanks were captured by the Germans as they pushed back the British. Impressed with the capabilities of the tanks, and lacking their own counterparts, the Germans rushed the captured machines to their depot at Charleroi for refurbishment and re-arming: the 6pdr (57mm) guns were replaced by Sokol 57mm guns captured from the Russians, and the 0.303in (7.7mm) machine-guns by 7.92mm (0.31in) MG08 weapons. The vehicles were then issued to the Germans' fledgling tank arm with the designation Beutepanzerwagen IV, the comparative extent of British and German tank production at this time being indicated by the fact that captured tanks equipped four of the Germans' seven tank companies in December 1917.

As noted above, Stern appreciated from the early days of the Mk I that the weakest point of the tank was its transmission/gearing and associated Foster-Daimler petrol engine. To meet operational requirements, the Mk IV was rushed into production and service even as Stern was investigating alternative powerplants, and from October 1917 the Tank Supply Department had a modest breathing space in which to consider other tank automotive systems. These included a Wilson mechanical transmission and steering system using epicyclic gears and brakes instead of the standard change-speed gearing, which offered the possibility of one-man control without the potential problems of the petrol-electric systems.

Wilson was entrusted with the overall design of the tank to use his epicyclic gearbox, and this emerged as the Tank Mk V with hull and armament based on those of the Mk IV but fitted with the Wilson gearbox and a new 150hp (112kW) Ricardo petrol engine. The Tank Mk V Male weighed 29.466 tonnes and the Tank Mk V Female 28.45 tonnes, but the use of a more powerful engine and additional fuel tankage boosted maximum speed and range. The Mk V went into production at the Birmingham works of the Metropolitan Carriage, Wagon and Finance Co. during December 1917, and began to reach service

Designed as a fast tank to undertake the cavalry role of exploiting any breakthrough created by its larger brethren, the medium tank was based on a higher power/weight ratio, lower trackwork, and a lighter armament operated by a smaller crew. This cutaway view reveals the salient details of the first such type to enter service, namely the Tank Medium Mk A otherwise known as the Whippet or Tritton Chaser, the latter referring to its designer, William (later Sir William) Tritton of William Foster & Co. Ltd. The type first ran in October 1917, and was notable for the location of the engine and fuel tank at the front, with the fighting compartment, carrying three or four Hotchkiss machine-guns with 5,400 rounds of ammunition, at the rear. The other details of the three-man Whippet included a weight of 14 tons, length of 20ft (6.1m), width of 8ft 7in (2.62m), height of 9ft (2.74m), and speed of 8.3mph (13.35 km/h) on its two 45 hp (33.6kW) Tylor JB petrol engines.

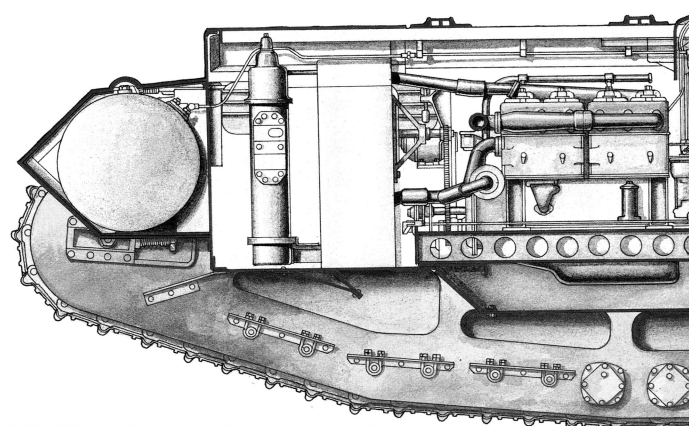

units in May 1918 in equal numbers of male and female tanks, of which a proportion were converted in the field to Tank Mk V Hermaphrodite standard. One-man control of the Mk V's automotive system greatly improved control and manoeuvrability, and the more powerful engine made useful contribution to performance, but the Mk V was also considerably advanced over its predecessors in its better engine cooling and ventilation system; the provision of a cupola above the roof at the rear for the commander, who thus had far better fields of vision than in earlier tanks; and facility for the unditching beam to be connected and disconnected from inside the vehicle, thereby obviating the need for at least two crew members to leave the vehicle.

The Mk V first went into action at Hamel in July 1918, and thereafter partnered the more numerous Mk IV for the rest of World War I. The tank was dimensionally similar to the Mk IV, and suffered the same limitations when faced with a wide trench. Consequently, the Mk V was evaluated with a 'tadpole tail' as pioneered on the Tank Mk IV to improve trench-crossing capability, but a better expedient was adopted after development by the Tank Corps Central Workshops in France from February 1918. This resulted in the Tank Mk V*, in which the vehicle was cut in half to allow the insertion of a

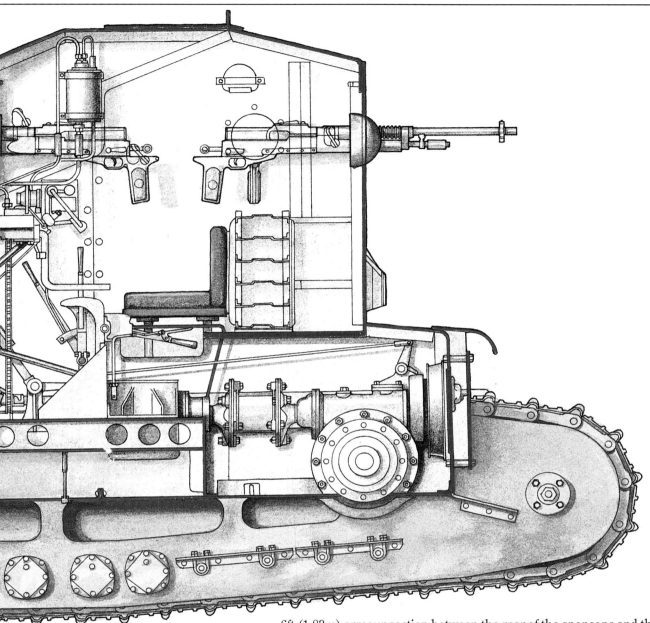

6ft (1.83m) armour section between the rear of the sponsons and the epicyclic gearbox, increasing ground length and providing a 13ft (3.96m) trench-crossing capability, at an increase in weight of 4.064 tonnes. The additional section carried two machine-gun positions to complement the standard fit based on that of the Mk IV, already boosted by the provision of two positions in the new commander's cupola. The extra weight reduced performance slightly and manoeuvrability considerably, but the additional length increased internal volume to the extent that the Mk V* could be used to carry either 25 troops (who suffered badly from the heat and the poor ventilation), or a substantial load of supplies. Production was undertaken by Metropolitan from May 1918, and 579 examples had been built by the time of the Armistice.

The Mk V* was the ultimate version of British mainstream battle tank development to see service in World War I, no fewer than 324 Mk V and Mk V* tanks spearheading the decisive breakthrough offensive of 8 August 1918 in the Battle of Amiens, which the German commander, General Erich Ludendorff, characterized as 'the black day of the German army'. In this offensive the Mk IV and Mk V variants were partnered by a number of light tanks.

The Allied concept of military operations after November 1914 had been posited without significant deviation on a breakthrough of the German line and exploitation into the enemy rear. Even before the battle tank had begun to prove itself as a weapon for the breakthrough phase, tank advocates had begun to work on a lighter and more mobile tank suitable for the exploitation phase, for the battle tank was too slow and too short-ranged for any but the most direct battlefield tasks. In 1916, Tritton designed a high-speed tank with light armour for the task of co-operating with the cavalry, and this initial 'Whippet' scheme was revised from December 1916 as the Tritton Chaser or, more prosaically, the Tritton No.2 Light Machine. The type first ran in February 1917, and trials were generally successful. Various changes were required before a firm order was placed in June 1917. The definitive version became the Medium Tank Mk A, generally named the Whippet, and deliveries from Foster's began in October 1917, to meet the initial requirement for 200 machines. This order was subsequently increased to 385, but then reduced once more to 200 when it became clear that the double automotive system of the Mk A was both expensive to produce and difficult to maintain at a reasonable standard of reliability.

The overall design of the Whippet was totally different to that of the battle tank, with long low-set unsprung tracks whose shoes were based on those of battle tanks but were of lighter construction and fitted with provision for spuds: the tracks were long enough to provide a 7ft (2.13m) trench-crossing capability. The track units were fitted on each side with four chutes along much of the length of the top run to keep the tracks clear of mud. The long forward section of the hull above the upper run of the tracks accommodated two 45hp (33.6kW) Tyler petrol engines, located side by side and each provided with its own clutch and gearbox to drive one track. Twin throttles were located on the steering wheel, their movement together controlling acceleration of this 14.225 tonne vehicle to a maximum speed of 8.3mph (13.4km/h). Movement of the driver's steering wheel worked on the throttles to increase the power of one engine and decrease that of the other (to a maximum variation of 12hp/8.95kW), and so providing additional power to one track or the other. The system was complex and extremely demanding on the driver, who often stalled one engine in a tight turn and then shed a track, thus immobilizing his vehicle.

The fighting compartment at the rear of the vehicle, was essentially a fixed barbette (the original notion of a rotating turret having been abandoned to simplify production), and was occupied by the driver, commander and one or two gunners, and equipped with three or four

The Tank Mk IV (Female) was designed to accompany infantry and to protect the Tank Mk IV (Male) from attack by enemy infantry. It was soon appreciated that such tanks were vulnerable to destruction by the heavier guns carried by German tanks, and a number were therefore adapted to Tank Mk IV (Hermaphrodite) standard with one of the standard machine gun-armed female sponsons replaced by a male sponson carrying one 6pdr (57mm) gun and one machine-gun. Others were adapted to the Tank Mk IV (Fascine) standard illustrated here. This was designed to create passages over the extra-wide trenches of the Germans' Hindenburg Line defences by dropping a fascine: this was a chain-wrapped bundle of wooden rods some 10ft (3.05m) long and 4ft 6in (1.37m)in diameter. Variations on the basic fascine theme were a hexagonal wooden crib and a steel crib.

Medium Tank Mk B Whippet

PRODUCTION of the Medium Tank Mk A was limited to 200 vehicles by the appearance of the more advanced Medium Tank Mk B, which was also nicknamed Whippet. This was based on a new automotive system using a single 100 hp (74.6kW) Ricardo petrol engine located, for the first time in a tank, in a dedicated compartment of its own at the rear of the vehicle and driving the tracks by means of epicyclic gearing. This resulted in greater manoeuvrability, improved reliability and reduced production cost. The Mk B was designed by Major Wilson, and differed from the Mk A in being a larger vehicle based on the rhomboidal shape of the larger tanks with all-round tracks. Mounted on the front of the hull was a large turret :in the Mk B (Male) form that was not built this would have been a revolving unit carrying one 2pdr (40mm) gun, and in the Mk B (Female) form it was a fixed unit carrying four Hotchkiss machine guns with 7,500 rounds of ammunition. Design work was completed late in 1917, but in mid-1918 before an order was placed for 450 such vehicles, of which the first ran in September 1918. Only 45 had been completed by the time of the armistice in November 1918, when further production was cancelled as the Mk B had lower performance than the Mk A, provided cramped conditions for its four-man crew, and offered an engine compartment whose advantages in terms of reduced interior noise and fume levels were offset by a very cramped design that made working on the engine all but impossible unless it was removed.

Hotchkiss machine-guns for all-round fire. The second gunner and the
Hotchkiss in the rear of the barbette were usually omitted by operational
units to mitigate the appalling conditions inside the barbette.

The type first saw action in March 1918 near Herbertune in northern
France, and was used up to the end of the war. The type's greatest moment
came in the Battle of Amiens on 8 August 1918, when the 3rd Tank Brigade's
two battalions were fully equipped with 96 Mk A machines. The brigade was
tasked with support of the Cavalry Corps, and although liaison was poor
some useful results were gained. The major tactical problem was apparent
in good conditions, when the cavalry was faster than the tank brigade and
had to deal with the opposition whilst waiting for the tanks to catch up. As

17

The Germans' first tank design was notably unsuccessful, and the German army therefore pressed into service a number of British vehicles, often captured after suffering a mechanical breakdown and revised to Beutepanzerwagen IV standard with the 6pdr (57mm) guns replaced by 57mm Sokol cannon captured from the Russians and the machine-guns replaced by 0.312in (7.92mm) MG 08/15 machine-guns.

a result, the tanks were not employed in a homogeneous mass that might have completely destroyed the German rear areas to a depth of 10 miles (16km) or more. The Mk As were used in small numbers attached to specific cavalry units, but nonetheless achieved the successes that fully vindicated their overall capabilities.

The type was limited by its use of two low-powered engines and unsprung tracks, and in an effort to overcome these limitations, Major Philip Johnson, an Army Service Corps officer serving at the Tank Corps Central Workshops in France, reworked the design with sprung tracks and a 360hp (268kW) Rolls-Royce Eagle aero engine working through the transmission of a Mk V battle tank: speeds well over 20mph (32km/h) were achieved, but this important advance failed to find favour.

At much the same time that Colonel Swinton was first pleading his case to the War Office for armoured fighting vehicles, the same pattern of events was emerging in France where Colonel J. E. Estienne had seen the cross-country capability of the Holt tractor and, working from this conceptual basis, advocated the development of what he called a cuirassé terrestre (land battleship) to unlock the static nature of trench warfare. Estienne's ideas found ready acceptance in the mind of General Joseph Joffre, the French field commander, who saw great tactical use for Estienne's original concept for a 4 tonne armoured tractor with a crew of four, and able to drag a 7 tonne armoured sled carrying 20 infantrymen. The similarity to Swinton's original thinking is strong, and Estienne's tactical notion was that such an armoured force could 'sandwich' the occupants of the desired trench by pushing half its strength across the trench to isolate it and keep it under machine-gun fire.

Joffre appreciated the advantages of such a combination but was sufficiently astute to realize its impracticality. Ultimately, the French army reached the same conclusions as the British about the need for a tracked armoured vehicle that could cross barbed wire and knock out German machine-gun posts, and so open the way for the attacking infantry. Joffre therefore ordered Estienne to Paris where he was to liaise in the development of France's first tank with Eugene Brillie of the Schneider-Creusot company. This was the French licensee of the American Holt company, which had supplied one 45hp (33.6kW) and one 75hp (55.9kW) machine for trials purposes in May 1915. The basic design made extensive use of Holt components and practices, and was completed towards the end of 1915; on 31 January 1916 an order was placed for 400 of these tanks, to be designated Char d'Assaut 1 (CA 1) Schneider and delivered by November 1916. The Artillerie d'Assaut, as the French tank arm was named, was created in August 1916, and the first CA 1 Schneiders were delivered in September, just before Estienne was appointed commander of the tank arm.

The CA 1 Schneider was based on the Holt track system, which in this application was sprung by vertical coil springs and notable for its short overall length and very limited forward rise. The all-important trench-crossing and parapet-climbing capabilities were therefore wholly indifferent, and ground clearance was insufficient to give the tank useful performance under adverse conditions. The hull was basically rectangular, with a boat-hull nose section to aid parapet-climbing and reduce the tank's chances of embedding its nose in mud, and terminated at its front with a large serrated wire cutter. At the rear were a pair of upward-curving projections, designed to increase trench-crossing capability by increasing the tank's effective length. The CA 1 Schneider massed 13.50 tonnes under combat conditions, and was powered by a 55hp (41kW) Schneider petrol engine located at the front left of the vehicle (with the driver to its right), driving the tracks via a crash gearbox: steering was effected by clutches and brakes on the half shafts. As in the British Mk I, the petrol tank was located internally, to feed the engine by gravity. The CA 1 Schneider had a crew of six (an officer as commander/driver, an NCO as second-in-command, and four enlisted men in the form of a gunner, a loader and two machine-gunners), who entered and left the tank via large double doors in the rear. The armament was planned originally as one 37mm gun plus machine-guns, but the definitive fit comprised one short-barrel 75mm (2.95in) Schneider gun and two 8mm (0.315in) Hotchkiss machine-guns.

The CA 1 Schneider first saw action at Berry-au-Bac near the Chemin des Dames on 16 April 1917: of the 132 tanks committed, no fewer than 57 were destroyed and many others were damaged beyond economical repair. The primary culprits for this disaster were a combination of poor design and the

Schneider CA 1

DESIGNED for the assault role, namely the breakthrough of the Germans' trench lines so that the infantry and the cavalry could pour through the breech as undertake a deep exploitation into the enemy's rear areas to destroy artillery positions and supply lines, the Schneider CA 1 was not notably successful because of its poor trackwork. This was too short and too low to provide adequate trench-crossing and parapet-climbing capabilities, which were only 5ft 9in (1.75m) and 2ft 7in (0.787m) respectively despite the use of a lower hull with a boat-shaped 'stern' and 'bow', the latter with a tall wire breaker projecting upward and forward from the structure. The Schneider CA 1 was based on a maximum 11.5mm (0.45in) of armour, and its dimensions included a length of 20ft 8.75in (6.32m), width of 6ft 7in (2.05m) and height of 7ft 6.5in (2.30m). The tank had a crew of six, and its armament comprised one 2.95in (75mm) gun with 90 rounds of ammunition in a right-hand side sponson, and two 0.315in (8mm) machine-guns with 4,000 rounds of ammunition. The Schneider CA 1 was powered by a 55hp (41kW) Schneider petrol engine, and this was sufficient for a speed of 4.6mph (7.5km/h) on roads.

Germans' special 'K' bullet with its tungsten carbide core, which could penetrate the French armour without undue difficulty. The poor design concerned mainly the dismal ventilation and the location of the fuel tankage next to the machine-guns. After several tanks had blown up, the CA 1 Schneider was dubbed the 'mobile crematorium', an epithet that was slow to disappear even after the internal tankage had been replaced by two armoured external tanks; ventilation was also improved, but remained a problem under certain conditions. Protection was enhanced by the addition of rudimentary spaced armour over the most vulnerable areas.

Development and production of the CA 1 Schneider had bypassed the French army's normal vehicle procurement executive, the Service Technique Automobile (STA), which was sufficiently piqued to instigate the design and construction of another battle tank. This was the Char d'Assaut Saint Chamond, designed by Colonel Rimailho and ordered from the Compagnie des Forges et Acieries de la Marine et Homecourt (FAMH) at Saint Chamond. The first prototype was completed in February 1916, and two months later the STA ordered 400 of the type. Like the CA 1 Schneider, the CA Saint Chamond was based on the Holt sprung tractor system, although in this application with the track length increased by about 0.3m (0.98ft). This was clearly a basic improvement over the trackwork of the CA 1 Schneider, but was totally offset by the superimposition of an extraordinarily long hull: the result was cross-country performance still worse than that of the CA 1, with the tendency to ditch, even on slightly undulating ground; in terms of performance in front-line conditions, this translated into abysmally poor trench-crossing and parapet-climbing capabilities.

Two unusual features of the CA Saint Chamond were its provision for a unique rear driving position and its use of electric drive for the tracks. The Crochat-Collardeau electric generator was driven by a 90hp (67.1kW) Panhard petrol engine, and current was supplied to the electric motor attached to each track's drive sprocket. Differential powering of the tracks provided considerable agility within the limitations imposed by the hull, and

Built in very large numbers during World War I for the French and several of their allies, and maintained in production after the war in many variants for the French and a number of export customers, the Renault FT17 was the first successful light tank developed anywhere in the world, and was a simple yet effective and reliable vehicle with a two-man crew and an armament of one cannon or one machine-gun. This is an FT 17 in service with a unit of the US Army during the Argonne fighting of 1917.

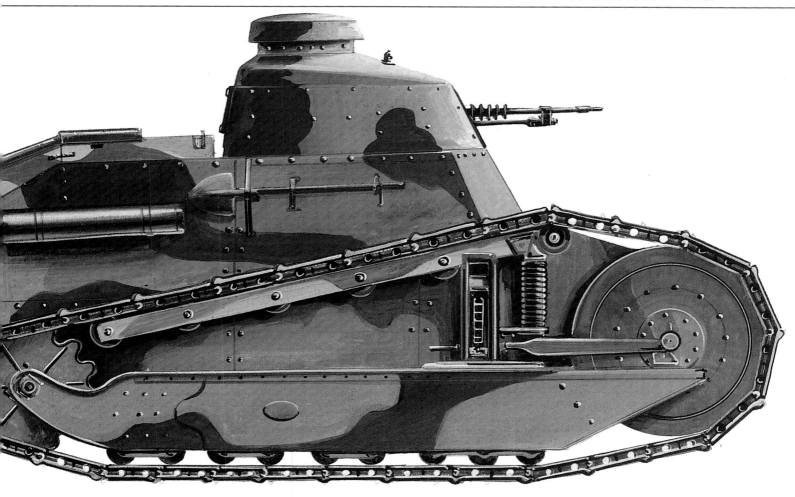

despite a combat weight of 22.00 tonnes the CA Saint Chamond had useful performance. The primary disadvantage of the electric drive system was its weight, which added to the mobility problems engendered by the long hull, which terminated at its forward end in a well-sloped glacis plate above an angled-back vee-shaped lower surface designed to help the tank ride over earth banks .

The CA Saint Chamond possessed a crew of eight including the driver and commander, who each had a small cupola at the front of the vehicle; access to the vehicle was provided by a door in each side plus another in the tail plate. The armament comprised one 75mm (2.95in) Saint Chamond TR commercial gun (first 165 vehicles) or one 75mm (2.95in) Modèle 1897 gun (last 235 vehicles), and four 8mm (0.315in) Hotchkiss machine-guns. The main gun was located in a limited-traverse mounting in the glacis plate, and the machine-guns were placed one in the bow (on the lower right-hand side), one in the tail plate, and one on each side of the hull. Deliveries of the CA Saint Chamond began in late 1916, and the type was first used in action in May 1917 at Moule de Laffaulx. In this first engagement, the limitations of the design became all too apparent: of 16 CA Saint Chamonds committed, 15 ditched in the first line of German trenches. Further action confirmed the need for modifications, which included: increasing the armour thickness against the effect of the German 'K' anti-tank bullet, a raised forward section of the hull, the elimination of the commander's cupola, the replacement of the original flat roof with a pitched roof so that grenades would roll off, and the use of wider tracks. These measures improved the tank's capabilities,

Weighing 6.7 tons, the FT 17 light tank had its driver in the forward lower part of the hull and its commander/gunner in the revolving turret. The vehicle was 16ft 5in (5.0m) long with the optional tail that increased its lower-hull length and thus its trench-crossing capability, 5ft 8.5in (1.74m) wide and 7ft 0.25in (2.14m) high, and was powered by a 35hp (26kW) Renault petrol engine for a speed of 4.8mph (7.7km/h). The armament illustrated here is a 0.315in (8mm) Hotchkiss machine-gun, for which 4,800 rounds of ammunition were supplied, and the alternative installation was one 37mm cannon for which 237 rounds of ammunition were supplied.

but nothing could be done about the basic design flaw in the vehicle's configuration, and from May 1918, when the final deliveries were made, the type was stripped of its main gun and used for supply tasks as the Char Saint Chamond de Ravitaillement.

Both the French chars d'assaut were perhaps ahead of their British contemporaries in gun calibre and in locating this single weapon in a central mounting, but the French designers had been too impressed with the cross-country capabilities of the Holt tractor to realize that a long track length combined with a large forward rise were essential elements for adequate trench performance. The two French tanks were thus little more than incidentals to the French army's war effort, although they did play an important part in the development of 'tank consciousness' and in the evolution of tank tactics and organization. However, the most important French tank of World War I was an altogether different machine, the Renault FT light tank, the designation indicating Faible Tonnage (light weight). The concept stemmed from Estienne's desire for a lightweight partner to his CA 1: the heavy tank would crush barbed wire and deal with the German strongpoints, and the lightweight machine would accompany the attacking infantry to suppress any surviving pockets of German resistance and develop the exploitation phase of any breakthrough.

Yet again, Estienne bypassed the normal channels of procurement, and in October 1917 went straight to Joffre with his scheme for 1,000 examples of a 4.00 tonne light tank carrying one 8mm (0.315in) machine-gun or a smaller number carrying one 37mm gun in a 360-degree traverse turret, armoured against small-arms fire, and possessing a maximum speed of

The FT 17 and its successors were comparatively cheap to build and possessed the advantages of useful manoeuvrability and considerable agility. Another advantage was the revolving turret, although this was limited in its utility by its ability to carry only one man, who had to double as the commander and gunner. Even so, the advanced nature of the FT series was reflected in the type's retention in service by several nations right into the opening part of World War II, some 25 years after the type had been designed.

The Dilemma of Turret Size

WITH the development of the turret on the Renault FT series, tank designers first encountered a problem that still remains, namely the optimum size of the turret. In essence, the answer to this dilemma is that there is no complete solution other than the fact that the designer must arrive at a judicious compromise. On the one hand, a large turret allows the incorporation of a larger and therefore more destructive and longer-ranged gun, allows the addition of the extra equipment that is inevitably required during the tank's operational life, and offers better working conditions for a larger and therefore tactically superior crew, which under ideal conditions can include a commander who controls the operation of the vehicle and looks for targets, a gunner and a separate loader. On the other hand, a large turret is more visible to the enemy and therefore more vulnerable, is heavier and therefore tends to destabilize the tank as well as degrade performance on the power of a given engine, and is also more expensive to produce in terms of material and man hours required. The designer therefore has to consider all these factors and arrive at a design that offers the blend of protection, gun size, crew size and working volume that best satisfies the requirements of his country's army.

12km/h (7.5mph). Estienne also proposed, in a very far-sighted manner, that a number of the machines should be completed with wireless equipment to allow communication between commanders and their mobile forces. Despite considerable resistance from some parts of the French war ministry, Estienne's notion found sufficient favour to secure authorization of prototype production after a mock-up had been completed at the end of 1916. The first prototypes appeared in February and March 1917, and immediately displayed excellent qualities in trials at the Champlieu camp. An initial order for 150 FTs was placed on 22 February 1917, but at the insistence of General Henri Pétain, the French commander-in-chief, the order was increased to 3,500 vehicles for delivery by the end of 1918, and additional orders increased the planned production run to more than double this figure. It was clear that Renault could not handle the orders on its own, and this important programme soon involved Belleville, Berliet, Delaunay, Renault and SOMUA as manufacturers, with a large number of other companies (including some in the United Kingdom) as subcontractors.

The FT was an unusual but interesting and successful tank in its technical and tactical features. Technically, the tank lacked a conventional chassis but was rather a monocoque of riveted armour plate, a box-like structure to which were attached the major internal and external components, terminating at the tail in an upswept plate that increased the effective length of the vehicle as an aid to trench crossing. The hull accommodated the driver at the front, the turret in the centre, and the combined engine and transmission assembly at the rear. The turret, surmounted at its rear by a mushroom-shaped observation cupola, was the world's first to offer 360-degree traverse. The engine was a 35hp (26.1kW) Renault petrol unit, and drove the tracks by means of a crash gearbox, with a clutch-and-brake system used for steering.

The first production tanks were completed in September 1917, but the whole programme was hampered by shortages of the special cast steel turret and by arguments within the army about the precise nature of the armament to be fitted. By the end of the year, Renault had delivered only 83 examples of the initial variant, which was designated the Char Mitrailleuse Renault FT 17 and was first used in combat on 31 May 1918 in the Forêt de Retz. The turret problem proved insoluble in the short term, and after the delivery of some pre-production vehicles with cast turrets, the producers designed their own eight-sided turrets of riveted plate construction, allowing larger-scale production from mid-1918 for the delivery of 3,177 tanks before the Armistice, against orders that currently totalled 7,820 including 3,940 from Renault. When the cast turret began to arrive in useful numbers it was installed on a version generally designated FT 18. The FT 17

Above: The LK.II was the German equivalent of the Medium Tank in British service, but was somewhat more heavily armed with a single 57mm gun in the front face of the fixed barbette above the hull rear. The vehicle was built only in small numbers, and was based on the chassis and axles of the Daimler car.

and FT 18 remained in service until the opening stages of World War II (1939-45), and were also exported in large numbers.

Such was the mainstream of French tank development in World War I, although a few experimental types were tested, including the Char 1, developed in two forms as a char de rupture (breakthrough tank) for the planned 1919 offensives and most importantly as the precursor of the Char 2C discussed below.

Given the dominant role played by German armour in the first half of World War II, it is interesting to note that Germany was not an outstanding tank operator in World War I. This cautious approach to the tank was not for lack of encouragement, for many army officers and civilians had advocated the development of tracked armoured vehicles. In was only after the British introduction of the tank as an operational weapon, however, that a major effort was launched towards the creation of a German tank superior in all significant capabilities to the British tank. Initial contracts were placed in

November 1916. Herr Steiner, the German representative of the Holt company, was appointed as adviser on the tracks, and the initial specification called for a Gelandespanzerwagen (all-terrain armoured machine) weighing 30.00 tonnes, powered by a 100hp (74.6kW) engine and armed with two guns (one in the front and the other in the rear) plus flank-mounted machine-guns or, in unarmed form, a payload of 4.00 tonnes.

The specification was hopelessly unrealistic, and failed to take into account the geography of front-line terrain. The Germans had to make an enormous technical effort in their attempt to catch up with the British, but like the French they made a large mistake in relying on the existing Holt track system as the core of their new vehicle, regardless of the fact that it lacked the cross-country capabilities required for parapet climbing and trench crossing. Working with Steiner, who was primarily tasked with the much-lengthened Holt track system, Josef Vollmer designed a massive machine, accommodating a crew of 18, that first ran in prototype form in April 1917. A wooden mock-up of the definitive version was inspected by the German general staff representatives in May 1917, and the design was accepted for production as the Sturmpanzerwagen A7V. The prototypes were thoroughly tested during the summer, and provided striking evidence of the design's failings, particularly in the tracks, and in the cooling system for the two 100hp (74.6kW) Daimler petrol engines that were located in the centre of the vehicle under the driver and commander. It was a practical but heavy drive system, decidedly lacking in power for a vehicle weighing 32.51 tonnes laden. This led to limited engine life and to overheating under all but the best of road conditions.

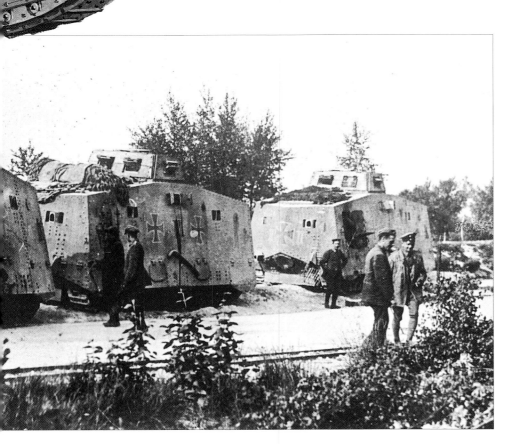

Slow and very unwieldy, the A7V was the only German heavy tank to enter production and service in World War I. The type had a large 18-man crew drawn from several branches of the German army, and this made the effective integration of the crew all but impossible. The tank's primary armament was a 57mm Sokol gun of which large numbers had been captured from the Russians, and a secondary armament of six 0.312in (7.92mm) MG 08/15 machine-guns was scattered round the sides of the large and highly vulnerable hull.

The Legacy of World War I

To most of the officers who reached senior rank during the war and remained in service after it, World War I was regarded as something of a military oddity that would, for reasons that they were unable to explain, not recur. Thus, in the opinion of these officers, never again would there be the conditions of trench warfare that required heavy tanks for assault purposes and light tanks for the exploitation of the breeches effected by these heavy tanks. The inevitable result of this thinking meant that there was little real demand for the retention of a tank arm after the war, or for the considerable expense of developing and producing more advanced tanks, especially of the heavy type for which no real role was foreseen. This woolly-headed belief in a return to the type of mobile warfare that hadt been seen as the norm in the second half of the 19th century, but which was now rendered impossible by the advent of barbed wire, the machine-gun and fast-firing artillery, was gladly seized upon by treasury departments desperate to reduce the scale of military spending in the 1920s, and led to the virtual end of tank development during this period. More advanced thinkers appreciated the potential of the tank, however, but these were generally more junior or middle-ranking officers whose opinions were usuallu condemned as having been tainted by the virtual heresy of armoured warfare.

The tracks lacked significant rise at their forward ends, limiting the A7V's parapet-climbing capability, while their short lengths provided only a disappointing trench-crossing ability. The low ground clearance also meant that the tank bellied on all but the levellest of hard surfaces; its performance on soft ground was poorer still. In short, therefore, the A7V had been designed as an armoured fort to co-operate with the infantry, but the German designers had neglected the aspect of mobility. The main armament, located in the bow plate, was a 57mm Sokol cannon from captured stocks, while the secondary armament comprised six 7.92mm (0.31in) MG08 machine-guns located as two in each side and two in the rear. The large crew was drawn from three separate army branches rather than from a homogeneous tank corps: the driver and two mechanics were engineers, the two men on the 57mm gun were artillerymen, and the commander and 12 machine-gunners were infantrymen.

The first vehicle was delivered in September 1917, the first fully-armoured example following in October. Daimler of Berlin was responsible for manufacture, the armour supplied by Krupp in Essen and from Steffens & Noelle in Berlin. There was considerable variation in the quality and nature of the armour plate supplied, some A7Vs having a hull made of a few large plates, but most having hulls in which smaller plates were riveted together (splash being a particular problem with these). There were still a large number of difficulties with the type, but the German general staff decided that it could wait no longer for improvements, and ordered 100 A7Vs on 1 December 1917, with delivery to be completed by the time of the great Spring offensives planned for 1918. Daimler, on the other hand, thought that a delivery rate of five per month was more practical, and only 35 or less machines had been delivered by the time of the Armistice. The type was first used operationally in the Battle of St Quentin in March 1918, and proved to be of little use for any task other than boosting the morale of the German infantry.

The only other countries to develop tanks to the hardware stage during World War I were Italy and the United States, which made determined efforts but achieved little success. The conditions in which the Italians were fighting the Austro-Hungarians were totally unlike those of the Western Front and therefore were not relevant to the armoured concept developed by the British and French. Neither the Italian nor the American types reached operational service in World War I.

Troubled Development

THE world's new tank arms had to ensure their survival, and secure emancipation from their positions subordinate to one of the armies' other arms. It was to be a difficult task occupying the 1920s and most of the 1930s. To the politicians, the tank could embody the concept of 'an engine of war' and thus smacked too strongly of militarism; to the economists, the tank represented a high level of development cost, followed by high production and operating costs; and to the professional heads of the world's most important armies the tank was an unessential embarrassment. The more far-sighted were content to see the retention of the tank in small numbers as an adjunct of the infantry (medium tank) and the cavalry (light tank), while the majority of soldiers wished to return to the pre-1914 pattern in which they had trained and gained most experience of practical soldiering. As a young arm, the tank service of most countries had attracted relatively junior officers with an interest in the mechanization that was becoming important in the period up to World War I, but without 'entrenched' attitudes to military operations. These men were able and eloquent, but had generally risen only into the lower levels of field rank, and were therefore able to achieve little but keep up a constant but carefully-controlled stream of propaganda to keep their tank arm alive pending the day it could prove itself.

Development of the tank in the period immediately following World War I was hindered by political, economic and social antipathy, and it was left to more far-sighted men to press ahead on shoestring budgets. One result was the Morris-Martel Tankette designed under the supervision of Major Sir Gifford Le.Q. Martel on the basis of commercial components supplied by the Morris company, which also undertook the construction of these prototype vehicles. This is the Two-Man Tankette of 1926, which was a half-tracked type with rear steering wheels.

The British squandered the technical and tactical lead they had established in World War I by a programme of parsimony so extreme that it could well have proved disastrous. Yet the British tank arm was saved by the twin efforts of men working solely within the professional confines of the army (middle-ranking officers such as P. Hobart, C. Q. Martel and Ernest Swinton), and a smaller number of men such as Colonel J.F.C. Fuller and Captain B. H. Liddell Hart, working mainly on the outside of the army framework to develop and promote their theories of armoured warfare.

Within the army, the middle-ranking advocates of armoured warfare worked to convince their largely sceptical superiors that the era of fully-mechanized warfare had arrived, and that the cornerstone of this new type of warfare was the tank. The army protagonists promoted the concept of the tank as embodying the primary virtues of firepower, protection and mobility in a package of unrivalled versatility; and at the same time they urged that the army opened its mind to the possibility of merging the new weapon with a new set of tactical doctrines whose absence would negate all the advantages of a tank force.

This accorded with the role played by Fuller and Liddell Hart, who were concerned not only with the practicalities of armoured warfare with present and future weapons, but with the 'ideal' of armoured warfare, and therefore the course in which the long-term development of tanks should be directed. At the core of the thinking of both Fuller and Liddell Hart was the concept that the tank was a new weapon, perhaps presaged in other weapons, but in its post-World War I form a weapon different from those of the infantry, cavalry and artillery, and as such requiring the formulation of a new set of tactical precepts.

Fuller was the tactical thinker par excellence, and his ideas stemmed directly from the British experience at Cambrai and Amiens: if it made full use of its mobility, the tank was unstoppable, giving its operating country

Seen coming to grief during its trials, the Fiat 3000 was the Italian-built development of the Renault FT with the engine mounted lower and transversely in the rear part of the hull. The original variant was the Fiat 3000 Modello 1921 with an armament of two machine-guns, but the vehicle seen here is the Fiat 3000 Modello 1930 (or Fiat 3000B) with a more powerful engine, exhaust silencers, a 37mm gun and a large vision cupola for the commander/gunner. The type was built in moderately large numbers for Italy, was exported to Albania, Ethiopia and Latvia, and was evaluated but not adopted by Denmark, Greece and Spain.

The DD (Duplex Drive) system was the British-developed method for creating an amphibious tank out of a conventional tank (here an M4 Sherman) without affecting its primary capabilities. The addition of a propeller provided propulsion on the water, and buoyancy was created by the addition of a folding canvas screen attached in a watertight fashion to the hull and erected only when waterborne operation was contemplated. The screen was lowered once the tank had reached land, thereby restoring the vehicle to full tank capability. The canvas screen could be discarded as the situation permitted.

the ability to strike at will against different points in the enemy's line; this would force the enemy onto the defensive and dilute his strength to the point that he would find it impossible to counter the tank attack and consequent breakthrough at the offensive's chosen point. The threat thus posed to the enemy's lines of communication would in turn force the enemy to retreat, the accumulation of such retreats leading inevitably to the enemy's defeat. Fuller was the great advocate of the 'all-tank' school of thinking, which averred that the evolution of the tank had rendered obsolete all other combat arms: cavalry had been rendered manifestly obsolete by the advent of mechanization, infantry was required merely to garrison that which the tanks had captured, and artillery should be replaced by special versions of tanks – fitted with large-calibre ordnances (self-propelled artillery) yet able to match the tank force for speed and mobility. In this last concept Fuller went too far, and in the process so threatened (or appeared to threaten) the established arms that they coalesced to frustrate Fuller's notions. In the long term, therefore, Fuller had a partially counterproductive effect on the development of the British tank arm when he moved out of the province of tactics into the more difficult intellectual and moral terrain of operational doctrine.

Working from the same basis of operational experience as Fuller, Liddell Hart transferred more easily from tactics into the field of operations and strategy, which were based on exploitation of the tank's speed (mobility) combined with its shock effect (firepower and protection). The key to Liddell Hart's concept was tactical and operational surprise: the initial offensive could be a hammer blow by massed armour into and through the enemy's front line, followed by an unrelenting exploitation in which the key was outright speed. Tanks must therefore be organized to push straight through the opposition or, if the opposition was too strong, to bypass and isolate it for elimination by the follow-up forces. By maintaining its impetus, Liddell Hart demonstrated, the tank force could punch through to the enemy's rear areas on a narrow front and then fan out in an 'expanding torrent' that would prevent the enemy's reserves from moving up in effective support: and then by destroying, capturing or incapacitating his command and logistic centres, the tank force would crush the enemy's capability to sustain the defence. It is worth noting here that Liddell Hart appreciated the full potential of the aeroplane for a battlefield role. Fuller had rightly realized the value of the aeroplane for reconnaissance and communication, but Liddell Hart recognized that the aeroplane was the ideal substitute for artillery in his 'expanding torrent', possessing greater mobility than the tank and having the three-dimensional agility to negate the effect of the enemy's anti-aircraft artillery while delivering attacks of great accuracy.

Liddell Hart's concept was remarkably far-sighted, but was not accepted in his own country as anything but an idealized picture of future warfare. This was a reaction with immense consequences.

The most important successes gained by the tank advocates were in the development of new vehicles, which possessed far greater mobility than their World War I predecessors in terms of agility, speed and range. The development programme was severely limited by lack of financial resources, and evolved via two main streams, namely the one- or two-man tankettes from Morris-Martel and Crossley-Martel, and the two- or three-man light tanks from Carden-Loyd and Vickers.

The tankette concept was forced on countries unable or unwilling to fund the development of larger and more capable vehicles, and was a conceptual dead-end, unimportant except as the precursor of the light tank.

The first practical light tank design was the Carden-Loyd Mk VII, a two-man vehicle that appeared in 1929 for evaluation as the A4E1. Although evolved from the earlier Carden-Loyd vehicles, the Mk VII provided striking proof of the pace of armoured vehicle development in the later 1920s, for it was a machine markedly superior to its predecessors in all respects. The armament was still a single 0.303in (7.7mm) Vickers machine-gun, but this was located in an exceptionally trim turret with bevelled edges on its top to reduce its silhouette. More notable, perhaps, was the increase in performance generated by the new running gear and more powerful engine.

Perpetuation of an Obsolete Doctrine

In the aftermath of World War I, Germany was prohibited from the possession and/or the development of tanks, and none of her allies of the defeated Central Powers had started work on such vehicles. Of the victorious Allies, the USA's tank-building industry was its its earliest infancy, the British, French and Italians were financially exhausted, and Russia (now the USSR after the Soviet Revolution of 1917) had yet to start on the design and production of tanks. It was France and the United Kingdom that were the only major powers capable of large-scale development of more advanced tanks. This was denied to them by a combination of financial retrenchment, moral and industrial exhaustion, and combined political and public antipathy to the concept of war and the weapons necessary for it. In the circumstances it was inevitable that tank development, such as it was, would be concentrated on small, and therefore cheap, vehicles designed to explore potentials and to keep alive the concept of armoured warfare. The resulting tankettes and light tanks inherited the mantle of World War I's medium tank in the 'cavalry' role, while tank designers and advocates pressed for the development of heavier tanks that inevitably came to be regarded as ideal for the 'infantry' role in two forms as the medium tank for the support task and the heavy tank for the breakthrough task. As funds for the development and procurement of these heavier tanks were made available in the late 1920s and early 1930s, the lighter tanks were retained in service rather than being discarded, and thus there emerged armoured forces based on two widely differing types of tank. The fallacy of this concept would be revealed only by World War II, which showed that the bulk of the armoured force should comprise multi-role battle tanks with good firepower, protection and mobility, with the balance comprising light tanks for the reconnaissance role with modest firepower and protection but very good mobility.

The former comprised four large road wheels in leafsprung pairs connected by an external girder, and the latter a 59hp (44kW) Meadows petrol engine: the result was a maximum speed of 35mph (56km/h) for this 2.54 tonne vehicle. Trials confirmed the overall suitability of the A4E1, which was developed for small-scale production as the Carden-Loyd/Vickers Light Tank Mk VIII, and accepted as the British army's first light tank in 1930 under the designation Light Tank Mk I. The running gear was revised and the new 58hp (43kW) Meadows EPT petrol engine provided a maximum speed of 30mph (48.3km/h) in a vehicle that weighed 4.88 tonnes.

The family directly evolved from the Carden-Loyd Mk VII ended with the Light Tank Mk III and Light Tank Mk IV. The Mk III entered service in 1933 as a Mk II with its superstructure lengthened to the rear, and the Mk IV series was produced in 1934 with a monocoque chassis to which components were directly attached.

By this time, the Royal Tank Corps had amassed a considerable volume of experimental and operational data with its first series of light tanks. Generally, it was satisfied that the light tank had a valuable role to play, although operational experience was limited to parts of the world where there was no effective opposition. However, while the monocoque hull, powerplant and running gear of the Mk IV still had value, the vehicle was limited in operational capacity by its one-man turret and its single machine-gun. An important step was thus taken with the 1935 adoption of the Light Tank Mk V. This was another Vickers-Armstrongs product, and was in practical terms the hull of the Mk IV with an enlarged fighting compartment surmounted by a new two-man turret. This was the first such unit fitted on a light tank, and for ease of traverse was mounted on a ball race: the armament comprised two Vickers machine-guns, one of 0.303in (7.7mm) and the other of 0.5in (12.7mm) calibre, and the turret was surmounted by a commander's cupola.

The Light Tank Mk VI entered service in 1936, and with it came the end of development by Vickers-Armstrongs on the basis of the Carden-Loyd Mk VII. The Mk VI was modelled closely on the Mk V, but with a longer hull

The Tank Mk IV was an effective weapon against barbed wire and machine gun strongpoints, and possessed the ability to traverse rough terrain and trench lines at modest speed. Even so, such behemoths could become bogged down, and in such circumstances the unditching beam carried on the top of the hull could be attached by chains to the tracks and thus brought forward, down and round to the underside of the trackwork to provide considerably greater traction for unditching purposes.

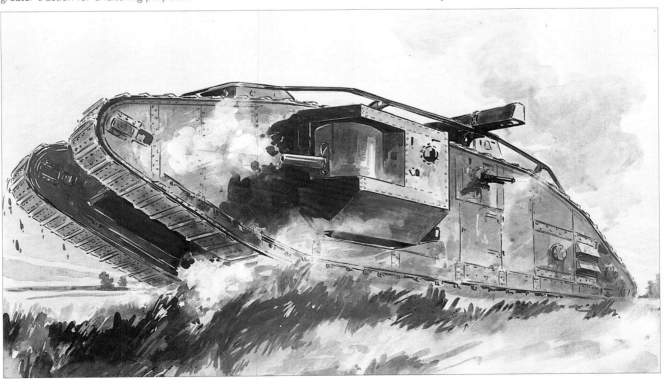

Lack of Operational Experience

PART of the problem with the develoment of tanks in the period between the two world wars was the operational vacuum in which the designers and operators lived. In the absence of major conflicts, at least up to the time of the outbreak of the Spanish Civil War in 1936, tank protagonists were forced to rely on their own conceptual thinking and on lessons that might be gleaned from the limited use of tanks in smaller wars such as the Gran Chaco War (1932-35) between Bolivia and Paraguay. These were hardly front-rank military nations even by South American standards, and the war was fought bitterly but inefficiently with tactical methods that resembled those of World War I and helped persuade those who followed such matters that the static nature of trench warfare was still relevant. The one occasion in which tanks were used, albeit in modest numbers, was in the Battle of Ayala (July 1933). Here the Bolivians attacked with three Vickers Six-Ton Tanks and two Carden Loyd tankettes, which operated in the support role: of the Six-Ton Tanks, one was finally knocked out by artillery fire, another by mechanical problems, and the third after an armour-piercing bullet had jammed its turret, and of the tankettes one was knocked out early in the engagement and the other was turned over in a trench. Two of the Six-Ton Tanks were repaired and committed again on the following day, but were withdrawn after all six crew members had been wounded by armour spall and bullet splash. The larger Six-Ton Tank was deemed to have been moderately successful, but the consensus was that the artillery shell and the armour-piercing bullet had the measure of the tank.

and the turret increased in length rearwards to allow the installation of a radio set. The type was mechanically reliable and cheap to produce, a combination that prompted large-scale orders: indeed, during the first month of World War II in September 1939, the British army fielded about 1,000 examples of the Mk VI family. Given the army's lack of recent combat experience against a high-quality enemy, these modest vehicles were used extensively in Europe, the Middle East and North Africa, and suffered heavy losses because of their lack of offensive and defensive capabilities.

The final pair of British three-man light tanks were both Vickers-Armstrongs designs: the Light Tank Mk VII Tetrarch of 1938 and its successor the Light Tank Mk VIII Harry Hopkins of 1941. The two types were built only in small numbers, and were similar in concept, being based on four independently-sprung road wheels of which the rear units served as drive sprockets and the front units as idlers; the steering was unusual, sharp turns were acheived by the standard skid occasioned by braking of the inside track, but gentle turns were effected by pivoting of the road wheels to curve the tracks. The Mk VII was armed with a 2pdr (40mm) main gun plus co-axial 7.92mm (0.31in) Besa machine-gun in a trim turret. The Mk VII had little practical application in World War II, its only real use being the provision of armoured support for airborne forces after their arrival in specially designed General Aircraft Hamilcar gliders. The type was also used in small numbers as the Tetrarch Infantry Close Support (ICS) with a 3in (76.2mm) howitzer instead of a 2pdr (40mm) turret gun.

The Mk VIII was intended to overcome the Mk VII's vulnerability by the adoption of armour that was both thicker and of superior ballistic shape: this increased weight to 8.64 tonnes, and Mk VIII production amounted to 100 machines, but these were never issued for service.

Such was the mainstream of British light tank development in the period between the two world wars. It is worth noting that, in addition to its Carden-Loyd derivatives for the British army, Vickers-Armstrongs also developed and produced two private-venture series of light tanks that enjoyed considerable export success. The first of these was the six-ton Tank Mk E powered by an 87hp (64.8kW) Armstrong-Siddeley engine. The second series was similar to the Light Tank Mk IV, although fitted with a bewildering array of armaments.

Further up the weight scale was the medium tank, for which the light tank provided reconnaissance and support: thus while the light tank was the inheritor of the World War I medium tank's mantle, the medium tank succeeded the (battle) tank of World War I. Initial British efforts in the period after World War I were the Medium Tank Mk D, continuing the effort already well under way in the war, and the Light Infantry Tank. The latter was again the work of Colonel P. Johnson of the government's Tank Design Department, and similar to the Mk D although smaller and lighter: its role was machine-gun support of infantry assaults, but work was ended in 1923 when the Tank Design Department was closed down as part of the government's financial retrenchment programme.

By this time, Vickers-Armstrongs had been invited to join the medium tank development programme, and its first design in this important field was the five-man Vickers Tank, produced in Nos 1 and 2 variants during 1921 and 1922. The overall configuration was akin to that of the Medium Tank Mk B, but the Vickers Tank sported a roof-mounted domed turret surmounted by a commander's cupola, and was the first British armoured fighting vehicle with its main armament in a 360-degree traverse turret. In the No.1 variant, the turret accommodated three 0.303in (7.7mm) Hotchkiss machine-guns in ball mountings, and in the No.2, one 3pdr (47mm) gun and four Hotchkiss machine-guns including one for anti-aircraft fire.

The Vickers Tank was mechanically unreliable, but experience with this type was invaluable for the company, and its next design was one of extreme importance in the evolution of tank design: the new vehicle was the world's first fast tank, allowing the type's use in the manoeuvres that validated the tactical and operational concepts of Fuller and Liddell Hart. The tank's body was positioned above the tracks so that adequate armament could be located in a revolving turret without loss of fields of fire, and reduction of length and weight allowed higher performance on the same power as earlier tanks. Designed in 1922 as the first British tank of genuine post-war concept, the five-man Light Tank Mk I was redesignated the Vickers Medium Tank Mk I after the army's decision to buy the Carden-Loyd/Vickers Mk VIII (the Light Tank Mk I). The 11.94 tonne Medium Tank Mk I entered service in 1924, and in its various forms was built to a total of about 160 machines that formed the mainstay of the Royal Tank Corps in the later 1920s and early 1930s, and remained in service until the period just before World War II. The Mk I was the first British service tank to have a 360-degree traverse turret and geared elevation for the main armament, and is also notable for the high speed made possible by sprung suspension. The tank had a box-like hull in which the driver was located at the front of the vehicle next to the engine, and the other four crew members were located in the fighting compartment and turret to deal with command, operation of the radio, and the handling of the armament. However, there were advanced and obsolescent features: the powerful 3pdr (47mm) Mk 1 L/31.4 main gun, was partnered by the

The Vickers Medium Tank Mk III of 1928 combined old and new features. The semi-rhomboidal trackwork with large mud chutes made for good mobility under adverse conditions, the large turret allowed the incorporation of both radio and wireless telegraphy equipment for better and more flexible control in battle, and a separate commander's cupola was installed over the turret for improved visibility in battle. The armament comprised a 3pdr (47mm) main gun and co-axial 0.303in (7.7mm) machine-gun in the main turret, and single 0.303in (7.7mm) machine-guns in each of the two subsidiary turrets located ahead and to each side of the main turret. The crew was seven men, and 'production' was limited to three 16 ton development vehicles.

obsolescent secondary armament of four 0.303in (7.7mm) Hotchkiss guns in the turret plus a pair of Vickers guns of the same calibre in the hull sides.

Given the type's longevity of service, it is not surprising that the basic machine was developed into variants with a number of mechanical and operational improvements.

In 1925 Vickers-Armstrongs introduced the improved Medium Tank Mk II with thicker armour (at the penalty of a weight increase to 13.415 tonnes), and the longer 3pdr (47mm) Mk 2 L/40.05 gun with a higher muzzle velocity for better armour penetration; the driver was located farther forward for improved fields of vision, and the suspension was protected by skirt armour. This basic type was also developed in a number of improved forms.

During 1925 as the Medium Tank Mk II was entering service, Vickers-

Armstrongs was involved in the design of the Vickers Independent Tank that pioneered a number of advanced features and had a profound effect on tank design outside the United Kingdom. This tank inaugurated the new British system of tank nomenclature, being officially designated the A1E1, and was delivered to the Mechanical Warfare Experimental Establishment in 1926 for exhaustive trials, but which did not lead to a production order because of financial restrictions rather than any major problem with the tank itself. Among the Independent Tank's more advanced features were intercommunication among the eight-man crew by throat-mounted laryngaphone, a long wheelbase with the hull built up between the suspension assemblies, hydraulically powered controls and wheel steering for all but the sharpest turns. For its time, the Independent was a massive machine, weighing 32.01 tonnes and measuring 25.42ft (7.75m) in overall length. Power was provided by a 398hp (267kW) Armstrong-Siddeley petrol engine. Most unusual (and widely copied in Germany and the USSR) was the armament system, which comprised one main turret with four subsidiary turrets clustered round it. The main turret was fitted with a 3pdr (47mm) Mk 2 gun and incorporated a cupola for the commander, whose laryngaphone communication with all other crew members was

Despite its limitations, the Medium Tank Mk A, otherwise known as the Whippet, was well suited to the exploitation of the breakthroughs secured by the British army after the Battle of Amiens during August 1918, roaming ahead of the advancing infantry to keep the beaten Germans off balance and cut their lines of communication.

complemented by a pointer system to indicate targets to any of the turrets. The subsidiary turrets were each fitted with a single 0.303in (7.7mm) Vickers machine-gun.

Until the early 1930s the British had remained confident that they had the right 'mix' of armoured vehicles in the form of the light tank for reconnaissance, and the medium tank for independent mobile operations and support of the infantry. The realization of the need for a rapid re-armament programme, forced by Germany's growing strength and belligerence, drove the army towards the decision that it could best cater for the independent mobile and infantry support roles with different tank types. As a result, the medium tank was supplanted by the cruiser tank for mobile operations and by the infantry tank for support operations.

The first cruiser tank was the A9, otherwise known as the Cruiser Tank Mk I, and designed by Sir John Carden of Vickers-Armstrongs in 1934. The type entered small-scale production in 1937 as a 12.70 tonne vehicle with a crew of six, a 150hp (112kW) AEC Type 179 petrol engine, and an armament of one 2pdr (40mm) gun plus one 0.303in (7.7mm) machine-gun in the power-traversed main turret and one Vickers machine-gun in each of two subsidiary turrets. The use of a 2pdr (40mm) gun in place of the previous standard 3pdr (47mm) weapon may appear a retrograde step, but was in fact a highly sensible move, as the smaller-calibre weapon had far higher muzzle velocity and armour-penetrating capability than the larger weapon.

Production of the A9 amounted to only 125 vehicles, and the type remained in service up to 1941, seeing operational use in France and North Africa.

At much the same time, Vickers-Armstrongs undertook design of the A10 as an infantry tank, using the A9 as its basis but increasing the armour thickness: the additional armour took the form of plates attached to the hull (the first use of appliqué armour on a British tank), and increased the weight of the vehicle to 13.97 tonnes. The engine remained unaltered, and this led to a reduction in maximum speed. The subsidiary turrets of the A9 were not retained, and in 1940 the Vickers co-axial machine-gun was replaced by a 7.92mm (0.31in) Besa, a weapon of the same type which was sometimes added in the nose in place of some of the ammunition stowage. By the time the A10 was ready for production it was clear that the time lacked adequate protection for the infantry role, and the type was classified as the Heavy Cruiser Tank Mk II.

A turning point in British tank design was heralded in 1936 by the decision to develop new cruiser tanks on the basis of the suspension system devised in the USA by J. Walter Christie and already adopted with a high degree of success by the Soviets for their BT series. The Christie suspension used large-diameter road wheels attached to swinging arms supported by long coil springs: this gave the individual road wheels great vertical movement. In its basic form the Christie suspension system provided for high speed over adverse terrain, but considerable work had to be undertaken to turn the system into a battleworthy suspension for the new cruiser tanks. The result was incorporated in the A13. The prototype was completed in 1937 and performed excellently as a result of the Christie suspension combined with a high power-to-weight ratio: the A13 was powered by a 340hp (253.5kW) derivative of the World War I Liberty aero engine and weighed 14.43 tonnes, which resulted in a high maximum speed combined with unprecedented cross-country performance. Only moderate armour and armament were provided, as the tank was intended to rely on performance and agility for its protection. Armament comprised a turret-mounted 2pdr (40mm) gun and a 0.303in (7.7mm) Vickers co-axial machine-gun. The reduction in the number of machine-guns did not seriously affect

35

the tank's ability to defend itself against infantry attack, and had the advantage of allowing a reduction in crew to just four men.

Deliveries of the resultant Cruiser Tank Mk III started in December 1938 and were completed in 1939, when the improved Cruiser Tank Mk IV began to appear. The Mk III was used in France during 1940 and in North Africa during 1941, but proved a failure because of its wholly inadequate armour.

It was this failing that the Mk IV (also designated the A13 Mk II) was designed to overcome through the provision of additional armour in its more important areas. Even so, the Mk IV was decidedly under-armoured by the standards of its contemporaries. The Mk IVA introduced a 7.92mm (0.31in) Besa co-axial machine-gun in place of the original Vickers, and also featured a Wilson combined gearchange and steering gearbox. As with the Mk III, range was too limited for effective independent operations, and the angular design of the box-like hull and Vee-sided turret provided many shot traps.

The next British cruiser tank was the A13 Mk III, otherwise known as the Cruiser Tank Mk V Covenanter. This resulted from official dissatisfaction with the speed of an unsuccessful type, the A14 prototype, and the LMS Railway Co. was asked to develop a cruiser tank with considerably better speed than the 29.97 tonne A14. The Covenanter was essentially the A13 Mk II with a purpose-designed 300hp (224kW) Meadows engine, thicker armour, and a low-silhouette turret designed to optimize ballistic protection by increasing armour angles. The tank was a combat vehicle of some potential, and production eventually totalled 1,771, but the type was beset by intractable problems with engine cooling and, despite evolution through four marks in an effort to overcome these difficulties, was never used in combat. The Covenanter nevertheless proved invaluable as a training tank. The standard armament was one 2pdr (40mm) gun and one 7.92mm (0.31in) Besa co-axial machine-gun, but the close-support variant of each of the four marks was fitted with a 3in (76.2mm) howitzer.

The A12 Infantry Tank Mk II, otherwise known as the Matilda II, epitomises all that was right and wrong with British tank design in the late 1930s. Ordered 'off the drawing board' in 1937 as a breakthrough tank and built to the extent of 2,987 vehicles between 1940 and 1943, the 26.5 ton Matilda II was reliable but slow, was very well protected with armour ranging in thickness between 20 and 78mm (0.79 and 3.07in) for virtual invulnerability to German anti-tanks guns of the period except at very short ranges, but was also very decidedly underarmed with a 2pdr (40mm) main gun supported by just one 0.303in (7.7mm) machine-gun.

In the mid-1930s the British realized that, whereas previous tanks had been fitted with the 14mm (0.55in) armour deemed sufficient to stop the anti-tank projectiles fired by small arms, the advent of specialist anti-tank guns in calibres of 37mm or greater posed a new threat. The cruiser tank was evolved as successor to the medium tank in its mobile independent role, but with only modest armour as it was to rely on agility and speed for its main protection. The infantry support role demanded a new type of tank with considerably greater armour protection, as agility and speed would not be appropriate to the operational task envisaged. The division of the medium tank role into the cruiser and infantry roles coincided with the appointment of General Sir Hugh Elles (commander of the Tank Corps in World War I) to the position of Master General of the Ordnance. Elles thus had considerable operational experience of the direct infantry support role, and despite the technical and financial objections of many interested parties, Elles was insistent that a new breed of infantry tank should be evolved: the primary requirements being invulnerability to the fire of 37mm anti-tank guns, and good performance in adverse conditions.

The design task was entrusted to Sir John Carden of Vickers-Armstrongs, but the predetermined unit cost of each vehicle dictated that Carden had to work to very fine limits. The resulting A11, or Infantry Tank Mk I Matilda, gave every indication of having been designed down to a price rather than up to a specification, yet it managed to achieve one of the concept's primary requirements, through the use of armour varying in thickness between 10mm and 60mm (0.39in and 2.36in). It is acknowledged that, up to the end of 1940, the A11 was among the world's most heavily armoured tanks, and this helped to reduce losses. This was fortunate perhaps, for the A11 was not adequately planned in terms of armament, the limiting price having forced Carden to design a small vehicle whose two-man crew dictated the use of a one-man cast turret armed with a single 0.303in (7.7mm) Vickers machine-gun, later altered to one 0.5in (12.7mm) Vickers machine-gun in a move that increased firepower but further cramped the already uncomfortable turret.

Even as the A11 was starting prototype trials in 1936, the War Office was concluding that the infantry tank should not only be well protected but also sufficiently well armed to deal with enemy positions as well as infantry. A cursory examination showed that the A11 could not be evolved in such a fashion, and it was decided to limit A11 production to 139 machines that would serve as interim types pending the arrival of a superior infantry tank. This was the A12, otherwise known as the Infantry Tank Mk II Matilda II and designed by the Tank Design Department of the Mechanisation Board on the basis of the 1932 A7 prototype, using the same running gear (strengthened for greater weights) and powerplant of two 87hp (64.9kW) AEC diesels driving through a Wilson gearbox. The design was ordered straight into production, and for lack of tank-experienced companies with the capability for making large armour castings, manufacture was entrusted to the Vulcan Foundry of Warrington, with other companies brought in as the programme expanded. Most of the castings for the heavy hull and turret armour were produced by Vulcan, which was responsible for final assembly. Production eventually amounted to 2,987 vehicles, and the risky decision to order the type 'off the drawing board' was validated by generally successful capabilities from the beginning of trials. The 26.97 tonne Matilda II was of course heavier than its predecessor, but this allowed the carriage of a four-man crew and the installation of a larger turret accommodating a 2pdr (40mm) gun and one co-axial machine-gun. Improvement during World War II was undertaken wherever possible, resulting in the Mk IIA* Matilda III

Tank Warfare on the Outer Mongolian Frontier

ALTHOUGH they were the main producers and exponents of the tank in the 1920s, France and the UK could not pursue their chosen course on the basis of lessons learned in contemporary armoured warfare, for such warfare was virtually nonexistent in that decade. The same problem affected American, British and French developments in the 1930s, but did not apply to countries such as Germany, Italy, Japan and, more importantly, the USSR. Japan used her tanks in the somewhat atypical fighting of her campaign to conquer China, but then in the late 1930s came up against the altogether more formidable Soviet armoured capability in two major campaigns along the river borders between the Japanese-occupied Korea and Siberia in 1938, and the Japanese puppet state of Manchukuo (Manchuria) and the Soviet client state of Mongolia in 1939. The more serious of the clashes took place between May and September 1939 along the Khalkin Gol river near Nomonhan, and here the Japanese made the mistake of using their light and medium tanks to support conventional infantry assaults, which were severely handled by the Soviet infantry with generally superior artillery support. Meanwhile the Soviets had been massing a major armoured force in the form of the 4th Tank, 6th Tank, 7th Mechanised, 8th Mechanised, 9th Mechanised and 11th Tank Brigades. (The mechanised brigade was a tank brigade with a battalion of motorised infantry.) This force was allocated to the Soviet left and right wings which, once the Japanese had been pinned by the advance of the Soviet centre, were to sweep round the flanks and take the Japanese in the rear after cutting their lines of communication. The plan was devised by the local commander, General Georgi Zhukov, and introduced the type of tactic used with overwhelming success in World War II. This success was presaged by its triumph in the Nomonhan fighting, in which the Soviets virtually destroyed the Japanese 6th Army in the type of combined-arms fighting that received little attention at the time but was to portend with some exactitude the nature of armoured warfare used in World War II.

with two 95hp (70.8kW) Leyland diesels, the Matilda III CS with a 3in (76.2mm) howitzer, the Matilda IV with mechanical improvements over the Matilda III, the Matilda IV CS with mechanical improvements over the Matilda III CS, and the Matilda V which was identical to the Matilda IV but with a directly-operated pneumatic gearbox.

So far as the situation in 1939 was concerned, one must conclude that official indifference and lack of funding were responsible for the parlous condition of British tank strength: the light reconnaissance tank was available in useful numbers but was obsolete, the medium tank was outdated, the cruiser tank was unproven in concept and was too lightly armed and armoured, and the infantry tank was also unproven and was too slow. This dangerous situation was compounded by lack of adequate design and manufacturing capabilities, and by the failure of the higher authorities to grasp the nettle of German tank superiority when this became evident.

Like the United Kingdom, France was faced with problems of how to develop its armoured force after World War I, especially as financial resources were in short supply and the role of the tank was in question. Most production orders were cancelled at the end of World War I, and much of the in-service tank fleet was in fact unserviceable because of the cumulative mechanical defects of designs that had been rushed into production too hastily. General J. E. Estienne, meanwhile, set to work on the tactical and operational roles of an independent tank arm evolved from the Artillerie d'Assaut of World War I, using a derivative of the Char 1 as its first major vehicle. However, the Artillerie d'Assaut was disestablished in 1920 and the tank arm subordinated to the infantry, tank units thereafter serving as components of infantry formations.

Opposite top: Variously known as the Renault Type ZT or AMR 35, this vehicle was a light tank developed from the Type VM with slightly lower overall performance and reduced versatility offset by better crew comfort and improved vision devices. The type was of bolted construction, and was generally armed with one 0.295 or 0.512in (7.5 or 13.2mm) machine-gun or, as illustrated here, a 25mm Hotchkiss anti-tank gun. Production totalled 200 vehicles.

Opposite bottom: Also known as the Renault Type VM or AMR 33, this vehicle was a light tank of bolted construction and was optimised for the reconnaissance role with an armament limited to one 0.295in (7.5mm) machine-gun carried in the revolving turret mounted centrally above the superstructure above the rear of the hull.

The main heavy battle tank of the French army at the time of the German invasion of May 1940, the Char B1-bis was a 32-ton development of the Char B1, itself a development of the Char B prototype. The type was built from 1937 by Renault. The four-man type was costly to produce but was considered to be highly effective with cast and bolted steel armour varying in thickness between 20 and 60mm (0.79 and 2.26in), and an armament that comprised one 2.95in (75mm) gun with 74 rounds in the hull front, one 47mm gun with 50 rounds in the revolving turret, and two 0.295in (7.5mm) machine-guns with 5,100 rounds. The Char B1-bis was 21ft 4.75in (6.52m) long, 8ft 2.5in (8.2m) wide and 9ft 2in (2.79m) high, and its 180hp (134kW) Renault petrol engine provided a speed of 17.4mph (28km/h).

In 1921 the French formulated their first programme for tank development, calling for a char de rupture (breakthrough tank) and a char de bataille (battle tank), the latter to succeed the Renault FT in the infantry support role. Under the auspices of the Section Technique des Chars de Combat, this programme produced one breakthrough tank (the Forges et Chantiers de la Mediterranée 2C of which only a few were built) and five possible battle tanks from Delaunay-Belleville, FAMH (Saint Chamond), FCM and Renault/Schneider.

After assessment of the five char de bataille proposals and examination of four mock-ups in 1924, the Section Technique des Chars de Combat ordered single Char B prototypes from FAMH, FCM and Renault/Schneider in 1927. The specification had called for a weight of 15.00 tonnes, a crew of four, and a main armament of one hull-mounted 47mm or 75mm (2.95in) gun. The prototypes appeared between 1929 and 1931, with a weight of 25.00 tonnes, a hull-mounted 75mm (2.95in) SA 35 main gun, and a secondary armament of four 7.5mm (0.295in) Chatellerault machine-guns (two fixed in the forward hull and two flexible in the turret). After exhaustive trials in the 1932 French army manoeuvres, the Char B was ordered into production in a revised form as the Char B1. This entered service in 1935 with a main gun fixed in traverse (the whole tank having to be slewed to bring the gun to bear on the target) but movable in elevation, while the turret accommodated one 37mm gun plus a 7.5mm (0.295in) co-axial machine-gun. Only 36 Chars B1 had been produced before the considerably revised Char B1-bis was introduced with heavier armour, revised armament, and a more powerful

The logic behind the design of the Char B series was the creation of a tank that would be virtually invulnerable to enemy anti-tank fire as a result of its heavy armour, and able to serve as a breakthrough tank with the fire of its general-purpose main gun located in the hull front, with the smaller turreted gun providing capability against tanks and strongpoints. The concept had some merit, but resulted in a tall and somewhat cumbersome vehicle whose main gun was fixed in azimuth so that the whole vehicle had to be slewed to bring the gun to bear on its intended target.

The PzKpfw I was a light reconnaissance tank with machine-gun armament, and was intended not so much as a combat vehicle but as a type on which German industry could cut its teeth and the new German armoured arm could develop some experience in the operation and use of armoured fighting vehicles.

engine. The Char B1-bis weighed 30.00 tonnes, was armoured more extensively with bolted-together castings to the maximum of 40mm (1.575in), had a revised turret accommodating one 47mm gun and one 7.5mm (0.295in) co-axial machine-gun, and featured a 250hp rather than a 180hp (186kw rather than 134kW) Renault petrol engine: production amounted to 365 vehicles by June 1940.

The last development of this potent armoured fighting vehicle, still one of the most formidable weapons of its type in 1940, was the Char B1-ter of which five were produced. This featured a 310hp (231kW) Renault engine, a maximum armour thickness of 70mm (2.76in), a main gun provided with limited traverse, and a crew increased to five by inclusion of a mechanic in the enlarged fighting compartment.

In 1926 the French produced a new tank programme providing for three tank types, in the form of the char léger (light tank) with one 37mm gun and 7.5mm (0.295in) machine-guns, the char de bataille with a main gun of 47mm calibre or more, and the char lourd (heavy tank) with thicker armour than the char de bataille. Little money was available to the French army during this period, most available resources being devoted to the fixed defences of the 'Maginot Line', and the programme was generally unsuccessful. The main results were the Renault Chars NC1 and NC2 improved versions of the FT, which secured export orders but failed to win French approval. Considerable development of tactical ideas followed in the early 1930s as the infantry and cavalry expanded their thinking about the nature and employment of armour, but France's sole armoured warfare visionary, Colonel Charles de Gaulle, fell into political oblivion after the publication of his *Vers l'Armée de Métier*. This called for a professional rather than a conscript army of mechanized shock troops centred on armoured divisions, and ran counter to all the tenets of France's pacifist government.

In 1931 the infantry organized its armoured force by type of equipment in service or under development, all such infantry vehicles being designated

chars: the chars légers (light tanks) were the Renault R-35 and R-40, FCM-36 and Hotchkiss H-35; the new category chars moyens (medium tanks) were the Renault D1 and D2, and AMX-38; the chars de bataille were the Char B series; and the chars lourds were the Char 2C series. The cavalry followed suit in 1932 with a wider-ranging classification of auto-mitrailleuses (machine-gun cars) that included wheeled armoured cars: the AMD (Auto-Mitrailleuse de Decouverte) category comprised long-range armoured cars; the AMR (Auto-Mitrailleuse de Reconnaissance) category comprised cross-country light reconnaissance tanks with machine-gun armament, such as the Renault Type VM and Type ZT; the AMC (Auto-Mitrailleuse de Combat) category comprised gun-armed tanks such as the Renault Type YR and Type ACG1; and the char de cavalerie category added in 1935 covered heavier gun-armed tanks such as the Hotchkiss H-35 and H-38/39, and the SOMUA S-35 and S-40.

Compared with their German opponents in 1940, the PzKpfw I and II, the French tanks had generally superior armament and protection, but were let down tactically by their two-man crews, their use in small non-homogeneous units, and (with the exception of the R-35 series) their comparatively small numbers.

The chars moyens were intended as medium-weight infantry support tanks. The most important of these was the Char D produced by Renault in

Whereas the PzKpfw I was limited to an armament of two 0.312in (7.92mm) machine-guns, the PzKpfw II was somewhat better armed with a 20mm cannon and co-axial 0.312in (7.92mm) machine-gun. The vehicle had a crew of three, and is seen here in its first definitive model, the PzKpfw II Ausf C of which some 2,000 were produced mainly for the development of the German armoured force but also for limited operational use in the Spanish Civil War and, as a result of tank shortages, in the first part of World War II. This model differed from its predecessors mainly in the adoption of revised running gear with five road wheels and elliptical springs on each side for improved cross-country mobility.

response to the 1926 new tank programme and based mechanically on the Renault NC 1 (NC27) light tank that secured export rather than domestic sales. The first prototype appeared in 1931, and production of 160 tanks was undertaken between 1932 and 1935. The key to this model was the use of a two-man cast turret (one of the first such units in French service) on a riveted hull with skirt armour to protect the running gear. The crew of three was well provided with vision devices, and a radio with a distinctive triangular antenna was standard. The Char D1A was armed with a 37mm main gun and a co-axial 7.5mm (0.295in) machine-gun, plus a fixed machine-gun of the same calibre fired by the driver, and at a weight of 12.00 tonnes the tank had a maximum speed of 18km/h (11.2mph) on its 65hp (48.5kW) Renault petrol engine.

Technically one of the best tanks fielded by any of the combatants at the beginning of World War II was the SOMUA S-35, which was a char de cavalerie. This was the world's first tank with all-cast hull and turret construction, and was arguably one of the ablest armoured fighting vehicles of its day anywhere in the world. The turret was an electrically traversed unit with a maximum thickness of 56mm (2.2in), and was identical with the turret used by the Char B1-bis and Char D2: the main armament was the 47mm SA 35 gun, and the secondary armament comprised a 7.5mm (0.295in) co-axial machine-gun in an unusual mounting that allowed limited traverse independent of the turret; there was also provision for mounting a second 7.5mm (0.295in) machine-gun on the commander's cupola for anti-aircraft defence. The S-35 had a combat weight of 20.05 tonnes, was powered by a 190hp (142kW) SOMUA petrol engine, and had a crew of three.

Of all the countries which were to become the Allied powers of World War II, that making the greatest strides in the development of armoured fighting vehicles in the interwar period was the USSR. As in other countries, ideas for armoured fighting vehicles abounded in the years before and during World War I, considerable numbers of armoured cars being placed in service and some development towards genuine tanks being undertaken as supplies of British and French tanks were received. But the first tanks were not produced until after World War I, by which time revolution had replaced Tsarist Russia with the Soviet state. The Soviets were impressed

The Char D2 was a French medium tank intended for the infantry support role. Deliveries of the type from the Renault production line began in 1934, although production was limited to just 50 vehicles produced by 1936 as the new SOMUA S-35 offered better all-round capabilities. The three-man Char D2 weighed 18.5 tons, was powered by a 150hp (112kW) Renault petrol engine for a speed of 14mph (22.5km/h), and was armed with one 47mm gun in the revolving turret supplemented by one 0.295in (7.5mm) machine-gun that could be a co-axial weapon or a fixed weapon in the nose plate

Strv m/37 was the Swedish designation for a Czechoslovak light tank, the CKD/Praga AH-IV-Sv. Weighing 4.5 tons and armed with two machine-guns in the revolving turret, the two-man Strv m/37 was produced to the extent of 50 vehicles assembled in Sweden by Jungner from components delivered in crates from Czechoslovakia.

Designed as successor to the T-32 heavy tank, the T-35 remains the classic example of the multi-turret tank in the period leading up to World War II. Weighing 45 tons and manned by a crew of 10, the tank was powered by a 500hp (373kW) petrol engine for a speed of 18mph (29km/h), and its armament was centred on a main turret and four subsidiary turrets. The main turret carried a 3in (7.62mm) gun, the right-hand forward and left-hand rear auxiliary turrets each carried a 37mm (later 45mm) gun, and the left-hand forward and right-hand rear auxiliary turrets carried two of the six 0.3in (7.62mm) machine-guns that constituted the tertiary armament. Production was limited to about 30 tanks, some of which were later stripped of some if not all of their auxiliary turrets in an effort to improve performance and agility.

with the capabilities of tanks, and avidly seized those left behind by the departing 'interventionist' Allied forces. The Renault FT suited their requirements admirably, and in 1919 they ordered an FT 'clone' into indigenous production as the Krasno-Sormova (KS), which was identical to the FT in exterior detail but featured an American gearbox and 45hp (33.6kW) Fiat engine. Production was limited by lack of Soviet industrial capacity, and this also affected the thinking towards the development of other tanks. In direct violation of the 1919 Treaty of Versailles, the Soviet authorities readily agreed to the establishment of a secret German tank centre at Kazan in the USSR, and thereby kept abreast of German developments. Combined with overt purchases of the best of foreign tanks, this allowed the Soviets to keep their tactical and technical thinking fully appraised on modern developments without the risks and costs of an indigenous tank programme. A wholly-Soviet design was also attempted, but nothing came of this effort before the Central Armoured Force Command was dissolved in the early 1920s and further design was entrusted to the War Department Tank Bureau created in 1923.

The consolidation of the Soviet state continued steadily during the 1920s, allowing the promulgation of the wide-ranging First Five-Year Plan in 1927. This included the notion of mechanizing the Red Army, and also of developing tanks in all categories now deemed essential for a modern army. The plan called for each division to have a supporting group of tanks, and the MS series was considered to be an adequate basis for the first generation. These vehicles included the T-17 one-man tankette, the T-19 and T-20 two-man light tanks, the T-21 two-man light tank, the T-23 two-man tankette, the T-24 three-man medium tank and the TG five-man heavy tank. All were failures for a variety of reasons, with lack of mechanical reliability proving the single most significant factor. The 25.40 tonne TG heavy tank was of notably advanced concept with low silhouette, armament of one 75mm (2.95 in) gun and four machine-guns, and a 300hp (224kW) petrol engine.

That the Soviets had appreciated the possible failure of this programme is given credence by the contemporary purchase of much of Vickers-Armstrongs' tank range, including Carden-Loyd tankettes, Six-Ton Light Tanks, Medium Tank Mk IIs, Carden-Loyd A4E11 amphibious tanks and tractors. A thorough technical and tactical analysis of these vehicles provided the Soviets with the starting point for a new generation of designs based on sound principles rather than the assumptions of World War I. Just as significantly, however, several of these British tanks were passed to the Germans for evaluation at Kazan, and it is not surprising therefore that Carden-Loyd and Vickers-Armstrongs features appeared in several German tank designs of the early 1930s. It is also worth noting that at this time the Soviets were astute enough to investigate tank developments of other sorts, exemplified by their purchase of licences for German BMW engines and the US Christie suspension in 1930.

Evaluation of these tanks and associated components was completed at the beginning of 1931, and the decision was made to cancel production of the T-19 to T-24 series in favour of the Six-Ton Light Tank (as the T-26 light tank), the Carden-Loyd Mk VI (as the T-27 tankette), and the Carden-Loyd A4E11 (as the T-37 and improved T-38 light amphibious tanks). All were produced in large numbers and as several steadily improving variants, providing the Soviets with a first-rate introduction to modern design, manufacturing and operating principles. The Christie M1931 (T-3) medium tank was also accepted for production as the BT-1, the first variant of the BT (Bistrokhodny Tank, or fast tank) series, although the Soviets were mindful that this was not a tank well suited to operational use. Modest production was undertaken, however, to provide Soviet designers with a data base of experience with the Christie suspension which, unlike the complete Christie tank, was clearly well suited to the nature and extent of the theatres likely to be forced on the Soviets in any future war.

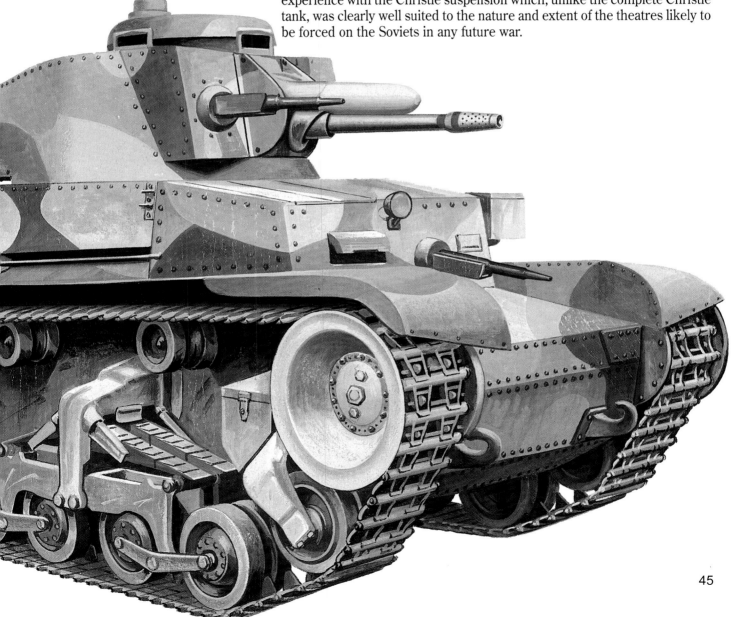

Germany Enters the Scene

A FTER the Armistice of 11 November 1918, the German army's tank force was disbanded, and the Treaty of Versailles of June 1919 included, among its many provisions, a total ban on the development of tanks. Yet the German army was already well established on its programme of intelligence-gathering about foreign developments, clandestine evaluation of tank-capable components in Germany, and secret links with countries not unsympathetic to German liaison in the development of their own tank forces. In this last respect the Swedes were the Germans' most important 'allies' in the early 1920s, when the LK.II was readied for Swedish production and service as the Strv m/21 under the leadership of Vollmer and a German army team. As the 1920s progressed the Germans became increasingly involved with the Soviets, both parties thinking that a fair deal had been struck when the Germans were given use of the Kazan tank school as an experimental and proving ground, in return for technical information and training provided to the fledgling Soviet tank arm.

Between 1926 and 1929 the Germans broke the strictures of the Treaty of Versailles to produce a number of experimental tanks. These were commissioned in great secrecy from major engineering and arms companies as a means of evaluating trends in the design of armoured fighting vehicles, and also of regaining a manufacturing capability pending the day that Germany would move into the field as a major armoured force.

Accompanying this technical and manufacturing effort was a great deal of theoretical thinking about the operational and tactical employment of armour. By a paradox typical of military history, the Germans were well served by their lack of armour in this period: it left them without the entrenched thinking and existing hardware that inevitably accompanies the existence of in-service weapons, and opened the way for radical and professionally competent thought about the nature and employment of a future tank force. Coupled with a realistic analysis of the German army's performance in World War I, this paved the way for the adoption of the Blitzkrieg (lightning war) concept of operations, derived ultimately from the thinking of Fuller and Liddell Hart towards massive breakthroughs or bypassing of the enemy's major front-line assets by massed armour, with substantial air support as the first step in fast-moving operations into the enemy's rear areas.

While these tactical and operational concepts were still in their embryonic phases, the Germans were moving towards the creation of new hardware with a number of prototype vehicles such as the Leichte Traktor VK31 and Grosstraktor, so designated to convey the impression of an agricultural role and thus not contrary to the provisions of the Treaty of Versailles.

The German army began to plan its overt growth to world capability in 1932, and an accelerating implementation and augmentation of this plan followed the Nazis' rise to power. Plans had already been laid for the

The PzKpfw I was too poorly armed and armoured to be of usefull service with the German armoured divisions in the first part of World War II, but a number of the vehicles such as this PzKpfw I Ausf B were adapted as command tanks with additional radio equipment.

development of a tank force based on existing prototypes, but the recommendations of men such as Oberst Heinz Guderian for a massive force of comparatively light armour used in the Blitzkrieg concept of fast-moving operations found favour with the army's political masters, who recognized the military and propaganda value in a multitude of smaller vehicles that could be obtained for the same financial and industrial outlay as a considerably smaller number of heavier vehicles. In 1933, therefore, the German army started to plan a family of tactically interrelated armoured fighting vehicles for development over the next few years. However, the need to train large numbers of tank crews and support personnel, and the development of the appropriate tactical doctrines through practical training, coincided with political demands that Germany must be seen to be developing a tank force. The result was a requirement for a nominal 5 tonne light tank with a crew of two and an armament of two turret-mounted 7.92mm (0.31in) MG13 machine-guns. Designs were commissioned from Daimler-Benz, Henschel, Krupp, MAN and Rheinmetall for a light tank weighing between 4.00 and 7.00 tonnes; the Krupp LKA I design (with features of the Carden-Loyd Mk VI tankette in its running gear) was accepted and construction by Henschel of three LaS prototypes began in December 1933. The first mild-steel prototype was running by February

The first tank to enter production in
Germany after World War I, the PzKpfw I
was intended as little more than a training
type on which the new Panzer divisions
could begin to learn their trade. The vehicle
illustrated here is a PzKpfw I Ausf A, which
was the pre-production model produced
to the extent of 100 vehicles in three
subvariants for the evaluation of different
suspensions and other details.

1934, and after successful trials, an initial production contract for 150
vehicles was placed in July 1934, later contracts raising the total to about
1,800. Of this number about 300 were of the initial PzKpfw I Ausf A model
with four road wheels, and the remainder were of the more powerfully
engined PzKpfw I Ausf B variant with five road wheels.

The PzKpfw I was the main vehicle used by the German tank force up to
the beginning of World War II, and was largely responsible for the high
quality of German tank tactics, maintenance and overall capability at the
beginning of the war. The type was also used operationally in the Spanish
Civil War (1936-39), and confirmed the tactical limitations imposed by a two-
man crew and armament of only two machine-guns. The armour varied from
7mm to 13mm (0.28in to 0.51in) in thickness, which was confirmed as too
thin for genuine operational capability. The total obsolescence of the design
led to the PzKpfw I's retirement from front-line roles from 1941.

In 1934 it became clear that the German army's definitive PzKpfw III
battle tanks and PzKpfw IV medium tanks would take longer to develop than
anticipated, and it was decided to produce an interim type to succeed the
PzKpfw I, which would offer superior operational qualities with a crew of
three and an increased nominal weight of 10 tonnes. Designs and prototypes
were tendered by Henschel, Krupp and MAN, that eventually selected for
development as the LaS 100 being the MAN design with a 130hp (96.9kW)
engine and a turret-mounted armament of one 20mm KWK 30 cannon and
one 7.92mm (0.31in) MG13 co-axial machine-gun. Trials were undertaken
with the pre-production LaS 100 a3 (PzKpfw II Ausf a3) and improved
PzKpfw II Ausf b with thicker armour and a 140hp (104kW) Maybach HL 62
TR engine. Extensive trials were continued in this period, together with
operational trials in the Spanish Civil War, and resulted in the 1937 arrival of
the PzKpfw II Ausf C with a full-width superstructure, a revised turret, and
completely remodelled suspension based on five larger-diameter road
wheels with independent elliptical springing.

This led to the first service model, the 7.305 tonne PzKpfw II Ausf A with improved protective features but otherwise similar to the Ausf c. The PzKpfw II Ausf B introduced a slightly more powerful engine and revised tracks, while the PzKpfw II Ausf C was similar except for thicker frontal armour for a weight of 9.50 tonnes. Full-scale deliveries began in 1937, and such was the pace of production that 1,000 PzKpfw IIs were available for the Polish campaign that started World War II. The type was clearly as good as any light tank in the world in the late 1930s, but by the beginning of the 1940s the position was changing, and when the PzKpfw II was used in the Western campaigns of May and June 1940, it maintained an admirable reconnaissance capability but was a liability when forced to fight: even the frontal armour was too thin to stop the British 2pdr (40mm) shot, and the kWK 30 cannon projectile could not penetrate the armour of British and French medium tanks.

Development of the basic machine was still continuing, however, and in 1939 Daimler-Benz produced the PzKpfw II Ausf D and Ausf E variants with revised running gear, which utilised the Christie pattern with four large road wheels. Cross-country performance was inferior to that of the Ausf A to Ausf C variants, and in 1940 most surviving vehicles were converted to other roles.

The main stream of development therefore evolved from the Ausf C, resulting in the 1940 introduction of the PzKpfw II Ausf F with solid conical-hubbed rear idlers in place of the previous open spoked type, and frontal armour thickened by the addition of spaced appliqué plates to defeat the hollow-charge anti-tank warhead that was becoming increasingly lethal to battlefield tanks. Further evolution of the same basic theme resulted in the PzKpfw II Ausf G and Ausf J variants with a stowage box on the turret bustle and other detail modifications. Production of the PzKpfw II series continued into 1941, when the start of the war against the USSR proved beyond doubt that the type was obsolete.

The PzKpfw III was the most important German medium tank in the first part of World War II, and was planned as the backbone of the Panzer divisions' strength with heavier support provided by the PzKpfw IV. The type had a crew of five, and in its various main forms had a weight of approximately 20 tons. The very first tanks of this type were armed with a 37mm main gun and had coil spring suspension, although all later vehicles had heavier armament (a 50mm or later a 75mm gun) and torsion bar suspension. The illustration shows a PzKpfw III, here armed with a short 50mm gun that was later replaced by a longer weapon of the same calibre, involved in the fighting around Tobruk on the North African coast during 1942.

By 1935 the German designers and industrialists had gained sufficient experience with the PzKpfw I and II light tanks to embark upon the first of Germany's definitive battle tanks, the five-man PzKpfw III with a nominal weight of 15 tonnes. The German army's plan at this time was to field a force based on two main types, one a battle tank with a high-velocity anti-tank gun backed by machine-guns, and the other a medium tank with a medium-velocity gun backed by machine-guns and intended mainly for the support role; the battle tank became the PzKpfw III with a 37mm gun (later a 50mm gun), while the medium tank became the PzKpfw IV with a 75mm (2.95in) gun. The standard tank battalion had four companies, and it was planned that three of these would field the battle tank and the fourth would use the medium tank.

Development of the battle tank was undertaken with the cover designation ZW, and prototype orders were placed with Daimler-Benz, Krupp, MAN and Rheinmetall during 1936. The Inspectorate for Mechanized Troops wished the ZW to be fitted with a 50mm gun, but the Ordnance Department pointed out that the infantry's standard anti-tank gun was a 37mm weapon: a compromise announced that the type would carry the 37mm KWK L/45 gun but with a turret ring of adequate diameter to allow later substitution of the 50mm KWK 39 gun if tactical conditions altered. This was an extremely far-sighted move, and allowed the PzKpfw III to be retained as an effective weapon for about two years longer than would otherwise have been the case.

It proved impossible to design a battle tank down to the desired weight of 15 tonnes, so the upper limit was raised to the 24 tonne rating of Germany's

In a definitive form such as the Ausf F and G, the PzKpfw III was armed with an L/42 gun of 50mm calibre that was replaced in models such as the PzKpfw III Ausf J, L and M by an L/60 weapon of the same calibre. The PzKpfw III Ausf H, which was first produced in 1941 with the L/42 gun but later switched to the L/60 weapon, carried two 0.312in (7.92mm) machine-guns as its secondary armament, weighed 21.6 tonnes, was protected by armour varying in thickness between 30 and 80mm (1.18 and 3.15in), and possessed dimensions that included a length of 18ft 1in (5.52m), width of 9ft 8in (2.95m) and height of 9ft 8in (2.95m). The PzKpfw III Ausf H was powered by a 300hp (224kW) Maybach HL 120 TRM petrol engine for a maximum speed of 25mph (40km/h).

road bridges, and the selection battle settled down to a choice between Krupp and Daimler-Benz; the latter was selected for production of the PzKpfw III Ausf A after features of the Krupp MKA prototype had been incorporated into the design. In overall layout the PzKpfw III followed the pattern finalized in the PzKpfw I: the five men of the crew were favoured with considerable working space by comparison with contemporary tanks of the same basic type, and the driver had the useful advantage of a preselector gearbox: this required more maintenance than the crash gearbox used in most other tanks, but offered greater flexibility of operation in conjunction with the 230hp (171.5kW) Maybach HL 108 TR petrol engine. The sensible layout of the vehicle was echoed in the construction of high-grade chrome/molybdenum steel armour: the hull was a bolted-together assembly of three welded subassemblies (the lower hull, the forward upper hull and the rear upper hull), and the turret was another welded assembly. The armament rather let down the potential of the tank, being the 37mm KWK L/45 gun and three 7.92mm (0.31in) MG34 machine-guns (two co-axial with the main armament and the third in the bow).

The first production model (or perhaps the last pre-production model as only 440 were built) was the PzKpfw III Ausf E, which appeared in 1938 with the 320hp (239kW) Maybach HL 120 TR engine.

At about this time the Ordnance Department finally appreciated its short-sightedness in pressing for a 37mm main armament, and instructed Krupp to proceed with the design of a new turret to accommodate the 50mm KWK 39 gun. The development had not been completed, however, when the next variant of the tank III was being readied for production in early 1940 as the PzKpfw III Ausf F. This 20.30 tonne variant therefore had to retain the 37mm

The PzKpfw IV was conceived as the heavier partner to the PzKpfw III with a larger gun for the support rather than the anti-tank role, and in all its variants was delivered with a 2.95in (75mm) gun that was gradually increased in length and lethality as the PzKpfw IV superseded the PzKpfw III as the standard tank of the Panzer divisions. The PzKpfw IV had the distinction of remaining in production right through World War II.

gun, and its main improvements over the Ausf E comprised better ventilation, a stowage box on the turret and the HL 120 TRM engine rated at 300hp (224kW). The new main armament was still not ready when the PzKpfw III Ausf G was introduced later in 1940, so this variant also retained the 37mm main gun. It had the same weight and improvements as the Ausf F, but also featured a revised commander's cupola with improved protection for the vision ports.

All three of these variants were retrofitted with the new kWK L/42 gun as this became available, to the annoyance of Hitler who appreciated the pace of armoured warfare development and thus demanded the longer and more powerful kWK 39 L/60 gun of the same calibre. Development of the PzKpfw III continued after 1940, and details of the ultimate extension of the PzKpfw III's capabilities are discussed in the next chapter.

The last of Germany's main tanks with a pre-war pedigree was the PzKpfw IV, which possesses the distinction of being the only German tank to have remained in production right through World War II, with an overall total in excess of 8,500 examples. The type was planned at the same time as the PzKpfw III, and was essentially similar apart from its main armament, which was the 75mm (2.95in) kWK L/24 designed to provide the lighter PzKpfw III with high-explosive (HE) fire support.

The design was fixed at a weight not exceeding 24 tonnes, and prototype vehicles were ordered in 1934 under the cover designation BW, from Krupp as the VK2001(K), MAN as the VK2002(MAN) and Rheinmetall as the

Based on the Krupp VK.2001 prototype, the PzKpfw IV was numerically and tactically the most important tank fielded by the German forces in World War II. The type entered production as the PzKpfw IV Ausf A during 1937, and went through a number of forms with a 2.95in (75mm) gun of steadily increasing length, thicker and better disposed armour protection, uprated engines, and other enhanced operational features. Typical of the later variants was the longer gun (originally an L/43 weapon but later an L/48 ordnance) fitted with a muzzle brake for reduced recoil loads. Common to all variants was the trackwork, with four track-return rollers and eight small bogie wheels in pairs on each side.

VK2001(Rh). The Krupp submission was selected in 1936 for production after the incorporation of features from the Rheinmetall prototype, including the simpler running gear, on each side consisting of eight small road wheels in two-wheel bogies with leafsprings.

The crew was disposed in much the same way as in the PzKpfw III, but whereas the battle tank had a manually operated turret, that of the medium tank was traversed electrically. Before the PzKpfw IV entered large-scale production, a number of features were trialled in small pre-production batches, and it was only late in 1939 that the type entered full-scale production as the PzKpfw IV Ausf D, which differed from its predecessors primarily in general improvement of its protection. This indicated that the German army was now becoming seriously worried about the comparatively thin armour of its primary tanks, and this strengthening was continued with the PzKpfw IV Ausf E that was identical to the Ausf D in all but its improved protection and its new turret. The protective features included the thickening of the nose plate and, once a suitable machine-gun mounting had been evolved, the front plate; the turret protection was also improved by the addition of face-hardened panels, and spaced armour of various types was often added as a retrofit.

The Ausf E introduced the type of turret that remained standard on production vehicles for the rest of World War II. Some criticism had been levelled at the inadequate protection offered by the commander's cupola, and this was improved in the revised turret. The cupola was also moved forwards, allowing the installation of a smoothly curved back plate without the distinctive cut-out previously necessary to accommodate the rear of the cupola. Finally, the turret was fitted with an electrical ventilation fan, replacing the original ventilator flap. The PzKpfw IV went through later marks and developments, but these fall within the context of World War II and are therefore described in the next chapter.

Germany's design and industrial capabilities were severely tested by the virtually simultaneous development and production of four major service tanks, yet despite a prodigious effort, they could not satisfy the army's requirement in terms of volume and speed of production. To this extent, the army was fortunate that Hitler's territorial ambitions encompassed the overrunning of Czechoslovakia's rump in March 1939, after the ignominious British and French abandonment of the Czech Sudetenland to German demands in the Munich agreement of September 1938. The German army was able to absorb much of the Czech army's capable tank fleet, and the

During the German invasion and conquest of France in May and June 1940, the PzKpfw IV was used in its initial support role with a short 2.95in (75mm) gun firing an assortment of ammunition types including HE shell.

Czech production capabilities were completely at the disposal of the German war machine, which accepted two tanks of Czech design and manufacture, namely the CKD/Praga TNHP (otherwise LT-38) and Skoda LT-35 light tanks.

The spur for the development of the TNHP was the Czech army's reaction to a rapidly worsening European situation, by the creation in October 1937 of a committee to evaluate current Czech tank production capability and to recommend a new type of high-performance light tank to complement and later to supplant the Skoda LT-35, a 1935 type of exceptional performance but notable mechanical complexity.

The 8.00 tonne TNHP was the classic light tank of the period immediately before World War II, with a balanced blend of firepower, protection and mobility to optimize its capabilities in the twin roles of reconnaissance and support for the more powerfully armed medium tank. The weakest points of the design were the riveted construction (with the exception of the bolted-on upper surfaces to the superstructure) and the modest 37mm Skoda A7 gun. In layout the tank was conventional, with the driver in the forward compartment, the commander, gunner and loader/radio operator in the fighting compartment, and the powerplant in the rear compartment under a comparatively high rear decking. The turret was surmounted by a fixed cupola, and its weapons comprised one 37mm gun and one 7.92mm (0.31in) vz37 co-axial machine-gun; another vz37 machine-gun was located in the bow for operation by the driver. The engine was a 125hp (93.2kW) Praga EPA unit.

PzKpfw 35(t) was the German designation given to the Skoda S-IIa/T-II light tank after the occupation of Czechoslovakia in 1938. This advanced four-man light tank was armed with a 37mm main gun supported by two 0.312in (7.92mm) machine-guns, and was notable for the comparative spaciousness of its fighting compartment. Production was continued after the German occupation to provide the Panzer divisions with additional vehicles pending the delivery of larger numbers of German tanks.

When Czechoslovakia was occupied by Germany in 1939, the TNHP was just entering service with the Czech army and was taken into German service as the PzKpfw 38(t). Production was then continued against German plans for 40 such vehicles per month, ending only in 1942 after the production of 1,168 vehicles for the German army within an overall chassis production figure of 1,590. The Germans were concerned with the TNHP's comparatively light protection, and ordered increases in the basic protection to produce the 9.70 tonne TNHP-S, the suffix standing for Schwer (heavy). In many vehicles the German 37mm KWK L/45 gun was used in place of the Skoda L/47.8 weapon, and considerable revisions were made to the internal equipment to modify the vehicle to German standards. In the last 500 chassis, an uprated powerplant was installed in the form of the 150hp (112kW) EPA/AC engine.

The LT-35 (sometimes LTM-35) was designed by Skoda to satisfy operational requirements, such as rear drive to leave the fighting compartment uncluttered by transmission elements, a short engine to allow as much floor area as possible for the fighting compartment, a pneumatically-operated gearbox for transmission flexibility and ease of driving, pneumatically powered steering to permit the coverage of long distances without excessive driver fatigue, new running gear to ensure equal pressure on all road wheels, and duplication of all major accessories to increase system reliability in sustained operations. For its time the design was highly advanced, but suffered the consequences of its mechanical complexity in low serviceability. Nonetheless, the performance of the type in prototype trials was so impressive that at the end of 1935 the tank was ordered into production for the Czech army. The hull and turret were of riveted and bolted construction. The driver and bow gunner were located in the forward compartment, the latter to operate the 7.92mm

Inspired by the Soviet T-34 tank with its well-sloped armour and long-barrel gun, the PzKpfw V Panther was one of the classic tanks of World War II and may be credited with establishing the tank concept that was later adopted by the Western nations in the closing stages of World War II for the new generation of tanks that entered service in the late 1940s and early 1950s. The four-man Panther was notable for its good performance and agility as a result of the high power-to-weight ratio offered by its 650hp (485kW) petrol engine, the thickness and sloped nature of its armour, and the use of a long-barrel 2.95in (75mm) gun that provided excellent armour-penetration capability and which because of its twin-baffle muzzle brake, did not provide undue recoil forces.

55

(0.31in) bow machine-gun, and the commander/gunner and loader/radio operator were placed in the first 360-degree traverse turret to be installed on a Skoda tank. This turret, tactically limited by its two-man crew, was fitted with a fixed cupola, and was armed with a 37mm Skoda A3 L/40 semi-automatic gun and a 7.92mm (0.31in) co-axial machine-gun.

After German occupation of Czechoslovakia the LT-35 was taken into German service as the PzKpfw 35(t). The type continued to suffer reliability problems, and the Germans redesigned the tank's transmission and steering systems. From 1942, however, the type was phased out of front-line service for the less exacting but important role of mortar and artillery tractor.

After the rise of the Fascist party in Italy under Benito Mussolini, Italy increasingly swayed from its World War I alliance with France and the UK towards a political adherence to Germany, especially after the rise of the Nazi party in Germany. This consensus of right-wing political beliefs led to a formal alliance between Germany and Italy in May 1939. As noted above, Italy had perceived little utility for the tank in the context of its particular operational scenario in World War I, but nevertheless developed one important type (the limited-production Fiat 2000 heavy tank), improved on the Renault FT amongst others. With the end of World War I, Italian orders were immediately curtailed from 1,400 to a mere 100 examples of Italy's modified FT, the Fiat 3000. This served the Italian army well into the 1930s, and it was the late 1920s before serious consideration was given to a successor.

For a variety of economic, tactical and industrial reasons, Italy was drawn to the example of the Carden-Loyd Mk VI tankette, which offered useful if limited capabilities and also the possibility of large-scale production at modest cost by an automotive and armament industry with only small capacity for heavy engineering. The result was the CV (Carro Veloce, fast vehicle, or tankette) series, which began in 1929 with the CV.29, a vehicle

Italy was never able to match either the number or quality of the tanks produced by Germany in World War II, as evidenced by the fairly antiquated design of the Carro Armato M13/40 medium tank, which was based on riveted armour of inadequate thickness. Production amounted to 1,960 vehicles including a number completed to the standard illustrated here, namely the Semovente 40 da 75/18. This was a three-man self-propelled gun with a 2.95in (75mm) gun/howitzer in the front of the superstructure.

that was similar to the Mk VI and built only in small numbers (25 examples) as the precursor of an improved version of Italian origin, produced in prototype form as the CV.3 and, after evaluation in 1932 and 1933 with different running gear and water- or air-cooled machine-gun armament, was standardized for service as the CV.33 (alternatively the CV.3-33). The order was for 1,300 vehicles, of which 1,100 under the designation CV.33 Serie I were armed with a 6.5mm (0.26in) machine-gun, and the remaining 200, under the designation CV.33 Serie II, were armed with two 8mm (0.315in) machine-guns. Most Serie I tankettes were later brought up to Serie II standard, but this could not disguise the overall obsolescence of the type. Considerable development was undertaken on the basis of this simple vehicle. The CV.35 (sometimes designated CV.3-35) had a redesigned hull of bolted rather than riveted construction and slightly revised suspension, but was otherwise unaltered from the CV.33, while the L.38 of 1938 was a more ambitious updating of the basic concept with strengthened suspension, new tracks, improved vision devices, and an armament of one 13.2mm (0.52in) Breda machine-gun revised in 1940 to one 20mm Solothurn s13-1000 cannon. The 1938 system of nomenclature led to the redesignation of the CV.33 as the L.3-33 and of the CV.35 as the L.3-35 in the L-series of Leggero (light) tanks.

The CV.33 was intended primarily for security and reconnaissance duties in association with heavier tanks, but the nature of the Italian industrial machine dictated that when Italy entered World War II in June 1940, her armoured forces were still equipped with the L.3, which therefore had to be used for the type of combat role for which it was not designed and consequent losses were very high.

The replacement for the L.3 was the Fiat-Ansaldo L.6/40 light tank, of which 283 were ordered. The first prototype ran in 1940 and production began in 1941. The riveted turret, manned by the single commander/gunner, carried one Breda 20mm cannon and one 8mm

Japan's relative lack of industrial capacity combined with the nature of the war in China, which Japan launched in 1937 to gain a major empire on the Asian mainland, to persuade the Japanese army that it did not need advanced tanks. It was content, therefore, to retain obsolescent vehicles such as this two-man Tankette Type 94 that first appeared in 1934 with a welded and riveted hull carrying a turreted machine-gun of 0.303in (7.7mm) calibre.

(0.315in) co-axial machine-gun. The only other crew member was the driver who sat at the front of the 6.80 tonne vehicle, which was powered by a 70hp (52.2kW) SPA 180 petrol engine for a maximum speed of 42km/h (26.1mph).

Another stream of development from the Ansaldo light tank of 1935 resulted in the Carro Armato M.11/39, which was the first of the M-series of Medio (medium) tanks and destined to become Italy's most important tank of World War II. The design was started in 1936, and then pursued with considerable vigour after combat experience in the Spanish Civil War had revealed to the Italians the total inadequacy of the CV.35, in face of even moderate anti-tank capability. The first prototype was completed in 1937, and used running gear modelled on that of the CV.33/CV.35 series combined with the 105hp (78.3kW) SPA 8T diesel engine and armament layout of the 1935 light tank. The M.11/39 entered service in 1940, but an alarming loss rate revealed its concept to be obsolete.

The third of the Axis powers in World War II was Japan, which had fought on the Allied side in World War I but then fell under the sway of increasingly right-wing military administrations and drifted into the same political arena as Germany and Italy; in 1940 the three countries signed the German-Italian-Japanese Axis agreement, a 10-year mutual assistance pact. Japan was slow to enter the field of armoured warfare, and thereafter produced a number of vehicles that were adequate for her operations on the Asian mainland but were considerably inferior to their Western counterparts in overall capabilities.

The best of these vehicles was the Light Tank Type 95 (Ha-Go), without doubt the best tank produced and deployed in quantity by the Japanese in World War II. The prototype was built either by the Sagami Arsenal or Mitsubishi, and was extensively evaluated in Japan and under the operational conditions encountered in China before production was entrusted to Mitsubishi, which built about 1,250 examples from its own and subcontracted assemblies. The type entered service in 1935, and for its time was a capable machine and as good as any light tank in the world, the provision of an interior layer of asbestos proving useful in reducing interior heat and protecting the crew from injury as the tank moved at speed across country.

Otherwise known as the Ha-Go, the Light Tank Type 95 was the best vehicle of its category available to the Japanese in any numbers during World War II, and was a 7.4-ton vehicle with a crew of three, an armament of one 37mm gun and two 0.303in (7.7mm) machine-guns, and a 110hp (82kW) diesel engine for a speed of 25mph (40km/h).

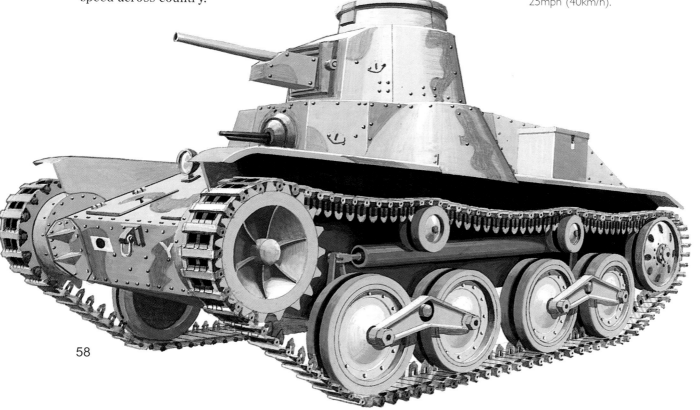

The 7.40 tonne machine was based on a welded and riveted hull, with a forward compartment for the driver and a gunner, and had a 6.5mm (0.26in) bow machine-gun. Behind this was the turret, also of welded and riveted construction, which accommodated the commander who, in addition to his command responsibilities, had the task of loading, aiming and firing the 37mm Type 94 main gun. At the rear were the 120hp (89.5kW) Mitsubishi NVD 6120 diesel engine and transmission.

Operational use in Manchuria and China confirmed that better armament was desirable, and the 6.5mm (0.26in) bow machine-gun was replaced by a 7.7mm (0.303in) weapon, another 7.7mm machine-gun was added on the right-hand side of the turret rear for use by the already overworked commander/gunner, and the original Type 94 main gun was replaced by a Type 98 weapon of the same calibre but with higher muzzle velocity.

The Light Tank Type 95 proved moderately successful in campaigns such as that during late 1941 and early 1942 in which the Japanese overran Malaya and seized the fortress city of Singapore.

The Type 95 was a major improvement over the Japanese army's previous light tanks, but was soon involved in an intensive programme to produce improved variants. The first of these was the Light Tank Type 98-Ko (Ke-Ni) that entered production in 1942 for construction of perhaps 200 vehicles, although some sources suggest only 100. The Ke-Ni used a greater proportion of welding than the Ha-Go, was better armoured, and carried an armament comprising one 37mm Type 100 high-velocity gun and two 7.7mm (0.303in) machine-guns.

The Japanese viewed the medium tank as a battle tank with modest armour, good armament and only limited performance as a battlefield support weapon for the infantry. The best of these vehicles was the Medium Tank Type 97 (Chi-Ha), a four-man machine weighing 15.00 tonnes. In basic concept the Type 97 was a scaled-up version of the Light Tank Type 95 with a two-man turret, thicker armour and greater power to maintain performance despite the considerably greater weight. The hull was of riveted and welded construction, with the driver and gunner for the 7.7mm (0.303in) bow machine-gun in the forward compartment, the fighting compartment in the centre, and the engine and transmission in the rear compartment. The turret was surmounted by the commander's cupola, and its weapons comprised one 57mm Type 97 short-barrelled tank gun and, in the rear face, one 7.7mm (0.303in) machine-gun. The turret provided 360-degree traverse, but the main gun had a second pair of trunnions allowing a maximum 10-degree traverse independently of the turret. The Type 97 entered service in 1938 and remained in major service until the end of World War II.

The Japanese were not unaware of the progress in tank tactics, however, and sensibly provided the Type 97 with a turret ring of greater diameter than required by the 57mm medium-velocity gun. This allowed for the later development of the Type 97 (Shinhoto Chi-Ha), which was essentially the hull of the Type 97 fitted with the turret of the Medium Tank Type 1 complete with its 47mm Type 1 long-barrel gun. This increased combat weight to 16.00 tonnes, but the longer gun provided a higher muzzle velocity and greater armour-penetration capability.

Blitzkrieg

THE last chapter described the main stream of tank development in the period between the two world wars. There had been some armoured conflict during this period, most notably between the Soviets and the Japanese in a number of border clashes in eastern Asia, and between the Nationalist and Republican forces in the Spanish Civil War, but these conflicts lacked the sustained intensity neccessary for any valuable long-term conclusions to be drawn. It was clear from these conflicts, however, that armour had a potentially decisive part to play if reliability could be improved, numbers increased and offensive power boosted. The two countries to recognize these implications were Germany and the USSR: Germany used the Spanish Civil War to validate the basic premises of its

The best-known German tank of World War II, the PzKpfw VI Tiger is revealed in this cutaway illustration, which highlights the central location of the large turret and the size of the rear-mounted engine. Notable features of this monumental tank were the thickness of the armour, which was not significantly sloped for additional ballistic protection, the massive nature of the very powerful 3.465in (88mm) gun, and the relatively low power-to-weight ratio that rsulted in indifferent performance coupled with poor range owing to a relatively small fuel capacity.

new Blitzkrieg concept, and the USSR decided that its considerable capacity for tank design and production would be best used in development of a new generation of high-speed tanks with superb cross-country performance, hard-hitting main armament, good protection and reliability enhanced by the ruthless elimination of less essential items of equipment.

From late 1940, the mainstay of the German army's Panzer battalions were the PzKpfw III battle tank and the PzKpfw IV medium tank, as the PzKpfw I and II had become obsolescent and were relegated to secondary roles. The PzKpfw III was designed as the German army's standard battle tank, and entered its stride as a production weapon with the PzKpfw III Ausführung H, the main production variant in the period between late 1940 and the end of 1941. The first large-scale production variant, the PzKpfw III Ausf E, had been allocated for production to several companies with little experience in the manufacture of armoured fighting vehicles, and had suffered in terms of production quantity and quality because of the comparatively complex manufacturing techniques required. The PzKpfw III Ausf H incorporated features to ease mass production, the most important being new idlers and drive sprockets, and a transmission arrangement with a six-speed manual gearbox in place of the original 10-speed preselector box. As a result of combat experience in Poland and the Western campaign, extra protection was added in the form of bolt-on plates as well as a measure of spaced armour to defeat hollow-charge warheads. This boosted the PzKpfw III Ausf H's combat weight to 21.60 tonnes, and wider tracks were fitted to reduce ground pressure. The 300hp (224kW) Maybach HL 120 TRM petrol engine

PzKpfw VI Ausf E Tiger

THE only tank variant of the original Tiger model to enter production and service was the PzKpfw VI Ausf E, which was a heavy battle tank with a weight of 56.9 tonnes and a crew of five. This vehicle had a length of 27ft 9in (8.46m) with the gun trained directly ahead, a width of 12ft 3in (3.73m) and height of 9ft 6in (2.90m), and in its definitive later form was powered by a 694hp (517kW) Maybach HL 230 P45 petrol engine for a speed of 23mph (37km/h) and a range of 73 miles (117km) with 125 Imp gal (567 litres) of fuel. The vehicle had minimum and maximum armour thicknesses of 26 and 110mm (1.02 and 4.33in) respectively, and the armour was of welded steel with mortised joints. The primary armament was one 3.465in (88mm) L/56 gun with a total of 92 rounds of ammunition, and the secondary armament comprised two or three 0.312in (7.82mm) machine-guns with a total of 5,100 rounds of ammunition: these guns were disposed as one co-axial weapon, one weapon in the bow plate, and one optional weapon in the anti-aircraft position on top of the turret.

introduced on the Ausf E was used in this and all later variants. Early examples of the PzKpfw III Ausf H retained the 50mm KWK L/42 gun, but later examples were produced with the more capable kWK 39 L/60 weapon of the same calibre and this was retrofitted to tanks already in service.

By the beginning of the campaign against the USSR in June 1941, some 1,500 PzKpfw III tanks were in service, and these performed creditably in the opening stages of the campaign. The experience of the crews and the relative maturity of the basic design swept Soviet armour away without difficulty. But from the end of 1941, the new breed of Soviet tanks, epitomized by the T-34 medium and KV heavy types, began to appear in growing numbers: the Soviet tank crews were of better tactical quality, but more importantly, the protection of their vehicles proved too thick for effective penetration by the L/42 gun. A crash programme was launched to retrofit the German tanks with the L/60 gun. To the dismay of the German authorities this longer version of the 50mm gun also proved inadequate to the task of tackling the T-34 and KV, except at point-blank ranges that were seldom achievable on the Eastern Front. A longer-term implication was that Hitler, on learning that his earlier instructions to fit the L/60 weapon had not been obeyed immediately, began to take a more personal interest in the design and manufacture of German tanks, as well as in their deployment and tactical use.

The comparatively small diameter of the PzKpfw III's turret ring now proved the decisive factor in developing a more capable variant: the 50mm Krupp gun was not entirely satisfactory, but the turret ring diameter effectively prohibited the installation of a high-velocity gun of greater calibre. All the Germans could do, therefore, was to step up production of better-protected models in the forlorn hope that numbers would provide the Panzer arm with an edge over the Soviet tank force. The next production variant was thus the PzKpfw III Ausf J, which was similar to the Ausf H apart from a reduction in hull and turret vision slots to ease manufacture, and an increase in armour protection, resulting in an increased weight of 22.30 tonnes and a slight but significant deterioration in cross-country performance and agility.

The Panzerjäger 38(t), otherwise known as the Marder III, was a specialised anti-tank weapon with a 2.95in (75mm) high-velocity gun located in a fixed barbette mounted above the hull rear of the obsolescent PzKpfw 38(t), which was the German designation for the CKD/Praga TNHP or LT-38 light tank.

The next variant was the Ausf L, which entered production in 1942, the year in which PzKpfw III production attained 2,600 machines. The Ausf L was similar to the late-production Ausf J (with the L/60 main gun) in every external respect but armour, which now included a spaced layer above the superstructure and mantlet. This further increased the nose heaviness already evident in the Ausf J and earlier models retrofitted with the L/60 gun.

In 1942 the PzKpfw III Ausf M also appeared, this being a variant of the Ausf L optimized for mass production by the elimination of the hull vision ports and escape doors. Although the elimination of the hull escape doors might be considered a retrograde step, it should be remembered that these were generally inoperable when essential skirt armour was fitted.

Production of the Ausf M continued into the beginning of 1943, but in 1942 the first examples of the ultimate PzKpfw III variant had appeared. This was the Ausf N, identical to the Ausf M in all respects but armament. In July 1942, Hitler had ordered that the Ausf L should be fitted with the obsolescent 75mm (2.95in)kWK L/24 gun in place of its current 50mm weapon. The German leader's intention was to provide a support tank for heavier tanks such as the PzKpfw VI Tiger, and the designated weapon was the ordnance of early models of the PzKpfw IV. But whereas the 50mm weapon was limited to HE and armour-piercing ammunition, the 75mm (2.95in) weapon could fire armour-piercing, HEAT, HE, Smoke and Case projectiles. The same ordnance was used in the Ausf N, which had revised ammunition stowage. Production amounted to 660 Ausf N tanks in the period from July 1942 to August 1943, the 213 vehicles built in 1943 being modified in production with definitive Schürzen (aprons), comprising 8mm (0.315in) skirts over the running gear and 5mm (0.2in) panels around the turret. Further protection was afforded by Zimmerit paste, of which a 100kg

A similar process was used to create the Panzerjäger IV Nashorn, which was the hull of the PzKpfw IV medium tank used as the basis for a 3.465in (88mm) anti-tank gun on a limited-traverse mounting in the rear-mounted barbette.

(220lb) coating provided protection against magnetically attached mines.

Total production of the PzKpfw III was 5,644, and the type's importance on the development of armoured warfare cannot be exaggerated as it was the primary weapon of the Panzer divisions in their heady days of triumph between 1939 and 1941.

The PzKpfw III's partner through the first half of the war was the PzKpfw IV, whose development up to the Ausf E has been covered in the previous chapter. The first definitive variant of the PzKpfw IV was the PzKpfw Ausf F. Although modelled on the preceding Ausf E, this variant was planned with thicker armour and a longer-barreled 75mm (2.95in) main gun. The armour was to a 50mm (1.97in) rather than 30mm (1.18in) basis, but the longer ordnance was not available in time and the standard kWK L/24 gun had to be fitted. The variant, weighing 22.30 tonnes, was built throughout 1941. When the far superior kWK 40 L/43 gun became available, it was introduced on an Ausf F variant known as the PzKpfw IV Ausf F2, earlier models being retrospectively redesignated PzKpfw IV Ausf F1. The Ausf F2 weighed 23.60 tonnes, and its advent marked an apex in German tank capability.

The Ausf F2 was succeeded by the Ausf G, which was basically similar to its predecessor apart from detail modifications and improved armour, the latter including a thicker top to the superstructure. Field additions often included spaced frontal armour and Schürzen of the types used in the PzKpfw III's later variants for protection against hollow-charge warheads. The L/48 version of the kWK 40 gun was introduced on the Ausf H version of this increasingly important tank. The Ausf H began to leave the production lines in March 1943, and was similar to the Ausf F2 and Ausf G, apart from its use of the longer gun, a revised turret hatch cover, cast rather than fabricated drive sprockets, improved frontal armour of the spaced type, and as a measure of protection for the increasingly vulnerable flanks, 8mm (0.315in) turret and 5mm (0.2in) skirt armour. This resulted in an increase in combat weight to 25.00 tonnes, but the retention of the same 300hp (224kW) engine inevitably caused a loss of performance and agility.

The Panzerjäger concept, in which a large-calibre anti-tank gun was mounted on a limited-traverse mounting in an open-topped barbette built up on the rear hull of an obsolescent tank, proved moderately successful at first, but increasing losses to heavier-armed tanks, artillery fire and aircraft attack later led to the demand for more fully optimised Jagdpanzer types with a lower silhouette, thicker armour and overhead protection. An excellent example of this type is the Jagdpanzer IV, which was the chassis and lower hull of the PzKpfw IV tank with a new upper hull of well-sloped and comparatively thick armour carrying a 2.95in (75mm) high-velocity anti-tank gun.

The PzKpfw VI Tiger, sometimes called the Tiger I to differentiate it from the later and far superior Tiger II or Königstiger, was a very formidable battle tank whose potent gun, thick armour but indifferent performance and agility made it better suited to ambush rather than truly mobile armoured warfare.

By the beginning of 1943, the limitations of the PzKpfw III and IV were clear to field commanders and procurement authorities alike, and in February it was proposed that the PzKpfw IV be entirely supplanted in production by the new PzKpfw V Panther and PzKpfw VI Tiger tanks. In essence the notion was correct, but as men such as General Heinz Guderian were swift to point out, production rates of the newer vehicles were so low that the PzKpfw IV should be retained to maintain the numerical strength of the Panzer arm in the decisive year of 1943, which in the event saw the strategic initiative swing firmly to the Allied nations. Hitler therefore decided that production of the PzKpfw IV should continue at least to the beginning of 1944, and this paved the way for the evolution of the final production variant, the PzKpfw IV Ausf J that began to reach combat units in March 1944.

The designers had taken the lessons of combat firmly to heart and created a variant that was easier to produce and more effective in combat, with higher performance and greater cross-country agility. The Ausf J had thicker frontal armour combined with flank protection by wire mesh screens in place of the heavy skirts of the Ausf F, G and H variants. Earlier models had been provided with a power system plus manual back-up for turret traverse, but in the Ausf J the power traverse system was removed (and the manual system supplanted by a two-speed geared unit) to provide greater fuel capacity. The Ausf J was thus a more capable machine than the Ausf H, and remained in production right to the end of World War II, the total for the two models reaching almost 6,000 chassis (from a total of 9,000 PzKpfw IV tanks) in the last two years of the war.

The PzKpfw IV fought on every German front in World War II, and proved itself one of the most important tanks ever produced. Although it was always armed with a 75mm (2.95in) main gun, the adoption of longer-

The designation Sturmgeschütz III was used for obsolescent PzKpfw III battle tanks converted to the assault gun role with a short-barrel 2.95in (75mm) gun in a low barbette replacing the revolving turret of the baseline tank.

barreled ordnances of this calibre allowed the designers to keep the tank up to date with most Western and many Soviet tanks, and when properly handled the PzKpfw IV was a capable adversary.

Up to 1940 the German army was highly satisfied with the versatility of the PzKpfw IV, and was content to opt for the exploitation its development potential rather than the creation of a wholly new type. The army had little reason to doubt the wisdom of its decision until the autumn of 1941, when the German forces driving towards Moscow began to encounter small but increasing numbers of the new Soviet T-34 tank, which immediately displayed itself superior to the PzKpfw IV in all aspects of firepower, protection and mobility. And it was clear to the German army that this was a new tank already mature in its mechanical aspects yet full of development potential in terms of firepower and protection.

This is a PzKpfw IV medium tank of the World War II period.

In November 1941 a German investigation team assessed a captured T-34 and came to the conclusion that the Soviet tank had significant advantages over German tanks in its sloped armour, large road wheels and long gun. The sloping of the armour offered an effective increase in thickness without the weight penalty of vertical protection of this actual thickness; the large road wheels offered a superior ride, especially across country; and the long gun, hitherto rejected by the Germans as impractical for a number of reasons, offered very high muzzle velocity and therefore a devastating armour-penetrating capability. The inevitable conclusion was that all current German tanks were obsolete in the technical sense, and an immediate programme was launched to produce a counter to the T-34: within days the German armaments ministry contracted with Daimler-Benz and MAN for VK3002 designs to meet a specification that demanded a 30/35 tonne battle tank with a 75mm (2.95in) main gun, well sloped armour to a maximum thickness of 40mm (1.57in) on the sides and 60mm (2.36in) on the front, and a maximum speed of 55km/h (34.1mph). In January 1942 the specification was revised, to include a 60km/h (37.3mph) maximum speed and frontal armour of 60mm (2.36in) on the hull and 100mm (3.94in) on the turret.

The VK3002(DB) and VK3002(MAN) designs were completed in April 1942. The VK3002(DB) was essentially a copy of the T-34, with the turret

This is a PzKpfw IV medium tank of the World War II period

located so far forward that the driver sat inside the turret cage and had to use a hydraulically operated remote steering system. The VK3002(DB) was a design of great potential, with a diesel engine offering lower susceptibility to fire as well as longer range, but an initial order for 200 vehicles, placed at the instigation of Hitler, was cancelled later in 1942.

The armament ministry, on the other hand, preferred the VK3002(MAN), which was specifically a German solution to the requirement, was powered by a proved petrol engine and, in the short term at least, was better suited to German production practices. The VK3002(MAN) had a basic layout similar to that of the PzKpfw IV, but was considerably more powerful than earlier German tanks, having more than twice the horsepower of the PzKpfW IV, and a special gearbox was developed to allow optimum use of this potential. The rubber-tyred road wheels were of sufficiently great diameter to negate the need for track-return rollers. The turret was located as far back as possible to reduce the type of mobility and tactical problems that might otherwise have been caused by a long barrel overhang of the L/60 gun originally planned for the vehicle (but later replaced by an L/70 weapon).

The first prototype of the VK3002(MAN) appeared in September 1942. It was launched on a large-scale evaluation programme, and such was the seriousness of Germany's armour position on the Eastern Front (compounded by technical problems with the new PzKpfw VI Tiger heavy tank) that the type was ordered into immediate production as the PzKpfw V Panther. The first production Panther appeared in November 1942, and the ambitious production rate of 250 vehicles per month was quickly raised to 600 per month. This figure was never achieved, despite the launch of a large-scale co-production system involving four major

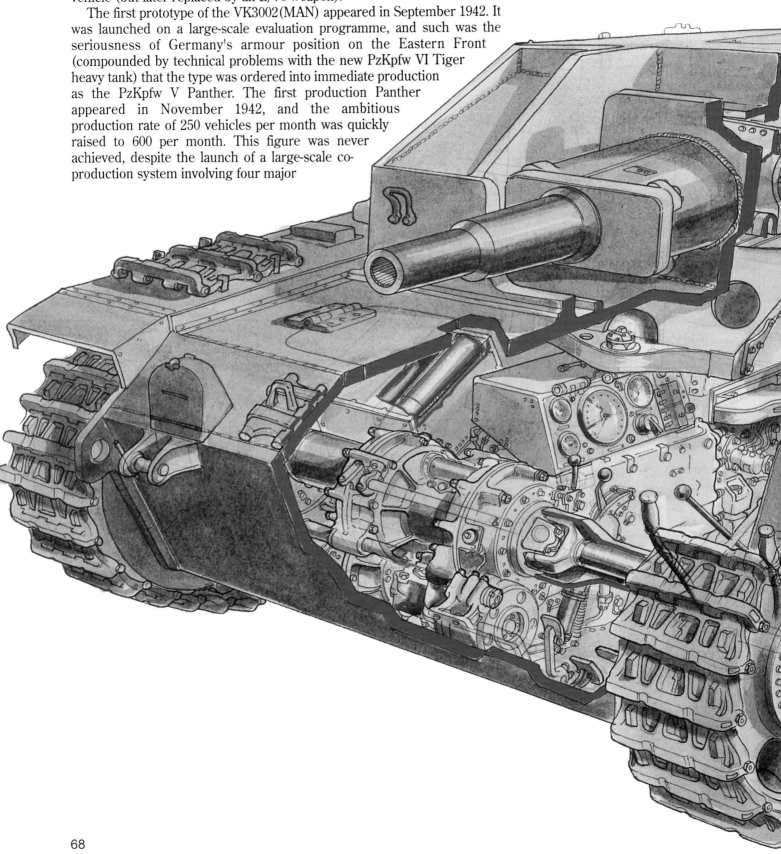

This cutaway view illustrates the major features of the early pattern of Sturmgeschütz III assault gun with an armoured barbette carrying the 2.95in (75mm) short-barrel L/24 gun without a muzzle brake. The lower hull, chassis and tracks were essentially unaltered from those of the PzKpfw III tank on which the vehicle was based.

The PzKpfw VI Tiger was a potent tank killer in confined country, but when caught in the open could be out manoeuvred by larger numbers of Allied tanks and destroyed with shots to the tracks or to the rear of the hull. This is a Tiger destroyed during the closing stages of the fighting in the North African campaign.

manufacturers, and the 1944 monthly average was 330, leading to an overall total of 5,590 Panthers by the end of World War II, comprising 1,850 in the first year of production and 3,740 between January 1944 and May 1945. An additional 679 chassis were completed for use in roles such as recovery, command, artillery observation and tank destroying.

The desired maximum weight limit of 35 tonnes had proved impossible to meet, and the Panther turned the scales at 45.50 tonnes on its service debut. This weight was due mainly to Hitler's insistence on thicker armour, and plans were made for use of the bored-out HL 230 in place of the originally specified HL 210 engine; despite this, the reduced maximum speed of 45km/h (28mph) had to be accepted.

The first 20 Panthers were designated PzKpfw V Panther Ausf A, and were in reality pre-production machines with the thinner frontal armour as demanded by the original specification, a 642hp (479kW) HL 210 engine, an early model of the L/70 main gun and the commander's cupola at the extreme left of the Rheinmetall turret. Considerable development work was undertaken with these first Panthers, which were redesignated PzKpfw V Panther Ausf D1 early in 1943. The proposed second and third production models were the Ausf B with a Maybach Olvar gearbox, and the Ausf C of which no details have been found. Trials with the Ausf A revealed a number of problems, but the importance of the programme was such that no delay in production was authorized to rectify any deficiencies before they were built into service tanks.

The first real production variant was therefore the PzKpfw V Panther Ausf D, which was redesignated PzKpfw V Panther Ausf D2 at the same time that the Ausf A became the Ausf D1. The type appeared in January 1943, and featured the standard type of 'dustbin' cupola, a vision port and machine-gun port in the glacis plate, the definitive L/70 main gun with a double-baffle muzzle brake to reduce recoil distance in an already cramped turret, smoke-dischargers on each side of the turret and, on later production examples, skirt armour added during construction, together with a coating of Zimmerit anti-mine paste.

The next variant appeared in July 1943, and should have been the Ausf E, but for reasons which remain unexplained was in fact designated the

PzKpfw V Panther Ausf A. This incorporated features that had been omitted in order to increase production of the Ausf D2 in preparation for the Germans' final effort to regain the strategic initiative on the Eastern Front in the Battle of Kursk of July 1943, the world's most comprehensive tank battle to date. Kursk was the Panther's combat debut, most available vehicles serving with one army and three SS divisions of the 4th Panzerarmee; when they ran well, the Panthers were more than a match for the Soviets' T-34s, but they seldom travelled for more than a few miles without a mechanical problem, due to the type having been rushed into service prematurely.

The Ausf A introduced the definitive commander's cupola with better ballistic shaping and armoured periscopes, a fully-engineered ball mounting for the hull machine-gun, a monocular rather than binocular gunner's sight in the turret, and elimination of all turret pistol spent-case ejection ports.

The final production variant of the original Panther series was the PzKpfw Panther Ausf G, so designated because Hitler, on 27 February 1944, had ordered the roman numeral in the original designation to be omitted. The origins of this model lay with the February 1942 instruction of the German armaments ministry that MAN was to co-operate with Henschel in the development of a Panther variant, incorporating as many PzKpfw VI Tiger components as possible. The programme would have resulted in the Panther II Ausf F with the interleaved steel wheels of the Tiger II, thicker armour on the hull top, a turret modelled on that of the Tiger Ausf B with stereoscopic rangefinder and gun stabilization system, a higher-rated gearbox, and greater power in the form of the HL 230 rated to 800hp (596kW) with petrol injection and a higher compression ratio, and to 900hp (671kW) with a supercharger.

Known to the Allies as the Royal Tiger or King Tiger, the PzKpfw VI Tiger II or Königstiger was one of the most formidable tanks of World War II, but appeared in only comparatively small numbers from late 1944. The Tiger II carried a longer (L/71 rather than L/56) version of the same 3.465in (88mm) main gun as the Tiger for considerably enhanced offensive power, and was an altogether more capable fighting machine as it had sloped and therefore ballistically more effective armour than its predecessor.

It is hard to overestimate the importance of the Panther to armoured warfare in World War II or to the development of the tank since that time. An indication of the Panther's capabilities is exemplified by its frontal armour, which was impenetrable to the projectiles of the Allies' main gun tanks, while its own manoeuvrability and gun power allowed it to knock out the Allied tanks from stand-off range.

The largest German tanks to see combat in World War II were the variants of the PzKpfw VI Tiger series, which first appeared before the PzKpfw V Panther but which are treated after it because of their later numerical designation. In the late 1930s the German army had started to plan a heavy breakthrough tank, but in 1940 several early schemes were

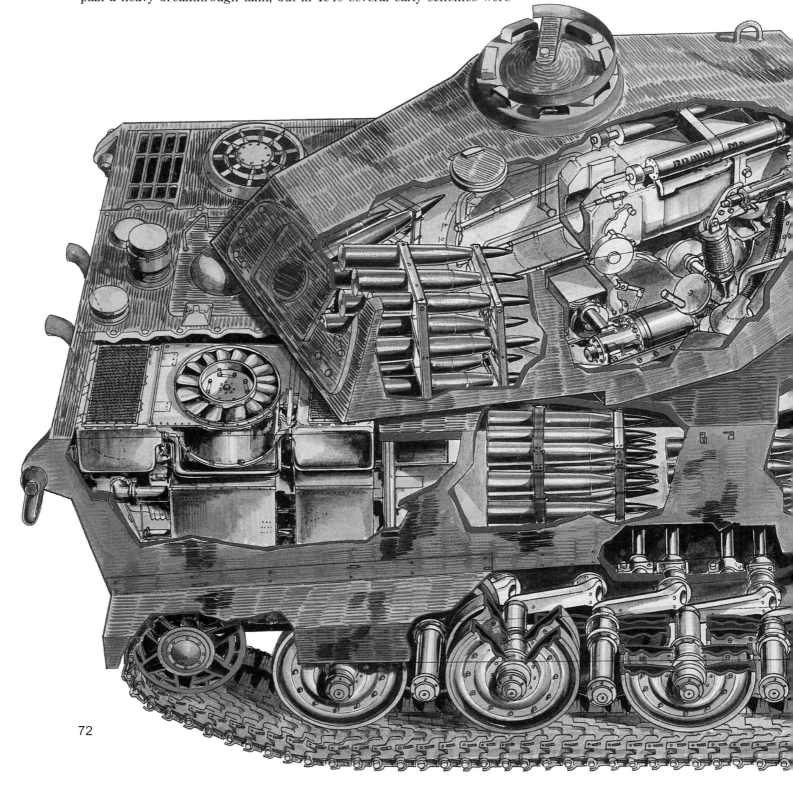

Although an extremely effective weapon in the type of defensive fighting forced on the Germans in the last campaigns of World War II, the PzKpfw VI Tiger II suffered to an even greater extent than the Tiger from a poor power-to-weight ratio, which adversely affected performance and agility, and at the same time placed so great a strain on the engine and transmission that reliability was worse than that of the Tiger.

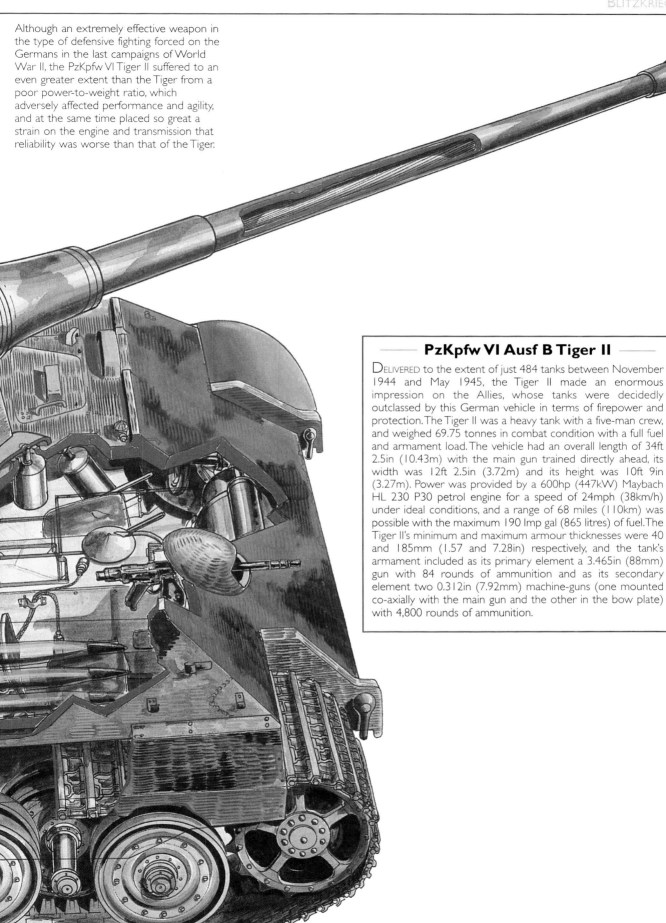

PzKpfw VI Ausf B Tiger II

DELIVERED to the extent of just 484 tanks between November 1944 and May 1945, the Tiger II made an enormous impression on the Allies, whose tanks were decidedly outclassed by this German vehicle in terms of firepower and protection. The Tiger II was a heavy tank with a five-man crew, and weighed 69.75 tonnes in combat condition with a full fuel and armament load. The vehicle had an overall length of 34ft 2.5in (10.43m) with the main gun trained directly ahead, its width was 12ft 2.5in (3.72m) and its height was 10ft 9in (3.27m). Power was provided by a 600hp (447kW) Maybach HL 230 P30 petrol engine for a speed of 24mph (38km/h) under ideal conditions, and a range of 68 miles (110km) was possible with the maximum 190 Imp gal (865 litres) of fuel. The Tiger II's minimum and maximum armour thicknesses were 40 and 185mm (1.57 and 7.28in) respectively, and the tank's armament included as its primary element a 3.465in (88mm) gun with 84 rounds of ammunition and as its secondary element two 0.312in (7.92mm) machine-guns (one mounted co-axially with the main gun and the other in the bow plate) with 4,800 rounds of ammunition.

discontinued in favour of a more advanced 30 tonne breakthrough tank armed with a 75mm (2.95in) main gun. Henschel and Porsche each received an order for four VK3001(H) and VK3001(P) prototypes respectively.

The Germans had been working concurrently on a heavier tank concept primarily to satisfy the demands of Hitler, who was becoming a firm advocate of heavy tanks with powerful armament and protection. Hitler's first choice for the main gun was a tank development of the 88mm (3.46in) FlaK 36 dual-role anti-aircraft/anti-tank gun, and armour was to provide protection against a similar gun. Competing VK4501(H) and VK4501(P) prototypes were introduced in May 1941. The contracts stipulated that the prototypes should be ready for Hitler's birthday on 20 April 1942: each type was to use a Krupp-designed turret accommodating the 88mm (3.46in) kWK 36 L/56 gun. The VK3601(H) was proposed as the VK3601(H1) with the Krupp turret and an 88mm (3.46in) gun and as the VK3601(H2) with a Rheinmetall turret and a 75mm (2.95in) kWK 42 L/70 gun. The H2 variant was never built, but the first prototypes of the VK3601(H1) variant appeared in March 1942.

The VK4501(P) appeared in the following month, and was modelled on the VK3001(P) with the same type of petrol-electric drive and longitudinal torsion bar suspension. Comparative trials confirmed the overall superiority of the VH4501(H), although it was as much as 11.00 tonnes over legend weight, and in August 1942 the type was ordered into production under the designation PzKpfw VI Tiger Ausf H and with the primary armament of onekWK 36 gun.

Variously known as the Sturmtiger and Sturmmörser Tiger, this extraordinary vehicle was the result of the German army's request for a very well protected 8.27in (210mm) self-propelled howitzer based on the PzKpfw VI Ausf E Tiger for the infantry support role and therefore able to tackle hard targets with high-angle fire. There was no suitable weapon for this vehicle, however, and it was therefore decided to develop a type offering basically similar capabilities by using the 14.96in (380mm) Raketenwerfer 61, which was an army development of a weapon initially developed for the German navy as an anti-submarine mortar. Only 10 such vehicles were completed, the raised superstructure carrying the massive mortar and 12 rounds.

Production of the Tiger lasted exactly two years from August 1942, and during that time amounted to 1,350 vehicles. Production peaked in April 1944, when 104 vehicles were delivered: the original rate planned by the armaments ministry had been 12 vehicles per month, but at Hitler's insistence this figure had been increased to 25 vehicles per month by November 1942, increasing again as the type proved itself in combat. In February 1944 the designation was revised, and the vehicle became the PzKpfw Tiger Ausf E (SdKfz 181), this change being contemporary with a modification of the production standard to include a new cupola, simplified fittings and resilient steel wheels in place of the original type with rubber tyres.

The Tiger was truly a massive machine, and its design epitomizes that of the classic 'German tank' of World War II: this was evolved before the T-34 hammered home the advantages of sloped armour, and the Tiger was thus the next in logical sequence from the PzKpfw IV with basically upright armour. In so large and heavy a machine the designers were faced with acute problems of hull rigidity, especially against the torsional effect of recoil when the gun was fired at any angle off the centreline. For this reason the basic structure made use of the largest possible one-piece plates. The overall impression conveyed by the vehicle was one of angular strength, and was confirmed by the minimal armour inclination and maximum armour thickness for a combat weight of 55.00 tonnes or more. The movement of this mass required considerable power: the first 250 vehicles had the 642hp (479kW) Maybach HL 210 P45 petrol engine, and the remainder had the 694hp (517.5kW) HL 230 P45 from the same manufacturer.

The main tactical limitations of the Tiger were the use of hydraulic power from an engine-driven motor for turret traverse, meaning that the heavy turret had to be moved in secondary manual mode when the engine was shut down, and the prodigious thirst of the engine, which resulted in very short range and the general use of the Tiger as an ambush tank rather than a mobile warfare tank, and the high points of its career were thus in the close-country campaigns such as those waged in Normandy (June and July 1944) and the Ardennes (December 1944).

As the Tiger entered production, the Germans decided to develop a new model with better armament and protection in case the Soviets produced another surprise after the T-34. Henschel and Porsche were asked to develop competing designs with sloped armour and the new kWK 43 88mm (3.46in) gun. This weapon was considerably heavier and longer than the kWK 36, but its L/71 barrel provided a much higher muzzle velocity for enhanced armour-penetrating capability.

Porsche responded with the VK4502(P), based on the VK4501(P) but carrying a beautifully shaped turret offering excellent ballistic protection and initially intended for a 150mm (5.91in) L/37 or 105mm (4.13in) L/70 gun, later revised to an 88mm (3.46in) L/71 gun in line with the army's thinking of the period. The VK4502(P) was considered the likely winner by Porsche, which organized the casting process for the turret before the receipt of any production order: but whereas the petrol-electric drive of the VK4501(P) had been rejected largely for its novelty, the basically similar system of the VK4502(P) was now rejected because the copper required for its electric motors was, by late 1943, in very short supply.

The winning design was therefore Henschel's VK4503(H), although the first 50 production vehicles were fitted with the Porsche turret before the comparable Henschel type became standard. The Porsche turret was recognizable by the cut-away lower edge of the turret front, creating a dangerous shot trap between the gun and the roof of the hull; the Henschel turret had a straight front dropping right down to the hull roof without the Porsche turret's dangerous re-entrant. The Henschel design had been completed later than anticipated, the delay to October 1943 being attributable mainly to the armament ministry's desire to standardize as many parts as possible between the new tank and the planned Panther II. Henschel thereby lost a considerable amount of time in liaison with MAN. Production finally began in December 1943, alongside the Tiger (now sometimes known as the Tiger I to differentiate it from its more powerful companion), and the type entered service in the spring of 1944, first seeing action on the Eastern Front in May 1944. Production continued to the end of World War II, and amounted to 485 vehicles, known to the Allies as the Royal Tiger or King Tiger, to the German soldiers as the Königstiger (King Tiger) and to German officialdom as the PzKpfw VI Tiger II Ausf B, this was revised at about the time of the tank's introduction to PzKpfw Tiger II Ausf B.

To a certain extent, the Tiger II should be regarded as the heavyweight counterpart to the Panther rather than as a successor to the Tiger; certainly, the Tiger II had similarities to the Panther in its configuration, sloped armour, and powerplant. This comprised a 694hp (517kW) Maybach HL 230 P30 petrol engine for a 69.70 tonne vehicle, considerably heavier than the 45.50 tonne Panther and the 55.00 tonne Tiger I. The results were inevitable: reduced performance and agility as the power-to-weight ratio was poorer than that of the Panther and Tiger, unreliability because the engine and transmission were overstressed, and a dismal maximum range. These failings were perhaps excusable in a tank now used for defensive warfare, its sole offensive outing being the 'Battle of the Bulge' of December 1944, when many Tiger IIs broke down or ran out of fuel.

On the credit side, however, the Tiger II was the heaviest, the best-armed and best-protected tank of World War II. The construction of the vehicle was of welded and well-sloped armour varying in thickness from 25mm (0.98in) on the belly to a maximum of 150mm (5.91in) on the hull upper front; the turret was also welded of armour up to 100mm (3.94in) thick.

Germany's massive tanks of the Panther and Tiger series were good vehicles, using their firepower and protection to counter the Allies' numerical superiority in armoured vehicles of all types, but were finally immobilized for want of petrol. The significance of these operational tanks is proved by the interest with which captured examples were examined by the victorious Western Allies, their many good features being assessed for incorporation into the new generation of American and British post-war tanks.

Germany's primary allies in World War II were Italy and Japan, but these fell far behind Germany in the development and employment of armour as the cornerstone of their land operations. It has to be admitted that both countries lacked an industrial base comparable in size with that of Germany, but this merely compounded the problem that neither country had seriously considered the tank as an offensive weapon in its own right, and therefore laid the organizational and tactical groundwork for significant armoured forces in the early to mid-1930s.

The best Italian tank of the period was the 14.50 tonne Carro Armato M.14/41 of which 1,103 examples were built with the 145hp (108kW) SPA 15 TM41 engine, sand-removing air filters, and a primary armament of one 47mm gun. The final development in this design sequence was the 15.50 tonne Carro Armato M.15/42, which entered service in 1943. This was modelled closely on the M.14/41, but had a hull lengthened to permit the installation of a 192hp (143kW) SPA 15 TBM42 petrol engine. Several detail modifications (such as additional attachment points for external stowage,

The Japanese fighting vehicle known as the Medium Tank Type 89 was powered by a diesel engine for reduced vulnerability and for the better fuel economy typical of this type of powerplant, but was otherwise of undistinguished design with riveted armour and a forward-mounted turret carrying the main armament, which was a 57mm gun that was complemented by two machine-guns.

and a revised exhaust system) were introduced and the turret was provided with a power traverse system. The armament was also modernized, the 47/32 gun of the M.13/40 and M.14/41 being replaced in the M 15/42 by a 47/40 gun whose additional eight calibres of barrel length provided a higher muzzle velocity for greater armour penetration without any sacrifice of fire rate, which remained about seven or eight rounds per minute. Production of the M.15/42 totalled about 90 examples by March 1943, after which time the Italians decided to halt manufacture.

The best Japanese tank of the World War II period was the Medium Tank Type 3 (Chi-Nu). This was based on the hull of the Chi-He with a new turret designed around the Type 3 gun and installed on the basic hull. The larger main gun and its turret (without a machine-gun in its rear face) increased combat weight to 18.80 tonnes, but as the 240hp (179kW) diesel engine remained unchanged, the overall effect was a slight reduction in performance. Production started in 1944, but Japan's increasingly acute production problems limited manufacture to between 50 and 60 of these improved tanks.

Given their failure to appreciate the true course of development in armoured warfare in the 1930s, the Italian and Japanese tank arms could not emulate that of Germany either operationally or technically. Italian and Japanese tanks were therefore only of limited use in World War II, and generally failed to inspire post-war trends.

The Allies Fight Back

A T the outbreak of World War II in September 1939, British armoured regiments were equipped with tanks developed in the 1930s, but the increasingly rapid pace of re-armament since 1936 was beginning to pay dividends in newer tank types, which the army hoped would be better suited to the type of operations likely to be encountered in Britain's worldwide commitments. These commitments required tanks that could operate in terrains, climates and logistical situations as diverse as northern Europe, North Africa and the Middle/Near East, and South-East Asia.

The tank types serving in greatest numbers at the beginning of World War II were the Light Tank Mk VI, the Infantry Tanks Mk I and Mk II, and the Cruiser Tanks Mk I, Mk II, Mk III and Mk IV. The best of these, without doubt, were the A13 Cruiser Tank Mk III and A13 Mk II Cruiser Tank Mk IV, and the A12 Infantry Tank Mk II Matilda II, all of which werel discussed in the second chapter.

In the cruiser category, great things had been expected of the A13 Mk III Cruiser Tank Mk V Covenanter, but this machine had not performed well and in 1937 the basic design was developed into the A15 Cruiser Tank Mk VI Crusader, first of the so-called heavy cruiser tanks but with the same 2pdr (40mm) main armament as the earlier tanks together with the 340hp (253.5kW) Liberty Mk III engine used in the A13. Even as it appeared, the type was recognized as being too lightly armed and too poorly armoured. The Crusader was nonetheless ordered 'off the drawing board' in July 1939, nine companies being involved in manufacture of an eventual 5,300 examples in various marks.

The hull was similar to that of the Covenanter, with a long low decking and a well-angled glacis, and the Christie type of running gear was also similar to that of the Covenanter, although with the addition of an extra road wheel on each side and with the springs located inside rather than outside the hull. The running gear proved to be excellent, and the Crusader was able to exceed its legend speed of 27mph (43.5km/h) by a considerable margin: some Crusaders were capable of speeds over 40mph (64.4km/h), but high speeds often caused mechanical failure in the engine. The forward compartment was occupied by the driver and bow machine-gunner, the latter operating a single 7.92mm (0.31in) Besa machine-gun in a small turret to the left of the driver. The rear compartment was occupied by the Liberty engine, a de-rated version of the aero engine designed in World War II as a 400hp (298kW) unit. The centre of the vehicle housed the fighting compartment with the multi-side and angular (though well sloped) turret above it: this power-traversed turret was extremely cramped with its complement of commander, gunner and loader/radio operator, and carried only a 2pdr (40mm) main gun, whose limitations were becoming apparent

This cutaway illustration highlights the most important structural and conceptual features of the classic Sherman medium tank in its M4A4 variant that was standardized in February 1942 and powered by a 30-cylinder Chrysler petrol engine that comprised five six-cylinder car engines geared together to operate as a single unit offering 425hp (317kW) for a speed of 25mph (40km/h). The M4A4 had a crew of five and a combat weight of 31.7 tons, and its armament comprised one 2.95in (75mm) main gun and three machine-guns.

even in 1939. A 7.92mm (0.31in) Besa machine-gun was mounted co-axially with the main armament, and there was also a 0.303in (7.7mm) Bren light machine-gun on the roof for anti-aircraft defence. In the Cruiser Tank Mk VICS Crusader ICS the 2pdr (40mm) gun was replaced by a 3 in (76.2mm) howitzer for use in the close-support role.

The Crusader was rushed into production and service before all its mechanical problems had been eliminated, and in its first combat operations, the 'Battleaxe' fighting of June 1941, more Crusaders were immobilized by mechanical failure than by enemy action. There was also criticism of the Crusader's cramped interior and thin armour, resulting in the Cruiser Tank Mk VIA Crusader II. The first criticism was alleviated by omission of the machine-gun turret, although the space was frequently used to increase the 2pdr (40mm) ammunition stowage; the second was ameliorated by increasing the maximum armour thickness on the frontal arc to 49mm (1.93in). The loss of the turret was balanced by the thicker armour, and the combat weight therefore remained steady at 19.30 tonnes. There was also a Cruiser Tank Mk VIA Crusader IICS with a 3in (76.2mm) close-support howitzer replacing the 2pdr (40mm) gun.

The ultimate development of the Crusader gun tank was the 20.07 tonne Cruiser Tank Crusader III, with much improved armament and the improved Liberty Mk IV engine. In this model all provision for the machine-gun turret was removed, the frontal armour was thickened and the main gun became a 6pdr (57mm) weapon. This gun was both longer and heavier than its predecessor, and this led to revision of the turret for two-man operation by the gunner and commander/loader/radio operator. The Crusader III was

available in time for the decisive 2nd Battle of El Alamein in October and November 1942, but was severely hampered operationally by the overtaxing of the commander. Nevertheless, the Crusader was a vital element of the eventual British success in the North African campaign, and although a few were used in the opening stages of the Italian campaign, the Crusader disappeared rapidly as a first-line gun tank from mid-1943.

The origins of the cruiser concept lay with the lightweight cavalry tank, designed for reconnaissance and deep penetration, using its speed and mobility to avoid the type of trouble that could be handled by thin armour and light armament. The Crusader was the last cruiser tank to be designed to this concept, whose fallacies were evidenced by the efforts made to step up the Crusader's protection and firepower.

The 6pdr (57mm) gun offered the firepower required, so the main problem to be addressed in the next cruiser tank was the deficiency in protection. Early in 1941, the War Office issued a requirement for a new heavy cruiser tank, to be called the Cromwell.

This requirement demanded armour on a 2.75in (70mm) basis, thereby offering some 50 per cent more protection than available on the Crusader, and a 6pdr (57mm) main armament in a turret using a 60in (1.52m) diameter turret ring so that there would be adequate space for the commander, gunner and loader. The requirement also specified a combat weight of about 25.2 tonnes for the new tank, which was to be powered by a Rolls-Royce Meteor (a derivative of the Merlin aero engine) to provide cruiser-type performance. Progress was hindered because the Meteor engine was still at an early stage of development by Leyland and Rolls-Royce.

Known to its American originators as the Light Tank M3 and to the British as the General Stuart, this attractive little vehicle was universally known as the 'Honey' for its pleasant nature and great reliability. Carrying a four-man crew and weighing some 12.3 tons, the M3 was powered by a 250hp (186kW) Continental radial engine for a speed of 35mph (56km/h), was armed with a 37mm main gun equipped with a primitive stabilisation system, and also had between three and five machine-guns.

Development of the A27M Cruiser Tank Mk VIII Cromwell was also delayed by the exhaustive evaluation programme demanded by the War Office following the problems with the production runs of the Liberty-engined interim Crusader and Cavalier models. Although the first Cromwell prototype had run in January 1942, it was January 1943 before the first Cromwell I gun tanks came off the production line. The first vehicles had the 600hp (447kW) Meteor engine built by Rolls-Royce, although production of this important engine was switched as rapidly as possible to other manufacturers so that Rolls-Royce could concentrate on its aero engine development and production programmes. The availability of the new engine finally gave British tanks the performance fillip they needed: there was now great reliability and ample power, and the engine rarely needed to be run at the high power settings that had caused the less powerful Liberty to break down with such regularity.

The Cromwell had been planned with the 6pdr (57mm) gun, but during 1942 there was a gradual change in popularity from the dedicated anti-tank gun to a weapon capable of firing anti-tank and HE rounds. Officers with experience of the American M3 Grant and M4 Sherman tanks were unanimous in their praise for the 75mm (2.95in) M2 and M3 weapons used in these vehicles, and their pressure finally convinced the War Office. In January 1943 it was decided that the majority of medium tanks should be fitted with a dual-capable weapon, and be supported in action by smaller numbers of tanks with role-specific anti-tank and close-support weapons. The result in the armament field was the rapid procurement of the 75mm (2.95in) Mk 5/5A gun, derived from the 6pdr (57mm) weapon with the barrel bored out, shortened and fitted with a single-baffle muzzle brake and firing the standard range of US ammunition for the M2/M3 guns.

It was planned to fit this weapon in the Cromwell, whose generous turret ring diameter made such a move possible without undue modification, but as the weapon did not become available until October 1943, the first Cromwells were delivered with the 6pdr (57mm) gun. In overall

Seen here with a flail-type mineclearing system extended in front of its nose, the M4A1 was the second production version of the Sherman medium tank, and was powered by a 400hp (298kW) Continental R-975 radial engine for a speed of 24mph (39km/h) at a weight of 29.7 tons and with a crew of five. The armament was of the standard type for these early variants, namely one 2.95in (75mm) main gun and three machine-guns.

configuration the Cromwell was of typical British tank layout, with Christie-type running gear derived from that of the A13 with suitable strengthening.

The Cromwell remained in service until 1950, and went through an extensive development programme, involving the introduction of the Cromwell I with an armament of one 6pdr (57mm) gun and two 7.92mm (0.31in) Besa machine-guns; the Cromwell II with tracks 15.5in (394mm) rather than 14in (356mm) wide to reduce ground pressure and promote agility; the Cromwell III (originally designated Cromwell X) produced by converting the Centaur I with the Meteor engine; the Cromwell IV conversion of the Centaur III with the Meteor engine and a 75mm (2.95in) gun; the Cromwell V improvement of the basic tank with the 75mm gun; the Cromwell Vw with a welded rather than riveted hull; the Cromwell VI close-support version fitted with a 3.7in (94mm) howitzer in place of the 75mm (2.95in) gun; the Cromwell VII based on the Mk IV but fitted with wider tracks, a reduced ratio final drive and increased armour thickness for a combat weight of 28.45 tonnes; the Cromwell VIIw with a welded hull; and the final-production Cromwell VIII development of the Cromwell VI close-support version with the improvements of the Cromwell VII.

The Cromwell proved itself an excellent tank in terms of protection and mobility, and when properly handled could evade the more powerfully armed German tanks. But this could not disguise the fact, recognized at the beginning of 1942, that the type would soon lack the firepower necessary to combat new German tanks likely to appear in service from late 1942. This

The A27M, otherwise known as the Cruiser Tank Mk VIII Cromwell, was the full-development version of the A27L or Cruiser Tank Mk VIII Centaur with the earlier tank's 395hp (294.5kW) Liberty engine replaced by the considerably more powerful 600hp (447kW) Rolls-Royce Meteor engine for a maximum speed of 40mph (64km/h) at a weight of 28 tons. The Cromwell had a crew of five, and its main armament was one 2.95in (75mm) gun.

resulted in a development known as the A30 Cruiser Tank Challenger, designed to carry the very powerful 17pdr (3in/76.2mm) anti-tank gun in a new and enlarged turret. This turret was characterized by its height rather than its width, and despite the lengthening of the Cromwell's basic hull by the addition of a sixth road wheel on each side, the 32.00 tonne Challenger was too small for its turret and performance suffered as a consequence. The pressures of the situation demanded production, however, and in 1943 some 260 Challengers were ordered: these were generally used to strengthen the capabilities of Cromwell cruiser tank regiments in the North-West European campaign of 1944-45.

The last operational cruiser tank was another heavy type, the A34 Cruiser Tank Comet. The specific spur for the specification that led to development of the Comet was the nature of the armoured battles fought in the Western Desert early in 1942, when it became clear that current British tanks lacked a gun capable of defeating the armour of Germany's latest tanks. Just as worrying was the fact that the new generation of British tanks was designed round the 6pdr (57mm) gun, which was only marginally superior to current German protection. The answer was a larger-calibre gun, and the ideal weapon was found in the 17pdr (3in/76.2mm) towed anti-tank gun. Plans to upgrade the Cromwell with this weapon proved impossible, and the hybrid Challenger was also unsuccessful. Just one month after the appearance of the prototype Challenger in August 1942, the decline of the British situation in North Africa further emphasized the need for an up-gunned cruiser tank, and in September, Leyland was commissioned to design a new A34 heavy cruiser tank with the 17pdr gun and good armour on a chassis that was to use as many Cromwell features as possible in order to reduce costs and speed development.

Leyland had completed its A34 mock-up by September 1943 after starting definitive work in July, and production was scheduled for mid-1944. The hull was based on that of the Cromwell (and thereby perpetuated the vertical front plate and bow machine-gun that had caused a certain amount of justified criticism), but the armour was thickened and the construction was all-welded. The same 600hp (447kW) Meteor engine and associated transmission were used, and the running gear was ultimately revised to include four track-return rollers on each side. The major improvement, however, was the welded turret with a cast front plate and mantlet: this turret was more spacious, had better access, supported a 360-degree vision cupola for the commander, was fitted with an electrical traverse system, and had provision for the ready-use rounds to be stowed in armoured bins for additional protection.

The prototype appeared in February 1944 with running gear akin to that of the Cromwell. But the need to strengthen the suspension for the Comet's weight of 33.34 tonnes combined with other modifications to delay production into the late summer, the first production tanks reaching the

Although not a tank in any real sense of the word, the Landing Vehicle Tracked may be regarded in some respects as the analogue of the tank and armoured personnel carrier for the amphibious assault role, and some later types were indeed fitted with the turreted armament of a light tank for the direct support of landed troops. This is an LVT(A) armed with two 20mm cannon.

To the British and US armies the US Navy's LVT(A)4 was known as the Alligator Mk IV, and was a six-man vehicle used mainly in the support role with the power-traversed turret of the M8 Howitzer Motor Carriage with its short 2.95in (75mm) howitzer. The LVT(A)4 weighed 18.3 tons fully laden, and with a 250hp (186kW) Continental radial engine had water and land speeds of 7 and 16mph (11.25 and 25.75km/h) respectively.

regiments in September 1944. Thereafter the Comet proved itself an excellent machine that remained in British service until 1958, and apart from the high-quality main armament, its most notable features were its cross-country speed and agility: these factors were often too great for the crew to endure, and the tank therefore has the distinction of being limited by crew rather than by mechanical considerations.

The British army's first two infantry tanks, the Matilda I and II, had resulted from official requirements and specifications. The same cannot be said for their successor, the Valentine, which was a private venture by Vickers-Armstrongs, based on the A10 Cruiser Tank Mk II with components from a number of other Vickers-Armstrongs tanks of the period, notably the A9 Cruiser Tank Mk I and A11 Infantry Tank Mk I. The resulting vehicle was a hybrid of the pure infantry tank and the cruiser tank: the protection and armament were to infantry tank standards, but the performance fell between infantry and cruiser tank requirements, an unfortunate feature that led the War Office to regard the machine as a well-protected cruiser, allocating it to the new armoured divisions being raised in expectation of the open warfare for which the Valentine really lacked the performance.

The company presented its design to the War Office in February 1938, but it was July 1939 before a production order for the Infantry Tank Mk III Valentine was placed and, given the exigencies of the situation, this order demanded 275 tanks delivered in the shortest possible time. No prototype was required as the basic features of the design had already been well proved, and the first Valentine I entered service in May 1940, coinciding with the German offensive against the West. Production ended in the early months of 1944 after some 8,275 had been built. Of these, almost 2,700 (including all but 30 of the 1,420 Canadian-built machines) were supplied to the USSR. The Red Army approved the Valentine's simplicity, reliability and protection, but found the main armament hopelessly inadequate: the standard 2pdr (40mm) gun of the British tanks was often replaced in Soviet service by a 76.2mm (3in) weapon which boosted offensive performance to a considerable degree, but made the already small turret yet more cramped.

Mention has been made of some of the Valentine's virtues, and to these must be added the type's enormous advantage of easy upgrading in terms of armament and motive power. Up to the Mk VIII model, all Valentines

weighed 16.26 tonnes. The Valentine I was powered by a 135hp (101kW) AEC petrol engine, had a crew of three, and the small turret accommodated commander and the gunner for the 2pdr (40mm) main gun, which was supported by a 7.92mm (0.31in) Besa co-axial machine-gun: the commander also acted as gunner and radio operator, and this proved a serious hindrance to the proper exercise of his basic function. The Valentine II had a 131hp (97.7kW) AEC diesel engine, but was otherwise similar to the Valentine I although often fitted with sand shields for desert operations. The Valentine III was identical with the Valentine II in everything except its turret, which was a modified type allowing a three-man fighting crew: the turret had the appearance of the original turret, but was modified internally by pushing the front plate forward and the rear plate backward. The Valentine IV and V were identical with the Mk II and Mk III respectively except in the engine, which was a 138hp (103kW) General Motors diesel. The Valentine VI and VII were produced in Canada, and were in effect versions of the Valentine IV with a General Motors diesel engine, a cast rather than riveted nose plate, and a 0.3in (7.62mm) Browning rather than a Besa co-axial machine-gun: the Mk VII differed from the Mk VI in having a remote-control system for the machine-gun. The Valentine VIIA was a derivative of the Mk VII with studded tracks and jettisonable external fuel tanks.

Seen with its flotation skirt lowered, this is a Duplex Drive version of the infantry Tank Mk III Valentine XI with all-welded construction and a primary armament of one 2.95in (75mm) gun. Attached in watertight fashion to the hull, the skirt was erected by release of compressed gas into tubes that thus straightened and lifted the canvas screen (skirt) attached to them.

The Valentine VIII received a considerable improvement in firepower by the adoption of a 6pdr (57mm) main gun, although its installation sacrificed the co-axial machine-gun in the two-man turret; the 6pdr (57mm) gun was controlled in elevation via a geared manual system, the original 2pdr (40mm) weapon having been operated directly via a gunner's shoulder rest. Weight was increased to 17.27 tonnes, and power was provided by the AEC diesel, switched in the otherwise identical Valentine IX to the General Motors diesel. Some Mk IXs were later fitted with a 165hp (123kW) General Motors diesel, and this engine was also used in the last two production models, the Valentine X with a 6pdr (57mm) main gun and Besa co-axial machine-gun, and the Valentine XI with a cast nose plate and a 75mm (2.95in) gun in place of the 6pdr (57mm) weapon.

After the Valentine came the United Kingdom's most important infantry tank of World War II, the A22 Infantry Tank Mk IV Churchill. This vehicle was planned in 1939 as a replacement for the Matilda II, the operational scenario envisaged by the War Office comprising a Western Front not dissimilar to that in France during World War I. This scenario called for a tank that was in essence a modern version of the rhomboidal tanks of that war, with thick armour, good but not exceptional armament, and the ability to move without undue difficulty in a heavily shelled area. In September 1939 the specification for an A20 infantry tank was issued, and design work was entrusted to Harland & Wolff in Belfast, as part of the government's policy of diversifying tank design and construction capability. Harland & Wolff built four prototypes by June 1940, and these revealed a striking similarity to World War I practices, with a general rhomboidal shape for good trench-crossing capability, and a main armament of two 2pdr (40mm) guns located in side sponsons. The type was also planned with a central turret, but none of the prototypes was fitted with either turret or armament.

In June 1940 the French campaign ended, and with it the War Office discarded its notions of latter-day trench warfare, and thus the A20's *raison*

The Valentine Crocodile was a development vehicle for the armoured flamethrower concept, and was the basic gun tank revised with the flame gun in a small turret: fuel was supplied by gas pressure from an armoured two-wheel trailer towed behind the truck.

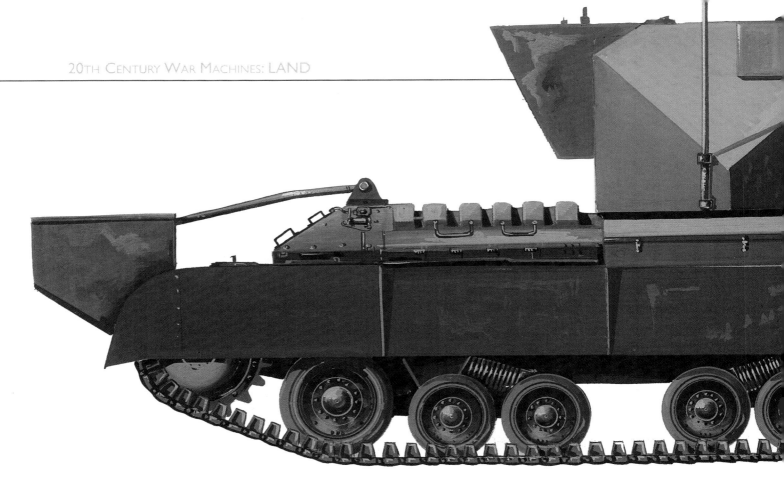

One of the many Valentine variants used for development purposes was this flail type, with a powered drum supported ahead of the vehicle to thrash the ground with the chains and explode any pressure-activated anti-tank mines buried there.

d'être. The design had good features in its hull and running gear, however, and these formed the basis of the tank designed to meet the revised A22 specification released to Vauxhall Motors. The country's desperate situation after the defeat at Dunkirk was reflected in the War Office's stipulation that production of the A22 should begin within one year, even though it realized that so hasty a programme would necessarily entail a number of inbuilt faults in the first model. Design began in July 1940 and the first A22 prototype appeared in December 1940, with the initial Churchill I production tanks appearing in June 1941, to inaugurate a programme that finally produced 5,640 Churchill tanks before production was completed in October 1945.

Results of tank development in the late 1930s, and the lessons of the Polish and Western campaigns waged and won by the Germans in 1939 and 1940, led to a tank that was both lower and better protected than its predecessors. In the first Churchills, the armour varied in thickness from 16mm (0.63in) to 102mm (4in), but two short-term limitations were the inadequate armament and the problem-prone engine. By 1940 it had been realized that the 2pdr (40mm) gun was too feeble a weapon for effective anti-tank employment, and lacked a significant HE shell capability; a considerably more effective weapon, the 6pdr (57mm) gun, was already in existence but not in production, and in the days after Dunkirk, a decision was made to keep the obsolescent gun in large-scale production rather than phase in the 6pdr (57mm) weapon. As far as the Churchill was concerned, this meant that a substantial 39.12 tonne vehicle was fitted with a turret carrying obsolescent armament. The situation was partially remedied in the Churchill I by the installation of a 3in (76.2mm) howitzer in the front plate of the hull: this howitzer had a useful support capability, although the installation was restricted by the limited traverse imposed by the semi-recessed position of the front plate behind the projecting forward horns of the running gear. The crew of five comprised the driver and gunner in the nose compartment, and the commander, gunner and loader in the spacious turret.

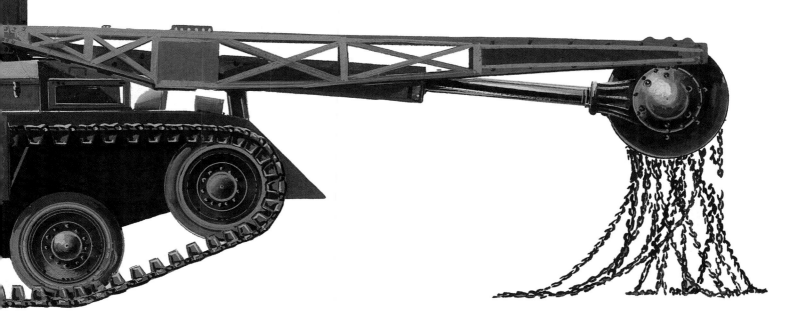

Many of the special-purpose 'funny' variants evolved with Valentine series prototypes were then developed into operational models based on the A22, otherwise known as the Infantry Tank Mk IV Churchill. One of the most important such variants of the Churchill was the AVRE (Armoured Vehicle Royal Engineers), which was a conversion from Churchill III or IV for assault engineer units with the main gun replaced by a petard mortar firing demolition bombs, with special stowage bins for engineer equipment, and with special exterior fittings on the front and sides for role-specific attachments. The vehicle illustrated here is a further development of the AVRE by the Canadian army as the Churchill AVRE Mk II SBG with a 34ft (10.4m) Standard Box Girder bridge that could be laid across a gap and then released.

The other major limitation was the engine, a custom-designed Bedford petrol unit that was essentially a pair of six-cylinder truck engines lying on their sides and married to a common crank-case. This petrol unit developed only 350hp (261kW), giving the Churchill a distinctly modest power-to-weight ratio, and was also plagued with reliability problems in its first year of service. Unreliability was a disadvantage in itself, but it was exacerbated by the Churchill's poor engine installation. The War Office had demanded a readily accessible engine compartment, but this failed to materialize and even comparatively minor problems demanded the removal of the entire engine. Development and service experience gradually eliminated the engine problems, and this in turn reduced the adverse effect of the poor engine installation. Ultimately the Churchill became a notably reliable tank.

The Churchill was in service with the British army from 1941 to 1952, and in this period underwent considerable development, especially during World War II. The Churchill I has already been described in basic detail, and there was also a Churchill I CS with a second 3in (76.2mm) howitzer in the turret in place of the 2pdr (40mm) gun. The Churchill II was similar to the Churchill I in all but armament, where the hull-mounted howitzer was replaced by a 7.92mm (0.31in) Besa machine-gun to complement the co-axial weapon in the turret. These first two marks may be regarded as pilot models, and the A22 design began to reach maturity in the Churchill III, which was a much improved 39.63 tonne model that appeared in March 1942 with an all-welded turret accommodating the 6pdr (57mm) gun for greater anti-tank capability; the Mk III also introduced the large mudguards that were fitted on all later marks and retrofitted to the first two variants.

The Churchill IV was similar to the Mk III except for its turret, which was cast rather than welded; in North Africa, some Mk IVs were revised to the so-called Churchill IV (NA 75) standard with the 75mm (2.95in) main gun and 0.3in (7.62mm) Browning co-axial

Another use for the Churchill AVRE was the creation of paths across dry gaps by the dropping of a large fascine.

machine-gun of the M3 Grant medium tank. The Churchill V was the first genuine close-support version of the series, and was armed with a 3.7in (94mm) Tank Howitzer Mk 1, the same weapon as that installed in the Centaur IV. The final variant of the initial Churchill series was the Churchill VI, another gun tank, and modelled on the Mk IV with the exception of the main armament, which was a 75mm (2.95in) Mk 5 weapon of the type installed on the Centaur III and on the Cromwell V, VI and VII.

The Churchill VI was essentially an interim variant pending deliveries of the considerably upgraded A22F (later A42) Infantry Tank Churchill VII. The origins of the variant date back to the War Office's realization that appliqué armour was not the optimum solution to the problem of improving protection. The A22F specification therefore called for a maximum armour thickness of 152mm (6in), but this was to be of the integral rather than appliqué type. The resultant Churchill VII retained the basic configuration and shape of the earlier marks, but was extensively revised to allow the incorporation of thicker armour in the structure and the addition of many features shown to be desirable in earlier variants. The armour varied in thickness from 25mm (0.98in) to 152mm (6in), and this increased the tank's basic weight to 40.64 tonnes. The engine remained unaltered so the performance was degraded, and the main armament was the same 75mm (2.95in) gun as fitted in the Mk VI, with a single-baffle muzzle brake; the turret was a composite unit with the horizontal roof welded to the cast vertical sections, and was the first

British example of a commander's cupola providing a 360-degree field of vision in the closed-down mode.

The close-support version of the Mk VII was the Churchill VIII, the last production variant. This was identical to the Mk VII in all but its armament, which was the same as that of the Mk V: one 3.7in (94mm) howitzer and two 7.92mm (0.31in) Besa machine-guns, one co-axial and the other in the bow plate.

The last three marks were earlier Churchills reworked to improved standards, with appliqué armour and the cast turret of the Mk VII complete with the 75mm (2.95in) gun. The designations Churchill IX, X and XI were used for Mks III and IV, Mk VI and Mk V tanks respectively, while the suffix LT (Light turret) was used for those that retained their original turrets (revised for the heavier main gun) but featured appliqué armour.

The United States shared the UK's lack of enthusiasm for large-scale technical and tactical development of armoured warfare in the 1920s and 1930s. During the late 1930s, however, the rapid worsening of world affairs prompted a re-evaluation of the situation. As previously mentioned, in the 1930s the US Army had sought to mitigate the worst effects of the USA's isolationist foreign policy and its lack of financing for the services, by pursuing an adventurous design philosophy with limited production allocated to industrial concerns capable of rapid expansion in times of need. This policy helped to keep the US Army abreast of overseas developments up to the mid-1930s, and the organization of the army's tank arm was also modified to consolidate tactical thinking.

The Churchill Crocodile was a conversion from the Churchill VII gun tank standard, with a flame gun installed in the forward part of the hull was supplied with 400 Imp gal (1,818 litres) of fuel from a two-wheel armoured tanker towed behind the vehicle by a quick-release mechanism. The fuel was forced to the flame gun by compressed nitrogen carried in five bottles in the trailer: flame could be projected to a typical range of 80yds (73m) and a maximum range of 120yds (110m).

The main tank types in service with the Armored Force in 1941 were the Light Tank M3 and the Medium Tank M3, both introduced to service in that year after standardization in 1940. The Light Tank M3 was a straightforward development of the Light Tank M2A4, which had been standardized in 1939 as the final expression of the basic concept pioneered in the M2A1 of 1935. The Americans had wished to develop a more capable light tank, perhaps armed with a 75mm (2.95in) main gun, but the need to undertake development as rapidly as possible to match potential enemies' numerical superiority necessitated an M2 update rather than a new vehicle; this removed any possibility of a larger-calibre main gun because of the M2's narrow hull, itself dictated by the width capability of the Engineer Corps' pontoon bridging equipment.

The M2A4 was a moderately useful machine. Its mobility and firepower were considered adequate, but there was concern about the level of protection provided by the riveted plate armour: overall thickness was satisfactory, but serious reservations were expressed about the protection offered against air attack, which the opening operations of World War II had shown to be considerably more devastating than had been expected. Thus the M2 was taken in hand for development with thicker armour on the upper surfaces, although the overall level of protection was improved by the adoption of reliable homogeneous armour rather than the brittle face-hardened armour of the M2 series. This improved armour was used for the all-riveted construction of the baseline M3A1, raising weight from the M2A4's 11.685 tonnes to 12.50 tonnes in the M3A1, standardized in July 1940.

Production of the M3 series continued until August 1942, the American Car and Foundry Company delivering some 5,811 M3 tanks in just over two years. The Americans failed to fall into the trap of three- rather than four-man crews, and the M3's complement consisted of a driver, assistant driver/hull gunner, commander and gunner. The turret therefore had a crew of two, a situation ameliorated by the comparative light weight of the ammunition for the 37mm main gun, which did not impose too great a burden on the gunner. Apart from the 37mm M5 or M6 main gun, the M3A1's armament comprised five 0.3in (7.62mm) Browning machine-guns located as a single co-axial weapon, a single bow weapon, a single anti-aircraft weapon on the commander's fixed turret-roof cupola, and two weapons in side sponsons fixed to deliver forward fire, (these two weapons

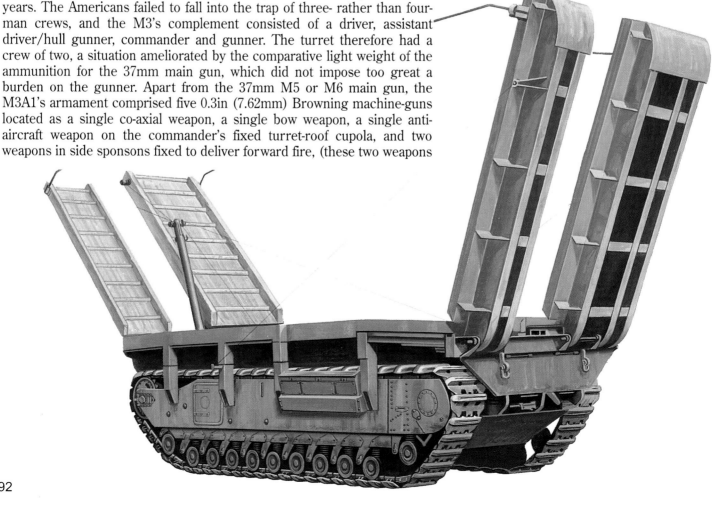

The Churchill Ark was a ramp-type bridging tank: the turret was removed and the upper part of the hull revised as a 'roadway' with folding ramps at each end. The vehicle was driven into the gap to be bridged and the ramps were then lowered, creating an 'instant road' across which other vehicles could pass.

Designed for the creation of a pathway over which infantry and trucks could cross barbed wire or poor ground, the carpet-laying concept was used in several forms by variants of the Churchill infantry tank, which could carry a large bobbin of reinforced hessian material for rapid laying under the tank's tracks.

were often omitted, especially in British service where sand-shields were usually installed in place of the machine-guns).

The M3 series was widely used by the British and dominion forces, and was given the name General Stuart whilst in British service. The tank was widely admired for its high level of protection, reliability, high speed and good agility in difficult terrain, and this admiration was reflected in the nickname 'Honey', which was generally used in preference to the official British name. Total production of the Light Tank M3 series up to October 1943 amounted to 13,859 tanks, making this the most prolific light tank series of World War II. The type was extensively used in most Allied theatres and, due to features such as its stabilized gun, was still an effective weapon against Japanese tanks in 1945. What cannot be ignored, however, are the type's several limitations, most notably its high silhouette and angular lines, the latter contributing significantly to the creation of several shot traps.

The next stage in US light tank development was inspired by the car industry rather than the Ordnance Department. The Light Tank M5 was suggested by Cadillac, which proposed to a sceptical Ordnance Department that the M3 could be revised without difficulty to accept a different powerplant and transmission: the powerplant would be a pair of Cadillac V-8 car engines, and the transmission the Cadillac Hydra-Matic automatic type. Cadillac converted an M3 to this standard as the M3E2. The conversion was completed in October 1941, and the revised model was standardized in February 1942 as the Light Tank M5 with a welded hull and the hull front thickened to a maximum of 64mm (2.5in). The turret was that of the M3A1, and the model weighed 14.97 tonnes with 220hp (164kW) available from the ganged Cadillac engines. The M5 was named the General Stuart VI by the British, and was succeeded in production from September 1942 by the M5A1 (also called the General Stuart VI). This final version weighed 15.38 tonnes, and differed from the M5 in having the turret of the M3A3 with radio bulge, improved main gun mounting, larger hatches for the driver and co-driver, and an escape hatch in the belly. Production of the M5 series amounted to 8,884 (2,074 M5s and 6,810 M5A1s) before production terminated in October 1944.

Designed from 1933 to meet a French army requirement for a light infantry support tank, the Renault Type ZM (otherwise known as the Char Léger R-35) was a two-man type weighing 10 tons and armed with a 37mm short-barrel gun in a small hand-operated turret. Some 2,000 were built for the French army, whose most important tank it was in 1940, and the type was also exported to Poland, Romania, Turkey and Yugoslavia.

Unofficially known as the CV35 and more formally as the Carro Veloce 33/II, this was a simple and generally ineffective tankette with an armament of two 0.303in (7.7mm) machine-guns in the front of the 'fighting compartment'.

The next US light tank to enter large-scale production was the result of a carefully planned programme designed to yield a high-quality successor to the M3 and M5 series. This was the Light Tank M24, which emerged as the best light tank of World War II: firepower was superior to that of all medium tanks of 1939 through the use of a lightweight 75mm (2.95in) T13E1 gun with concentric recoil mechanism derived from the M5 aircraft weapon; protection was provided by a considerable lowering of silhouette combined with careful design of thinner (and lighter) armour, offering a high level of ballistic protection with few shot traps; and mobility was at least equal to that of the highly praised M5.

Launched in April 1943, the programme that led to the M24 incorporated the engine and transmission that had proved so successful in the M5, and the running gear of the 76mm Gun Motor Carriage M18 'Hellcat', a high-mobility tank destroyer using torsion bar suspension for five medium-diameter road wheels on each side. Such a vehicle was proposed by the Cadillac Motor Car Division of the General Motors Corporation, and two prototypes were ordered under the designation Light Tank T24. These were delivered in October 1943, and proved so successful during initial running trials that 1,000 were ordered even before the full service trials had begun. The tank was standardized as the Light Tank M24 in July 1944, and production orders eventually totalled 5,000 units, of which 4,070 had been built by June 1945. The M24 entered service with the US Army in 1944, and in 1945 a small quantity was supplied to the British army, which gave the name Chaffee to the type.

The US Army expended enormous development and production effort on medium tanks, which were the mainstay of the service's armoured divisions in World War II. In the late 1930s the US Army's principal vehicles in this class were the Medium Tank M2, and the similar M2A1 armed with a 37mm main gun, but in 1940 it was realized that despite their recent development, these machines were obsolete by the standard now set by German tank development and operations. In August 1940, therefore, the heads of the Armored Force and Ordnance Department decided on the specification for a new medium tank with armour on a 38mm (1.5in) basis and a 75mm (2.95in) main gun. So far as these features were concerned the specification was adequate: problems arose with the realization that the US Army had lagged behind the European nations in developing large-diameter turrets of the type required for a 75mm (2.95in) gun, and that an alternative installation would have to be considered. It was decided, therefore, to upgrade the M2 as the new Medium Tank M3, with thicker armour and a 75mm (2.95in) sponson-mounted gun in addition to the existing 37mm weapon (in a cast rather than welded turret surmounted by a secondary turret accommodating the commander and a 0.3in/7.62mm machine-gun). Late in August 1940 a recently placed order for 1,000 M2A1s was modified to the same number of M3s.

The key to the new tank was the M2 gun, which was in fact an interim model, the definitive weapon in this calibre being the M3 which was ready for installation on later M3 tanks, and was also earmarked for the M3's successor, the legendary M4. The primary limitation of the 75mm (2.95in) gun mounting in the M3 was its small traverse in its casemate, while a useful feature was the provision (for the first time in an operational tank) of a Westinghouse stabilization system for the main and secondary guns in elevation: this allowed moderately accurate fire even with the tank on the move, a feature impossible with previous shoulder- or gear-controlled guns. In tactical terms, the location of the main gun in a sponson meant that much of the tank's considerable height had to be exposed in order to bring the gun into action, while the engagement of targets more than a small angle off the centreline involved manoeuvring the whole vehicle.

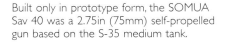

Built only in prototype form, the SOMUA Sav 40 was a 2.75in (75mm) self-propelled gun based on the S-35 medium tank.

Prototypes of the new M3 were delivered in January 1941 by Chrysler, additional vehicles following from American Locomotive (Alco) and Baldwin by April. Production was launched in August 1941, and 6,258 M3s were built before production ceased in December 1942. The six-man M3 bore a marked similarity to the M2, retaining the massive and angular hull, the aero engine-derived powerplant, and the running gear. Curiously, given the fact that the 23.37 tonne M2A1 was powered by a 400hp (298kW) Wright radial engine, the 27.22 tonne M3 had only a 340hp (253.5kW) version of the same unit.

The M3 entered US service in 1941, and was also delivered in substantial numbers to the British, primarily for service in North Africa and the Far East. Although the M3 medium tank's production life was comparatively short, the appearance of several important variants reflected the rapid pace of development in the first half of World War II, and the ability of American manufacturing companies to respond to these developments.

The original M3 (General Lee I in British service) had a riveted hull and

A French medium tank, the SOMUA S-35 was one of the best tanks in the world at the time of introduction in the second half of the 1930s. This 20-ton vehicle was the first tank in the world with all-cast hull and turret construction, and with a crew of three was armed with a 47mm gun and co-axial 0.295in (7.5mm) machine-gun in an electrically traversed turret. Production totalled 500 tanks.

Right and below right: The American
solution to the creation of a medium tank
with a large-calibre gun, at a time when
insufficient development had been
undertaken of the appropriate turret and
traverse mechanism, was the adoption of a
2.75in (75mm) gun in a casemated
installation on the right-hand side of the
hull. This resulted in the Medium Tank M3
that was known to the British as the
General Lee: the main gun was installed in
a cast casemate that allowed only limited
traverse, requiring the whole tank to be
slewed to achieve large changes in gun
azimuth, and was complemented by a
37mm gun in a cast turret. The rest of the
tank was of riveted construction changed in
later variants to a riveted lower hull and
cast upper hull, and finally to all-welded
construction for greater integrity and
reduced weight. The upper photograph is
of the first M3, and the lower photograph
shows an M3 off the production line. The
six-man production model weighed 26.8
tons, and with a 340hp (253.5kW)
Continental R-975 radial engine had a
speed of 26mph (42km/h).

a Wright R-975 radial petrol engine, although some M3 (Diesel) tanks were
fitted with a Guiberson T-1400 diesel engine to overcome shortages of the
Wright engine. Next came the M3A1 (General Lee II), mechanically
identical to the M3 with Wright or Guiberson engine, but built to the extent
of 300 vehicles exclusively by Alco, the only company in the programme
able to produce this variant's cast upper hull (whose side hatches were later
eliminated to provide extra strength, an escape hatch then being added in
the belly). The M3A2 was not used by the British, although the designation
General Lee III had been allocated, and the variant was mechanically
identical with the M3 but based on a welded rather than riveted hull. M3A2
production amounted to only 12 vehicles before Baldwin switched to the
28.58 tonne M3A3 (General Lee IV) with a welded hull and a completely
revised powerplant. This powerplant comprised two General Motors 6-71
diesels coupled to deliver 375hp (280kW): the larger engine installation
reduced fuel capacity, but the efficiency of the diesel powerplant boosted
range. Baldwin's production totalled 322 vehicles, and some British-

operated M3A3s were re-engined with the Wright radial and given the designation General Lee V. The M3A4 (General Lee VI) was identical to the original M3 in everything but its engine, which was a 370hp (276kW) Chrysler A-57 multibank petrol unit made by combining five car cylinder blocks on a common crankshaft; the engine was longer than the earlier units, and to provide an adequate engine compartment, the hull had to be enlarged and the weight increased to 29.03 tonnes. Production of 109 vehicles was undertaken by Chrysler. The final production variant was the M3A5, identical to the M3A3 in every respect but its hull, which was riveted rather than welded for a weight of 29.03 tonnes, and had the side doors either welded shut or eliminated: Baldwin delivered 591 of these vehicles, the last of them with the longer M3 gun fitted with a counterbalance weight at the muzzle.

As mentioned earlier, tanks of the M3 series were delivered to the UK under Lend-Lease, and with the name General Lee. The British also bought a variant of the basic M3 with a number of modifications (the General Grant). The most notable of these modifications was to the 360-degree traverse turret, which was lengthened to the rear so that a radio could be installed, and stripped of its secondary turret to reduce overall height. Similar modification was later made to the M3A5 to produce the General Grant II, whereupon the original variant became the General Grant I. It was as the General Grant that the type made its combat debut in the Battle of Gazala in May 1942. Here for the first time the British had a tank with a gun matching that of the Germans' PzKpfw IV. The importance of the Lee/Grant to the British was considerable, and although there were problems with the fuses and filling of the type's HE shell earlier in 1942, the tank played a significant part in the British success at the second Battle of El Alamein in October and November 1942.

The M3 was of tactical importance in its own right, but was also significant in buying time for the development of the Americans' most important medium tank of World War II. It had been appreciated from the beginning of the M3 programme that the sponson-mounted main gun was a potent limitation, and on 29 August 1940 (just one day after the first production order for the M3 had been placed), design work began on an M3

Together with its Light Tank M5 successor with a different type of powerplant, the Light Tank M3 was built in very large numbers for the USA and also for a number of American allies.

successor with its 75mm (2.95in) main gun in a 360-degree traverse turret. This would in itself provide great tactical improvement, while elimination of the sponson reduced the volume requiring armour protection, thereby allowing a lighter weight of armour for a more sprightly vehicle or, more practically, greater weight of armour over the protected volume that now accommodated five rather than six men. As much as possible of the M3 was retained, and the result was the Medium Tank T6 development model with a short-barrel M2 gun in a cast turret on a cast hull. The machine weighed 30.48 tonnes, was powered by a 400hp (298kW) Wright radial engine, and in addition to its main gun possessed an armament of four 0.3in (7.62mm) machine-guns, located as one co-axial, one bow and two fixed forward-firing nose guns. Prototype vehicles were delivered in September 1941, and trials confirmed the expectations of the designers and the army. In October 1941, a slightly modified version of the T6 (with a belly hatch and an additional driver's hatch in place of the side doors) was standardized as the Medium Tank M4, better known by the name Sherman (bestowed initially by the British within their system of naming US tanks after famous American generals). The M4 was planned to supersede the M3 on all current medium tank production lines, with additional sources coming on stream as production tempo increased. It was then realized that adequate casting facilities were not available for the anticipated number of hulls (at one time planned as 2,000 vehicles per month), and a more box-like upper hull of welded construction was developed as an alternative. Vehicles with the welded hull were designated M4, and those with the cast hull M4A1: both used the same one-piece cast turret, which had a maximum frontal thickness of 76mm (3in), an Oilgear hydraulic or Westinghouse electric power traverse system, and a stabilization system for the main gun in elevation. The main gun was the longer-barreled M3 weapon rather than the M2 used in the T6 vehicle.

In overall layout the Sherman was typical of its era, with a forward compartment for the driver and co-driver/nose gunner (the two fixed guns of the T6 were abandoned soon after the M4A1 came into production), a

The Medium Tank M4 Sherman was never the equal of its better German opponents in qualitative terms, but was reliable and available in very large numbers to equip the US Army and several other armies.

central fighting compartment for the commander, gunner and loader, and a rear compartment for the engine. On each side the running gear comprised three twin-wheel bogies with vertical volute spring suspension, three track-return rollers – one located at the top of each bogie attachment unit ('first-type suspension'), a front drive sprocket and a rear idler. The standard engine was the 400hp (298kW) Wright R-975 radial petrol engine.

The Sherman ran through a large number of variants and subvariants, and these are listed below in order of designation rather than production by the M3 manufacturers, who included Federal Machine and Welder, Fisher Body, the Ford Motor Company, and Pacific Car and Foundry. First in the designation sequence was the M4, designated Sherman I by the British: 8,389 of this model were built, 6,748 of them with the standard 75mm (2.95in) M3 gun and 1,641 with the 105mm (4.13in) M4 howitzer in the close-support role; the British designated the latter version the Sherman IB, and the suffix 'B' was used thereafter to denote Shermans with the howitzer. The M4 was standardized in October 1941 but became only the third model to go into production, and was distinguishable by its all-welded hull.

Next in designation sequence, but actually the first to enter production, was the M4A1 (Sherman II in British terms) with a cast hull. During the course of production the M4A1 received differential and hull front modifications parallel to those of the M4, and the track-return rollers were later shifted to the rear of the bogie attachment units ('second-type suspension'). Like the M4, the combat weight was 30.16 tonnes. Production of this variant totalled 9,677, of which 6,281 were completed with the M3 gun and the other 3,396 with the 76.2mm (3in) M1 high-velocity gun, whose installation was signified in British terminology by the designation Sherman IIA. This gun resulted from the realization by both the Armored Force and the Ordnance Department that the M3 gun was relatively indifferent in armour-penetration capability by comparison with the guns of contemporary

Opposite: The Medium Tank M4 Sherman was based on the same basic chassis as the Medium Tank M3, and was built in a large number of variants with different main guns, a cast or welded hull, vertical volute suspension that was later replaced by horizontal volute suspension, and a wide assortment of engine types so that deliveries of this war-winning weapon were not delayed when production of the chassis and hull exceeded that of the original Continental R-975 radial engine.

Seen after being knocked out on the beach of Normandy in June 1944, this is a Sherman of the 'Crab' type in which power from the main engine rotated chain flails which struck the ground in front of the tank and thereby detonated any pressure-activated mines. The tank otherwise possessed full combat capability through retention of its standard turreted gun.

German tanks. Over two months, the M1 was evolved from an anti-aircraft weapon, and tested during September 1942 in a standard M4 turret. This proved too small for the more powerful weapon, which was then installed in the cylindrical turret designed for the 90mm (3.54in) gun of the Medium Tank T23. This turret proved excellent, and could be installed on the M4 without modification. The gun/turret combination was authorized for the M4A3 in February 1944, deliveries beginning in the following month; the gun/turret combination was also used on the M4, M4A1 and M4A2, all signified in British usage by the suffix 'A' after the roman mark number.

The M4A2 was called Sherman III or Sherman IIIA by the British, depending on armament, and after standardization in December 1941 became the second Sherman variant to enter production. This 31.30 tonne type was similar to the M4 with a welded hull, but had a different powerplant in the form of a 410hp (306kW) General Motors 6046 diesel engine, comprising two General Motors 6-71 diesels geared to a common propeller shaft. Production amounted to 11,283 tanks, 8,053 of them with the 75mm (2.95in) gun and 3,230 with the 76.2mm (3in) gun.

In January 1942 a new variant was standardized as the M4A3, designated Sherman IV by the British. This again was similar to the M4 with a welded hull, but was fitted with a custom-designed engine, the 500hp (373kW) Ford GAA. This powerful and reliable petrol unit was instrumental in making the M4A3 the single most important Sherman variant: 11,424 were built, 5,015 with the 75mm (2.95in) gun, 3,370 with the 76.2mm (3in) gun and the other 3,039 with the 105mm (4.13in) howitzer. Once the M4A3 was available, the Americans generally reserved this model for themselves and disbursed the types with other engines to their Lend-Lease allies.

The M4A4 (Sherman V) was the main type supplied to the UK. The type was standardized in February 1942 as an M4 variant with a 425hp (317kW) Chrysler multi-bank engine, created by marrying five car engine cylinder blocks to a common crank-case. This was the same engine as used in the M3A4, and required a lengthening of the rear hull and an additional four track shoes on each side. The type was phased out of production in September 1943, and all 7,499 examples had the 75mm (2.95in) gun.

The designation M4A5 was used in the United States for the Ram tank that was a Canadian-built derivative of the M4, so the next production Sherman was the M4A6, designated Sherman VII by the British. The type was standardized in October 1943, and may be considered a variant of the M4A4 with the 497hp (371kW) Caterpillar D-200A diesel engine: the longer hull, more widely spaced bogies, extended tracks and 32.21 tonne weight were retained, and the 75mm (2.95in) gun was standard. Production amounted to only 75 tanks, for at the end of 1943 it was decided to cease powerplant experimentation and concentrate all production effort on the Wright- and Ford-engined models. Total production of Sherman gun tanks was 48,347, but this is by no means the whole of the Sherman story (or even of the Sherman gun tank story), for there were a large number of important variants produced by production-line, depot or field modification.

The best known of these variants is perhaps the Sherman 'Firefly', a British conversion with the 17pdr (3in/76.2mm) high-velocity anti-tank gun (indicated by the suffix 'C') for enhanced tank-destroying capability. Most Fireflies were of the Sherman VC variety, but there were also Sherman IC, IIC, IIIC and IVC versions, and the family proved highly important in the Normandy and North-West European campaigns as the Allied tanks best able to tackle the Panther and Tiger on anything approaching equal firepower .

The importance of the M4 Sherman tank in the Allied victory of World War II cannot be overemphasized. The Sherman may not have been a

The most capable version of the Medium Tank M4 Sherman was a hybrid Anglo-American model, the Sherman Firefly that was a conversion of the M4A1 (Sherman II), M4A2 (Sherman III), M4A3 (Sherman IV) and M4A4 (Sherman V) with the standard American gun replaced by the British 17pdr anti-tank gun. This turned the basic Sherman, which was an indifferent anti-tank weapon, into a devastating killer of German tanks.

qualititive match for the best German tanks (it lacked the all-round fighting capabilities of the Panther, and was not as heavily armed and protected as the Tiger), but it was adequate to its tasks, and was produced in the vast numbers that allowed Allied tank formations to overwhelm the Germans and, to a lesser extent, the Japanese. The Sherman remained in widespread service into the 1970s, and is still used by a number of armies.

The last category of American tank to be discussed is the heavy tank, of which the only type to enter more than token US service was the T26, which had been designed as a medium tank but increased in weight to the point at which it had to be reclassified as a heavy tank (in June 1944). This vehicle was the culmination of a development programme that had encompassed the T20, T22, T23, T25 and T26 medium tanks in all their variations, and to avoid confusion the first heavy tank model was classified Heavy Tank T26E3 and standardized for limited procurement in November 1944. The T26 was subjected to intensive combat evaluation, and in January 1945 was declared battleworthy, leading to the type's standardization in March 1945 as the Heavy Tank M26 General Pershing. The M26 was considered the primary US tank in the armoured battles with the Germans' Tiger tanks, though experience in Europe confirmed that while the M26 was equal to the Tiger in protection and superior in mobility, it was decidedly inferior in firepower, where the German 88mm (3.46in)kWK 36 and 43 weapons reigned supreme.

There were a number of variants of the M26 in its basic gun tank role, and just as there was a 'Lightweight Combat Team' derived from the M24 Chaffee, there was a 'Heavyweight Combat Team' derived from the M26 Pershing. In the basic line of development as a gun tank, the M26 spawned five derivatives. The M26A1 was very similar to the M26 but had a revised M3A1 main gun with bore evacuator and single-baffle muzzle brake; some of the type were fitted with a system to stabilize the main gun in elevation. The M26E1 was the basic vehicle fitted with the 90mm (3.54in) T54 gun: this had a concentric recoil system and used fixed rather than separate-loading ammunition, requiring the ammunition stowage inside the tank to be revised. The T26E2 was a close-support version with a 105mm (4.13in) howitzer as stabilized main armament; in July 1945 the T26E2 was standardized for limited production as the M45. The T26E4 was also very similar to the M26 but had a 90mm (3.54 in) T15E2 gun in place of the M26's

Built only in small numbers, the Cruiser Tank Ram was a Canadian effort to combine what was best in American and British tank thinking and to create a vehicle suitable for production in Canada. The Ram Mk I therefore combined the chassis, engine, transmission and trackwork of the Medium Tank M3, a cast upper hull and turret of Canadian design and manufacture, and British main armament in the form of the 2pdr (40mm) main gun. Production amounted to 50 vehicles between 1941 and 1943, but these were used only for training and were superseded from 1942 by the Ram Mk II (illustrated) with a number of improvements including a 6pdr (57mm) main gun. Production of the Ram Mk II totalled 1,899 vehicles.

M3 of the same calibre. And the T26E5 was the heavy tank counterpart to the M4A3E2 'Jumbo', a dedicated assault version with the frontal armour thickened to a maximum of 279mm (11in) on the mantlet, 190.5mm (7.5in) on the turret and 152mm (6in) on the hull, increasing weight to 46.27 tonnes; production amounted to only 27 vehicles.

Production of the M26 totalled 2,432, but the type saw only limited service in World War II. In May 1946 it was reclassified as a medium tank once again, and served with considerable distinction in the Korean War (1950-53). The Pershing marked a decisive turning point in the design of American medium tanks: namely the culmination of the evolutionary design process from the M2 series, yet its divergence from the main sequence in terms of its large road wheels, torsion bar suspension, hull-mounted track-return rollers and rear drive sprockets heralded the beginning of the post-World War II series of medium and battle tanks, from the M47 to the M60.

Seen during the course of desert manoeuvres, the Light Tank M5 was standardised in February 1942 as a development of the Light Tank M3 with a powerplant of two Cadillac car engines driving an automatic transmission.

American tanks made an enormous contribution to the Allied victory in World War II. The Americans themselves fielded large numbers of armoured divisions and independent tank battalions – and also provided their allies with enormous numbers of tanks. The hallmarks of the American tanks were initially their availability, reliability and comparatively heavy armament. And as the war progressed, the capabilities of American tank designers and the vast industrial machine that supported them combined to develop better designs that were put into production without hampering the flow of existing designs.

The nation that stands out as the most important exponent of armoured warfare in World War II, however, must be the USSR. The Soviets had devoted their energies in the 1920s and early 1930s to absorbing as much imported technology as possible, while at the same time pursuing a policy of limited indigenous development. By the mid-1930s the Soviets had built up a considerable armoured force, backed by a substantial industrial machine capable of supporting and expanding the in-service tank fleet. In the later 1930s the Soviets consciously turned away from their policy of mass production, and concentrated on the development of tanks that were qualitatively equal or superior to the best of Western tanks, but which could still be manufactured in large numbers.

At the beginning of World War II, the Soviets were undertaking a complete overhaul of their tank fleet, with the development and introduction of a new generation to replace the derivative designs of the 1930s. Given the geographical nature of the USSR, with its poor road and rail communications over vast areas indented by large rivers and split by extensive marshes, it was inevitable that the Soviets would place great emphasis for reconnaissance on the light tank, which should preferably be an amphibious type. In the late 1930s the most important in-service types were the T-27, T-37A and T-38, and to replace these the two-man T-40 light amphibious tank was developed, its prototype appearing in 1936: this resembled the BT-IS in overall configuration, and was a complete departure from earlier Soviet light tank designs in its welded construction,

The final expression of American thinking about heavy tanks in World War II was the M26 General Pershing that was used in limited numbers during the final stages of the war against Germany. After the end of the war the type was reclassified as a medium tank, and became a mainstay of the US armoured forces until the mid-1950s. This is an M26 in the Korean War.

independent torsion bar suspension for the arrangement of four road wheels on each side, and truncated conical turret accommodating the commander and the armament of one 12.7mm (0.5in) and one 7.62mm (0.3in) co-axial machine-gun. Standard components were used wherever possible, as in the 85hp (63.3kW) GAZ-202 petrol engine, and the type was buoyant without aid, being propelled in the water by a single propeller. Weight was 5.59 tonnes with a maximum armour thickness of 13mm (0.51in). The original T-40 had a blunt nose, but the later T-40A had a more streamlined nose, and the non-amphibious T-40S of 1942 had slightly thicker armour and provision for a 20mm main gun. The T-40 series served from 1941 to 1946.

The T-40 was planned for only modest service as the Soviets envisaged that the T-60 light tank should supplement and then supplant all in-service light tanks from 1942. Design of this vehicle was already in hand when the lessons of the Germans' 1941 invasion became understood. These suggested that the primary requirement of the light tank should not be mobility (including amphibious capability) to the exclusion of firepower and protection, but rather a more judicious blend of all three components. The design of the two-man T-60 was therefore revised to produce a more capable machine of all-welded construction with thicker armour and greater firepower. The Soviets had hoped to instal a 37mm gun, but the recoil forces of this weapon could not be absorbed by the small turret ring: in its place the designers fitted the exceptional 20mm ShVAK cannon, and a 7.62mm (0.3in) machine-gun was installed co-axially. The T-60 entered production in November 1941, and nearly 6,000 were built before the type was superseded in production by the T-70 light tank during 1943. The T-60 weighed 5.15 tonnes and was powered by an 85hp (63.3kW) GAZ-202 petrol, and its only tank variant was the T-60A of 1942 with thicker frontal armour and solid

The Soviet heavy tank mainstay at the time of the Germans' June 1941 invasion of the USSR, the KV-1 was based closely on the design of the T-100 and SMK heavy tanks with these two vehicles' forward turret removed and the tall barbette carrying the superfiring main turret eliminated to create a considerably more effective tank. The KV-1 was well protected, and its armament comprised one 3in (7.62mm) main gun and three machine-guns. The 46.35-ton vehicle had a crew of five and was powered by a 550hp (410kW) diesel engine for a speed of 22mph (35km/h).

The M24 Chaffee was the final expression of American light tank thinking in World War II, and was an exceptional vehicle of its type with well-disposed and well-sloped armour, a moderately powerful gun, and very good combination of performance and agility.

rather than spoked road wheels, although after the introduction of the T-70, surplus T-60s were converted as mountings for Katyusha rockets or as tractors for 57mm anti-tank guns.

Despite its improvement over the T-40 in firepower and protection, the T-60 was soon found to be inadequate in these respects for the military requirements of the Eastern Front. The replacement was the T-70 light tank, which retained the basic chassis of the T-60, but with the drive sprockets shifted from the rear to the front and the armour revised in shape and angle to generate better protection. The modified turret still accommodated a single, tactically overtaxed commander/gunner/loader: this one man had to command the tank and operate the armament of one 45mm L/46 high-velocity gun and one 7.62mm (0.3in) co-axial machine-gun. The T-70 weighed 9.96 tonnes but had better performance than its predecessor due to improved runnning gear and a powerplant of two 70hp (52.2kW) ZIS-202 petrol engines. Production of the T-70 started late in 1941, and ended in the autumn of 1943 after the delivery of 8,225 vehicles, including the improved T-70A with thicker armour.

The core of the Soviets' armoured thinking was the medium tank, and in this category was the legendary T-34, which was acknowledged as the most important tank of World War II, and was arguably the most influential tank ever developed. By Western standards the tank was mechanically unsophisticated, with its four-speed gearbox and clutch/brake steering, but the power train and running gear/suspension were ruthlessly reliable, the armament formidable, and the protection far superior to that of the German PzKpfw IV tank. Small-scale encounters with the T-34 units were recorded by the Germans as early as June 1941, and fully operational T-34 units appeared with increasing frequency in the autumn of the same year. The advent of the T-34 was an enormous and thoroughly unpleasant surprise to the Germans: up to this point in World War II, their Panzer divisions had enjoyed an unequalled blend of tactical superiority and technical advantage; from this time the Germans' technical edge was eroded, and their tactical expertise was slowly matched by the Soviets.

The T-34 (often called the T-34/76 in Western terminology for the calibre of its main gun) appeared in prototype form at the end of 1939 for exhaustive evaluation and proving trials in the first six months of 1940. The T-34/76 was a further development of the T-32 prototype vehicle with a number of detail modifications, and slightly thicker protection on the least protected areas for a weight of 26.725 tonnes. The hull and turret were of welded construction, and the type was powered by a 500hp (373kW) diesel engine.

The hull was sectioned into three compartments. The forward compartment provided side-by-side seating for the driver and bow machine-gunner, who doubled as radio operator in the company and platoon commanders' vehicles that were the only tanks fitted with this equipment. The fighting compartment was just behind the short forward compartment rather than in the centre, and the engine compartment was at the rear. The transmission to the rear drive sprockets was also located in the rear compartment, and proved the least reliable single component of the T-34. The least successful tactical feature of the T-34/76 in its initial form was the turret, a small unit with manual or electric traverse. Mounted co-axially with the main armament was a 7.62mm (0.3in) DT machine-gun, and the bow machine-gun was a similar weapon.

The T-34/76 entered production in the middle of 1940, and although exact figures are not available, year totals seem to have been in the order of 115 machines in 1940, 2,800 in 1941, 5,000 in 1942, 10,000 in 1943, 11,750 in 1944 and 10,000 in 1945, giving a grand total of about 39,665 T-34s of all types.

The first production variant had the Western designation T-34/76A, and was the version described above with a welded turret carrying the Model 1939 L11 main gun. The welded turret was somewhat complex to build, and as the Soviets possessed good capability for the production of large castings a cast turret (still with the same L/30.5 gun in a rolled plate mounting) was introduced to allow turret production to match the steadily increasing tempo of hull production. During 1941, the Germans began to field an increasing number of 50mm PaK 38 anti-tank guns whose projectiles could pierce the T-34's armour at short ranges, and in response the Soviets increased the thickness of the T-34's frontal armour. In 1942 the Soviets introduced to the T-34 series the improved Model 1940 F34 gun with a longer barrel, a weapon that had been pioneered in the 1930s for the T-28 and T-35 tanks. This Soviet gun compared favourably with the 75mm (2.95in)kWK L/24 and kWK 40 L/43 weapons carried by the Germans' contemporary PzKpfw IV tanks, but the T-34 still scored decisively over its German adversaries in protection, range and cross-country performance.

Throughout its history, the USSR placed considerable emphasis on evolutionary development of proved designs for ease of manufacture, reduced spares holding requirements, and simplification of training. Thus clear links to earlier battle tank types can be found in the T-54, which first appeared in 1947 as a development of the T-44, which itself was a 1944 prototype that drew extensively on the T-34 that was the Soviets' primary medium tank of World War II.

Seen in the form of a vehicle operated by the Finnish army, the T-55 was a simple development of the T-54 and first appeared in 1960 with a number of detail improvements and other major enhancements, such as a more powerful engine and the same 3.94in (100mm) main gun now in a stabilised mounting and provided with a greater quantity of ammunition.

The use of the longer 76.2mm (3in) gun in the T-34 is signalled in Western terminology by the designation T-34/76B, and T-34/76Bs are associated with welded as well as cast turrets. Thicker armour and the cast turret increased the T-34/76B's weight to 28.50 tonnes without any serious degradation of performance.

Some criticism had been levelled at the provision of a single large forward-hingeing hatch in the turret roof of these first models, and this deficiency was remedied in the T-34/76C that began to appear in 1943. This variant had twin hatches, which slightly increased overall height, and weight was boosted to 30.50 tonnes with a consequent decrease in speed. Other features of the T-34/76C were spudded tracks, improved vision devices and an armoured sleeve for the bow machine-gun.

By the time the T-34/76C was beginning to enter service, the Soviets were well advanced with the development of the up-gunned T-34/85 version, but saw considerable merit in maintaining the combat capability of the T-34/76 series with a number of improved features. The first of these was a revised hexagonal turret with a wider gun mounting/mantlet in a version known to the West as the T-34/76D: the new turret provided greater internal volume and, perhaps just as significant, removed the earlier turrets' rear overhang, whose slight horizontal separation from the rear decking had given German assault pioneers an ideal spot for the placement of anti-tank mines. The new turret increased tank weight to 31.40 tonnes, and another feature introduced on this variant (and retrofitted without delay on earlier marks) was provision for jettisonable external fuel tanks to increase the T-34/76's already considerable range. The T-34/76E was basically similar, but had a welded turret complete with a commander's cupola. The final T-34/76F had a cast turret with the commander's cupola, and also introduced a five-speed gearbox; only very limited production was undertaken before the T-34/76 series was superseded by the T-34/85.

The T-34/85 appeared in the autumn of 1943, with the new 85mm (3.35in) gun designated initially as the D-5T85, or in upgraded form as the ZIS-S53; the gun was used with a turret adapted from that of the KV-85 heavy tank. With either of these weapons the T-34/85 was a devastating tank, completely outclassing the PzKpfw IV and providing a match for the Panther and Tiger in all but outright firepower at medium and long ranges. The main gun was backed by two 7.62mm (0.3in) machine-guns (one bow and the other co-axial). The larger turret had the considerable advantage of allowing a tactical crew of three, the availability of a gunner and loader permitting the commander to concentrate on his primary function.

The T-34/85 was authorized for production in December 1943, and 283 had been built by the end of the year. By the end of 1944 some 11,000 T-34/85s had been delivered, and production continued into the post-war period: the type served with the Soviet armies until the mid-1950s, and is still in use in many parts of the world.

The T-34 series was produced in greater numbers than any other tank in history, and formed the most important part of the Soviets' tank inventory in World War II. The success of the series did not prevent the Soviets from developing a successor in the form of the T-44, but as this was placed in production only after the end of the war as recursor of a new family of tanks, it is discussed below.

The Soviets were long-term advocates of the heavy tank, and during the 1930s they conceived the massive T-100 and SMK types, with their main turrets on barbettes to give them a superfiring capability over the auxiliary turret. The fallacy of this practice was fully revealed in the Russo-Finnish 'Winter War' (1939-40). Yet at the beginning of World War II the USSR

The affinity of the T-62 to the preceding T-54 and T-55 series is clear in the general configuration of the tank and in the ballistic shaping of the turret, but major changes were the longer and wider hull, the improved shaping of the turret, and the use of a larger-calibre 4.53in (115mm) main gun.

was the only country to have placed such monsters into full-scale production, the initial type being the KV-1, named after Klimenti Voroshilov. Design of the KV-1 began during February 1939 at the Kirov factory in Leningrad, the intention of the design team being a heavy tank less tall than its predecessors, and therefore overcoming their stability and visibility problems. The KV-1 was modelled on the T-100 and SMK (especially in the design and structure of the hull, and the nature of the running gear with torsion bar suspension), but excluded the auxiliary turret and its 45mm gun, thereby removing the need for the main turret's barbette and allowing a general reduction in overall dimensions and weight.

The prototype KV-1 was built between April and September 1939, and ordered into production in December, at the same time as the T-34 medium

Soviet Tank Philosophy

THROUGHOUT its existence, the Soviet Union worked to a single main principle for the design of the weapons used by its armed forces: a basic simplicity of core design that yet possessed the capability for considerable evolutionary development in the course of protracted production and service lives. This policy, so different from the 'gold plating' tendency of the Western nations in general and the USA in particular, meant that a weapon could be designed for its specific purpose with adequate volume for vital equipment but no provision for 'frills', and this translated into a thoroughly utilitarian weapon in which particular attention was paid to features such as reliability, high performance and, in the case of a tank, good protection and a large-calibre main gun provided with a large number of rounds.

Habitability came well down the designers' list of priorities, and although it has been argued in Western circles that this lack of 'comfort' soon began to degrade the capabilities of Soviet tank crews, it should be realized that such tank crews were used to conditions considerably more spartan than those of their Western counterparts and they were therefore better able to cope with the lack of creature comforts typical of Soviet armoured fighting vehicles.

The basic simplicity of Soviet tanks facilitated mass production at a rapid rate, eased the task of training crews with only modest technical skills, and also made less troublesome the task of upgrading the tanks as new generations of equipment became available. This should not be construed, however, to mean that the Soviets paid no attention to the safety of their tanks and their crews, for the Soviet authorities fully appreciated the investment that had been made in men and equipment. Thus Soviet tanks were generally notable for their good armour protection both in terms of thickness and inclination, their use from the late 1930s of a diesel engine running on low-volatility fuel for reduced fire hazard in combat as well as greater range on a given volume of fuel, and their use of a main gun generally one step up in calibre from that used by most of their Western contemporaries.

tank. The machine had a crew of five, a weight of 47.50 tonnes and a powerplant of one 600hp (447kW) V-2K diesel engine. The massive turret was made of welded armour between 30mm and 75mm (1.18in and 2.95in) thick with a 25mm (0.98in) cast mantlet, and was fitted with the same main armament as the T-34/76; the secondary armament comprised three 7.62mm (0.3in) machine-guns.

The KV-1 entered production in February 1940, and 245 had been produced by the end of the year. A few were sent for operational evaluation in the Finnish campaign, proving successful in the breakthrough of the Finns' Mannerheim Line defences. After the German invasion, the Kirov factory was evacuated to Chelyabinsk, in whose Tankograd all subsequent production was undertaken, to the extent of 13,500 chassis used for assault guns and heavy tanks. Variants of the KV-1 were the KV-1A of 1940 with the L/41.2 main gun, resilient road wheels and thicker frontal armour; the KV-1B of 1941 with even thicker frontal and lateral armour and later with a cast turret, increasing weight to 48.775 tonnes; the KV-1C of 1942 with the cast turret, wider tracks, an uprated engine and maximum armour thicknesses increased to 130mm (5.12in) on the hull and 120mm (4.72in) on the turret; and the KV-1s (skorostnoy, or fast) of 1942 with weight reduced to 43.185 tonnes by the omission of the appliqué armour used on the previous models.

The ultimate development of the Soviet heavy tank was the Iosef Stalin (IS, sometimes rendered JS) series, initially conceived to counteract the German development of new tank types with heavy protection and powerful armament. It was appreciated by the Soviets that their current service and development tanks might not be able to cope with these new German tanks, and early in 1943 a novel IS series was planned at the Kirov factory. Design was entrusted to the KV team, who used features of the KV series to reduce technical risk and to speed the design and development programme. Weight no greater than that of the KV was demanded, and as initial plans called for an 85mm (3.35in) main gun the designation IS-85 was allocated. The first of three prototypes appeared in the autumn of 1943, and although clearly derived from the KV series in its hull, powerplant and running gear, it was an altogether more formidable machine with highly sloped armour that was also extremelythick; hull armour was welded while the turret was the same cast unit as fitted on the KV-85. By comparison with the KV-85, the hull of the IS-85 had lower running gear to permit the use of a superstructure that overhung the tracks and allowed a larger turret ring. The care taken in component as well as overall design is indicated by the fact that the IS-85 emerged with 50mm (1.98in) more armour than the KV-85 but weighed some 2.00 tonnes less, allowing a higher maximum speed on a less powerful engine. It is believed that the IS-85 saw very limited operational service as the IS-1.

It was considered inappropriate for a heavy tank to have the same armament as the current medium tank, so it was proposed that a variant should be developed as the IS-100 with a 100mm (3.94in) main gun, in a process made very straightforward by the initial adoption of a large turret ring. A small number of IS-100 tanks were evaluated, but the type proceeded no further as an even more formidable machine had been proposed, with a new turret of superior ballistic shape and fitted with the 122mm (4.8in) D-25 gun. After development as the IS-122, the type was placed in production as the IS-2, and the considerably more potent turret/armament combination was also retrofitted to the small number of IS-100s that had been built to create the variant known in the West as the IS-1B, the original IS-1 being redesignated IS-1A to avoid confusion. The IS-2 was accepted for production at the end of October 1943 after an extremely rapid development programme, and by the end of the year some 100 IS-2 tanks had been delivered.

The Post-War Years

AFTER World War II, the victorious Allies undertook an intensive analysis of armoured warfare, especially the German technical research into all aspects of tank technology. The Soviets were content with the tactical and technical performance of their armoured forces in the last two years of the war, but the Western Allies had cause for considerable revision in their thinking, although there were many good features that could be retained for future development.

World War II had nearly bankrupted the UK, and the vast demobilization after the end of the war forced economies on the army and further straitened the situation at home. This position was worsened after 1947, when the grant of independence to India signalled the start of a rapid dissolution of the British empire: the departure of India removed the need for many of the imperial 'way stations' on the sea and air routes to the old viceroyalty, and after about 15 years, the British empires in Africa, the Near East, Middle East and Far East had disappeared, further reducing the UK's need for a large military capability. This capability had demanded a high-quality regular army supported by a territorial force, designed for high levels of strategic mobility so that any threat could be met by adequate strength and with minimum delay. The dissolution of the empire led to a reassessment of the role of the British army, the inevitable conclusion being that while the dwindling imperial commitment had still to be met, the new role of the army was in Europe as part of the NATO alliance. Like the imperial role, this demanded a modest but high-quality army, fielding the best of heavy weapons rather than ordnance designed for use against an unsophisticated enemy. The anticipated foe was now the USSR, and the vast tank fleet mustered and constantly improved by the Soviets represented a serious threat.

After the end of World War II the Heavy Tank M26 was reclassified as the Medium Tank M26, and further development at this time resulted in the M46. These two types were the US Army's standard battle tanks at the time of the Korean War, and further work on the M46 resulted in the M47 Patton, which was the chassis and hull of the M46 combined with the new turret and 3.54in (90mm) gun designed for the new T42 battle tank that was not yet ready for production. The M47 was essentially an interim type, although a very good one and a type that is still in limited service with a number of Third-world armies. As soon at it had entered production, work started on the development of a successor, which was basically the turret and main gun of the M47 combined with a new chassis and hull to create the M48 Patton. This entered service with the US Army in 1953, and remained in service with this force until superseded by the M60 that was in essence the M48 revised with a 4.13in (105mm) main gun. This is an M48 operating in Cambodia in the early 1970s.

Armed with a 2.95in (75mm) main gun, the M24 Chaffee had considerable firepower for a light tank.

The light tank concept had fallen out of favour with the British during World War II, and in the period immediately after the war the reconnaissance role was entrusted to wheeled scout cars and wheeled armoured cars. In the short term, and so far as tracked vehicles were concerned, the British kept in service the best of the cruiser and infantry tanks of World War II while working on replacements. These two types were the A41 Cruiser Tank Centurion and the A45 Infantry Tank Conqueror, both launched on their development careers in 1944.

After basic formulation by the Department of Tank Design in 1943, the A41 was entrusted to AEC for detail design with the object of producing a high-mobility cruiser tank characterized by improved Horstmann suspension, better protection through the adoption of thicker and better-sloped armour, and heavier firepower through the use of the 17pdr (76.2mm/3in) high-velocity gun in a mounting that would be readily adaptable to larger-calibre weapons; the secondary armament was also increased in the prototypes to a 20mm Polsten co-axial cannon, but it was eventually decided to revert to the standard 7.92mm (0.31in) Besa machine-gun, which was then replaced by a 0.3in (7.62mm) Browning machine-gun. Not included in the original concept were high road speed or anything more than minimal range, and these two factors were to be the Centurion's main limitations throughout its highly successful and lengthy service career.

Production of the Centurion was entrusted to the Royal Ordnance Factory in Leeds, Vickers-Armstrongs at Elswick and Leyland Motors at

All the British experience in armoured warfare during the course of World War II was used in the creation of the A41 Centurion battle tank, which remains one of the classic armoured fighting vehicles of the period after World War II with a good record of combat success in several wars. Illustrated here are Centurion Mk 5 tanks in which the problem of the earlier models' acute shortage of range was addressed by provision for an armoured monowheel trailer carrying additional fuel. The Centurion Mk 5 was also armed with a 20pdr (3.28in/83.4mm) main gun in place of the earlier models' 17pdr (3in/76.2mm) gun.

Leyland: by the time Centurion production ended in 1962, these companies had built over 4,400 of the series, including about 2,500 for export to countries such as Australia, Canada, Denmark, India, Iraq, Israel, Jordan, Kuwait, Lebanon, the Netherlands, South Africa, Sweden and Switzerland. The type is still in service with several of these countries, and is still being upgraded to maintain it as a viable weapon with a better fire-control system, modern armament and (in many cases) a diesel powerplant. Although limited in speed and range, the Centurion has proved to be a remarkably long-lived weapon because of its capability for up-armouring and up-gunning.

Six prototypes were completed before the end of World War II, but although these were shipped to Germany they arrived too late for combat. An extended period of development followed World War II as the concept of a battlefield team of cruiser and infantry tanks faded in face of the notion of the single battle tank that could undertake both halves of what was becoming a unified role, and the initial Centurion Mk 1 entered service in 1949 with a main armament of one 17pdr (76.2mm/3in) Tank Gun Mk 3, a considerably more powerful weapon than the 17pdr Tank Gun Mk 2 used in the Sherman 'Firefly', and radically more devastating than the slightly shorter 77mm Tank Gun Mk 2 used in the Comet.

Further development of the baseline model produced the Centurion Mk 2 with improved armour, but a major change came with the Centurion Mk 3, armed with the 20pdr (83.4mm/3.28in) Tank Gun Mk 1 offering still greater armour-penetrating capability. The Centurion Mk 4 was to have been the close-support counterpart of the Mk 3 with a 3.7in (94mm) Tank Howitzer Mk 1, but was not built, so the next production variant was the Centurion Mk 5, which was the first definitive version. It was a Vickers-designed counterpart to the Mk 3 vehicles, which were all brought up to this operationally improved standard. Further development produced the up-armoured Centurion Mk 5/1, and the Centurion Mk 5/2 which entered service in 1959 and was armed with the magnificent 105mm (4.13in) Tank Gun L7, a product of the Royal Ordnance Factories, fitted in a mounting that provided full stabilization in elevation to complement the turret's stabilization in azimuth.

The Centurion was probably produced in more variants than any other tank in the period after World War II, and after the Mk 5 variants, the sequence continued with the Centurion Mk 6, which was the Mk 5/2 up-armoured and fitted with additional fuel tankage; subvariants of the Mk 6 were the Centurion Mk 6/1 with a stowage basket on the turret rear and infra-red equipment to provide a limited night-driving and night-fighting capability, and the Centurion Mk 6/2 which introduced a ranging machine-gun for the main armament. The Centurion Mk 7 was a Leyland model with the 20pdr (83.4mm/3.28in) gun fitted with a fume extractor, and which was subsequently designed FV4007 in the Fighting Vehicle designation system; subvariants of the Mk 7 were the Centurion Mk 7/1 (FV4012) with improved armour, and the Centurion Mk 7/2 with the L7 gun. The Centurion Mk 8 was essentially the Mk 7 with a revised gun mounting, contra-rotating commander's cupola and provision for the commander's twin hatch covers to be raised for overhead protection when the commander's torso was out of the turret; subvariants of the Mk 8 were the Centurion Mk 8/1 with improved armour, and the Centurion Mk 8/2 with the L7 gun. The Centurion Mk 9 (FV4015) was the Mk 7 with thicker armour and the L7 gun; subvariants of the Mk 9 were the Centurion Mk 9/1 with the stowage basket and infra-red vision devices, and the Centurion Mk 9/2 had the ranging machine-gun. Following this was the Centurion Mk 10 (FV4017), essentially

Armour Penetration

THE initial solution to the task of penetrating enemy tanks' armour protection was the use of kinetic energy, in the form of a solid shot fired at high velocity to punch a hole through the armour or, failing that, to cause the inside of the armour to spall (flake into a large number of high-velocity fragments) and thereby wounding the crew.

Armour designers responded by toughening the armour and using it in thicker plates, and gun designers countered with denser shot fired at higher velocity. This see-saw battle between gun and armour designers continued into World War II, when the establishment of a plateau in gun and armour performance resulted in a switch to another means of offence in the form of the chemical-energy round.

This was developed during and after World War II in two basic forms as the HEAT and HESH rounds. In the HEAT (High Explosive Anti-Tank) round, a warhead with a specially shaped and copper-lined hollow in the forward edge of its explosive filling is detonated with as little spin as possible at precisely the optimum distance from the armour, the shaping of the explosive charge creating a jet of vaporised copper and very hot gases that burns its way through the armour to incinerate the crew and ignite the ammunition. in the HESH (High Explosive Squash Head) round, the warhead includes a mass of plastic explosive that is plastered onto the outside of the armour by the force of the impact, and then detonated to create a massive spall effect inside the tank.

The response of the armour designers was initially spaced armour, in which the force of the HEAT or HESH round's explosion is absorbed by an outer layer of armour separated by an air gap from the main armour that is therefore little affected, and then by composite armour in which a classified mix of metal, ceramics, fibrous matter and composite materials is used to make it difficult if not impossible for the explosive jet to find a path into the interior of the vehicle. The gun designer's response, already under development before the advent of composite armour, has been the kinetic-energy dart, which is made of dense material such as tungsten or depleted uranium, and fired from the main gun in bore-filling sabots that fall away as the projectile leaves the muzzle, allowing the small-diameter dart to travel to the target at extremely high velocity and punch a hole through the armour.

113

the Mk 8 with improved armour; subvariants of the Mk 10 were the Centurion Mk 10/1 with stowage basket and infra-red vision devices, and the Centurion Mk 10/2 with the ranging machine-gun. The Centurion Mk 11 was the Mk 6 with stowage basket, infra-red vision devices and ranging machine-gun, while the Centurion Mk 12 was the Mk 9 with the same improvements, and the final Centurion Mk 13 was the Mk 10 with infra-red vision devices and the ranging machine-gun.

The Centurion remains one of the classic tanks of all time, proving that the United Kingdom can produce a tank matching the best anywhere in the world. The same cannot be said of the A45, which was conceived as the Centurion's heavy companion and then planned as the baseline model in the Universal Tank series, which would have used the same hull for flamethrowing, dozing and amphibious variants. The A45 was not adopted, however, although its chassis became the core of a new heavy tank planned to tackle the IS-3 and its succesors in Soviet service. This was developed as the Conqueror (FV214), initial proof of concept being undertaken in a model called the Caernarvon (FV221), which was the hull of the Conqueror and the turret of the Centurion. The definitive Conqueror appeared in 1950, and the obsolescence of the concept that led to its development is indicated by the fact that production of only 180 vehicles was undertaken in the period between 1956 and 1959. Weighing 66.04 tonnes attributable mostly to very thick armour, the Conqueror was powered by the 810hp (604kW) Meteor 120 No. 2 Mk 1A petrol engine. It had a crew of four, and the massive cast turret accommodated a 120mm (4.72in) Tank Gun L11, one 0.3in (7.62mm) co-axial machine-gun and one 0.3in (7.62mm) machine-gun on the commander's cupola.

French tank developments had effectively ceased by June 1940, resuming only after the liberation of France had begun in 1944. Just before the fall of France, designers had completed preliminary work on the ARL-40, a project originated in 1938 for a Char B1 successor using the same hull

The M46 was in essence a product-improved M26, and was the first step in the evolutionary design process that provided the US Army's battle tanks from the M26 of World War II to the M60 that entered service in 1960 and is still in widespread service.

The M47 Patton is still in extensive service, many older vehicles having been upgraded for continued capability by the replacement of the original petrol engine with a diesel powerplant, revision of the suspension system, and replacement of the original 3.54in (90mm) main gun with a 4.13in (105mm) weapon. This is an M47 of the Italian army.

but with the 75mm (2.95in) gun located in a revolving turret rather than in a limited-traverse hull mounting. During the war the design was modified and modernized at the Atelier de Construction de Rueil (ARL) with different hull (retaining the Char B1's running gear and tracks), and a revised power-traversed Schneider turret accommodating a 90mm (3.54in) gun, and after the liberation this was placed in production as the Char de Transition ARL-44. The prototype appeared in 1946 as a 48.00 tonne heavy tank with thick armour and a 700hp (522kW) Maybach petrol engine. Only 60 out of a planned 300 were built, and these served between 1947 and 1953, eventually being replaced not by the proposed AMX-50 but by US medium tanks, as France began to develop its own concept of combined-arms warfare and a new type of tank.

The first French tank of post-war design to enter service was the Char AMX-13 light tank, designed at the Atelier de Construction d'Issy-les-Moulineaux (AMX), and built first by the Atelier de Construction de Roanne before construction was transferred to Creusot-Loire at Chalon-sur-Saône. The origins of the AMX-13 lay with a 1946 requirement of the French airborne forces for a tank that could provide their forces with medium fire-support: the requirement therefore demanded a high-velocity 75mm (2.95in) gun, air-portability and a maximum weight of 13.00 tonnes. This attractive combination of features appealed both to the French army, which became the major operator of the resultant type for reconnaissance and tank-destroying roles, and to a number of other armies, who appreciated the AMX-13's heavy firepower and modest cost: the cost, combined with the vehicle's simplicity and reliability, attracted armies that were in the process of establishing armoured forces for the first time.

The prototype appeared in 1948, and revealed its origins in its lightweight construction, configuration, and the use of a low-profile oscillating turret. The hull was of all-welded construction, supported on each side by five road wheels with torsion bar suspension. The hull accommodated the driver (left) and engine (right) at the front together with the transmission to the front drive sprockets; there were two or three track-return rollers on each side. The centre and rear of the hull housed the Fives-Cail Babcock FL-10 turret, an oscillating type whose fixed lower portion (located on the turret ring) had the trunnions that carry the oscillating upper portion together with the 75mm (2.95in) fixed gun, plus the commander (left) and gunner (right). Traverse was achieved hydraulically or manually by the complete turret, while elevation was achieved hydraulically or manually by the upper portion. This had the advantage of minimising the overall height of the vehicle, and permitted the use of an automatic loader for the main gun. The adoption of an automatic loader ensured that no tactical capability was lost in having only a three-man crew, which in turn allowed the designers to keep the tank smaller and lighter than would have been the case with a four-man crew. A variant of the AMX-13 intended for North African operations had the FL-11 turret with a manually loaded gun, and was distinguishable by its lack of a turret bustle. The next variant was fitted with the FL-12 turret carrying a 105mm (4.13in) GIAT 105/57 gun, a rifled weapon designed to fire non-rotating rounds. Most older AMX-13s in French service were revised with the 90mm (3.54in) GIAT CN90F3 gun able to fire a more advanced range of modern ammunition types, but some retained the smaller gun and in recompense gained four SS.11 wire-guided anti-tank missiles, which were replaced in the late 1960s by six more-advanced HOT anti-tank missiles.

The only other nation in the Western alliance to develop new tanks in the late 1940s and 1950s was the USA, which unlike the USSR, had ended World War II with a vast number of vehicles mostly designed in the early 1940s and which were approaching obsolescence. The USA could therefore not allow any delay in the development of new types (based mainly on the few types that entered service late in the war, but revised in the light of analysis of World War II operations and the emergence of the USSR as the main threat). The older tanks were acquired by the newly created armoured forces of American allies, allowing a new generation of armoured fighting vehicles to be adopted.

The most important of the late-World War II vehicles was the Heavy Tank M26 Pershing, which was reclassified as a medium tank in May 1946 following the final American recognition that the wartime classification of vehicles (medium tanks for the 'maid-of-all-work' roles, heavy tanks for the support role and tank destroyers for the tank-killing role) was spurious. The new medium tank classification used for the Pershing paved the way for what is now universally known as the main battle tank.

In 1947 it was decided to re-work the Pershing to a more workmanlike standard with the improved 90mm (3.54in) M3A1 gun in place of the original M3, and the 810hp (604kW) Continental AV-1790-5A petrol engine and Allison cross-drive transmission/steering in place of the original Ford GAF petrol engine with mechanical transmission and separate controlled-differential steering. In this guise the tank began to enter service in 1948 as the Medium Tank M46 Patton. The Patton was planned as an interim type pending deliveries of a new medium tank based on the T42 development model, but this model was still unavailable when the Korean War broke out in 1950, and the M26 and M46 therefore bore the brunt of operations in that war.

In 1949 the US Army decided to develop a new series of tanks to replace all World War II types and their derivatives still in service. These were placed under development as the Light Tank T41, the Medium Tank T42 and the Heavy Tank T43. The origins of the T41 were recognizable in the T37 light tank, whose design as a development model had been launched shortly after World War II. The T37 Phase I prototype with the 76.2mm (3in) M32 gun was completed in 1949, but already the T37 was involved in a development programme whose fruits were the T37 Phase II with a redesigned cast/welded turret, a new mantlet, revised ammunition stowage,

Entering service in 1951 and later named in honour of General Walker, the bulldog-like commander of the US forces in Korea at the beginning of the Korean War, the M41 was the last true light tank developed in the USA. This is still in service with a number of countries, and despite its small size offers moderately good protection, considerable performance and agility, and a 3in (76.2mm) main gun that was notably powerful at the time of the tank's adoption and is still an effective weapon for a vehicle now used mainly for the reconnaissance role.

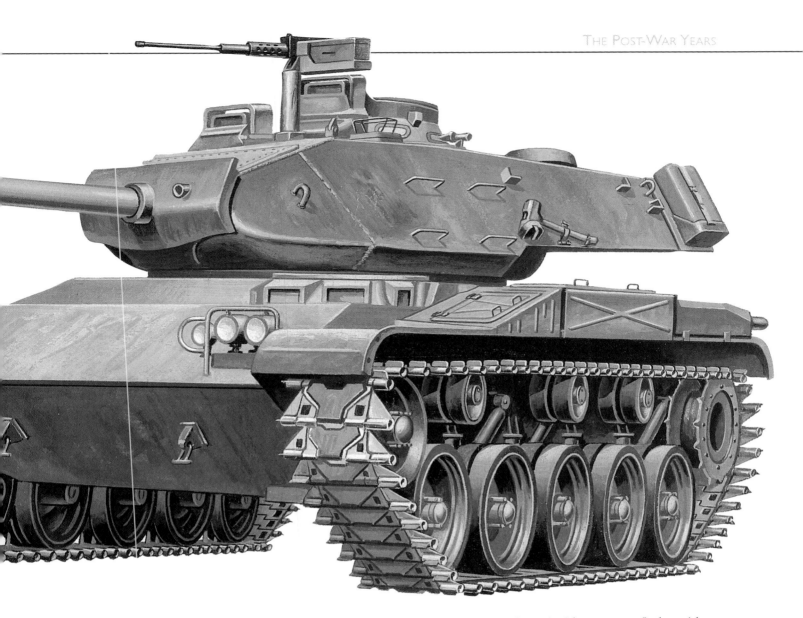

and a fire-control system that integrated a coincidence rangefinder with a Vickers stabilizer for the gun mounting, and the T27 Phase III with an automatic loader for the main armament, and an IBM stabilizer for the gun mounting. The T37 Phase II became the starting point for the T41, which was finally standardized in 1950 as the Light Tank M41 Little Bulldog, although the name was subsequently changed to Walker Bulldog in honour of the small but pugnacious US commander in Korea. Production began in 1950, and some 5,500 M51 series vehicles were built.

In design, the M41 made full use of US combat experience in World War II, and it is in many ways similar to the M24 it was designed to replace. The all-welded hull is arranged into the standard three compartments, with the driver in the forward compartment, the commander, gunner and loader in the turret/basket assembly over the central compartment, and the 500hp (373kW) Continental AOS-895-3 petrol engine in the rear compartment, to power the rear drive sprockets via the cross-drive transmission. The running gear consists on each side of five road wheels with independent torsion bar suspension, and there are three track-return rollers and a front idler. The powered turret is mainly of cast construction with a welded roof and bustle, and accommodates the M32 L/52/1 unstabilized gun. Later variants of the Walker Bulldog were the M41A1, M41A2 and M41A3 which differed only in detail, including an increase in main armament stowage.

117

The last variants had the AOSI-895-5 engine, a fuel-injected version of the standard unit.

The M41 and its derivatives are still in moderately extensive service, current update packages centring on the powerplant and armament, for which a diesel engine and a 90mm (3.54in) weapon are offered.

The T42 medium tank did not enjoy as successful a career. It had been realized fairly early in the M26's career that the turret lacked the ballistic shaping to provide adequate protection against the best anti-tank projectiles beginning to appear in the mid-1940s, and the T42 project was designed to remedy this deficiency. However, when the Korean War started the hull of the T42 was still not ready for production, and it was decided to produce another interim type by combining the hull of the M46 with the turret of the T42, complete with its 90mm (3.54in) M36 gun, to produce the M46A1 (converted models) and the Medium Tank M47 Patton (production models). The improved turret shape further highlighted the Americans' steady progress towards the Soviet pattern of battle tank, with a more curvaceous turret located well forward in front of an extensive rear decking: the increased length of current tank guns dictated that when the tank was out of combat, the turret was generally traversed to the rear as a means of reducing the vehicle's overall length. Despite its interim nature, the M47 was produced to a total of 8,576 examples. The M36 gun was a L/43/1 development of the M1 anti-aircraft gun.

The M47 entered service in 1952, but as an interim type did not remain in service for very long. As soon as supplies of M48s began to arrive in useful numbers, the M47 was withdrawn and reallocated to the USA's allies under the Military Aid Program. The tank is still in widespread service, and in many countries has been upgraded with a diesel powerplant and improved armament, the latter sometimes including the 105mm (4.13in) M68 gun with a more modern fire-control system.

Development of the Medium Tank M48 Patton began in October 1950 at the Detroit Arsenal, and as its name suggests this is an evolutionary development of the M46 and M47. The first T48 prototype appeared in December 1951, and the type was ordered into production during the following March at two major construction facilities, some 11,700 being built before production ended in 1959. The production commitment occurred at a time when the Americans were worried that the Korean War could escalate towards a third world war, and this demanded the rapid production of new battle tanks. However, when the tank began to reach service units in 1953 it became clear that the production decision had been reached too quickly, and most of the early M48s had to be virtually rebuilt in a costly programme to eliminate the mechanical teething problems that had not been obviated by the development programme.

By comparison with the M47, the M48 introduced a cast hull and a cast turret of revised shape for a vehicle that was slightly shorter, wider and lower than its predecessor. The same engine and transmission were used, but despite an increase in combat weight compared with the M47, the M48

The value of the M41 Walker Bulldog light tank lay not in the type of high-intensity warfare envisaged for Europe, where the two superpower blocs faced each other across Germany, but in the lower-intensity warfare that flared up in areas such as South-East Asia. These M41s are seen during a 1962 training deployment to Thailand.

The M48A3 was one of the most important M48 variants as it introduced a diesel-engined powerplant for greater range in combination with the greater operational safety associated with the low-volatility fuel used by this type of engine, and was also fitted with a more advanced fire-control system than earlier M48 variants. The type had a crew of four and a combat weight of 46.4 tons, its protection was afforded by steel armour varying in thickness between a minimum of 12.7mm (0.5in) and a maximum of 120mm (4.8in), and its armament comprised a 3.54in (90mm) main gun with 62 rounds of ammunition and two machine-guns: the latter comprised one 0.3in (7.62mm) weapon co-axial with the main gun and supplied with 6,000 rounds of ammunition, and one 0.5in (12.7mm) weapon with 630 rounds of ammunition on the commander's hatch for local protection and anti-aircraft use. The type was powered by a 750hp (559kW) Continental AVDS-1790-2A diesel engine for performance that included a speed of 30mph (48km/h) and a range of 288 miles (463km). The vehicle's overall dimensions included a length of 24ft 5in (7.442m) with the main gun trained directly forward, a width of 11ft 11in (3.63m) and a height of 10ft 3in (3.12m).

was slightly faster. The baseline M48 was followed by the M48A1 with detail improvements, the M48A2 with a fuel-injected engine and a larger fuel capacity, the M48A3 (rebuilt M48A1 and M48A2) with the 750hp (559kW) AVDS-1790-2A diesel engine, and the M48A5 (rebuilt M48A1 and M48A3) with a host of improvements pioneered on other models and a 105mm (4.13in) L68 main gun. Like other battle tanks of its period, the M48 was improved with operational additions such as infra-red lights and upgraded fire-control systems, and in more recent years several manufacturers in the USA and elsewhere have offered modernization packages for an updated diesel engine, a 105mm (4.13in) gun and other advanced features.

By the mid-1950s the M48 was maturing into a powerful battle tank, but in 1956 it was decided to press ahead with the development of an M48 derivative with greater firepower, superior mobility and reliability, and enhanced range. Greater firepower and superior mobility were clearly desirable in a tank whose primary object was to tackle and defeat main battle tanks of the type epitomized by the Soviet T-54 and T-55 series with their 100mm (3.94in) L/54 guns; whilst better reliability and enhanced range offered significant battlefield advantages at all operational levels. To date, the Americans had been relatively unconcerned by deficiencies in range and reliability: in World War II they had deployed so large a logistical back-up capability that any such shortfalls in their tanks did not seriously affect the tempo of operations. But by the mid-1950s, the changing nature of warfare persuaded the Americans that greater unrefuelled range (and greater reliability) were required, as these logistical services could no longer be guaranteed to front-line forces in the type of fluid warfare that seemed inevitable.

The hull and running gear of the M48 were deemed more than adequate as the basis of the new tank, which was thus an evolutionary development rather than a completely new design. In November 1956, an M48 hull was

re-engined with the AVDS-1790-P diesel engine, and extensive tests yielded highly successful results. In February 1958 the concept was taken a step further when three M48A2s were re-engined with the diesel powerplant as the prototypes for the XM60 series, and these were also successfully tested under a range of operational, climatic and geographical conditions.

The final part of the improvement package over the M48 rested with the new tank's firepower, which had to be markedly superior to that of the 90mm (3.54in) M41 L/48 gun of the M48 series, and in October and November 1958 a number of candidate weapons were trialled before the decision was made in favour of the 105mm (4.13in) M68, which combined the barrel of the British L7 with an American breech. Work had been developing on the refinement of the complete package, and the selection of the main armament allowed the Main Battle Tank M60 to be standardized in March 1959, with the initial production contract let to the Chrysler Corporation in June 1959 for 180 examples to be built at the Delaware Defense Plant. Production later switched to the Detroit Tank Plant, which then became the USA's only major tank production facility. Production continued into mid-1985, when the M60 production line was closed after the delivery of more than 15,000 vehicles for the US and export markets.

The M60 entered service with the US Army in 1960, and in numerical terms remained the most important US tank until it was supplemented and then largely supplanted in first-line units by the M1 Abrams during the 1980s and 1990s. The initial M60 variant weighed 46.27 tonnes and was powered by a 750hp (559kW) AVDS-1790-2A diesel engine. The M60 can be regarded only as an interim model, for it retained the basic turret of the M48 that was recognized as failing to provide adequate levels of ballistic protection. In October 1962, therefore, the M60 was replaced in production by the M60A1 with the new 'needle-nosed' turret that offered both superior ballistic protection and greater internal volume. This helped to increase the main armament's ammunition stowage and improve its elevation arc. The modified turret also altered the ammunition capacities for the 7.62mm (0.3in) co-axial and 0.5in (12.7mm) anti-aircraft machine-guns, the latter located on a trim commander's cupola. The overall weight of the M60A1 is 48.99 tonnes,

The US Army's current mainstay battle tank is the M1 Abrams with a gas turbine powerplant and a large measure of composite armour. The type is used in four main variants, namely the basic M1 (illustrated) with a 4.13in (105mm) rifled main gun, the M1A1 with a 4.72in (120mm) smooth-bore main gun, the M1A2 with an automatic loader allowing the reduction of the crew from four to three, and the M1A3 development of the M1A2 with a number of protection and mobility enhancements.

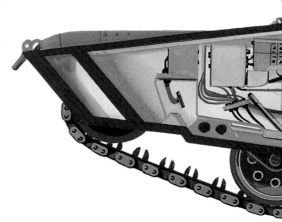

but the engine and performance remain unaltered despite a fractional reduction in fuel capacity.

The M60A1 was the initial definitive production model, and was made of large castings welded together to create the hull and turret. There is no stabilization system for the gun in either elevation or azimuth, but the necessities of modern war are reflected in the provision of night-vision equipment and, most importantly of all, a central filtration system that supplies air cleaned of NBC (nuclear, biological and chemical) warfare agents to the four crew members via individual tubes. And the requirements of independent operations are further reflected in provision of dozer blade attachments for the preparation of fire positions; in addition, the M60A1 possesses deep-wading capability.

The M60 was still at a comparatively early stage of its career (which has seen development well into the 1990s), but as its basic design lies with the philosophies of the 1950s, the tank's complete history is described here.

Whilst the M68 gun was being developed and accepted, the US Army was considering alternative anti-tank weapons for future armoured fighting vehicles, and decided that a better method of defeating modern armour might lie with the guided missile; this resulted in development by Philco-Ford of the MGM-51 Shillelagh tube-launched missile for use by the M551 Sheridan (often called a light tank although the US Army rightly designates it a reconnaissance vehicle). The missile was designed to be fired from a 152mm (6in) gun/launcher, and after leaving the gun/launcher deployed its control surfaces for guidance by an infra-red system that required the gunner merely to keep the crosshairs of his sight centred on the target until the missile impacted and the HEAT warhead detonated. Considerable development problems were encountered with the missile and also with the ammunition designed for use with the same gun/launcher.

It was decided to instal the same gun/launcher in an M60 variant, with 13 missiles and 33 conventional rounds of ammunition. This M60A2 variant

This cutaway illustration highlights the internal arrangement of the M1 Abrams battle tank with the gas turbine powerplant in the rear of the hull, and the ammunition supply for the main gun in the turret bustle behind fire- and flash-proof doors with blow-out panels in its upper surface so that the force of any ammunition explosion is vented upwards rather than forward into the fighting compartment. Less readily apparent are the relatively angular external appearance, resulting from the use of composite armour that currently can only be produced in flat panels, and the advanced main gun system. This system is based on a turret that can be stabilised in azimuth and a gun that can be stabilised in elevation to allow accurate fire with the tank on the move across country, and on an advanced fire-control system with a digital computer to generate high-quality solutions to any fire-control problem on the basis of data provided by stabilised day and night optical and thermal sensors, a laser ranger, sensors for ambient conditions (external temperature, air pressure, and wind speed and direction, and internal factors such as ammunition temperature) and standardised data for the various ammunition parameters.

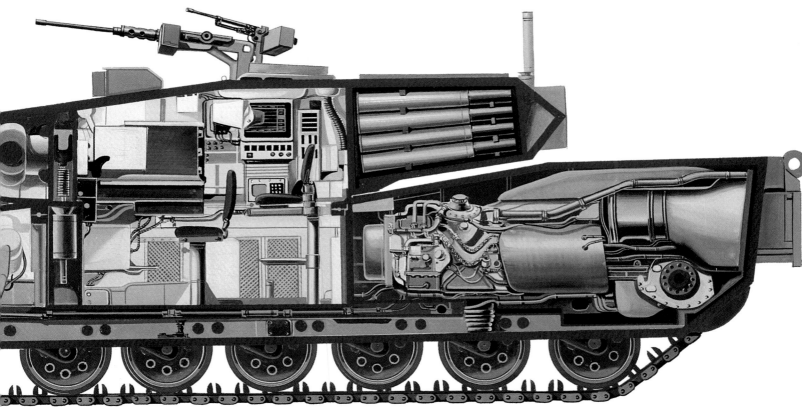

Most modern tanks, typified here by an M60, can be fitted with extra equipment such as a dozer blade for the creation of semi-concealed fire positions, with only the turret protruding above ground level, and for tasks such as the creation of ramps facilitating entry and exit to obstacles such as river banks.

was developed in 1964 and 1965 for its production debut in 1966: some indication of the gun/launcher and ammunition/missile development problems can be gained from the facts that the first M60A2 unit became operational only in 1972, and that total M60A2 production was a mere 526 vehicles, which were withdrawn after only a short first-line career for conversion as required into specialized derivatives of the M60 series, such as the M60 Armored Vehicle-Launched Bridge and M728 Combat Engineer Vehicle.

Service experience with the M60 and M60A1 had meanwhile suggested a variety of ways in which the basic tank could be upgraded mechanically, and a number of retrofit packages were developed. The most significant of these are the so-called RISE (Reliability Improved Selected Equipment) modification of the engine, two-axis stabilization for the main armament, an upgraded fire-control system, and improved night-vision equipment. These and other modifications are the hallmarks of the final variant, the M60A3, that is in essence a product-improved M60A1 that began to enter production in February 1978. New-production examples are complemented in service by M60A1 machines retrofitted to virtually the same standard with items such as a thermal sleeve to reduce main

The Pz 61 was the first battle tank of Swiss design, and was an unexceptional but very well made vehicle with an unstabilised 4.13in (105mm) main gun. Production of 150 such tanks was completed between 1964 and 1968.

armament barrel distortion caused by differential heating, a top-loading air cleaner, and passive night-vision devices.

The M60A3 incorporates all these features, as well as British-type smoke-dischargers on each side of the turret, an engine smoke generator, an automatic engine fire-extinguishing system, and a much improved fire-control system. This last system was developed by Hughes with a laser rather than optical rangefinder and a solid-state digital rather than mechanical analog computer. Like that of British tanks, the M60's success rests mainly with its good protection and firepower, although some reservations have been expressed about mobility and the M60's high silhouette, a factor exacerbated by the commander's substantial cupola.

The heavyweight companion to the M41 light and M60 medium (now main battle) tanks was the Heavy Tank M103, of which only 200 were produced. The cast hull was basically that of the M48 lengthened by the addition of an extra track-return roller and two road wheels on each side, and the turret was a very large cast unit that accommodated a crew of four (commander located immediately behind the gun, gunner and two loaders) and the massive 120mm (4.72in) M58 L/60gun. The vehicle was fitted with the powerplant and transmission of the M47 battle tank, and at a weight of 56.70 tonnes was underpowered to a serious degree and so lacked mobility. It was 1957 before the type was finally cleared for service as the M103A1, which was soon replaced by the M60. The other main operator of the type was the US Marine Corps, which used 156 M103A2 tanks produced by converting surplus M103A1s with AVDS-1790-2AD diesel engines.

The only other Western nation to develop an indigenous tank in the 1950s was Switzerland, a country with a long record of tank operation, although until the development of the first Swiss tank in the 1950s these had all been imported or licence-built machines. The Swiss programme resulted in the kW 30 prototype that appeared in 1958 with a Swiss-designed 90mm (3.54in) main gun and Belleville washer suspension for its arrangement of six road wheels on each side. The kW 30 was joined by a similar prototype in 1959, and later by 10 examples of the Pz 58 pre-production version with the British 20pdr (83.4mm/3.28in) gun. The pace of tank development in this period was unrelenting, and the Pz 61 production model that entered service in 1965 mounted a British 105mm (4.13in) L7 gun. This model had a cast hull and turret, each an impressive single-piece casting, weighed 38.00 tonnes and was powered by a 630hp (470kW) MTU MB 837 diesel engine.

After 150 Pz 61s the production line switched to the improved Pz 68, which

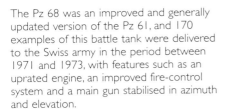

The Pz 68 was an improved and generally updated version of the Pz 61, and 170 examples of this battle tank were delivered to the Swiss army in the period between 1971 and 1973, with features such as an uprated engine, an improved fire-control system and a main gun stabilised in azimuth and elevation.

first appeared in 1968 and was then built to the extent of 170 tanks. This model is similar to the Pz 61 in all essential details but for the addition of a two-axis stabilization system for the main gun, and a 650hp (485kW) MB 837 diesel powerplant for superior performance at a weight of 39.70 tonnes. Gun-armed variants of this initial model, which was redesignated the Pz 68 Mk 1 when the later variants appeared, are the Pz 68 Mk 2 with a thermal sleeve for the main armament (50 built), the Pz 58 Mk 3 based on the Mk 2 but with a larger turret (110 built), and the Pz 68 Mk 4 based on the Mk 3 (60 built).

On the other side of the Iron Curtain all tank development was concentrated in Soviet hands, and pressed ahead feverishly on the basis of late-World War II developments. The two most important types in Soviet service at the end of World War II were the T-34/85 medium tank and IS-3 heavy tank, which were deemed adequate for first-line service through the remainder of the 1940s. But the Soviets were not content to rest on their laurels, and a classic new tank was developed from the T-44 medium tank (that was built in small numbers during 1945 and 1946 but proved mechanically unreliable). This was the Main Battle Tank T-54, which appeared in prototype form during 1946 and entered production at Kharkov in 1947 for service in 1949 or 1950. The T-54 and its Main Battle Tank T-55 derivative were built in larger numbers than any other tank in the period after World War II, and it is estimated that before production ceased in 1981, more than 50,000 examples had come off the main production lines in Kharkov and Omsk in the USSR, and off other lines in China (as the Type 59), Czechoslovakia and Poland.

The driver is seated in a forward compartment on the left, and there is a fixed 7.62mm (0.3in) machine-gun for use by the driver. To the driver's right, instead of the bow machine-gun and its gunner of earlier tanks, are

The M113 series of tracked armoured personnel carriers is the most important of its type anywhere in the Western world, and is an amphibious type of largely aluminium construction. This American basic vehicle has been used as the core of a host of important armed and unarmed variants.

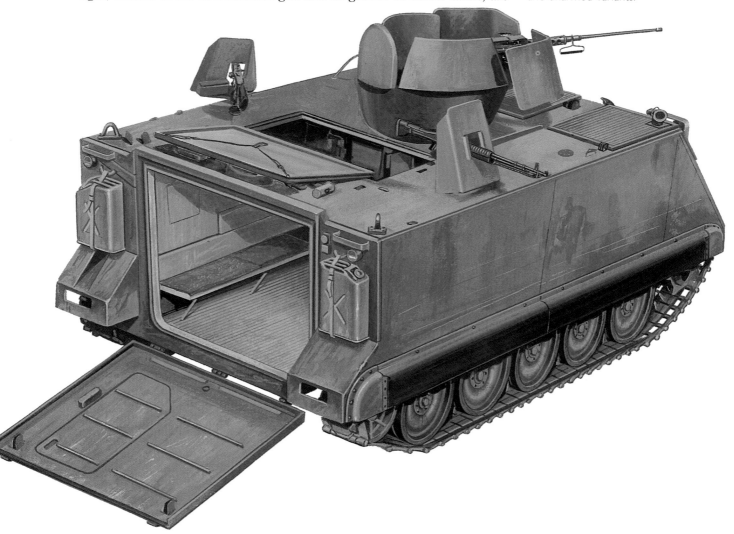

main armament ammunition stowage, the vehicle's batteries and a modest quantity of fuel. At the rear of the vehicle is the compartment for the 520hp (388kW) V-54 diesel engine and transmission. This overall arrangement leaves the centre of the vehicle for the fighting compartment, whose elegantly shaped turret had a manual traverse system in early models, revised to an electro-hydraulic system with manual back-up in later models. The turret is a single casting with a welded two-piece roof and a rotating floor rather than a turret basket, and accommodates the commander, gunner and loader together with the 100mm (3.94in) D-10T gun in somewhat cramped conditions. This is still a useful weapon, but in the T-54 is now let down by its simple fire-control system, which relies on optical sighting by the commander and gunner. This was considered adequate when the T-54 was introduced, but increasingly became a limiting feature as the type remained in service. The other main limitations suffered by T-54 crews include the small main armament ammunition stowage of 34 rounds, the use of external (and highly vulnerable) fuel tanks to boost range, and the poor elevation arc of the main gun, which makes it all but impossible for the T-54 to adopt a hull-down tactical position, and this places great emphasis on the good ballistic protection provided by the tank's shaping.

Given the longevity of its production and service careers, the T-54 has inevitably undergone a number of modifications and improvements, including an NBC system on later models (also retrofitted to earlier models). Most T-54s were later fitted with infra-red driving equipment and received the revised designation T-54(M). First seen in the mid-1950s, the T-54A has improved main armament in the form of the D-10TG gun with a bore evacuator, stabilization in the vertical plane and powered elevation; when retrofitted with infra-red driving lights it is designated the T-54A(M). In 1957 the Soviets introduced the T-54B and, apart from being the first model produced with infra-red night-vision devices as standard, it has the D-10T2S main gun with two-axis stabilization. Variously described as the T-54C or T-54X, the next model is identical with the T-54B except that the gunner's cupola is replaced by a plain forward-opening hatch.

These collective modifications resulted in a basically similar tank with the revised designation Main Battle Tank T-55, which was introduced in the late 1950s with standard features such as no loader's cupola with its 12.7mm (0.5in) anti-aircraft machine-gun, no turret dome ventilator, and a 580hp (432kW) V-55 diesel engine of 500km (311 miles) range rather than 400km (249 miles); the 12.7mm (0.5in) machine-gun was reinstated on some tanks which were then designated T-55(M). Seen for the first time in 1963, the T-55A is the final production version, and is similar to the T-55 apart from having a 7.62mm (0.3in) PKT co-axial machine-gun in place of the original SGMT of the same calibre, an increase in main armament ammunition stowage due to removal of the bow machine-gun, and a number of detail improvements such as an anti-radiation lining; when fitted with the 12.7mm (0.5in) anti-aircraft machine-gun this model is designated the T-55A(M).

The T-54 and T-55 are no longer in service with the former-Soviet forces, but are widely used by many of the former-USSR's clients and allies, who have often carried out their own modification and update programmes. The most important of these have included replacement of the Soviet 100mm (3.94in) main gun with a British or American 105mm (4.13in) weapon. Despite its tactical failings by comparison with the latest Western tanks, the T-54 and T-55 remain important weapons and the very simplicity that makes them obsolescent against the West is an invaluable asset in countries with limited mechanical resources and trained manpower. In general, the T-54 and T-55 can be equated with the American M60A1.

The Soviets' best heavy tank at the end of World War II was the IS-3.

Advent of the Mechanised Infantry Fighting Vehicle

ONE of the most important lessons of World War II was that armoured formations could generally move faster than their companion infantry formations, even when the latter were of the motorised type carried in trucks until they approached the scene of action and disembarked to fight as standard infantry, and that tanks without infantry support were relatively easy targets for the enemy's artillery.

This led to the creation of the first truly mechanised formations that combined tank and infantry units in tracked or, in the case of the infantry unit, half-tracked vehicles that provided the embarked troops with protection against small-arms fire and shell fragments and could match their tank brethren in basic cross-country mobility.

The most important vehicle for this infantry task in World War II was the half-track carrier epitomised by the American M2 and M3 vehicles, although small-scale use was also made of obsolete tanks stripped of their turrets so that the fighting compartment could be used for the accommodation of a small number of infantrymen. So successful were these first attempts that after World War II considerable attention was paid to the creation of specialised armoured personnel carriers (APCs) based on multi-wheeled or, wherever possible, fully tracked chassis. Although some of the early APCs had open-topped accommodation, it was soon realised that overhead protection was vital, and in its fully fledged form the APC soon became a box-like tracked vehicle with a rear compartment for the carriage of infantry, who could disembark with considerable speed through a large door or, in vehicles such as the M113, a rear wall that was designed to hinge down to create a large ramp.

It was not long before these APCs began to be seen as more than mere infantry transports, and a trainable machine-gun was therefore provided for the vehicle commander, who could therefore provide covering fire for the troops as they disembarked, and could also provide a measure of self-protection against the attentions of enemy infantry. Further expansion of this concept led to the mechanized infantry fighting vehicle (MCV) such as the German Marder, with a turreted cannon for genuine if limited offensive capability against other light armoured fightinf vehicles, trucks and other 'soft' targets.

Immediately after the end of the war the Soviet army began to receive the improved IS-4 with the same 122mm (4.8in) main gun. This was the starting point for IS-5, IS-6, IS-7, IS-8 and IS-9 prototypes in the late 1940s and early 1950s. Stalin died in 1953, and when the IS-9 was placed in production during 1956 the letter prefix was altered to 'T', so that the service version of the IS-9 became the T-10, which began to reach operational units in 1957. Production amounted to some 2,500 such tanks in the late 1950s, and its role was heavy support for the T-54 and T-55. The hull was of the same rolled armour construction as the IS-3, but was lengthened by the addition of a seventh road wheel on each side. The main armament was an improved version of the IS-3's 122mm (4.8in) D-25 L/43 gun, in this instance designated D-74. The other armament was a pair of 12.7mm (0.5in) machine-guns, one located co-axially and the other on the turret roof as an anti-aircraft weapon.

The 49.80 tonne T-10 was succeeded by the more capable T-10M with 14.5mm (0.57in) rather than 12.7mm (0.5in) machine-guns, a multi-baffle rather than double-baffle muzzle brake on the main armament, two-axis stabilization for the main armament, enhanced night-vision capability, and an NBC system. The revised T-10M weighed 46.25 tonnes, and maintained the T-10's striking resemblance to the IS-3, although its armour was revised and thickened, while the use of a 690hp (515kW) V-2-IS (otherwise V-2K) diesel engine provided for a higher maximum speed.

The M551 Sheridan remains something of an oddity, for it was basically a light tank fitted with a 5.98in (152mm) main 'gun' designed either to fire a low-velocity anti-tank projectile or serve as the launch tube for the MGM-51 Shillelagh anti-tank missile, which used an infra-red link for command to line of sight guidance. The missile was never completely satisfactory, but the M551 was retained in American service as it is easily air-portable and therefore well suited to the requirement of the US airborne forces, which operate the type in the reconnaissance role.

This inside view of the M551 Sheridan's turret reveals the relative complexity of a type designed in the late 1950s and early 1960s.

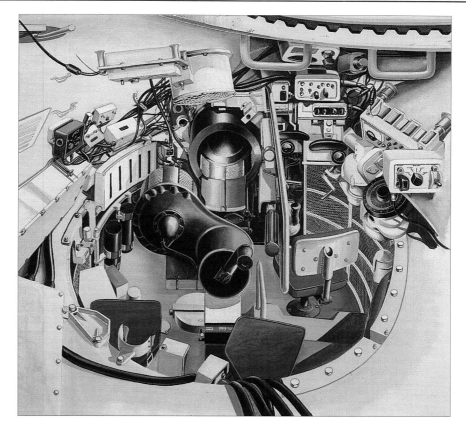

Falling outside this main sequence of tank development is the Light Tank PT-76, which appeared in service during 1952 as evidence of the Soviets' return to the concept of a light amphibious vehicle for deep reconnaissance. Developed from a lightweight cross-country vehicle and Soviet light tanks of the late World War II period, the PT-76 has the advantages of simplicity and moderate offensive capability; this has made the type popular with former-Soviet client states requiring a machine matched to their poor communications and lack of a large industrialized base for the support and maintenance of more advanced tanks. The main failings of the PT-76 and other amphibious light tanks include their large size to provide adequate volume for buoyancy, thin armour which leaves the PT-76 vulnerable even to heavy machine-gun fire, and the sacrifice to weight-saving of features such as an NBC system and night-vision equipment. The welded hull of the 14.00 tonne PT-76 accommodates the driver in a forward compartment, the fighting compartment in the centre and the engine compartment at the rear. The 240hp (179kW) V-6 diesel engine is essentially half of the V-2 used in the T-54/T-55 series, and provides maximum land and water speeds of 44km/h and 10km/h (27.3mph and 6.2mph) respectively. The electrically/manually-powered turret is of welded steel, and accommodates the commander, who doubles as gunner, and the loader for the 76.2mm (3in) D-56T gun, which is a development of the weapon used in the T-34 and KV-1 tanks of World War II.

The PT-76 has appeared in a number of forms as the PT-76 Model 1 with a multiple-slotted muzzle brake, the PT-76 Model 2 with a double-baffle muzzle brake and a bore evacuator, the PT-76 Model 3 similar to the Model 2 but without a bore evacuator, and the PT-76 Model 4 (or PT-76B) with the D-56TM gun with two-axis stabilization. The PT-76 is still in very widespread service, and is likely to remain so for the foreseeable future due to the lack of an adequate replacement.

Modern Tanks

THE tanks of the 1950s may be characterized as logical developments of the best features to emerge from World War II: new features did appear, but in almost every instance these were grafted onto tanks that could have (and indeed often had) been developed in that war. Tanks were used extensively in the period up to 1960, especially by the Soviets in dealing with revolts and revolutions by their eastern European subjects, but true armoured warfare had been rare. The Korean War (1950-53) saw considerable use of tanks by the United Nations' forces, although mainly in the support rather than anti-tank role, and the most significant episodes of tank warfare in the period were the Arab-Israeli wars of 1947-48 and 1956. In these wars the Israelis secured major victories over larger and theoretically more powerful foes through the adventurous use of high-quality armoured forces in deep outflanking and penetration movements, destroying the Arab forces' cohesion and lines of communication. These were essentially the tactics of World War II with their pace quickened by ideal tank terrain, and confirmed the continued dominance of the tank under conditions of air superiority.

By 1960, however, a new generation of tanks had begun to emerge, which, whilst building on previous experience and practice, were notable for their adoption of the best of modern features that had been retrofitted into the tanks of the 1950s. Combined with these technical features (gun stabilization systems, computer-aided fire-control systems, night-vision equipment, NBC protection, and advanced ammunition) were improvements in protection, mobility and firepower. Armour continued to increase in thickness, and was also better conceived and designed for superior protection against the diversity of modern ammunition types, increasingly complemented by surface- and air-launched guided missiles. Mobility was enhanced by the adoption of increasingly powerful yet compact engines to improve power-to-weight ratios. And firepower was enhanced by the adoption of larger-calibre main guns, firing improved projectiles with the aid of increasingly sophisticated fire-control systems to create a significantly higher first-round hit probability. Typical of the improved projectiles are the comparatively

The Hagglund Ikv 91 is a relatively rare creature for a modern army, being a dedicated tank destroyer based on the Pbv 302 armoured personnel carrier chassis and hull with a revolving turret carrying a 3.54in (90mm) high-velocity gun.

Being relatively lightly protected and indifferently armed, the M551 Sheridan is best suited to the reconnaissance role in areas where it can exploit its performance and agility to avoid engagement by more powerfully armed opponents.

slow-moving HEAT warhead designed to generate an armour-piercing jet of super-hot gas and molten metal that can burn its way through protective armour, and the extremely fast-moving APFSDS designed as a fin-stabilized dart of heavy metal (normally tungsten or depleted uranium) that discards its supporting sabots on leaving the gun barrel, and delivers a devastating kinetic blow to the armour.

During the early 1950s the main tanks in service with the British forces were the Centurion medium and Conqueror heavy types. These were recognized as among the best vehicles in their classes, but it was also appreciated that Soviet developments would soon redress the USSR's qualitative inferiority, and the search was initiated for a single type to supersede both the Centurion and Conqueror, offering the mobility of the former with the firepower of the latter, but in a modern package. Various experimental designs were drawn up, but none of these progressed past the drawing board stage until Leyland produced two examples of its FV4202. This was perceived as a research rather than a pre-production design, but it pioneered two of the key features later adopted for the Chieftain: a turret without a gun mantlet, and a semi-reclined driver position, allowing considerable reduction in hull height.

The same reconnaissance task is performed for the British army by the Scorpion, otherwise known as the Combat Vehicle Reconnaissance (Tracked). The Scorpion is fast and nippy, and its 3in (76.2mm) main gun is a low-pressure type designed to fire the effective HESH round.

The Vickers Main Battle Tank is something of a rarity by modern standards for it was designed as a private venture, in this instance to meet a requirement issued by the Indian army for a battle tank that could be made under licence in India and maintained by unsophisticated troops, yet still offer a good account of itself on the modern battlefield. In its Mk 1 form the Vickers Main Battle Tank was sold to India and Kuwait, and in its Mk 3 form (illustrated) with a diesel rather than a petrol powerplant was delivered to Kenya and Nigeria.

When it was re-created in 1956, the West German army was equipped mostly with US weapons, including the M47 and M48A2 tanks: the M47 was already in widespread service, and was thus cheap, and presented even an inexperienced service with no problems, while the smaller number of M48A2s offered superior combat capabilities to crews who had mastered the M47. From the beginning, however, the West German army realized that its tactical concepts, inherited from its vast experience of European armoured warfare in World War II, were at variance with US concepts, which stressed firepower and protection to the detriment of agility and the battlefield advantages of modest weight and low overall silhouette. The US main battle tanks of the period turned the scales at about 50.80 tonnes, but the West German army thought that a figure nearer 30.00 tonnes should be the norm for operations in Western Europe. In 1957, therefore, the West German army called for a new tank weighing a maximum of 30.00 tonnes, powered by an air-cooled multi-fuel engine for a minimum power-to-weight ratio of 22kW/tonne (30hp/ton).

France and Italy had reached much the same conclusions as the West Germans, and France and West Germany were able to sign an interim

Developed by Thyssen Henschel in Germany, on the basis of the TAM medium battle tank it had designed for Argentina and using the chassis, hull and automotive system of the Marder mechanised infantry combat vehicle, the TH 301 was an improved prototype that failed to secure any production order.

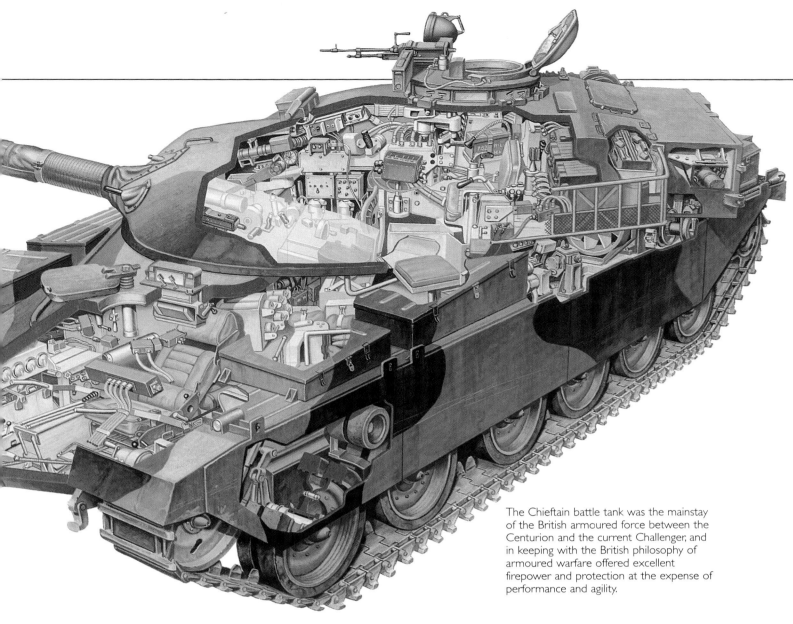

The Chieftain battle tank was the mainstay of the British armoured force between the Centurion and the current Challenger, and in keeping with the British philosophy of armoured warfare offered excellent firepower and protection at the expense of performance and agility.

understanding about the development of the new vehicle. Thus two prototypes were produced in France by AMX, and two different prototypes by each of two West German consortia: Gruppe A led by Porsche and Gruppe B by Ruhrstahl. A turret to suit all these prototypes was ordered from Rheinmetall. The two Gruppe A vehicles were delivered in January 1961 and the two Gruppe B machines in September of the same year. Given the nature of the specification, it was hardly surprising that the two vehicle types were similar in overall line, and were powered by the same Daimler-Benz MB 838 multi-fuel engine.

The Challenger is an altogether more formidable machine: an evolutionary development of the Chieftain with all the advantages that accrue from such a practice in terms of low technical risk, reduced development cost and contracted development time. The Challenger entered service in 1983 and is essentially the Shir 2 revised to accord with British operational requirements, and fitted with the Chobham composite armour first trialled during 1971 on a Chieftain derivative, the FV4211 prototype. Although based on the Chieftain in its structure and layout, the Challenger has a different appearance through the use of the special Chobham laminate armour, which comprises layers of special ceramics, metal and other material to provide a very high level of impenetrability to anti-armour weapons of both the chemical and kinetic varieties. To date, Chobham armour can be produced only in flat sheets, and this means that

131

The Chieftain was designed for service in the type of landscape seen here, namely the relatively close country of West Germany where any Soviet invasion of Western Europe was expected to materialise between the late 1950s and late 1980s. Optimisation for this type of battlefield meant that the Chieftain was well gunned and heavily armoured, but not notable for its performance.

specially shaped panels have to be laid over a steel inner structure to produce hull and turret contours less curvaceous than those of the Chieftain. The Challenger also has the Condor 12V 1200 diesel engine and an automatic transmission in an easily removed powerpack, revised suspension for a better cross-country ride, the TOGS sight and the IFCS fire-control system. The armament is currently the L11A5 gun, although the production version of the XL30 high-pressure gun is planned for retrofit as soon as possible.

Introduced in 1965, the Leopard 1 is in marked contrast to the Chieftain: whereas the priority list for the British tank was firepower, protection and mobility, that for the West German tank was firepower and mobility (as equal first) and then protection. Since 1965 the Leopard 1 has proved eminently successful, the total of 2,437 vehicles built for the West German army being complemented by export sales to Australia (90 vehicles), Belgium (334 vehicles), Canada (114), Denmark (120), Greece (106), Italy (920), the Netherlands (468), Norway (78) and Turkey (77).

Like the Chieftain, the Leopard 1 is of conventional layout but with only two compartments: that for the crew of four (the driver in the hull, and the commander, gunner and loader in the turret) at the front, and that for the powerpack at the rear. The manual transmission drives rear sprockets, and the running gear comprises, on each side, seven dual road wheels with independent torsion bar suspension and four track-return rollers. And as with the Chieftain, the Leopard 1 has night-vision devices, smoke-dischargers on each side of the turret (triple units), an overpressure NBC system, and metal-reinforced rubber skirts. The armament is a British-supplied 105mm (4.13in) L7A3 weapon firing the standard range of NATO ammunition, of which 55 rounds were carried; but when first delivered, the Leopard 1 lacked any gun stabilization and a sophisticated fire-control system.

Given that low weight was important to the Leopard 1, armour of only modest thickness was inevitable. The Leopard 1 has much in common with the German battle tanks of World War II, being fairly angular in shape and possessing sharply angled armour only on the hull front and upper sides. The hull is of welded construction, while the turret is a cast unit.

Just as the Chieftain paved the way for the Challenger in British service,

the Leopard 1 paved the way for the Leopard 2 in West German service. This resulted from the cancellation of the planned MBT-70 collaborative tank design, and the West Germans decided to develop a new main battle tank using MBT-70 components wherever possible: the most significant of these were the MTU MB 873 multi-fuel engine and the Renk transmission. Improved Leopard 1 components had also been developed, and wherever possible these were also worked into the design of the Krauss-Maffei Leopard 2, which may be compared favourably to the T-34 as being the only tank of its period to combine firepower, protection and mobility in equal proportions. The Leopard 2's main European rivals are the Chieftain and AMX-30. The Chieftain, as discussed above, has good firepower, good protection and poor mobility, while the AMX-30, as discussed below, has good mobility, adequate firepower and poor protection.

The 1960s were years of considerable development in the armoured field, and other main battle tanks to emerge from European manufacturers were the French AMX-30 and the Swedish Strv 103. The design of the AMX-30 was carried out by AMX, while production was entrusted to the Atelier de Construction de Roanne, which completed the first production tanks in 1966 to allow a service debut in the following year. The AMX-30 is a comparatively simple tank with a hull of welded rolled armour and a cast turret, and is the lightest main battle tank of its generation. Combined with a moderately powerful engine, this produces an impressive power-to-weight ratio and thus high performance and great agility, which are both features admired by the French armoured force. Such sprightliness is bought at the expense of protection, however, and the AMX-30 must now be judged obsolescent against the heavier modern weapons, especially in flank and overhead attacks. This tendency is exacerbated by the machine's comparatively tall silhouette, created by the considerable height of the commander's cupola and its 7.62mm (0.3in) anti-aircraft machine-gun on top of an otherwise admirably low hull and turret.

The main gun is the 105mm (4.13in) GIAT CN105F1 rifled ordnance, and the AMX-30 possesses an unusual secondary armament, for although the co-axial weapon was the standard 0.5 in (12.7mm) heavy machine-gun when the AMX-30 began to enter service, this was soon replaced by a 20mm GIAT

The first battle tank designed in Germany after World War II was the Leopard, which became the Leopard I after the introduction of the considerably superior Leopard II. The type is illustrated here by the Leopard armoured recovery vehicle, which is a turretless development fitted with front-mounted dozer blade, a winch, and a small crane, which was designed especially for tasks such as the changing of a Leopard I powerpack in the field.

M693 cannon to provide a potent capability against lightly armoured targets and helicopters. The AMX-30 lacks gun stabilization and an advanced fire-control system, but has standard features such as an NBC system and night-vision equipment. This results in a tank that is somewhat cheaper to buy and easier to maintain than equivalent American, British and West German main battle tanks, with consequent advantages in the export market to less developed countries: apart from France, AMX-30 operators include Chile, Cyprus, Greece, Iraq, Qatar, Saudi Arabia, Spain, the United Arab Emirates and Venezuela.

The series is still in production, the current variant being the upgraded AMX-30 B2 with improved transmission, a COTAC integrated fire-control system (with a laser rangefinder, low-light-level TV and lead-generating computer) and other operational enhancements such as skirts, and appliqué armour for the turret.

Another main battle tank in large-scale Western service is the Americans' most important weapon of this type, the M1 Abrams. This vehicle marks a turning point in main battle tank design as it is the world's first such machine to use a gas turbine as its sole automotive engine. The origins of the type lie with West Germany's 1970 decision to pull out of the Germano-American MBT-70 programme and to concentrate instead on an indigenous tank (the Leopard 2). This left the Americans with the need to develop an M60-series successor as rapidly as possible.

In basic layout the Abrams is completely conventional, but in structure the tank reflects recent advances in protection: the Abrams is constructed of the same type of composite armour as the Challenger and Leopard 2, which explains the angularity of the tank's external contours which are conditioned by the inflexibility of the protective material added over the core structure. The driver is located in the centre of the vehicle's forward compartment, and is seated in a semi-reclining position so that the hull front can be kept low and well angled against head-on fire. Behind the driver's position is the turret, which has electro-hydraulic traverse with manual

The OTO Melara/Fiat OF-40 is an Italian battle tank designed for the export market, and makes extensive use of components and assemblies from the Leopard I, which the companies built under licence in Italy.

controls for emergency use. The main armament is the 105mm (4.13in) M68 rifled gun, which is stabilized in two axes and has power elevation; the commander and gunner are located to the right of the weapon, and the loader to its left. The fire-control system includes a Computing Devices of Canada high-speed solid-state digital computer, a Hughes Aircraft Company laser rangefinder, stabilized day/night sight and automatic sensors for static cant and wind direction/speed.

Under the raised rear decking typical of most modern battle tanks is the unusual engine, a 1,500shp (1,118ekW) Lycoming AGT-1500 gas turbine. The power delivered to the rear drive sprockets by the gas turbine is greater than that from a similarly rated diesel engine because of the gas turbine's reduced cooling requirement; this, together with its compact size and supposedly high levels of reliability, was one of the reasons for this engine type's selection. The greater power of the gas turbine gives the M1 far livelier performance than the M60A3, however, and another advantage is the fact that the engine can be run on diesel oil or kerosene (or in an emergency on petrol); the fuel tanks are separated from the crew compartment by an armoured bulkhead for increased safety. On the debit side are the engine's comparative lack of ruggedness, its high thermal signature which makes the M1 more vulnerable to heat-seeking missiles, and a specific fuel consumption high enough to offset the additional fuel capacity made possible by the smaller engine.

The last 894 M1s were completed to the Improved M1 Abrams standard with enhanced protection. Production then switched to the definitive M1A1 Abrams, which began to enter service in August 1985. This has the enhanced protection of the Improved M1, a number of detail improvements, three rather than two blow-off panels in the turret roof, integral engine smoke generators, an integrated NBC system that provides the standard conditioned breathing air and also heating or cooling for those occasions when the crew are using NBC suits and face masks. The most important modification, however, is the use of the 120mm (4.72in) Rheinmetall Rh-120

Developed as a private venture by Vickers in the UK (turret, armament and fire-control system) and FMC in the USA (chassis, automotive system and hull), the VFM 5 is an interesting attempt to combine features of two tank types, namely the armament and protection of a main battle tank with the overall weight and dimensions of a light tank.

smooth-bore gun in place of the original 105mm (4.13in) M68 rifled weapon for greater offensive capability and longer range. The gun mounting was designed with this change in view, so the disruption to production caused by the armament change was minimal. The considerably larger ammunition of the 120mm (4.72in) gun made a reduction in ammunition capacities inevitable: in the M1 stowage is provided for 55 rounds (44 in left- and right-hand bustle compartments each surmounted by a blow-off panel, eight in a hull compartment and three in spallproof boxes on the turret basket) while in the M1A1 there is provision for only 40 rounds (36 in left-hand, central and right-hand bustle compartments each surmounted by a blow-off panel, and four in a rear hull box).

Enhancement of the M1A1 has continued at a steady pace. M1A1 Block II vehicles have a number of detail improvements as well as an improved commander's position with an independent thermal viewer, and the M1A1 Block III is a General Dynamics proposal with a three-man crew made possible by the addition of an automatic loading system, rapid refuelling and re-ammunitioning capabilities, and improved suspension. The Abrams has suffered its fair share of problems in service, but in its M1A1 form it is certainly one of the best tanks in the world today, with a large measure of development capacity still ahead of it

Within the Soviet bloc during the 1960s and 1970s, design and construction of heavy armour was retained exclusively by the USSR, which in the late 1950s had begun to plan a successor to the T-55 and T-55 series, with the same levels of protection and mobility, but with increased firepower in the form of a 115mm (4.53in) U-5TS (or 2A20) smooth-bore gun fitted with a fume extractor and two-axis stabilization: an unusual feature of this gun is its integral spent case ejection system, activated by the gun's recoil. This is a useful feature, but had to be bought by a limitation in fire rate to only four rounds per minute with the tank stationary, as the gun has to be brought to an exact elevation for the ejection system to function. Turret

Such was the versatility and mechanical reliability of the AMX-13 light tank that its lower hull and automotive system were used as the basis for a number of other armoured fighting vehicles such as a self-propelled gun, self-propelled anti-aircraft mounting, armoured personnel carrier, command vehicle, mortar vehicle, combat engineer vehicle and, as seen here, prototype mechanised infantry combat vehicle with a remotely controlled 20mm cannon over the rear of the hull.

Otherwise known as the S-tank, the Strv 103 was a highly ambitious and largely successful Swedish attempt to create a small and manoeuvrable battle tank without a turret. The 4.13in (105mm) main gun is fitted with an automatic loader and is fixed in the front of the vehicle: the weapon is brought to bear by slewing the complete vehicle, whose suspension is then adjusted to secure the desired elevation angle.

The M163 is a simple and moderately effective air-defence vehicle for the short-range protection of mobile forces, and is basically an M113 armoured personnel carrier with a 20mm Vulcan six-barrel rotary cannon on a traversing and elevating mounting above it.

risks are reduced by the carriage of only four ready-use rounds in the turret, the balance of 36 rounds being carried below the turret ring (16 to the right of the driver and 20 in the rear of the fighting compartment).

The cast turret resembles that of the T-54 and T-55 series, but the welded hull is both longer and wider than that of the earlier series, with a different spacing of the road wheels. In other essential respects the T-62 is very similar to the T-55 it succeeded, and began to enter production during 1961 for service in 1963. The construction programme in the USSR lasted until 1975 and accounted for about 20,000 tanks complemented by another 1,500 from a Czech line between 1973 and 1978, and an unknown number from a North Korean line that is currently producing tanks for the domestic and continued export markets.

The T-62 is still in very widespread service, and continues as one of the Warsaw Pact forces' most important first-line assets. The standard features of the tank include an NBC system, active night-vision equipment and a snorkel to permit wading to a maximum depth of 5.5m (18.05ft), and its adequate range on internal fuel can be boosted by auxiliary fuel carried in main and supplementary external tankage. The T-62 has been used extensively in combat, especially in the Middle East. The type has acquitted itself well, the high level of protection provided by its well-sloped armour. However, in common with other Soviet tanks, this protective capability is made all the more valuable by the main armament's poor elevation arc. The T-62 is also limited in offensive capability by its comparatively simple fire-control system.

Given its importance and longevity, it is hardly surprising that the T-62 has appeared in variant form, although few in number. The most important of these in numerical terms is the T-62A, which has a turret of revised shape and different size, together with a rotating cupola mounting (plus external 12.7mm/0.5in machine-gun) in place of the fixed loader's hatch of the T-62. It is also believed that an improved fire-control system and night-vision equipment have been fitted, the former to a standard comparable with that of the M60A3 with a ballistic computer, laser rangefinder and various sensors. A derivative of the T-62A is the T-62M with 'live' tracks for longer life and better performance.

Like the Americans and other major tank-producing nations, the USSR operated on the principle of starting the search for a successor as soon as any major type had entered production. In the case of the T-62 this process led to the development of the T-64. Several prototypes were trialled in the period up to 1966, when the decision was made to place the best in production as the T-64, which was designated the M1970 in Western terminology. It is uncertain when the T-64 began to enter service, but the type is believed to have been manufactured between 1966 and 1971, although the production line remained open until 1981 for the re-manufacture of earlier vehicles. Total production is thought to have been in the order of 8,000 vehicles. Taken in combination, factors such as a comparatively small production run, a late service entry date and an extensive re-manufacturing programme suggest that there were severe problems with the type. It is also probable that the Soviets had a high expectation of the type, which resulted in re-manufacture rather than cancellation of the project.

The initial M1970 version was probably a large-scale pre-production type with a turret basically similar to that of the T-64, but with a different hull, running gear and engine. The turret was located slightly farther to the rear, and the welded hull used a more advanced type of armour than the rolled plate used in the T-62. Whereas the T-54 and its immediate successors used medium-diameter road wheels without track-return rollers, the M1970 and its progeny have six small-diameter road wheels per side instead of the earlier tanks' five larger wheels, four track-return rollers per side to support the inside of the track, and hydropneumatic rather than torsion bar

The Merkava is one of the most advanced tanks in the world, and reflects the virtually unique experience of the Israeli army in fighting four major armoured campaigns since the creation of Israel in 1948.

suspension. The idlers were at the front, leaving the drive sprockets to be located at the rear, where they were powered by hydraulically-assisted transmission driven by a new type of engine, a five-cylinder opposed-piston diesel engine. The M1970 was armed with a 115mm (4.53in) smooth-bore gun, but the T-64 'definitive' production version has a 125mm (4.92in) D-81TM Rapira 3 (or 2A46) smooth-bore gun, an altogether more powerful weapon fitted with an automatic loader to allow a reduction in crew from the M1970's four to the T-64's three. The gun is stabilized in two axes, has a larger-than-usual elevation arc and is used with an advanced fire-control system including a ballistic computer, stabilized optics and a laser rangefinder. Other standard features are an NBC system, night-vision equipment and a snorkel for deep wading; it is also possible that a laser-warning receiver is fitted to provide the crew with advanced warning of attack by a tank fitted with a laser rangefinder, or by an air-launched 'smart' weapon with passive laser guidance to home onto any tank laser-illuminated by a third party.

There were considerable problems associated with the T-64's engine, suspension, automatic loader and fire-control system, and the type has evolved through a number of variants known only by their hybrid Western designations. Thus the initial T-64 was followed by the T-64A (M1981/1) with a revised gunner's sight, smoke-grenade dispensers on the turret and hinges for the attachment of skirt armour; there is also an M1981/2 subvariant fitted with permanent skirts rather than for the optional skirts of the M1981/1.

The next variant is believed to have been the most important production model, built as such but perhaps supplemented by older tanks re-manufactured to the improved standard. This variant is the T-64B, which has the improved 125mm (4.92in) weapon also carried by the T-72 and T-80, together with a revised and more reliable automatic loading system. The gun can also fire the AT-8 'Songster' missile, which is a dual-role weapon for use against tanks to a range of 4,000m (4,375yds) and against helicopters to a range of perhaps 8,000m (8,750yds). The missile is carried in the automatic loader in two sections, and fed into the main ordnance in exactly the same way as conventional ammunition. The precise balance of missiles

Reconnaissance for heavy armoured forces calls for a comparatively light and moderately protected vehicle whose survival is provided by levels of speed and agility greater than those of the more heavily gunned vehicles it may encounter, and by a main gun of larger calibre and greater strength than those carried by faster opponents. The British specialist in this important field is Alvis, which produces a number of tracked and wheeled vehicles characterized by the use of highly reliable commercial, rather than specifically military, components in their automotive systems.

The Strv 74 is an obsolete Swedish light tank.

and conventional ammunition will depend on the tactical situation, but it is likely that at least some tanks in any given unit will be tasked with a primary anti-helicopter role and therefore will field a higher-than-normal complement of missiles.

The T-64B became operational in 1980, with reactive armour first appearing in 1984. The problems faced by the T-64 series persuaded the Soviet authorities to attempt a comparable but lower-risk version, powered by a conventional diesel engine and fitted with torsion bar suspension for an arrangement of six larger-diameter road wheels on each side, together with only three track-return rollers. The hull was revised accordingly, with slightly less length, marginally more width and a modestly increased height. The result is the T-72, a main battle tank similar to the T-64 in operational capability, but offering greater reliability in its automotive system and, as a result of its lighter weight and improved power-to-weight ratio, superior mobility and performance.

The T-72 began to reach service operators in 1981, and is still in production at four former-Soviet plants and at plants in Czechoslovakia, India, Poland and the former Yugoslavia. Whereas the T-64 is used exclusively by the Russians, the T-72 has no provision for AT-8 missiles and is operated by the Warsaw Pact countries and non-Warsaw Pact operators such as Algeria, former Yugoslavia, Angola, Cuba, Finland, India, Iraq, Libya and Syria.

The T-72 has been developed in a number of forms and variants, and while some of these are known by their Soviet designations, others are best individualized by Western designations. The baseline model is the T-72 discussed above, and has an infra-red searchlight to the left of the main gun; there is also a T-72K command model. The T-72M is the main production variant, with the searchlight moved to the right of the main gun; there is also a T-72MK command model. The designation T-72 (M1981/2) is used for older T-72s retrofitted with side armour to prevent effective top attack of the engine compartment. The T-74 has been produced in several subvariants. The initial version lacks the optics port in the right-hand side of the turret front (presumably for a laser rangefinder), while the T-74 (M1980/1) is similar but has fabric skirt armour over the suspension and side containers. The T-74 (M1981/3) has appeared in two models, the initial type resembling the T-72 (M1980/1) but with thicker frontal armour, and the later type having smoke-grenade launchers. The latest model is the T-74 (T-72 M1984 or T-74M) based on the previous type but with appliqué armour and anti-radiation cladding.

The last main battle tank from the Soviet stable was the T-80, which is now known to be a further development of the missile-capable T-64B, and began to enter production in the early 1980s for service deliveries in 1984. By the end of 1987, it is believed that some 7,000 T-80s had been produced exclusively for the Soviet forces.

The tank is similar in configuration and shape to the T-64, with the driver's compartment at the front, the two-man turret in the centre and the engine compartment at the rear. But the T-80 has a considerable number of detail differences from the T-64B. The most important of these are a laminated glacis for improved protection against kinetic and chemical attack, a dozer blade retracting under the nose, a new pattern of road wheel with torsion bar suspension, a cast steel turret with an inside layer of 'special armour', a modified commander's hatch, revised stowage on the outside of the turret, a modified rear decking and, perhaps most significantly of all, a new powerplant in the form of a 985shp (734ekW) gas turbine with a manual transmission featuring five forward gears and one reverse, compared with the diesel-engined T-64's synchromesh transmission with seven forward gears and one reverse.

A Russian T-62 MBT. A typical Soviet design feature is the high rise of the forward track run to the forward idler.

The T-64 and T-80 are currently the most important main battle tank types in former Soviet service, but are more than ably backed by massive numbers of T-72s and T-62s.

Artillery

General-Purpose Artillery

RTILLERY is defined as a crew-served weapon firing a tube-launched projectile that was originally of the solid shot type, then the explosive-filled shell type, and can now be either of the shot or shell type depending on the purpose being served: the shot is used almost exclusively for the short-range destruction of hardened targets such as armoured fighting vehicles and strongpoints, while the shell (including its most recent cargo-carrying variant filled with submunitions) is used for virtually every other battlefield task.

The development of modern artillery began in the nineteenth century, when the well-established type of field and siege gun, loaded down its unrifled barrel first with black powder and then with its projectile (generally spherical although there were also cylindrical case and canister munitions), was gradually improved into a longer-ranged and more accurate weapon with a rifled barrel firing an elongated projectile that was loaded by means of an opening breech: this projectile was attached to the front of a brass case containing the propellant (originally black powder but then a nitrocellulose compound) to create a unitary round or, in the alternative separate-loading type of ammunition used for heavier guns, loaded in front of the one or more silk bags of propellant.

These developments did much to convert artillery from a short-ranged and relatively inaccurate type of weapon into a considerably longer-ranged and more accurate type that was standardised in two basic forms: as the gun and the howitzer. The gun is a direct-fire weapon used for the engagement of targets that are visible directly to the gunner, and fires at a higher muzzle velocity for a comparatively flat trajectory with the muzzle elevated to no more than 45 degrees. The howitzer, on the other hand, is an indirect-fire weapon used for the engagement of targets that are not directly visible to the gunner, and fires at a lower muzzle velocity for a high, lobbed trajectory with the muzzle elevated to more than 45 degrees. The gun is best suited to the destruction of shorter-range targets, while the howitzer is best suited to the engagement

Used in limited numbers during World War I, and most notably involved in the Japanese reduction of the German concession enclave at Tsingtao on the Chinese coast, the Army Howitzer Type 4 was typical of the heavier field artillery of the period. The weapon's details included a weight of 6,160lb (2,794kg), calibre of 149.1mm (5.87in) with an L/14.6 barrel, length of 20ft 9in (6.325m), elevation and traverse arcs of −5 to +65 degrees and 3 degrees left and right of the centreline, rate of fire of four rounds per minute for two minutes declining to one round per minute thereafter, muzzle velocity of 1,345ft (410m) per second, maximum range of 10,465yds (9,570m), and detachment of six or seven. The weapon could fire a number of projectile types each weighing some 80lb (36.32kg), their recoil being absorbed by a hydro-pneumatic recoil system, and while the howitzer could be moved over short distances as a complete unit on its two iron-tyred spoked wooden wheels, the standard method of longer-distance transport was in two loads each drawn by six horses.

of longer-range targets or positions that are hidden by natural or man-made obstructions such as a hill or village, over which the shell can pass before plummeting toward its target.

During the enhancement of the overall capabilities of artillery, the two features that proved difficult to solve – but which were seminal to the creation of modern artillery – were accurate weapon laying with the long-ranged type of fire now possible, and a method to control the recoil of the gun. Up to this time, the simple iron sight and then the slightly more advanced tangent sight had been sufficient for aiming purposes, but with a range in excess of 4,000yds (3,660m) now possible, something better than basic eyesight was required. The answer was found in the gun-laying methods developed for the Royal Navy by Captain Percy Scott, namely the telescopic sight: this was a telescope with

145

The Italian 149mm (5.87in) gun was a piece of heavy field artillery optimised for use in inhospitable regions. The weapon's details included a weight of 17,857 lb (8,100kg), elevation arc of −10 to +35 degrees, rate of fire of two rounds per minute, muzzle velocity of 2,198ft (670m) per second, and maximum range of 7,380yds (6,750m) with a 92.6lb (42kg) shell.

cross wires, that was clamped in a suitable position on the gun carriage and coupled to the gun so that movement of the gun moved the sight. It was a simple yet sufficient method of laying the gun with considerable accuracy, and is still the standard method albeit in modernised form.

Recoil had been a major problem right from the beginning of artillery's history. With the exception of heavy siege artillery, which was usually delivered to its tactical position in disassembled form and then erected on a prepared and fixed site that could absorb the recoil forces, artillery was generally intended for tactical operations on the battlefield and therefore had to be as light and as mobile as possible. This meant that most pieces of artillery were based on a two-wheeled carriage with a trail that carried the eye by which the gun was pulled by horses or other draught animals, and which helped to stabilize the gun in firing position. Even with black powder propellant, however, the recoil forces were so great that the gun recoiled several feet as it was fired: this meant that before it could be fired again, the crew had to manhandle the weapon back into position and then, after reloading, re-lay the weapon. This was a time-consuming process that reduced gun batteries' rates of fire, especially in the type of sustained battle in which stamina became a critical factor: at the Battle of Waterloo in 1815, for instance, the British gunners became so exhausted that they were unable to manhandle their weapons back into position, and therefore reloaded and fired from the positions into which their guns had recoiled. As might be expected, this seriously affected the accuracy of the gunfire.

The recoil problem became more acute as propellants were made more powerful and as the construction of guns was improved to reduce their weight (for reduced cost and better tactical mobility, without sacrificing the barrel strength on which depended the integrity of the weapon and thus the safety of its crew). The effect of these changes was to increase the tendency of guns

The Skoda 7.5cm Gebirgskanone M.15 mountain gun/howitzer was one of the best such equipments available in World War I. The weapon's details included a weight of 1,352lb (613kg), calibre of 75mm (2.95in) with an L/15.4 barrel, elevation and traverse arcs of −10 to +50 degrees and 3.5 degrees left and right of the centreline, muzzle velocity of 1,149ft (350m) per second with the HE projectile or 804ft (245m) per second with the shrapnel projectile, and maximum range of 9,025yds (8,250m).

to recoil out of position, especially when these guns were carried on a wheeled carriage. Early in the nineteenth century a French officer, the Chevalier de Beaulieu, suggested a muzzle brake system in which a gas deflection device was installed in front of the muzzle to trap some of the forward-rushing propellant gases and thus draw the gun forward as a means of partly counteracting the recoil forces. Trials with muskets fitted with a muzzle brake proved moderately successful, but the technology of the day was inadequate to make the muzzle brake effective with pieces of artillery.

Even if it had worked, the muzzle brake would have been little more than a palliative, as the weight of current guns was so high that the shot had departed and the force of the propellant gases had been dissipated before the effect of a muzzle brake could make itself felt. This is not to deny that the muzzle brake can have its uses, as proved from the 1930s when such devices have been used with considerable success on more advanced weapons based on a comparatively lighter gun fitted with a recoil system of the type discussed below; even in such guns, however, the effect of the muzzle brake is an addition rather than an alternative to the main recoil system.

The problem of recoil was becoming acute in the 1860s. At this time the United Kingdom, suddenly made aware of the inadequacy of its coastal defences against a re-emergent threat of hostilities with France, was building additional defences and improving existing fortifications with better guns (although the guns' existing casemates lacked the size to accommodate the recoil of modern guns). The current system comprised an inclined ramp up which a standard naval gun recoiled on its carriage with four small wheels: if the recoil appeared excessive, the gunners strewed sand on the ramp to increase friction; and if the recoil seemed inadequate, the gunners spread grease on the ramp to reduce friction. Faced with the same problem, the Americans developed the so-called 'compressor' system in which a series of metal plates was hung between the sides of the slide to interleave with another series of plates extending below the gun carriage: a screw jack was used to adjust the friction between these two sets of plates and thereby control the length of the recoil. In the British system the gun was checked at the moment of maximum recoil by a block-and-tackle device, and in the American system by a flick of the screw jack; in each system the gun used gravity to rumble down the ramp into position after being reloaded.

It was a workable although extremely cumbersome system that placed considerable emphasis on the crew's knowledge of a particular gun. What was needed was an automatic and therefore more reliable system that placed no demands on crew experience. The answer was found in a hydraulic system.

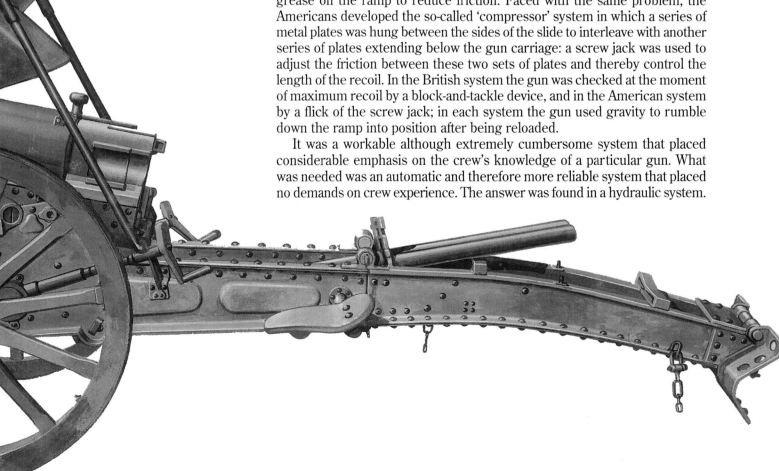

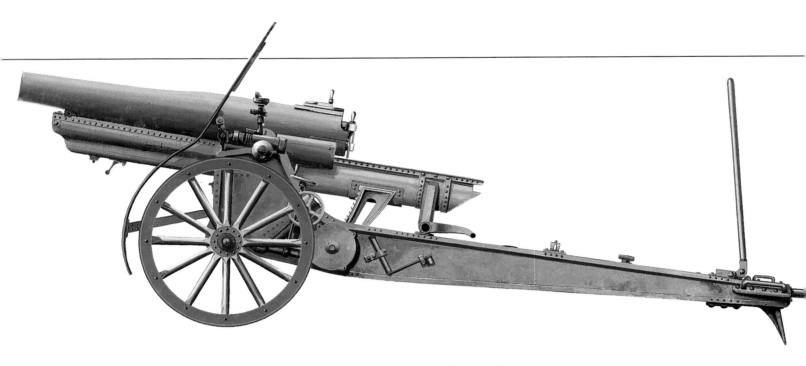

The Americans had already experimented with such a system: the recoiling gun ran back up its ramp until it struck a buffer piston rod, whereupon the buffer piston was driven back into the buffer cylinder in which water absorbed the recoil shock and brought the recoil to a halt. This system certainly achieved wonders in reducing the shock of the recoil, but did nothing to control or reduce recoil.

The hydraulic system provided the germ of an idea to a British team working at the Woolwich Arsenal under the supervision of Colonel Clerk. This team developed a new buffer system in which a cylinder of oil was attached to the ramp and the end of the piston rod was attached to the gun carriage: the piston head had a hole in it, and the recoil of the gun was controlled by the rate at which the oil passed from one side of the piston head to the other as the piston head moved through the oil. The system was still relatively primitive, but had the considerable advantages of not only stopping the recoil, but also of controlling the recoil and passing the recoil forces to the ramp and thus to the ground or the structure in which the gun was accommodated: this allowed the structure of the ramp (no longer required to carry the main recoil forces on its own) to be simplified and lightened with consequent improvements in the way it could be traversed, and also made it possible for the recoil of the gun to be controlled to the space available in existing casemates. It is worth noting, however, that the system included no provision for the gun to be returned automatically to battery, a task in which gravity, handspikes and the block and tackle still had to be employed.

This hydraulic buffer system was the basis of all future development in recoil systems, however, and was thus directly responsible for the evolution of the quick-firing gun which does not need to be re-laid between rounds. It was the quick-firing field gun that paved the way for developments in the years to come, and the type is therefore worthy of discussion in slightly greater detail.

The task set to designers in the creation of the quick-firing field gun was the production of a weapon that could achieve the maximum possible rate of fire under tactical conditions, and to this end the most desirable features were quickly established as unitary ammunition (the fused projectile crimped into the forward end of the brass case containing the propellant and its ignition system) so that the gun could be loaded quickly and simply as soon as the breech had been opened and the previous round's empty case extracted; a simple and fast-acting breech mechanism; an effective form of recoil control

The Russian 6in (152mm) howitzer of the World War I period was not an exceptional equipment, but was rugged, reliable and accurate.

Like other combatants in World War I, the Germans soon found themselves short of large-calibre field guns capable of firing at high velocity in the direct-fire role, and therefore adopted a similar expedient, namely a naval ordnance on a land carriage. This weapon was based on the gun originally designed as the secondary armament of German battleships, and its details included a weight of 25,408lb (11,525kg), calibre of 150mm (5.91in) with an L/40 barrel, elevation and traverse arcs of −8 to +32 degrees and 13.5 degrees left and right of the centreline, and maximum range of 19,000yds (17,375m) with the lighter of the two available projectiles.

An obsolete weapon that nonetheless served right through World War I was this French equipment in 120mm (4.72in) calibre. The gun was made in 1890, as suggested by its primitive recoil system.

so that the gun crew could remain in position round their weapon ready to reload as soon as the weapon had been fired; and some form of protection for the crew against the effects of small-arms fire and shell splinters.

Many weapons were designed and built in modest numbers as the artillery establishments of the world's most advanced nations sought to achieve this complex combination of features. The honours for being first to achieve this goal go to France, which standardised this Schneider weapon as the Canon de 75 modèle 1897. Generally known in the English-speaking world as the 'French 75', this gun was the result of a protracted evolutionary design process which incorporated a hydro-pneumatic recoil system that not only absorbed the gun's recoil but also returned the gun into battery after each shot; a quick-acting breech mechanism of the Nordenfeldt type (a breech block mounted eccentrically to the bore's axis with a cutaway portion that, aligned with the bore, permitted loading but was then rotated to swing a solid section of the block into position behind the cartridge case); fixed ammunition of the unitary type; a shield to protect the crew; provision for the wheel brake shoes to be dropped under the wheels to hold the carriage firmly in position; a pole trail fitted with a spade that dug into the ground and further stabilized the carriage in firing position; and an independent sighting system that permitted the gunner to lay the gun while an assistant controlled elevation.

The 'French 75' set the standard against which all other pieces of field artillery would now be measured. The primary details of this weapon included a calibre of 75mm (2.95in) with an L/36 barrel (barrel length of 36 calibres), weight of 4,343lb (1,970kg) in travelling order reducing to 2,513lb (1,140kg) in action, elevation and traverse arcs on the carriage of –11 to +18 degrees and 3 degrees left and right respectively, and a range of 12,140yds (11,100m) with a 13.66lb (6.195kg) shell fired at a muzzle velocity of 1,886ft (575m) per second.

The real key to the success of the 'French 75' was its advanced system to handle the recoil and return the gun to battery. Early observers were amazed at the steadiness of the weapon while it was being fired at 15 rounds or more per minute. Other such systems were already available, but these were based on a simple buffer (to control recoil) and large springs (compressed during recoil and then expanded to return the gun to battery). The effect of this primitive combination was to cut off recoil abruptly and then slam the gun back into battery: the net result was that the gun still leaped or rolled backward, although not as far as would have been the case without this system. The 'French 75', on the other hand, recoiled smoothly for between 3 and 4ft (0.9 and 1.2m) before coming to a halt and then sliding gently but quickly back into battery without the carriage moving. As details of the 'French 75' reached other countries, its operation became known as the 'long recoil' system and was adopted virtually universally: by Vickers and Coventry Ordnance Works in the UK, Krupp in Germany, Bofors in Sweden, Skoda in Austria-Hungary, Cockerill in Belgium, Vickers-Terni and Ansaldo in Italy, Putilov in Russia, Osaka Arsenal in Japan, and Bethlehem in the USA.

A weapon introduced in 1917 and known to the British as the 'Screaming Lizzie' for the high-pitched wail of its high-velocity shell, this was the 10cm Feldkanone 17 with a barrel characterised by a calibre of 105mm (4.13in), L/45 length, elevation arc of between –2 and +45 degrees, and traverse arc of 3 degrees left and right of the centreline. The weapon weighed 7,276lb (3,300kg), and fired a 40.8lb (18.5kg) shell with a muzzle velocity of 2,130ft (650m) per second to achieve a maximum range of 18,050yds (16,505m), and was notably accurate.

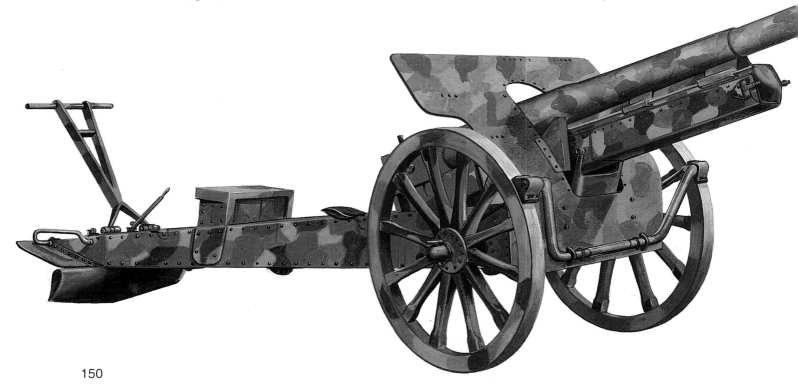

The Austro-Hungarian army's standard
heavy field howitzer was the Skoda-built
15cm schwere Feldhaubitze M.14 with a
barrel of 149.1mm (5.87in) calibre and only
L/14 length, elevation arc of –5 to +43
degrees, traverse arc of 2.5 degrees left and
right of the centreline, weight of 5,168lb
(2,345kg), muzzle velocity of 984ft (300m)
per second to fire a 90.4lb (41kg) shell to a
range of 7,550yds (6,905m), and
detachment of eight.

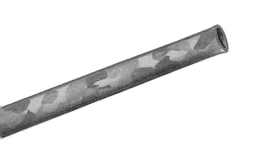

By the end of World War I (1914-18), the French pattern of quick-firing field gun had developed into a large number of weapons in calibres between 75mm (2.95in) and 105mm (4.13in). Among the classics of this breed were the German 77mm (3.03in) Feldkanone 16, 105mm Kanone 17/04 and 105mm Feldhaubitze 16; the Austro-Hungarian 76.5mm (3.012in) Skoda Kanone 17 and 100mm (3.94in) Skoda Kanone 14; and the British 76.2mm (3in) Ordnance, QF, 13pdr Gun and 83.8mm (3.3in) Ordnance, QF, 18pdr Gun used by the horse and field artillery respectively.

Further up the scale was heavy artillery with calibres in the range between 105mm (4.13in) and 210mm (8.27in). Despite their greater calibre, which ensured that a larger and heavier projectile could be fired to a considerably longer range than the smaller pieces of field artillery, these were conceptually related to the smaller-calibre weapons in their technical details. Being more massive, however, larger-calibre weapons were less mobile than their smaller-calibre counterparts, but came into their own later in World War I as the initial mobile operations gave way to attritional warfare after November 1914. The lines of parallel trenches had offered the soldiers of each side good protection against the direct fire of smaller-calibre weapons, but had placed greater emphasis on the more destructive capabilities provided by larger-calibre weapons. These fell into two classes, namely the larger-calibre guns that could engage point targets such as artillery dumps and the enemy's rear-area gun lines with direct fire at long range, and the larger-calibre howitzers that tackled front-line targets with plunging fire at somewhat shorter ranges.

The importance of these weapons grew as the static trench warfare of World War I dragged on, for up to the time of the tank's first appearance in September 1916, and its availability in substantial numbers from the summer of 1917, the only tactic that World War I commanders could imagine was the massive use of artillery. This was employed in great numbers and over protracted periods to lay down vast weights of fire designed to blast the enemy's trench lines, in preparation for the infantry assault that was designed to penetrate through the blasted section before the enemy could counterattack, and thereby create the gap into the enemy's rear areas that could be exploited by horsed cavalry (to cut the enemy's lines of communication and thereby facilitate the progress of the follow-up infantry).

Heavy guns and howitzers were essential to this process, and the middle stages of World War I were therefore dominated by these pieces of artillery. Good examples of such weapons were the Austro-Hungarian Skoda 149.1mm (5.87in) Haubitze 14 howitzer, Skoda 152.4mm (6in) Kanone 15/16 gun and Skoda 210mm (8.27in) Haubitze 18 howitzer; the French St Chamond 145mm (5.7in) Canon de 145L modèle 1916 gun, St Chamond 155mm (6.1in) Canon de 155L modèle 1916 gun, St Chamond 155mm Canon de 155C modèle 15 howitzer, St Chamond 155mm Canon de 155C modèle 1917 howitzer, and Filloux 155mm Canon de 155 Grande Puissance gun; the German 149.7mm (5.89in) schwere Feldhaubitze 13 howitzer, 149.3mm (5.878in) Kanone 16 gun, 152.4mm (6in) Haubitzen 09 and 10, and 211mm (8.3in) langer Mörser howitzer; the Italian 149.1mm (5.87in) Cannone da 149 gun; the British 4.5in (114.3mm) Ordnance, QF, Howitzer Mk I howitzer, 5in (127mm) Ordnance, BL, 60pdr Gun Mk I gun, 6in(152.4mm) Ordnance, BL, Gun Mk VIII gun, 6in Ordnance, BL, 6in 26cwt Howitzer Mk I howitzer, and 8in (203mm) Ordnance, BL, Howitzer Mk VII howitzer; and the American 155mm (6.1in) Howitzer M1918 howitzer.

Typical of these assorted weapons are the German Kanone 16, the British 60pdr gun and the American M1918 howitzer, the last an Americanised version of a French weapon, the Schneider Canon de 155C modèle 1917. The Kanone 16 was built in two almost identical versions by Krupp and Rheinmetall as the K 16 Kr with an L/42.7 barrel and the Kanone 16 Rh with an L/42.9 barrel: the details of the K 16 Kr included a weight of 22,445lb (10,180kg) in action, on-mounting elevation and traverse angles of 0 to +46 degrees and 4 degrees left and right respectively, and a range of 24,070yds (22,000m) with a 110.74lb (50.223kg) shell fired at a muzzle velocity of 2,440ft (744m) per second. The details of the 60pdr Gun Mk II gun, which was a post-war development of the 60pdr Gun Mk I, included a weight of 14,148lb (6,423kg) in travelling order and 12,048lb (5,470kg) in firing position, on-mounting elevation and traverse angles of –6 to +35 degrees and 4 degrees left and right respectively, and a range of 15,100yds (13,815m) with a 60lb (27.24kg) shell fired from the L/38.45 barrel with a muzzle velocity of 2,176ft (663m) per second. The details of the M1918 howitzer included a weight of 9,518lb

A thoroughly workmanlike weapon that survived right into World War II was the 15cm Kanone 16 Kr, the letters at the end indicating that this was the Krupp-built weapon that differed in slight details from the Rheinmetall-built 15cm Kanone 16 Rh. The details of this weapon, which was of moderately great importance in German operations during the later part of World War I, included a calibre of 149.3mm (5.878in), L/42.7 barrel length, weight of 22,445lb (10,180kg), elevation arc of between 0 and +46 degrees, traverse arc of 4 degrees left and right of the centreline, and muzzle velocity of 2,440ft (744m) per second to fire the 110.74lb (50.223kg) shell to a maximum range of 24,070yds (22,000m).

(4,321kg) in travelling order and 8,184lb (3,715kg) in firing position, on-mounting elevation and traverse angles of 0 to +42 degrees and 3 degrees left and right respectively, and a range of 12,295yds (11,250m) with a 94.27lb (42.8kg) shell fired from the L/13.64 barrel at a muzzle velocity of 1,478ft (451m) per second.

While most of the countries that would soon become embroiled in World War I were content in the first decade of the twentieth century to devote their artillery design and production efforts to such field artillery, the Germans and Austro-Hungarians appreciated that their longer-term offensive plans would require their armies to penetrate through bands of fixed defensive positions; therefore, they instructed their gun manufacturers to devote a significant part of their effort to the design and manufacture of modest numbers of heavy artillery pieces in the calibre range upward of 210mm (8.27in). These weapons were not designed for field use in mobile warfare, but rather for limited mobility or transport in dismantled state to the location of siege operations. The two most celebrated of these weapons were the Austro-Hungarian 'schlanke Emma' 305mm (12in) howitzer designed and built by Skoda, and the German 'dicke Bertha' 420mm (16.54in) howitzer designed and built by Krupp.

Both these weapons displayed prodigious capabilities in the task of penetrating and destroying concrete fortifications, and although there was little further demand for weapons of this specific type, especially as their mobility was so limited, further work on super-heavy artillery was based on wheeled carriages and later, as these became increasingly problematical with increasing gun calibre, on railway carriages. The British, for example, had been considering super-heavy artillery for some years, and the Coventry Ordnance Works 4.5in (114.3mm) howitzer was soon scaled up to 9.2in (233.7mm) calibre in a weapon that could be dismantled for movement on wagon bodies towed by steam traction engines. The weapon proved to be an excellent piece of ordnance through its combination of a durable barrel and considerable accuracy with a heavy shell. Further weapons, in calibres up to 15in (381mm), were produced by several of the combatants in semi-mobile gun and howitzer forms for dismantled movement or alternatively for installation on a railway carriage.

After World War I there was a considerable shift in the emphasis although not the technology of gun design, as national war ministries, which had become heavily involved in gun design during the war, were now loath to give up this capability. The effect was to reduce the gun design capabilities of manufacturers, who were now increasingly asked to implement the designs of the official design teams. Another change that was demanded at the highest

The 10.5cm leichte Feldhaubitze 13 was produced by Krupp, and its details included a calibre of 105mm (4.13in), L/20 barrel length, elevation arc of between –4 and +43 degrees, and a muzzle velocity of 1,410ft (430m) per second to fire a 35.34lb (16kg) shell to a maximum range of 9,735yds (8,900m).

153

military levels (but frequently not implemented as a result of financial stringencies during the 1920s and 1930s), was for larger-calibre guns: the tendency was therefore for medium field artillery to possess a calibre in the order of 85 to 105mm (3.34 to 4.13in) and for heavy field artillery to span the calibre bracket between 140 and 155mm (5.5 and 6.1in). An example of this tendency is provided by the British: the War Office decided that the army should adopt a 105mm weapon as its standard field howitzer, and the design of such a weapon was contracted to Vickers, which produced successful prototype weapons by 1930. At this point the Treasury stepped into the matter, objecting to the financial burden that would have to be suffered for the production and introduction of this wholly new weapon at a time when the army still had many hundreds of perfectly serviceable 18pdr (83.8mm/3.3in) guns. The final result was a compromise of the type so

typical in British history. The War Office had its way about the need for a more advanced gun, and the Treasury achieved its wish to avoid large capital expenditure: from 1935, therefore, more than 1,000 of the 18pdr guns had their barrels bored out to take a new and larger round of ammunition firing a 25pdr shell of 87.6mm (3.45in) calibre. The revised weapon was the Ordnance, QF, 25pdr Gun Mk 1, which thus retained the 18pdr gun's carriage (in a form revised with pneumatically tyred wheels in place of the original wooden-spoked and steel-tyred wheels) and thereby saved considerable expenditure.

Generally known as the 18/25pdr gun, this weapon was limited in elevation to a maximum of 30 degrees by its retention of the 18pdr's Mk IIITP carriage with its pole trail, but later the Mk IVP carriage was adopted, this having a box trail whose central gap allowed the breech of the gun to be lowered farther for a maximum elevation angle slightly in excess of 37 degrees, and there was also the Mk VP carriage of the type originally developed for the 25pdr Gun Mk 2. On the Mk IVP carriage, the 18/25pdr gun had a weight of 3,570lb (1,621kg), on-mounting elevation and traverse angles of –5 to +37 degrees and 4.5 degrees left and right respectively, and a range of 12,000yds (10,875m) with a 25lb (11.34kg) shell fired from the L/28.13 barrel at a muzzle velocity of 1,706ft (520m) per second.

In 1936 the range requirement for this 'new' standard field artillery weapon was increased to 13,500yds (12,345m), but this was beyond the capabilities of the 18/25pdr conversion: the maximum elevation angle was too low for the generation of the maximum range possible with the ammunition, and the carriage lacked the strength to cope with the full-charge cartridge designed for the 25pdr round. The 18/25pdr therefore used a round with a reduced propellant charge, but the full capabilities of the round were finally permitted by the adoption of a new carriage to create the Ordnance, QF, 25pdr Gun Mk 2. As originally planned, this was to have been of the split-trail type allowing a larger angle of on-mounting traverse, but

Just entering British service in the summer of 1916, when it was blooded in the Battle of the Somme as replacement for the 6in 30cwt howitzer, the 6in 26cwt howitzer (more formally the BL, 6in 26cwt Howitzer, Mk I) proved to be a well-designed and well-made weapon admirably suited to the warfare of World War I. The details of this important weapon, of which some 4,000 were in service by the time of the Armistice in November 1918, included a calibre of 6in (152.4mm), an L/14.6 barrel, weight of 9,849lb (4,467kg), elevation arc of between 0 and +45 degrees, traverse arc of 4 degrees left and right of the centreline, and muzzle velocity of 1,409ft (429m) per second to fire the 100.19lb (45.44kg) shell to a maximum range of 11,400yds (10,425m).

Opposite: The German 15cm schwere Feldhaubitze 13 was one of the best pieces of field artillery to be used in World War I, and remained in service right through the 1920s and 1930s to see limited service in World War II. The details of the type included a calibre of 149.7mm (5.89in), an L/17 barrel, weight of 4,961lb (2,250kg), elevation arc of between –5 and +45 degrees, traverse arc of 4.5 degrees left and right of the centreline, and muzzle velocity of 1,250ft (381m) per second to fire the 89.96lb (40.8kg) shell to a maximum range of 9,410yds (8,605m).

after a number of early trials this Mk VP carriage was abandoned in favour of the Carriage Mk 1 with a humped box trail and a circular firing platform. The humped box trail was extremely strong and allowed a greater ordnance elevation angle, and the complete weapon could easily be located on a circular firing platform on which the wheels could be moved, permitting rapid traverse through 360 degrees.

The details of the 25pdr Gun Mk 2 included a weight of 3,968lb (1,801kg), on-mounting elevation and traverse angles of –5 to +40 degrees and 4 degrees left and right respectively, and a range of 13,400yds (12,255m) with a 25lb (11.34kg) shell fired from the L/28.25 barrel at a muzzle velocity of 1,745ft (532m) per second. The weapon entered service in 1940, at about the time of the British reverse in France in May of that year, and before the end of World War II (1939-45) more than 12,000 such weapons had been delivered. Able to fire in the direct and indirect modes, the 25pdr was really a gun/howitzer, and proved very popular for its rugged reliability, handiness and generally excellent performance. So good was the type, moreover, that few changes were made during the course of its production run: some weapons that had to double in the anti-tank role in the North African campaign were fitted with muzzle brakes to offset the recoil of the larger propellant charge used with the anti-tank projectile, the Mk 2 carriage was introduced as a narrowed version of the Mk 1 carriage for use in jungle warfare, and the Mk 3 carriage introduced a hinged trail to permit a higher angle of elevation for mountain warfare. The 25pdr remained in service with the British and many of their Commonwealth allies until well into the 1970s, and the weapon is still used in several parts of the world.

Even the most cursory examination of the 25pdr gun/howitzer reveals a major difference in the concept of this and contemporary weapons

compared with those of World War I: this was the adoption of some sort of system to improve the weapons' traverse angles. World War I weapons generally had been fitted with a pole trail that limited the elevation angle of the gun and, perhaps more importantly, meant that the on-mounting traverse angle had to be kept small as the triangular footprint of the equipments' narrow-track main wheels and spade-fitted pole trail provided only marginal stability to lateral movement. This was sufficient for the purposes of World War I and its generally static warfare, but found disfavour during the 1920s as the lessons of the war were analysed. All modern armies decided that trench warfare had been an aberration that would not be repeated for a number of reasons, including a determination to ensure that mobile warfare of the type made possible in World War I by the advent of the tank would be enhanced by the availability of more modern tanks and greater numbers of lorries, so that the infantry and artillery could be motorised.

The determination to ensure that any future war did not bog down into static trench conditions meant that the artillery would have to deal with point targets that were moving, often at right angles to the artillery's line of fire. The ability to engage targets of this crossing type was beyond the artillery equipments of World War I with their very limited on-mounting traverse angles and traverse rates. There were two possible solutions to the need for larger traverse angles. One was the adoption of a turntable so that the whole weapon could be turned rapidly to approximately the right bearing before the on-mounting traverse capability was brought into play, and this system was used by the British for the 25pdr gun/howitzer, whose box trail was conceptually related to the pole trail although the central gap allowed greater on-mounting elevation and traverse angles than had been common in World War I. The other solution was the adoption of a carriage with wider-track wheels and split trails: the latter were brought together for towed movement of the weapon (using an eye on the joined trails for smaller weapons or a special eye-fitted axle for larger equipments), and in firing position were spread to their maximum width to provide a larger and therefore more stable firing footprint that could permit large on-mounting traverse angles without overturning as the gun was fired.

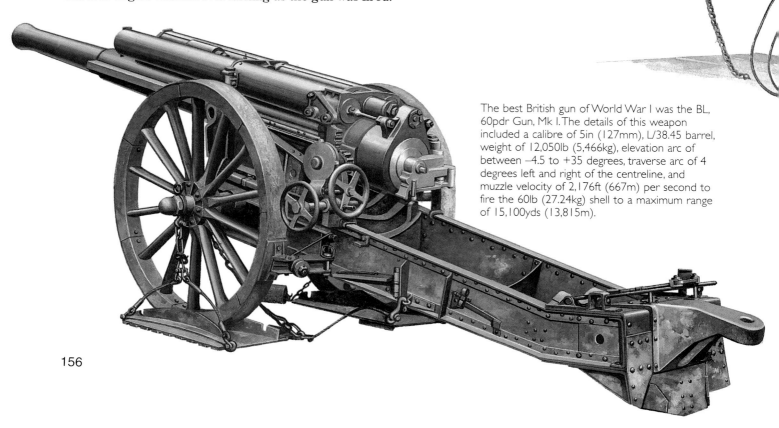

The best British gun of World War I was the BL, 60pdr Gun, Mk I. The details of this weapon included a calibre of 5in (127mm), L/38.45 barrel, weight of 12,050lb (5,466kg), elevation arc of between −4.5 to +35 degrees, traverse arc of 4 degrees left and right of the centreline, and muzzle velocity of 2,176ft (667m) per second to fire the 60lb (27.24kg) shell to a maximum range of 15,100yds (13,815m).

The static nature of World War I made feasible the use of virtually immobile super-heavy howitzers for the massive bombardment of key positions. Typical of this breed was the British 15in Howitzer Mk I, of which 12 were ordered by Winston Churchill, during November 1914. The weapons that were completed (six were in France at the time of the Armistice) fired 25,300 rounds and were manned by the men of the Royal Marine Howitzer Brigade. The details of these massive equipments included a calibre of 15in (381mm), a 1,450lb (658kg) shell fired to a maximum range of 10,000yds (9,145m), and a detachment of 12.

To complement the 25pdr gun, which was at best a medium field artillery piece and, as a result of the financial interference mentioned above, somewhat smaller in calibre than the equivalent weapons in service with countries such as Germany and the USA, the British operated a number of heavier field artillery weapons, including improved World War I howitzers as well as two more modern guns in the forms of the Ordnance, BL, 4.5in Gun Mk 2 and the Ordnance, BL, 5.5in Gun Mk 3. The 4.5in (114.3mm) weapon had its origins in the mid-1930s, when 76 Ordnance, BL, 4.5in Gun Mk I equipments were produced as new barrels on the modified carriage of the 60pdr gun of World War I, adapted with pneumatically tyred wheels with brakes. Further development led to the Mk II version with an improved version of the Mk I's ordnance on a derivative of the excellent carriage designed for the larger 5.5in (139.7mm) gun. The Mk II weapon proved

The Germans' super-heavy 'dicke Bertha' (fat Bertha) howitzers were semi-mobile equipments specially designed for the destruction of major fortifications, and proved admirably suited to this task as revealed by their demolition of the Belgian forts in 1914. The equipment had a calibre of 420mm (16.54in) and weighed 75 tons (76.2 tonnes), and was grouped in two-howitzer batteries with a strength of 280 men. The howitzer could fire ten 2,052lb (930kg) shells at the rate of 10 per hour to a maximum range of 15,530yds (14,200m).

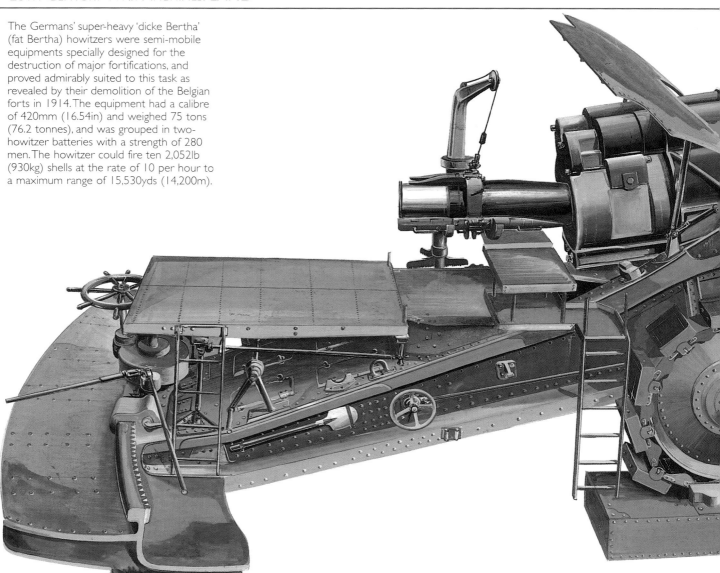

accurate and long-ranged, but was hampered by the small explosive filling of its 55lb (24.97kg) shell. Relatively few of these weapons (intended mainly for the counter-battery and interdiction roles) were made, as greater capability was provided by the 5.5in weapon.

The origins of this weapon can also be found in the mid-1930s, when the War Office issued a requirement for a new gun firing a 100lb (45.4kg) shell to a range of 16,000yds (14,630m). Design work on such a weapon was well advanced when in 1939 the War Office decided that a calibre of 5.5in rather than a shell weight of 100lb should be the critical factor; even so, the first such weapons were test-fired in 1940, soon revealing that the carriage designed for the originally planned 5in weapon was too light to handle the recoil forces of the 5.5in weapon. This led to delays in the production programme until a new carriage could be designed, and the 5.5in weapon finally entered service in 1941. The type then proved to be highly successful and examples of this weapon, which was in fact a gun/howitzer, remained in British service until the late 1970s. The details of the 5.5in gun included a weight of 12,768lb (5,796kg), on-mounting elevation and traverse angles of –5 to +45 degrees and 30 degrees left and right respectively, and a range of 16,200yds (14,815m) with an 80lb (36.32 kg) shell fired from the L/31.2

barrel at a muzzle velocity of 1,675ft (510m) per second; there was also a heavier 100lb shell that could be fired only to a shorter range.

The UK's main ally in World War II was the USA, which had devoted considerable thought and effort to the development of an effective artillery force in the 1920s and 1930s. As a result, the US Army's artillery arm was very ably equipped in World War II, with the 105mm Howitzer M2A1 as the main strength of its field artillery branch and its heavier units equipped mainly with the 155mm Howitzer M1, 155mm Gun M1918, 8in Howitzer M1, and 8in Gun M1.

The 105mm M2 howitzer was one of the main weapons proposed in 1919 by the Westerveldt Board, established immediately after World War I to consider ways in which the US Army's artillery arm could be improved in the light of its experiences in the war. The Board felt that the 75mm (2.95in) Field Gun M1917, the American copy of the 'French 75', was adequate in the short term for the battlefield direct-fire role, but thought that a larger-calibre howitzer would prove a useful adjunct. The truth of this conclusion was borne out by subsequent events, for the 105mm howitzer proved itself to be one of the classic weapons of World War II. In the short term, however, progress with the design and development of this weapon was painfully slow as a result of the severe financial restrictions imposed on the US military in the 1920s and early 1930s. It was only in 1939 that the design was finally completed by the Ordnance Department, but thereafter, progress was rapid. The weapon was placed in production during 1940, and up to the end of World War II some 8,536 such equipments were produced for use with the excellent split-trail M2A2 carriage, which was very sturdy and fitted with pneumatically tyred wheels on a number of self-propelled mountings. The details of this important weapon, which was used in every theatre involving American troops and could fire a useful 13 different types of projectile, included a weight of 4,260lb (1,934kg), on-mounting elevation and traverse angles of –5 to +65 degrees and 23 degrees left and right respectively, and a range of 12,500yds (11,430m) with the 33lb (14.98kg) shell fired from the L/22.5 barrel with a muzzle velocity of 1,550ft (473m) per second.

The 155mm Howitzer M1 was the heavier counterpart to the 105mm weapon, and was designed with extreme speed from 1939 by the Rock Island Arsenal for production from 1942. Up to 1945, 4,035 such equipments had been completed for service in every theatre involving American troops. Such was the success of the type, which soon acquired an excellent reputation for accuracy over its full range bracket, that it was retained in full service after the end of World War II with the revised designation M114, and is still in widespread service in many parts of the world. The weapon was extremely reliable, especially in its M1A1 version made of stronger steel, and was carried on the M1 carriage with pneumatically tyred wheels and a split-trail arrangement. The details of this weapon included a weight of 11,966lb (5,432kg), on-mounting elevation and traverse angles of –2 to +65 degrees and 26.5 degrees left and right respectively, and a range of

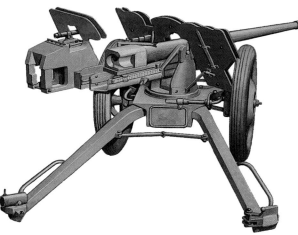

The Germans' 2.8cm schwere Panzerbüchse 41 was one of the most innovative weapons of World War II as it made use of the taper-bore barrel that decreased in calibre from 28mm at the breech to 20mm at the muzzle, to allow the pressure of the expanding propellant gases to work on an increasingly small base area and so accelerate the projectile to a muzzle velocity of 4,599ft (1,402m) per second.

The American 75mm Pack Howitzer M1A1 was an extremely compact weapon that could be broken down into nine loads for parachute delivery or animal transport over inhospitable terrain. The type was widely used in World War II, especially in regions such as Italy and the Pacific islands, and its details included a calibre of 75mm (2.95in), L/15.93 barrel, weight of 1,340lb (608kg), elevation arc of between –5 and +45 degrees, traverse arc of 3 degrees left and right of the centreline, and muzzle velocity of 1,250ft (381m) per second to fire the 13.76lb (6.24kg) shell to a maximum range of 9,760yds (8,925m).

16,000yds (14,630m) with a 95lb (43.14kg) shell fired from the L/20 barrel at a muzzle velocity of 1,850ft (564m) per second. One of the primary operational advantages of this weapon was the fact that, like its smaller 105mm counterpart, it could fire a wide range of projectile types to suit the particular tactical requirements.

The 155mm Gun M1918 was an American development of the 155mm Gun M1917, which was the American designation for a French weapon, the Filloux Canon de 155 Grande Puissance, of which a substantial number were transferred in the last part of World War I. The M1918 was the American-built version, and during the 1930s the type was revised with a more modern carriage in the form of the generally similar M2 and M3 units, designed for high-speed towing and therefore fitted with more modern wheels characterised by pneumatic tyres and pneumatic brakes. The details of this weapon included a weight of 25,550lb (11,589kg) in travelling order and about 20,100lb (9,117kg) in firing position, on-mounting elevation and traverse angles of 0 to +35 degrees and 30 degrees left and right respectively, and a range of 20,100yds (18,380m) with a 94.71lb (43kg) shell fired from the L/36.4 barrel with a muzzle velocity of 2,360ft (720m) per second.

Although built only in smaller numbers – 1,006 and 130 respectively – the 8in Howitzer M1 and Gun M1 were potent long-range weapons: the howitzer was well known for its long-range accuracy and good capability against concrete fortifications, while the gun was a very accurate long-range bombardment weapon. The howitzer was designed by the Hughes Tool Company on the basis of the British 8in Howitzer Mk VIII (numbers of which had been supplied to the US Army in World War I and remained in service up to 1940), and entered service in 1942 on a very substantial carriage with large split trails (carried in the towing position by a two-wheeled single axle) and two four-wheel axles. The details of this impressive equipment, which was retained in service after World War II with the revised designation M114, included a weight of 32,005lb (14,515kg) in travelling order and 29,703lb (13,471kg) in firing position, on-mounting traverse angles of –2 to +64 degrees and 30 degrees left and right respectively, and a range of 18,510yds (16,925m) with a 200lb (90.7kg) shell fired from the L/25 barrel with a muzzle velocity of 1,950ft (594m) per second.

The Gun M1 was a considerably more substantial weapon, and was first demanded by the Westerveldt Board in 1919, although financial restrictions meant that work on such a weapon was halted in 1924 for resumption only in 1939. The weapon was standardised in 1941 for service from 1942 as a massive equipment fired on a split-trail carriage installed on the ground after delivery by special transport wagons in disassembled form for erection with the aid of a 20-ton crane. The details of this impressive weapon included a weight of 69,300lb (31,434kg), on-mounting elevation and traverse angles of –10 to +50 degrees and 20 degrees left and right respectively, and a range of 32,025yds (29,285m) with a 240.37lb (109.03kg) shell fired from the L/50 barrel with a muzzle velocity of 2,950ft (899m) per second.

The other main exponent of artillery on the Allied side in World War II was the USSR, which had inherited a considerable capability in the design and tactical employment of artillery from Russia. (Russia had failed to exploit this capability to its best advantage during World War I because of ammunition shortages and the ineptitude of its generals). The equipments most widely used in World War I and retained in service thereafter, often in updated forms, were the 76.2mm (3in) Putilov Field Gun Model 1902, 107mm (4.21in) Field Gun Model 1910, 121.9mm

(4.8in) Field Howitzer Model 1910, 152.4mm Field Gun Model 1910, and 152.4mm Putilov Field Howitzer Model 1909.

With the worst of the economic problems resulting from the 1917 Bolshevik Revolution and subsequent civil war over by the mid-1930s, the Soviets decided that the time was ripe for the development of a new generation of artillery equipments to replace the updated versions of the weapons procured by the Russians before and during World War I. The result was a series of weapons that were generally highly impressive in their capabilities and therefore retained in service well after the end of World War II. The smallest of the new weapons was the 76.2mm Field Gun Model 1936 that was introduced to service in 1939 with details that included a weight of 5,291lb (2,400kg) in travelling order and 2,976lb (1,350kg) in firing position, on-mounting elevation and traverse angles of –5 to +75 degrees and 30 degrees left and right respectively, and a range of 14,850yds (13,580m) with a 14.11lb (6.4kg) shell fired from the L/43 barrel with a muzzle velocity of 2,316ft (706m) per second. This weapon was the mainstay of the Soviet field artillery units in the first part of the 'Great Patriotic War', as the Soviets called their part of World War II. In the later part of the war, the Model 1936 gun was supplemented and then largely supplanted by the classic 76.2mm Field Gun Model 1942 that was otherwise known as the SiS-3. This was basically a development of the Model 1936 gun with a muzzle brake and split pole trails for reduced weight, and the result was a weapon that was reliable,and potent for its calibre. The Model 1942 remained in widespread service to the late 1970s, and its details included a weight of 2,469lb (1,120kg), on-mounting elevation and traverse angles of –5 to +37 degrees and 27 degrees left and right respectively, and a range of 14,545yds (13,300m) with a 13.69lb (6.21kg) shell fired from the L/39.3 barrel with a muzzle velocity of 2,231ft (680m) per second.

The British BL, 5.5in Gun Mk III was an excellent piece of equipment introduced in the early part of World War II and remaining in limited service into the later 1970s. The details of this very popular and successful piece of heavy artillery included a calibre of 5.5in (139.7mm), L/31.2 barrel, weight of 12,768lb (5,792kg), elevation arc of between –5 and +45 degrees, traverse arc of 30 degrees left and right of the centreline, and muzzle velocity of 1,675ft (510m) per second to fire the 80lb (36.32kg) lightweight of two HE shell types to a maximum range of 16,200yds (14,813m).

During World War II, the Soviets decided that the artillery barrages with which they prefaced their offensives required a slightly heavier component at the lighter end of the scale, and the result was a pair of excellent weapons in 85mm (3.35in) calibre. These were the Field Gun Model 1943 and the Field Gun Model 1944, the latter otherwise known as the D-44. The Model 1943 weapon was produced in relatively modest numbers, and although generally classified as a divisional gun was in fact used mainly in the anti-tank role. The weapon's primary details included a weight of 3,757lb (1,704kg), on-mounting elevation and traverse angles of 0 to +40 degrees and 15 degrees left and right respectively, and a range of 18,155yds (16,600m) with a 20.95lb (9.5kg) shell fired from the L/55 barrel with a muzzle velocity of 2,608ft (795m) per second. Produced in far larger numbers and still used in many parts of the world, the Model 1944 weapon introduced a muzzle brake and split pole trails, and its salient details included a weight of 3,804lb (1,725kg), on-mounting elevation and traverse angles of –5 to +40 and 27 degrees left and right respectively, and a range of 16,950yds (15,500m) with a 20.95lb shell fired from the L/55 barrel with a muzzle velocity of 2,608ft per second.

A higher calibre for Soviet weapons produced in large numbers for the field artillery role was 121.9mm (4.8in). The first Soviet-designed weapon in this calibre was the Field Gun Model 1931 with a weight of 17,199lb (7,800kg) in travelling order and 15,656lb (7,100kg) in firing position, on-mounting elevation and traverse angles of —4 to +45 degrees and 28 degrees left and right respectively, and a range of 22,825yds (20,870m) with a 55.1lb (25kg) shell fired from the L/45 barrel with a muzzle velocity of 2,625ft (800m) per second. The ordnance of this equipment was later added to the carriage of the 152.4mm (6in) Gun/Howitzer Model 1937 to create the Field Gun Model 1931/37 otherwise known as the A-19.

Another weapon in the same 121.9mm calibre was the Field Howitzer Model 1938 that was one of the most important equipments of its type in Soviet service right through World War II. This weapon's primary details included a weight of 6,174lb (2,800kg) in

A powerful but little-known weapon, the Germans 21cm lange Mörser was introduced in the period before World War I as a heavy howitzer, and among the few known details of the type are a calibre of 210mm (8.27in) and a maximum range of between 10,280yds (9,400m) with the 1914 short shell and 11,155yds (10,200m) with the 1896 long shell.

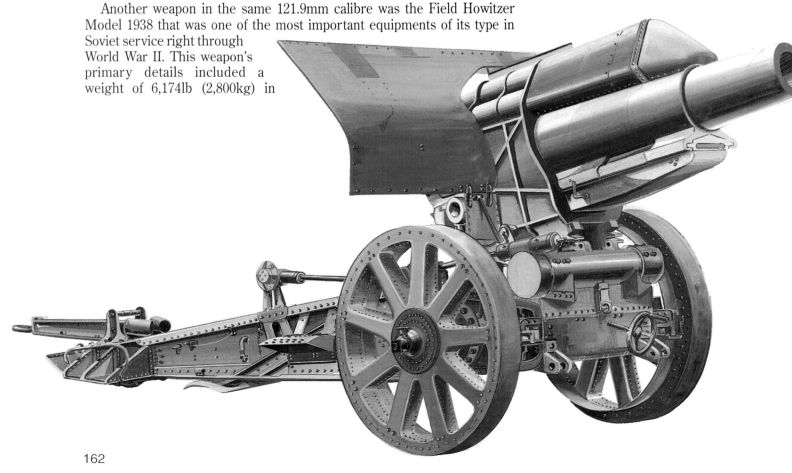

travelling order and 5,402lb (2,450kg) in firing position, on-mounting elevation and traverse angles of –3 to +63 degrees and 24.5 degrees left and right respectively, and a range of 12,910yds (11,800m) with a 47.98lb (21.76kg) shell fired from the L/21.9 barrel at a muzzle velocity of 1,690ft (515m) per second.

Next up the Soviet calibre ladder was 152.4mm (6in). An excellent weapon in this calibre was the Gun/Howitzer Model 1937, otherwise known as the ML-20 and intended for the counter-battery role on two types of carriage: one had spoked wooden wheels and was intended for horse traction, and the other had double-tyred steel wheels for tractor towing. The details of this weapon, which remained in service up to the 1980s, included a weight of 17,485lb (7,930kg) in travelling order and 15,717lb (7,128kg) in firing position, on-mounting elevation and traverse angles of –2 to +65 degrees and 29 degrees left and right respectively, and a range of 18,880yds (17,265m) with a 96.05lb (43.56kg) shell fired from an L/29 barrel at a muzzle velocity of 2,149ft (655m) per second.

The 152.4mm calibre bracket was completed by two other first-class weapons in the form of the Field Howitzer Model 1938 otherwise known as the M-10, and the Field Howitzer Model 1943 otherwise known as the D-1. The Model 1938 was designed from the outset for mechanical traction and featured a single axle with two double wheels, and its main details included a weight of 10,033lb (4,500kg) in travelling order and 9,150lb (4,150kg) in firing position, on-mounting elevation and traverse angles of –1 to +65 degrees and 25 degrees left and right respectively, and a range of 13,565yds (12,400m) with a 112.6lb (51.5kg) shell fired from the L/23.15 barrel at a muzzle velocity of 1,417ft (432m) per second, although the weapon could also be used in the anti-tank role with an 88.18lb (40kg) shot fired at 1,667ft (508m) per second. The Model 1943, which is still in moderately widespread service, was basically the carriage of the Model 1938 with a new ordnance carrying a double-baffle muzzle brake. The details of this weapon included a weight of 8,008lb (3,635kg) in travelling order and 7,940lb (3,600kg) in firing position, on-mounting elevation and traverse angles of –3 to +63

One of the many pieces of excellent artillery introduced by the Soviets in World War II was the 76.2mm Field Gun Model 1942, otherwise known as the SiS-3 and a development of the Model 1939 gun with a muzzle brake and a new carriage of the split-trail type with pole legs. The result was a light and therefore useful weapon that found considerable favour with the Soviet Army, which received the type in very large numbers for service into the late 1970s.

degrees and 17.5 degrees left and right respectively, and a range of 13,565yds with a 112.6lb shell fired from the L/24.6 barrel with a muzzle velocity of 1,667ft (508m) per second.

The largest of the standard Soviet artillery equipments used in World War II was the 203mm (8in) Howitzer Model 1931 otherwise known as the B-4. This was an enormous weapon produced in six variants, and was most notable for its tracked rather than wheeled carriage. The variants were differentiated mainly by the type of carriage and suspension used, but invariable details included on-mounting elevation and traverse angles of 0 to +60 degrees and 4 degrees left and right respectively, and a shell weight of 220.46lb (100kg) fired from the L/24 barrel at a muzzle velocity of between 1,765 and 1,991ft (538 and 607m) per second for a range of between 14,000 and 17,500yds (12,800 and 16,000m).

Of Germany, Italy and Japan, the three main combatants of the Axis forces ranged against the Allies in World War II, it was only Germany that made and operated high-quality artillery equipment, which often included weapons captured from the Allied powers. The smallest of the equipments operated by the Germans was the 105mm (4.13in) leichte Feldhaubitze (leFH) 18, which was designed by Rheinmetall and entered service in 1935. Although it was a reliable and rugged weapon with a number of modern features including split trails and a shield, it was given a faintly obsolescent appearance by the use of large steel-tyred wheels. The equipment had a weight of 5,589lb (2,535kg) in travelling order and 4,377lb (1,985kg) in firing position, on-mounting elevation and traverse angles of −6 to +40 degrees and 28 degrees left and right respectively, and a range of 11,675yds (10,675m) with a 32.65lb (14.81kg) shell fired from the L/25.8 barrel with a muzzle velocity of 1,542ft (470m) per second. The leFH 18 was undoubtedly a fine weapon in its basic capabilities, but there could be little doubt that it was also somewhat too heavy, as was made abundantly clear from the autumn of 1941 on the Eastern Front, where appallingly muddy Russian conditions often resulted in leFH 18 equipments becoming bogged down. In March 1942 the German army called for a weapon offering the same ballistic capabilities as the leFH 18 but with a considerably lighter overall weight without any sacrifice of strength, and the result was the leFH 18/40 which comprised the ordnance of the leFH 18 on a modified version of the carriage designed originally for the 75mm PaK 40 anti-tank guns. The le FH 18/40 initially retained the PaK 40's wheels, but later in the type's career these wheels

Not a piece of artillery in essence, but offering the German army of World War II some of its capabilities at a fraction of the cost, the 15cm Nebelwerfer 41 was a pioneering rocket launcher. The weapon weighed only 1,245lb (565kg) for towing on its two wheels, and was stabilized in firing position by the opening of its two pole-type trail legs and the lowering of the foot forward of the axle. The assembly of six 6.24in (158.5mm) barrels could be elevated through an arc between 5 and 45 degrees and traversed through an arc of 13.5 degrees left and right of the centreline, and could fire its six Wurfgranate 41 Spreng rockets in a rippled salvo at two-second intervals. This rocket weighed 70lb (31.8kg) with a 5.5lb (2.5kg) explosive load, and left the muzzle of the launch tube with a velocity of 1,120ft (342m) per second to reach a maximum range of 7,725yds (7,065m).

were replaced by units of greater diameter and increased width to reduce the tendency to bog down. The details of the leFH 18/40 included a weight of 4,310lb (1,955kg), on-mounting elevation and traverse angles of –6 to +40 degrees and 28 degrees left and right respectively, and a range of 13,485yds (12,325m) with a 32.65lb shell fired from the L/25.8 barrel with a muzzle velocity of 1,771ft (540m) per second.

The next German calibre was 128mm (5.04in), and in this calibre the Germans used small numbers of an exceptional weapon, the Kanone 44. This was developed in direct response to the Germans' belated realisation that, in general, the artillery of the Soviet army was superior not only in quantitative but also in qualitative terms to that of the German army. With a weight of 22,403lb (10,160kg) in firing position, the K 44 entered service in 1944 as a substantial direct- and indirect-fire weapon, really a gun/howitzer and anti-tank gun rather than just a gun, based on a large carriage supported when travelling by the four or six of two or three axles (on the more common Krupp or less common Rheinmetall versions respectively), and in firing position by two screw jacks under the axles and two outrigger legs that were extended from the sides of the carriage before large pads were extended to the ground by actuation of a screw system. This carriage carried the ordnance behind a substantial shield on a mounting that provided traverse through 360 degrees and elevation between –7.5 and +45 degrees. The ordnance was fitted with a 'pepperpot' muzzle brake, and fired a 62.4lb (28.3kg) HE shell or anti-tank shot from the L/51.75 barrel with a muzzle velocity of 3,018ft (920m) per second for a range of 26,710yds (24,415m).

The following German calibre was 150mm (5.91in), and in this calibre the Germans had a number of important weapons. The most numerous of these, and the standard heavy howitzer of the German armies throughout World War II, was the schwere Feldhaubitze (sFH) 18 with an ordnance designed by Rheinmetall on a Krupp-designed carriage. The sFH 18 was designed from 1926 and entered service in 1935 as a weapon that combined modern features with the type of apparently obsolete wheel that was standard in the German army: this was a solid steel unit, pierced with holes to reduce weight, of considerable diameter and surrounded by a solid rubber tyre. The carriage was of the split-trail type, the ends of the closed trails being carried on a small two-wheel limber for towing by horses or a tractor. The tactical versatility of this equipment was increased by the availability of several different types of projectile within the separate-loading ammunition, but when it became clear in 1942 that the sFH 18 was considerably outranged by Soviet artillery equipments, the ordnance was modified to accept two charges additional to the standard six. This modification certainly boosted range to the required figure, but also shortened barrel life and strained the recoil system. The weapon was therefore further adapted with a renewable chamber liner and a muzzle brake to become the sFH 18(M). The primary details of the sFH 18 included a weight of 12,154lb (5,512kg) in firing position, on-mounting elevation and traverse angles of –3 to +45 degrees and 32 degrees left and right respectively, and a range of 14,600yds (13,325m) with a 95.7lb (43.5kg) shell fired from the L/29.6 barrel at a maximum muzzle velocity of 1,710ft (521m) per second.

The gun counterparts to the sFH 18 were the Kanone 18 and Kanone 39. The K 18 was designed from 1933 by Rheinmetall and entered service in 1938 as a basically sound weapon whose efficiency in tactical operations was somewhat hindered by the fact that the gun had to be towed in two sections (involving considerable effort and delay in the process of getting the gun into and out of action), and was given 360-degree traverse capability by the provision of a two-piece platform onto which the gun had to be towed before

The Bofors 40L70 a development of the weapon that had proved so successful in World War II in a host of land-based and shipborne forms. The basic weapon seen here has been further developed into a number of more advanced forms with an on-mounting power supply and fire-control systems (fair- and all-weather types), but the core details of this system, which is based on a four-wheeled carriage for towing but is stabilized in firing position by four screw jacks (two of them on lateral outriggers), include an L/70 barrel with a calibre of 40mm, weight of 11,354lb (5,150kg), length of 23ft 11in (7.29m), elevation arc of between –4 and +90 degrees, traverse angle of 360 degrees, rate of fire of 240 (or in later models) 300 rounds per minute (cyclic), range of 13,670yds (12,500m) horizontal maximum and 4,375yds (4,000m) slant effective, and detachment of four to six.

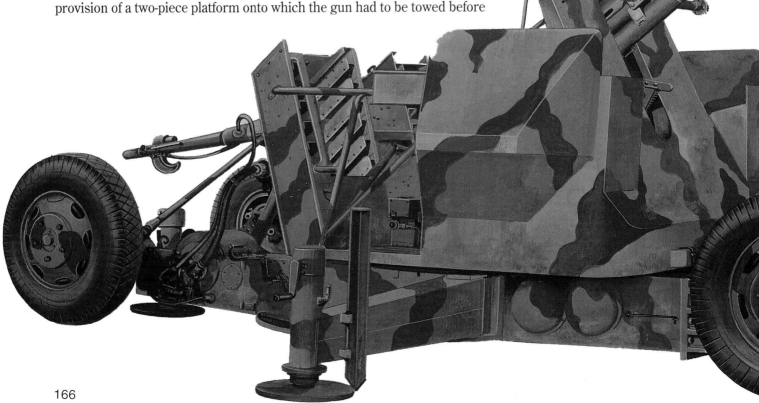

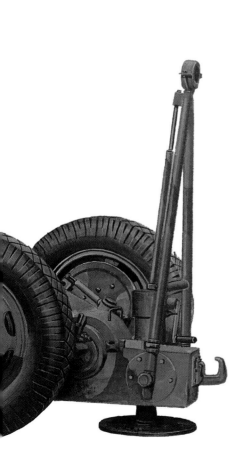

use. Details of this weapon included a weight of 28,131lb (12,760kg) in firing position, on-mounting elevation and traverse angles of –2 to +45 degrees and 5 degrees left and right respectively, and a range of 26,800yds (24,500m) with a 94.8lb (43kg) shell fired from the L/55 barrel with a muzzle velocity of 2,920ft (890m) per second; the type could also fire a special 95.9lb (43.5kg) shell for the penetration of concrete fortifications.

The K 39, which was used in smaller numbers, was a Krupp weapon originally designed for Turkey as a dual-role heavy field gun and coast-defence gun. The weapon was even more cumbersome than the K 18, having to be broken down into three loads for movement, and in firing position was installed on a portable turntable for 360-degree traverse. The location of the gun on this turntable was a laborious and slow process requiring a large amount of digging. The main details of the K 39 included a weight of 26,901lb (12,200kg), on-mounting elevation and traverse angles of –3 to +46 degrees and 30 degrees left and right respectively, and a range of 27,025yds (24,700m) with a 94.8lb shell fired from the L/55 barrel with a muzzle velocity of 2,838ft (865m) per second.

Entering service in 1941 and planned as a weapon to replace the German army's current 150 and 210mm (5.91 and 8.27in) guns, the 170mm (6.7in) Kanone 18 in Mörserlafette was a Krupp design using the same carriage as the Mrs 18 and the same recoil system as the K 38 (described below). The 170mm weapon proved to be an excellent piece of artillery, but demand constantly outstripped production and the weapon could not be employed as widely as had been hoped. The carriage was of the split-trail type with a single two-wheeled axle, and the primary details of the weapon included a weight of 38,632lb (17,520kg) in firing position, on-mounting elevation and traverse angles of 0 to +50 degrees and 8 degrees left and right respectively, and a range of 32,370yds (29,600m) with a 138.5lb (62.8kg) shell fired from the L/50 barrel with a muzzle velocity of 3,035ft (925m) per second; there was also a heavier and more destructive 149.9lb (68kg) shell for use at shorter ranges.

The largest standard calibre for German artillery was 210mm (8.27in), and in this bracket were two weapons in the form of the Mörser (Mrs) 18 and Kanone 38. The Mrs 18 was a Krupp design that used basically the same carriage as the 170mm Kanone 18. This carriage had two variants (one with two wheels carrying solid rubber tyres and the other with four wheels carrying pneumatic tyres), and the main details of this powerful weapon included a weight of 36,824lb (16,700kg) in firing position, on-mounting elevation and traverse angles of 0 to +70 degrees and 8 degrees left and right (increasing to 360 degrees when the whole equipment was placed on the special trail platform that allowed a single man to move the weapon), and a range of 18,270yds (16,700m) with a 266.8lb (121kg) shell fired from the L/31 barrel with a muzzle velocity of 1,854ft (565m) per second. The versatility of this weapon was considerably enhanced by the availability of several types of projectile (including a 285.3lb/129.4kg concrete-penetrating shell, a muzzle stick bomb, and the Röchling fin-stabilized shell) and a six-charge propellant system that offered a range capability upward of 3,280yds (3,000m).

The K 38 was another Krupp design, in this instance ordered in 1938 as eventual replacement for the Mrs 18 that did not completely fulfil the German army's requirement. The guns were to have been delivered from 1940, but in fact the weapons were delivered after this time and only seven had been completed before production was terminated in 1943. Despite this fact, the K 38 was a highly advanced and efficient weapon with features from the Krupp 170 and 210mm guns, including a dual-recoil system that comprised the standard barrel recoil system and a system installed on the gun platform to allow this unit to recoil along slides on the upper part of the trail. The weapon was broken down into two loads but could be emplaced using only hand-operated winches installed on the carriage, and the on-mounting traverse angle could be increased to 360 degrees by installation of the equipment on a large platform. The details of this impressive weapon included a weight of 55,787lb (25,300kg), on-mounting elevation and traverse angles of 0 to +50 degrees and 8.5 degrees left and right respectively, and a range of 37,075yds (33,900m) with a 265lb (120kg) shell fired from the L/55.5 barrel with a muzzle velocity of 2,970ft (905m) per second.

In World War II, towed artillery had reached a conceptual peak which was not readily exceeded in the period following the war. In the immediate aftermath of the war, the victorious Allies inevitably decided that armies should retain the equipments that had proved successful and which were still available in numbers larger than required by the smaller peacetime armies. Thus it was only in the late 1950s and early 1960s that significant development of the towed gun and howitzer was resumed in earnest, the concentration now being placed on 155mm (6.1in) as the primary calibre for field as well as heavier artillery. There was little conceptually new about the equipments that now began to reach the production stage, for the type of weapon that had performed well in World War II was still advanced enough for its purposes, so the emphasis of design and development was placed on improving the breed rather than evolving something completely new. The improvements that were effected were based on features such as better materials for high strength-weight ratios; increased durability in items such as barrels; more reliable and sophisticated recoil systems including more effective muzzle brakes; upgraded fire-control systems for improved accuracy in long-range fire; and a wider assortment of specialised projectiles (including nuclear rounds and also cargo-carrying rounds that dispense submunitions towards the end of the trajectory for the purpose of creating minefields or attacking individual members of an armoured formation) to make artillery more flexible in its tactical applications. This has been a continuing process and, even more recently, other changes have included longer barrels to allow the build-up of the higher pressures required for the additional muzzle velocity that produces greater projectile range; superior propellants that also contribute to increased range and burn more steadily

Left: The 210mm (8.27in) rail gun developed by the Germans was intended as a long-range bombardment weapon, but proved itself an impractical weapon and saw virtually no operational employment.

Opposite: Designed by Krupp in 1937, the 'Gustav Gerät' was an enormous German rail gun with a calibre of 280mm (11.02in) named in honour of Gustav von Bohlen und Krupp, but was generally known as the 'Dora Gerät' as German artillerymen preferred to give their equipments female names. This fact has often led to the suggestion that there were in fact two such guns, but this is definitely not the case. The whole equipment weighed 1,350 tons in firing order and was moved piecemeal to its operational position, where a dual track was laid and the gun mount was built up with the aid of an overhead crane in a process that took nearly six weeks! The gun was assembled, maintained, guarded and operated by a 1,420-man detachment under the command of a major general, and was provided with two types of shell. These were a smaller HE shell fired to a maximum range of 51,400 yards (47,000m) and a larger concrete-piercing shell fired to a maximum range of 22,965 yards (21,000m). The only two occasions on which it is known that the gun was used operationally were in the siege of Sevastopol in 1942 and the reduction of the Warsaw rising in 1944, in which it fired some 40 and 30 rounds respectively. The fate of this magnificent but completely extravagant weapon at the end of World War II remains unknown.

to produce greater stability as the projectile emerges from the muzzle, thereby enhancing accuracy at longer ranges; aerodynamically refined projectiles whose lower drag and greater stability also have an effect on range and accuracy; an auxiliary power unit that can operate a power loading system and also provide the equipment with the limited independent battlefield mobility required for rapid movement ('shoot-and-scoot') after a few rounds have been fired and before counter-fire can arrive; and considerably improved fire-control systems in which sensors provide data about ambient conditions (air pressure, air temperature, and wind speed and direction) and exact muzzle velocity for each round fired, so that the associated computer (with positional data provided by a land navigation system), can provide a high-quality solution to the fire-control problem and help to ensure that the target is hit as rapidly and effectively as possible for the expenditure of the minimum number of rounds.

Among the more important ammunition concepts to have emerged in recent years are rocket-assisted and base-bleed projectiles (the latter with a system to increase the pressure in the otherwise low-pressure area immediately to the rear of the projectile's flat base and so reduce drag) for considerably enhanced range without the need for a larger propellant charge.

Artillery equipments in service around the world, which provide striking evidence of the spread of artillery manufacturing capability, are detailed below by alphabetical order of the country of origin. The Austrian NORICUM GH N-45 155mm (6.1in) gun/howitzer is a towed gun/howitzer with a multi-baffle muzzle brake, a carriage of the split-trail type with four road wheels and two castors, a weight of 22,200lb (10,070kg), on-mounting elevation and traverse angles of –5 to +69 degrees and 30 and 40 degrees left and right respectively, a rate of fire of three rounds in 16 seconds (burst), two rounds per minute (normal) and seven rounds per minute (maximum), a range of 33,155yds (30,300m) with a normal round and 43,305yds (39,600m) with the base-bleed round, and a crew of six. Developed by Voerst-Alpine in Austria and marketed by NORICUM, this is an improved GC 45 (see below) with features designed to ease manufacture and to aid field reliability and handling; the most important modification is the optional addition of an auxiliary power unit (APU) for battlefield mobility. This APU

Ammunition Types for Tactical Flexibility

IN artillery with a calibre of more than 105mm (4.13in), it is standard for the ammunition to be of the separate-loading rather than fixed type, with the projectile loaded before one or more bagged propellant charges whose number is decided by the range required. This facilitates the task of the gun detachment in handling the ammunition and is more economical of propellant: in fixed ammunition, the propellant load is that required for maximum range and lower ranges are produced by alteration of the barrel's elevation, while with separate-loading ammunition the barrel elevation and propellant charge can be co-ordinated for maximum economy. The use of separate-loading ammunition also offers greater flexibility in the types of projectile that can be fired. In the standard NATO range for 155mm (6.1in) weapons, for instance, are the following projectiles produced by Talley Defense Systems Inc. that are in general matched by the products of other American and European companies: 110lb (49.91kg) M110 Chemical with an 11.68 or 9.68lb (5.3 or 4.39kg) load of Agent H or Agent HD; 103lb (46.7kg) M718 Anti-tank with nine M73 mines; 103lb M741 Anti-tank with nine M70 mines; 94.6lb (42.91kg) M107 HE with a 14.6 or 15.4lb (6.62 or 6.98kg) filling of TNT or Composition B; 95lb (43.09kg) M449 Anti-personnel with 60 M43 anti-personnel minelets; 102.6lb (46.54kg) M483A1 Anti-personnel/anti-vehicle with 64 M42 and 24 M46 dual-purpose minelets; 102.5lb (46.49kg) M692 Anti-personnel with 36 M67 minelets; 102.5lb M731 Anti-personnel with 36 M72 minelets; 103lb (46.72kg) M795 HE with a filling of cast TNT; 96lb (43.54kg) HE Rocket-assisted with 16 or 15lb (7.26 or 6.804kg) filling of Composition B or TNT; 102lb (46.26kg) M118 Illuminating with a 4.3lb (1.95kg) illuminant filling; 93.65lb (42.48kg) M485 Illuminating with a 5.95lb (2.7kg) illuminant filling; 93.1lb (42.22kg) M116 Smoke BE with a 25.84 or 17.88lb (11.72 or 8.11kg) filling of Agent HC or C; 97.9lb (44.4kg) M110 Smoke WP with 15.6lb (7.07kg) filling of white phosphorus; 96.75lb (43.88kg) M631 Tactical CS with a 14lb (6.35kg) filling of CS; and 98.9lb (44.86kg) M121 Chemical with a 15.87 or 6.48lb (7.2 or 2.94kg) filling of VX or GB.

is a 121hp (90kW) Porsche unit permitting a maximum speed of 18.6mph (30km/h) and a range of 93 miles (150km). The L/45 barrel has a semi-automatic breech with a pneumatically operated rammer, and optional features on the powered version are a powered traverse and elevation system, a six-round ammunition bracket, an ammunition-handling device and tracks to increase the traction of the wheels.

The Belgian SRC International GC 45 155mm (6.1in) gun/howitzer has an L.45 barrel with a multi-baffle muzzle brake, a split-trail carriage with four road wheels and two castors, a weight of 18,126lb (8,222kg), on-mounting elevation and traverse angles of –5 to +69 degrees and 80 degrees total respectively, a rate of fire of four rounds per minute (burst rate for 15 minutes) and two rounds per minute (normal), a range of 32,810yds (30,000m) with the normal round and 41,560yds (38,000m) with the base-bleed round, and a crew of eight. This weapon, designed in Canada and Belgium by the Space Research Corporation and PRB, is an advanced gun/howitzer designed to fire separate-loading ammunition (including all standard NATO 155mm/6.1in types) and fitted with an automatic breech and pneumatic rammer. The type is notable for the fact that its extended-range full-bore projectile reaches 32,810yds without rocket assistance, and this ERFB Mk 10 projectile weighs 100lb (45.4kg), contains 19.4lb (8.8kg) of HE and has a maximum muzzle velocity of 2,943ft (897m) per second.

The Chinese NORINCO Type 66 152mm (6in) gun/howitzer is a towed equipment with an L/34 barrel fitted with a single-baffle muzzle brake, a split-trail carriage with two road wheels and two castors, a weight of 12,610lb (5,720kg), on-mounting elevation and traverse arcs of –5 to +45 degrees and 58 degrees total respectively, a rate of fire of between six and eight rounds per minute under normal conditions, a maximum range of 18,845yds (17,230m), and a crew of 10 to 12. The Type 66 is the Chinese version of the Soviet D-20 equipment, and is notable for its light weight, comparatively large crew, and relatively short range for its calibre. The ordnance uses a variable six-charge propellant system, and can attain its maximum normal range with the 96lb (43.56kg) HE and smoke projectiles. The type can also fire an RAP of the same weight, range with this projectile being 23,930yds (21,880m) without any loss of accuracy.

The Chinese NORINCO Type 59-1 130mm (5.12in) gun is a towed equipment with an L/58.5 barrel fitted with a double-baffle muzzle brake, a split-trail carriage with two road wheels and two castors, a weight of 13,889lb (6,300kg),

The British 105mm (4.13in) Light Gun is typical of modern weapons optimised for maximum tactical versatility through the combination of an advanced ordnance and sight system, with a carriage that is sturdy enough for all tactical purposes but light enough for easy carriage by tactical transports of the fixed- and rotary-wing types.

on-mounting elevation and traverse angles of –2.5 to +45 degrees and 58 degrees total respectively, a rate of fire of between eight and 10 rounds per minute under normal conditions, a range of 30,065yds (27,490m) with the normal round, 34,995yds (32,000m) with the base-bleed round and 37,575yds (34,260m) with the rocket-assisted projectile, and a crew of between eight and 10. The Type 59 is the Chinese copy of the Soviet M-46 equipment. The Type 59-1 variant is a simple combination of the Type 59 with features of the Type 60 (Chinese copy of the Soviet D-74) to produce an equipment that is better disposed than the Type 59. The Type 59-1 uses a scaled-up version of the Type 60's muzzle brake, recoil system and breech on a carriage with a number of Type 60 features. In combination with a lighter shield, this produces an equipment that is more manoeuvrable and has the additional advantage of not requiring the Type 59's two-wheel limber; the Type 59-1 fires a 73.6lb (33.4kg) HE projectile with a muzzle velocity of 3,051ft (930m) per minute, an RAP of the same weight, a 71.45lb (32.4kg) RAP, and an illuminating projectile.

The Finnish Tampella M-60 122mm (4.8in) field gun is a towed equipment with an L/53 barrel fitted with a single-baffle muzzle brake, a split-trail carriage with four road wheels, a weight of 18,739lb (8,500kg), on-mounting elevation and traverse angles of –5 to +50 degrees and 90 degrees total respectively, a rate of fire of four rounds per minute, a range of 27,340yds (25,000m), and a crew of eight. Entering service in 1964, the M-60 is a powerful equipment with a semi-automatic breech and firing separate-loading ammunition including a 55.1lb HE projectile with a muzzle velocity of 3,117ft (950m) per second. The four-wheel bogie can be powered hydraulically from the towing vehicle for improved cross-country mobility.

The French GIAT TR 155mm (6.1in) gun is a towed equipment with an L/40 barrel fitted with a double-baffle muzzle brake, a split-trail carriage with two road wheels, a weight of about 23,479lb (10,650kg), on-mounting elevation and traverse angles of –5 to +66 and 27 and 38 degrees left and right respectively, a rate of fire of three rounds in 18 seconds with a cold barrel, six rounds per minute for 2 minutes and two rounds per minute under normal conditions, a range of 26,245yds (24,000m) with a hollow-base projectile and 36,090yds (33,000m) with an RAP, and a crew of eight. Entering production in 1984, the TR is a modern equipment designed for the support of motorised divisions. A hydraulically powered rammer is standard to reduce crew fatigue, and helps the equipment to generate a high initial rate of fire with its standard French separate-loading ammunition: types include HE with a projectile weight of 95.35lb (43.25kg) and a muzzle velocity of 2,723ft per second for a range of 26,245yds, HE RAP with a projectile weight of 95.9lb (43.5kg) and a muzzle velocity of 2,723f per second for a range of 36,090yds, anti-tank mine-launching with a projectile weight of 101.4lb (46kg) and a load of six 1.2lb (0.55kg) mines, smoke and illuminating. The TR can also fire the US M107 round and the ammunition of the FH-70 series, and a measure of battlefield mobility is provided by the 39hp (29kW) auxiliary power unit, which offers a road speed of 5mph (8km/h).

The German, Italian and British Rheinmetall/OTO Melara/Vickers FH-70 155mm (6.1in) field howitzer is typical of the modern practice of international collaboration to reduce the development and production costs of expensive primary equipment, and is a towed equipment with an L/38.85 barrel fitted with a single-baffle muzzle brake, a split-trail carriage with an auxiliary power unit, two road wheels and two castors, a weight of 20,503lb (9,300kg), on-mounting elevation and traverse angles of –5 to +70 and 56 degrees total respectively, a rate of fire of three rounds in eight seconds with the optional flick loader, three rounds in 13 seconds (bursts), six rounds per

minute (normal) and two rounds per minute (sustained fire), a range of 26,245yds with the standard projectile and 32,810yds with the RAP, and a crew of eight. Developed jointly by West Germany, Italy and the UK in the late 1960s and entering service from 1978, the FH-70 is an advanced field howitzer firing its own special separate-loading ammunition as well as standard NATO types and the Copperhead cannon-launched guided projectile. The type uses a semi-automatic breech and loader for reduced crew fatigue and high rates of fire, with a flick loader optional for even higher rates, while the addition of a Volkswagen petrol-engined auxiliary power unit provides power for getting the equipment into and out of action, and also gives good battlefield mobility at speeds of up to 10mph (16km/h), gradients of 34% and a fording depth of 0.75m (2.5ft). Included in the ammunition types are the 95.9lb FRAG-HE projectile with 24.9lb (11.3kg) of HE, HE RAP, smoke and illuminating. The use of an eight-charge propellant system allows muzzle velocities of between 700 and 2,715ft (213 and 827m) per second. The FH-70R is an improved model developed as a private venture by Rheinmetall. This has an L/46 barrel, making possible ranges of 32,810yds with the standard projectile and 39,370yds (36,000m) with a base-bleed projectile. Rheinmetall is also developing combustible charge containers for this weapon and other 155mm types.

The Israeli Soltam Model 839P 155mm (6.1in) gun/howitzer is a towed equipment with an L/43 barrel fitted with a single-baffle muzzle brake, a split-trail carriage with an auxiliary power unit, four road wheels and two castors, a weight of 23,920lb (10,850kg), on-mounting elevation and traverse angles of –3 to +70 degrees and 78 degrees total respectively, a rate of fire of four rounds per minute (short periods) and two rounds per minute (sustained fire), a range of 25,700yds (23,500m), and a crew of eight. This equipment, which is a development of the same company's M-71 weapon, is produced in two variants as the Model 839P and the Model 845P. The Model 839P entered service in 1984 and uses the same ordnance on a revised carriage fitted with an 80hp (60kW) Deutz diesel-engined auxiliary power unit for a road speed of 10.6mph (17km/h), has a range of 43.5 miles (70km) and a gradient capability of 34%, as well as power for trail-spreading/opening, wheel lifting/lowering and firing platform lowering/lifting. A pneumatically operated rammer eases crew fatigue and increases rate of fire, and the ordnance fires separate-loading ammunition of various types including the 95.9lb FRAG-HE with 18.74lb/8.5kg of HE and the HE RAP with 9.9lb/4.5kg of HE. Entering service in 1985, the Model 845P is a version of the Model 839P with an L/45 barrel and a range of 31,170yds (28,500m) with a 'special projectile'.

The Israeli Soltam M-71 155mm (6.1in) gun/howitzer is a towed equipment with an L/39 barrel fitted with a single-baffle muzzle brake, a split-trail carriage with four road wheels, a weight of 20,282lb (9,200kg), on-mounting elevation and traverse angles of –3 to +54 degrees and 84 degrees total respectively, a rate of fire of four rounds per minute (short periods) and two rounds per minute (sustained fire), a range of 25,700yds, and a crew of eight. The M-71 is a development of the same company's M-68 equipment with a longer ordnance and a compressed-air rammer for rapid reloading at all angles of elevation. The ammunition types used with the M-71 are those detailed for the M-68.

The Israeli Soltam M-68 155mm (6.1in) gun/howitzer is a towed equipment with an L/33 barrel fitted with a single-baffle muzzle brake, a split-trail carriage with four road wheels, a weight of 20,944lb (9,500kg) in travelling order and 18,739lb (8,500kg) in firing position, on-mounting elevation and traverse angles of –5 to +52 degrees and 90 degrees total respectively, a rate of fire of four rounds per minute (short periods) and two

One of the most advanced items of conventional towed artillery in current service, the 155mm (6.1in) FH-70 was developed jointly by British, German and Italian interests, and is a highly capable equipment offering considerable range and accuracy.

rounds per minute (sustained fire), a range of 22,965yds (21,000m) with NATO ammunition and 25,700yds with Tampella ammunition, and a crew of eight. The M-68 is the baseline variant of Israel's important 155mm gun/howitzer family, and combines an Israeli ordnance on a locally developed adaptation of the carriage of the Finnish M-60. Development of the M-68 was undertaken in the 1960s, final trials being completed in 1968 for the equipment to enter service in 1970. The ordnance fires all standard NATO projectiles of this calibre, the 96.3lb (43.7kg) HE projectile leaving the muzzle at 2,379ft (725m) per second to attain a range of 22,965yds, although the weapon can also use the more capable range of ammunition developed by Tampella, using a nine-charge propellant system to attain a maximum range of 25,700yds.

The South African Armscor G5 155mm gun/howitzer is a towed equipment with an L/45 barrel fitted with a single-baffle muzzle brake, a split-trail carriage with an auxiliary power unit, four road wheels and two castors, a weight of 29,762lb (13,510kg), on-mounting elevation and traverse angles of respectively –3 to +75 degrees and 84 degrees total up to +15 degrees of elevation to 65 degrees total above 15 degrees of elevation, a rate of fire of three rounds per minute (15-minute period) and two rounds per minute (normal), a range of 32,810yds with standard ammunition and 41,010yds (37,500m) with HE base-bleed ammunition, and a crew of eight. The G5 is an extremely potent piece of equipment, and was developed from

Although most modern armies have opted for the logistic simplicity of using mainly the 155mm (6.1in) calibre in weapons that can be used in the direct- and indirect-fire roles, the USA still has small numbers of larger-calibre weapons in service. These are typified here by the 175mm (6.89in) M107 self-propelled gun, which was used in Vietnam for the long-range bombardment of targets such as Viet Cong build-up areas and suspected supply dumps.

1975 on the basis of the GC 45, although the process altered virtually every feature of the Canadian/Belgian weapon. The weapon entered South African service in 1983 and has proved very successful in terms of range, accuracy and cross-country mobility. Battlefield capabilities are considerably aided by the installation of a 68hp (51kW) Magirus-Deutz diesel-engined auxiliary power unit for hydraulic functions such as lowering/raising the firing platform and castors, and for opening/closing the trails, while crew fatigue is reduced by the provision of a pneumatically operated rammer. A three-charge propellant system is used for muzzle velocities of between 820 and 2,943ft (250 and 897m) per second, and the projectile types are 100.3lb (45.5kg) HE, 103.6lb (47kg) base-bleed HE, smoke, illuminating, white phosphorus and cargo-carrying rounds.

The Swedish Bofors FH-77A 155mm (6.1in) field howitzer is a towed equipment with an L/38 barrel fitted with a 'pepperpot' muzzle brake, a split-trail carriage with an auxiliary power unit, two road wheels and two castors, a weight of 25,353lb (11,500kg), on-mounting elevation and traverse angles of respectively –3 to +50 degrees and 50 degrees total up to +5 degrees of elevation to 60 degrees total above 5 degrees of elevation, a rate of fire of three rounds in 6–8 seconds or six rounds in 20–25 seconds (bursts) and six rounds every other minute (20-minute period), a range of 24,060yds (22,000m), and a crew of six. The FH-77A entered production in 1975, and is a highly capable equipment although only at great cost and considerable size. One of the main features of the equipment is its use of a Volvo B20 auxiliary power unit for a hydraulic system that drives the road wheels and castors, providing good battlefield mobility (at a maximum speed of 5mph/8km/h) and competent into/out of action times. Elevation and traverse are also hydraulically powered, and a powered rammer is used in conjunction with a crane-supplied loading table (the crane delivering three projectiles at a time) and semi-automatic breech for very high burst rates of fire. The FH-77A fires particularly potent separate-loading ammunition, the HE projectile weighing 93lb (42.2kg). The weapon uses a six-charge propellant system offering muzzle velocities between 1,017 and 2,539ft (310 and 774m) per second with projectiles that include HE, base-bleed HE, smoke and illuminating. The FH-77B is the export version of the FH-77A with a longer L/39 barrel, a screw rather than vertical sliding wedge breech mechanism, a fully automatic ammunition-handling system, elevation to +70 degrees, and improvements to cross-country mobility (including power take-off from the tractor to provide full 8x8 drive for the tractor/ordnance combination). The weight is increased to 26,235lb (11,900kg), and a bagged rather than cartridge charge propellant system is used. The standard range of the FH-77B is 26,245yds (24,000m) rising to 32,810yds with an extended-range full-bore round. The FH-77B can also be fitted with the Ferranti FIN 1150 gyrostabilised land navigation system to permit autonomous positioning of the equipment: trials have confirmed the utility of such a system for 'shoot-and-scoot' tactics, one equipment (with a crew of four men) in a period of 5 minutes 10 seconds coming into action, firing four rounds, moving 55yds (50m) and firing another three rounds.

The Soviet (now Russian) S-23 180mm (7.09in) gun is a towed equipment with an L/48.9 barrel fitted with a 'pepperpot' muzzle brake, a split-trail carriage with four road wheels and a two-wheel limber, a weight of 47,288lb (21,450kg), on-mounting elevation and traverse angles of –2 to +50 degrees and 44 degrees total respectively, a rate of fire of one round per minute (bursts) and one round per two minutes (sustained fire), a range of 33,245yds (30,400m) with normal ammunition and 47,900yds (43,800m) with an RAP, and a crew of 16. Originally thought by Western analysts to be a 203mm (8in) weapon, the S-23 was at first known in US terminology as the M1955 and

The air portability of modern artillery is revealed here by the carriage of a 105mm (4.13in) Light Gun by an Aérospatiale SA 330 Puma medium-lift helicopter.

originated as a naval weapon in the early 1950s. To facilitate towed transport, the ordnance can be withdrawn from battery and the ends of the trails supported on a two-wheel limber. The type fires separate-loading ammunition with variable bag charges, and the projectiles include a 185.4lb (84.09kg) HE type fired at a muzzle velocity of 2,592ft (790m) per second, an HE RAP type fired at a muzzle velocity of 2,789ft (850m) per second, a 215.4lb (97.7kg) concrete-piercing type, and a nuclear type with a yield of 0.2 kilotons.

The Soviet (now Russian) 2A36 152mm (6in) field gun is a towed equipment with a barrel of unknown length fitted with a multi-baffle muzzle brake, a split-trail carriage with four road wheels, a weight of about 19,400lb (8,800kg), on-mounting elevation and traverse angles of –2 to +57 degrees and 25 degrees left and right respectively, a rate of fire of five or six rounds per minute, a range of 29,530yds (27,000m) with the standard projectile and 40,465yds (37,000m) with an RAP, and a crew of 10. The 2A46 is generally known in the West as the M1976, which is its designation in the US system of terminology. This equipment began to enter service in 1981 and is apparently the modern replacement for the 130mm (5.12in) M-46 gun in the counter-battery role with army-level artillery divisions and brigades. The ordnance can fire HE, RAP, HEAT, chemical and nuclear projectiles of the separate-loading type, and the 101.4lb (46kg) HE fragmentation projectile is fired at a muzzle velocity of 2,625ft (800m) per second.

The Soviet (now Russian) D-20 152mm (6in) gun/howitzer is a towed equipment with an L/37 barrel fitted with a double-baffle muzzle brake, a split-trail carriage with two road wheels and two castors, a weight of 12,556lb (5,700kg) in travelling order and 12,456lb (5,650kg) in firing position, on-mounting elevation and traverse angles of –5 to +63 degrees and 58 degrees total respectively, a rate of fire of five or six rounds per minute, a range of 19,030yds (17,400m) with a standard projectile and 26,245yds (24,000m) with an RAP, and a crew of 10. Developed after World War II for a service debut in the early 1950s, the D-20 was initially called the M1955 in the West and was designed as successor to the ML-20. The recoil system and carriage are identical to those of the D-74 field gun although supporting a shorter and considerably fatter ordnance. The equipment fires separate-loading case ammunition with several projectiles, including a 95.9lb (43.51kg) HE-FRAG type at a muzzle velocity of 2,149ft (655m) per second, an HE RAP type to a maximum range of 26,245yds, a 107.5lb (48.78kg) AP-T type at a muzzle velocity of 1,969ft (600m) per second to penetrate 124mm (4.88in) of armour at 1,095yds (1,000m), a HEAT type, a concrete-piercing type, a smoke type, an illuminating type, a chemical type and a nuclear type with a yield of 0.2 kilotons. The M84 is the Yugoslav-made version of the D-20. This uses the same carriage as the D-20 but possesses a number of improved features including a longer barrel and two hydraulic pumps used to locate the weapon on its circular firing platform and raise the wheels clear of the ground; maximum rate of fire is six rounds per minute, and the Yugoslav ordnance can fire the same ammunition as the Soviet weapon, including the OF-540 HE-FRAG projectile, but can also fire the new Yugoslav M84 HE projectile: this is fired with a muzzle velocity of 2,657ft (810m) per second to attain a maximum range of 26,245yds. Also available are an illuminating projectile and the new High Explosive/Improved Conventional Munition (HE/ICM), the latter carrying 63 KB-2 bomblets to a range of 24,605yds (22,500m): each of these top-attack anti-armour bomblets weighs 0.55lb (0.25kg). The Type 66 is the Chinese-made copy of the D-20.

The nature of the modern 155mm (6.1in) howitzer is exemplified by this American prototype weapon. The main picture shows the moment of firing, the projectile emerging from the muzzle whose brake is just capturing and diverting part of the propellant gases to reduce the recoil. Note (left) the small radar used to capture the exact velocity of the departing projectile.

The Soviet (now Russian) M-46 130mm (5.12in) field gun is a towed equipment with an L/55 barrel fitted with a 'pepperpot' muzzle brake, a split-trail carriage with two road wheels and a two-wheel limber, a weight of 18,629lb (8,450kg) in travelling order and 16,975lb (7,700kg) in firing position, on-mounting elevation and traverse angles of –2.5 to +45 degrees and 50 degrees total respectively, a rate of fire of five or six rounds per minute, a range of 29,690yds (27,150m), and a crew of nine. Introduced in the early 1950s as successor to the A-19 (M1931/37) gun, the M-46 has its ordnance pulled right back out of battery for towed transport. The type's ordnance is essentially similar to 130mm guns used in warships of the Soviet navy, and fires separate-loading case-type ammunition with projectiles such as a 73.6lb (33.4kg) HE-FRAG type fired at a muzzle velocity of 3,445ft (1,050m) per second and an APC-T type fired at the same muzzle velocity to penetrate 230mm (9.06in) of armour at a range of 1,095yds as well as HE RAP, smoke and illuminating types.

The Soviet (now Russian) D-74 122mm (4.8in) field gun is a towed equipment with an L/47 barrel fitted with a double-baffle muzzle brake, a split-trail carriage with two road wheels and two castors, a weight of 12,235lb (5,550kg) in travelling order and 12,125lb (5,500kg) in firing position, on-mounting elevation and traverse angles of –5 to +45 degrees and 58 degrees total respectively, a rate of fire of six or seven rounds per minute, a range of 26,245yds, and a crew of 10. Designed in the late 1940s as a possible successor to the A-19 (M1931/37) gun, the D-74 was at first known in the West as the M1955 but not adopted by the Soviet army, which instead accepted the 130mm M-46. The D-74 uses the same carriage as the D-20 152mm gun/howitzer, and was widely produced for export. The type is

Another photograph of the same development weapon for the M198 howitzer shows the compact design but sturdy construction.

installed on a circular firing platform for operation, and fires separate-loading case-type ammunition: among the projectiles available are a 60.2lb (27.3kg) HE-FRAG type fired at a muzzle velocity of 2,904ft (885m) per second and a 55.1lb (25kg) APC-T type fired at the same muzzle velocity to penetrate 185mm (7.28in) of armour at a range of 1,095yds as well as chemical, illuminating and smoke types. The Type 60 is the Chinese-made copy of the D-74.

The Soviet (now Russian) D-30 122mm (4.8in) howitzer is a towed equipment with an L/35.5 barrel fitted with a multi-baffle muzzle brake, a three-leg split-trail carriage with two road wheels, a weight of 7,077lb (3,210kg) in travelling order and 6,944lb (3,150kg) in firing position, on-mounting elevation and traverse angles of –7 to +70 degrees and 360 degrees respectively, a rate of fire of seven or eight rounds per minute, a range of 16,840yds (15,400m) with standard ammunition and 23,950yds (21,900m) with an RAP, and a crew of seven. Entering service in the early 1960s as successor to the M-30, the D-30 offers useful advantages such as 360-degree traverse (on its three-leg firing platform) and greater range. The weapon is towed by its muzzle and fires separate-loading case-type ammunition; among the projectiles available are a 47.97lb (21.76kg) HE-FRAG type fired at a muzzle velocity of 2,264ft (690m) per second and a 47.7lb (21.63kg) HEAT-FS type fired at a muzzle velocity of 2,428ft (740m) per second to penetrate 460mm (18.1in) of armour at any range, as well as HE RAP, chemical, illuminating and smoke types. The Type 83 is the Chinese-made version of the D-30.

The British L118A1 105mm (4.13in) Light Gun is a towed equipment with an L/29.2 barrel fitted with a double-baffle muzzle brake, a split-trail carriage with two road wheels, a weight of 4,100lb (1,860kg), on-mounting elevation and traverse angles of –5.5 to +70 degrees and 11 degrees total (increasing to 360 degrees on the firing platform) respectively, a rate of fire of eight rounds in 60 seconds (burst), six rounds per minute (three-minute period) and three rounds per minute (sustained fire), a range of 18,800yds (17,190m) and a crew of six. Introduced in 1974, the L118A1 Light Gun is the basic electrically fired British version of the Light Gun and is a thoroughly modern piece of equipment designed to fulfil the pack howitzer and gun roles while being air-portable under medium-lift helicopters. The ordnance fires semi-fixed ammunition with a seven-charge propellant system offering ranges between 2,750 and 18,800yds (2,515 and 17,190m). The projectile types available are 35.5lb (16.1kg) HE, 23.1lb (10.49kg) HESH, illuminating and three smoke varieties. The L118F1 Hamel is the version of the L118A1 built under licence in Australia for the Australian and New Zealand armies.

Above and below: Keys to modern artillery design include comparatively small wheels, a light but very rigid carriage and cradle allowing the ordnance to be reversed for towing, an effective muzzle brake (often including the towing eye in its lower edge), a stable firing platform created by the trail legs and/or outrigger legs, and often the ability to move short distances on the battlefield as a result of the incorporation of an auxiliary power unit.

The L119A1 Hamel is the version developed for the US M1 ammunition series with different rifling, a single-baffle muzzle brake, percussion firing and a maximum range of 12,000yds (10,975m): the type is used by Australia and New Zealand as a training weapon for the L118F1, using existing stocks of US-supplied ammunition, and its shorter range renders it more appropriate for operational training in battle areas. The L127A1 is the version developed for Switzerland with different rifling, a double-baffle muzzle brake and percussion firing.

The American M198 155mm (6.1in) howitzer is a towed equipment with an L/39.3 barrel fitted with a double-baffle muzzle brake, a split-trail carriage with two road wheels, a weight of 15,790lb (7,162kg), on-mounting elevation and traverse angles of –5 to +72 degrees and 45 degrees total respectively, a rate of fire of four rounds per minute, a range of 19,850yds (18,150m) with the HE grenade-launching projectile and 32,800yds (29,995m) with the HE RAP, and a crew of 11. The M198 was designed as successor to the M114 series and began to enter US service in 1978. The type is designed to fire the full range of standard NATO separate-loading ammunition, and projectiles that can be used are two types of HE mine-launcher each weighing 102.5lb (46.5kg) and carrying 36 anti-personnel mines, two types of HE grenade-launcher (a 102.57lb/46.52kg type with 88 dual-purpose grenades and a 95lb/43.09kg type with 60 anti-personnel grenades), a 96lb (43.54kg) HE RAP type fired at a muzzle velocity of 2,710ft (826m) per second, two types of HE mine-launcher each weighing 103lb (46.72kg) with nine anti-tank mines, the Copperhead laser-guided anti-tank projectile, three chemical/gas types, two illuminating types, two smoke types and the M454 nuclear type with a 0.1-kiloton W48 warhead (to have been replaced by the W82 enhanced-radiation 'neutron' warhead).

Modern towed artillery is designed for the long-range delivery of several accurately aimed projectiles within as short a space of time as possible, and then departure from the firing position before counter-fire can arrive and destroy the equipment.

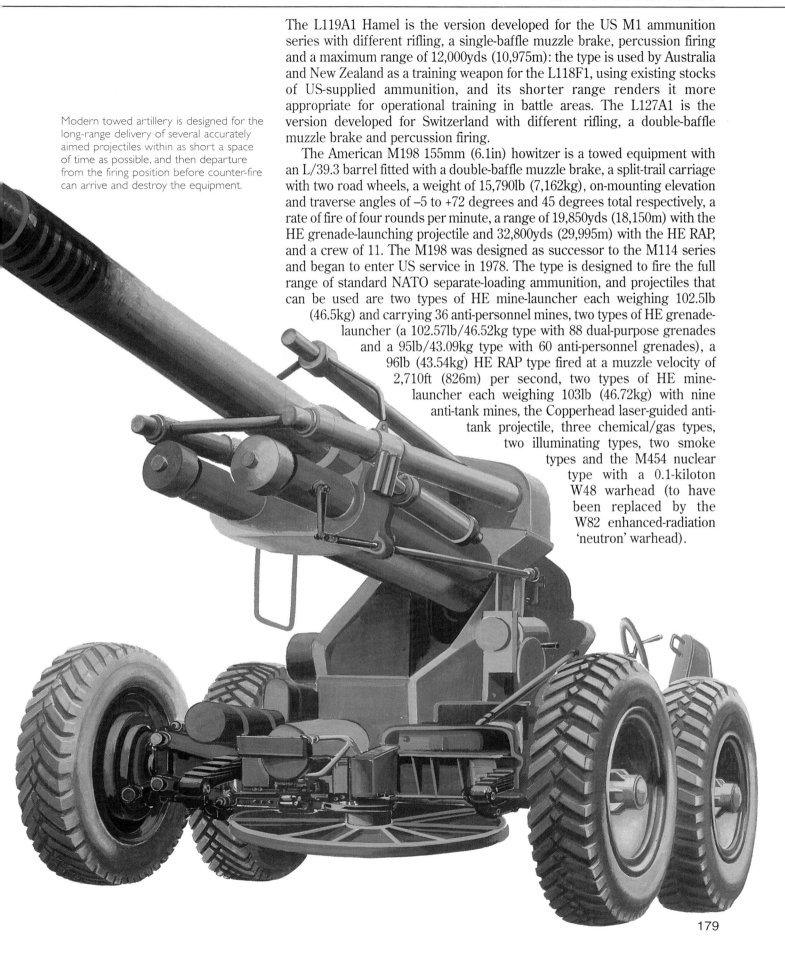

Special-Purpose Artillery

FIELD artillery of the light, medium and heavy types was designed for multi-purpose tactical use, but under certain circumstances could also be fired in more specialised roles such as the anti-tank and, to a lesser extent, anti-aircraft tasks. The Soviets in particular were avid exponents of the theory that every piece of artillery should be used for the anti-tank role when required, and therefore designed an anti-tank round for use with virtually every calibre of gun in the light, medium and heavy ranges. This was not allowed to disguise the fact that the anti-tank and anti-aircraft roles were best served by more specialised weapons, however, as these tasks required not only particular types of projectile but also a number of particular features in the guns themselves.

Both anti-tank and anti-aircraft guns were used in World War I, but these were not so much specialised weapons as lighter pieces of field artillery, either firing special ammunition, or being installed on dedicated mountings (often on the back of trucks for greater tactical mobility), allowing the guns to be elevated to a far higher angle than had been possible in the guns' original surface-to-surface role.

As the threat of the tank and the warplane increased during the 1920s and 1930s, specialised weapons (mostly of indigenous manufacture) began to appear on the equipment strengths of most European nations as well as the USA and Japan. The emphasis in this new type of specialised weapon was a high muzzle velocity as this was required by both the anti-tank gun and the aircraft gun: the former needed the velocity for the flattest and therefore most easily aimed fire with the maximum possible kinetic energy in the short-range task of penetrating armour with a solid shot, while the latter required velocity for the delivery of an explosive-filled shell to the desired altitude in the shortest possible time and with the straightest possible trajectory.

As the international situation began to decline in the 1930s with the rise of aggressive intention displayed by Germany, Italy and Japan, new generations of better protected tanks and faster- and higher-flying aircraft began to enter service, and this placed fresh emphasis on the need for high muzzle velocities for both anti-tank guns and anti-aircraft guns.

In World War II, the countries that developed, procured and used the most effective anti-tank guns were Germany, the UK, the USA and the USSR, whose primary weapons of this type are detailed below by country and in ascending order of calibre.

The smallest of the German weapons was the 28mm schwere Panzerbüchse (sPzB) 41 that entered service in 1941 as the world's first operational expression of the Gerlich-designed 'taper bore' concept. The sPzB 41 therefore fired a 28mm round whose 4.5oz (0.1305kg) solid projectile was fitted with collapsing annular skirts that allowed it to decrease in diameter as it was pushed up the tapered barrel to emerge from the 20mm muzzle with the very high velocity of 4,599ft (1,402m) per second for

Experience in World War II soon revealed what the prophets of armoured warfare had foretold, namely that armoured formations should be accompanied by self-propelled artillery as towed equipment could not keep pace with it. One of the best such equipments developed in World War II by the Americans was the Howitzer Motor Carriage M7, known to the British as 'the Priest' because of its 'pulpit' for the defensive machine gun: this was based on the chassis and lower hull of the M3 medium tank with a raised cupola carrying the 105mm (4.13in) M101 howitzer.

the ability to penetrate 56mm (2.2in) of armour at a range of 440yds (402m) at an impact angle of 30 degrees. The ordnance was installed in a light two-wheeled carriage of the split-trail type, had on-mounting elevation and traverse angles of -5 to +45 degrees and 90 degrees (reducing to 30 degrees at maximum elevation) total respectively, and a weight of 505lb (229kg). The sPzB 41 was an effective weapon offering good armour-penetration qualities for its weight, but the ordnance was difficult and therefore expensive to manufacture, and as Germany's supplies of strategic raw materials dwindled later in the war, the manufacture of the weapon was discontinued because of the difficulties of supplying its ammunition, which was based on a shot with a small-diameter tungsten core whose density and strength offered the best possible armour-penetration capability.

The smallest 'conventional' anti-tank gun used by the Germans was a Rheinmetall production, the 37mm Panzerabwehrkanone (PaK) 35/36. This was a simple weapon based on a two-wheeled light carriage of the split-trail type with a shield, and was developed from 1933 for a service debut during 1936 in the Spanish Civil War (1936-39). The L/45 barrel fired the 1.5lb (0.68kg) solid shot at a muzzle velocity of 2,499ft (762m) per second to penetrate 38mm (1.5in) of armour at a range of 440yds at an impact angle of 30 degrees: by 1940 the obsolescence of the weapon was realised in face of the latest British and French tanks, and the original ammunition was replaced by the AP40 type with a high-density tungsten core, and this 12.5oz (0.354kg) projectile was fired at a muzzle velocity of 3,378ft (1,030m) per second to penetrate 49mm (1.93in) of armour at a range of 440yds at an impact angle of 30 degrees. The complete equipment, of which more than 15,000 had been completed by 1941 for export as well as German use, weighed 952lb (432kg) in travelling order and 723lb (328kg) in firing position, and its on-mounting elevation and traverse angles were -8 to +25 degrees and 60 degrees total respectively. The AP40 shot was later supplemented by the Stielgranate spigot grenade in an effort to retain an operational effectiveness in the face of Allied tanks with thicker and better

Low and light, the British 6pdr anti-tank gun was a 57mm weapon that offered good capabilities within the limitation of its calibre but was already on the verge of obsolescence even as it entered service.

angled protective armour, but by 1943 the PaK 35/36 was obsolete even though it soldiered on to the end of the war in a number of second-line units. As well as being exported, the weapon was licensed for foreign production, and several other weapons were modelled closely on the German original, a good example being the American 37mm M3 weapon.

The 42mm leichte Panzerabwehrkanone 41 that entered service in 1941 was another taper-bore weapon based on a development of the PaK 35/36's carriage with sprung suspension and a spaced shield for improved protection against small-arms and shell fragments. The complete equipment weighed 992lb (450kg) and possessed on-mounting elevation and traverse angles of -8 to +25 degrees and 41 degrees total respectively, and the barrel tapered from 40.5mm at the breech to 29.4mm at the muzzle, resulting in the firing of the 11.75oz (0.336kg) shot at a muzzle velocity of 4,149ft (1,265m) per second to penetrate 72mm (2.84in) of armour at a range of 545yds (498m) at an impact angle of 30 degrees. This lightweight weapon was intended for use by the German air force's parachute arm, but supplies of tungsten for the core of the solid projectile were so limited that production was ended in 1942 after the delivery of only a small number of equipments.

The 50mm PaK 38 was designed by Rheinmetall from 1938 as successor to the PaK 35/36 with considerably improved armour-penetration capability, and entered service in the later part of 1940 as an excellent type that was later provided with improved ammunition that allowed it to remain in service up to the end of World War II. The PaK 38 was based on a two-wheel carriage of the split-trail type with a shield, the complete equipment weighed 2,174lb (986kg), and the on-mounting elevation and traverse angles were -8 to +27 degrees and 65 degrees total respectively. The L/60 barrel was fitted with a double-baffle muzzle brake and fired the 4.96lb (2.25kg) standard shot to penetrate 61mm (2.4in) of armour at a range of 545yds at an impact angle of 30 degrees, but the improved tungsten-cored 2.15lb (0.97kg) AP40 projectile left the muzzle with a velocity of 3,937ft (1,200m) per second to penetrate 86mm (3.39in) of armour at a range of 545yds at an impact angle of 30 degrees. The weight of the equipment was usefully reduced by the use of light alloys in place of steel for certain parts of the carriage and trail, and handling was facilitated by the use of a small castor inserted under the trails in the joined position.

The only weapon wholly designed in Japan for the anti-tank gun role, the 47mm Anti-Tank Gun Type 1 appeared in 1941, and although of moderately advanced design and appearance, was somewhat lacking in performance by comparison with other nations' towed anti-tank guns. The type had an L/54 barrel, weighed 1,660lb (753kg), possessed an elevation arc of between −11 and +19 degrees as well as a traverse of 30 degrees left and right of the centreline, and fired its 3.08lb (1.4kg) shot at a muzzle velocity of 2,701ft (825m) per second to penetrate 2in (50mm) of armour at 545yds (500m) at an angle of 30 degrees.

The Italian Semovente M.41M da 90/53 was produced only in small numbers, but was an impressive equipment that added the 90mm (3.54in) anti-aircraft gun in a low-angle traversing and shielded mounting on the hull of the M.14/41 medium tank chassis. The result was a powerful self-propelled anti-tank weapon.

Another Rheinmetall design, the PaK 40 was developed from 1939 in response to a German army requirement for a weapon offering significantly better armour-penetration capabilities than the PaK 38. The resulting weapon entered service in the later part of 1941 as a scaled-up version of the PaK 38, and was later provided with improved ammunition that allowed it to remain in service up to the end of World War II. The PaK 40 was based on a two-wheel carriage of the split-trail type with a shield (in this instance made of straight rather than curved sections of steel plate to simplify the production process), the complete equipment weighed 3,307lb (1,500kg), and the on-mounting elevation and traverse angles were –5 to +22 degrees and 65 degrees total respectively. The L/46 barrel was fitted with a double-baffle muzzle brake and fired the 15lb (6.8kg) standard shot to penetrate 106mm (4.17in) of armour at a range of 545yds at an impact angle of 30 degrees, but the improved tungsten-cored 7lb (3.2kg) AP40 projectile left the muzzle with a velocity of 3,068ft (935m) per second to penetrate 115mm (4.53in) of armour at a range of 545yds at an impact angle of 30 degrees.

Although the PaK 38 and PaK 40 offered a useful capability against the majority of Soviet tanks in the first phases of Germany's invasion of the USSR from June 1941, the rapid emergence of tanks such as the T-34 and KV series, which were soon available to the Soviets in very substantial numbers, presented the Germans with an increasingly acute problem in armour penetration with the tungsten-cored AP40 type of projectile. The Germans were therefore steadily reduced from the later part of 1942 to the ambush type of engagement in which the less well protected flanks and rear of the Soviet's tanks could be attacked as they passed the German anti-tank gun positions. The German army had anticipated this eventuality, although somewhat belatedly, and the result was the devastating 88mm (3.465in) PaK 43 that was in overall terms the finest anti-tank gun of World War II. Designed by Krupp, the PaK 43 was based on a four-wheel carriage of the four-trail type with a wide and well-sloped shield, the complete equipment weighed 11,023lb (5,000kg), and the on-mounting elevation and traverse angles were –8 to +40 degrees and 60 degrees total respectively. The L/71 barrel was fitted with a double-baffle muzzle brake and fired the 16.1lb

(7.3kg) standard shot with a muzzle velocity of 3,708ft (1,130m) per second to penetrate 226mm (8.9in) of armour at a range of 545yds at an impact angle of 30 degrees. In firing position the trails were opened out into a large cruciform and then lowered to the ground with the wheels removed, to create a firing platform of great stability and weapon traverse of 360 degrees, and the weapon was also a general-purpose utility being provided with a 30.8lb (13.97kg) HE shell. The overall effect of this powerful weapon, whose carriage was based on that of the 88mm anti-aircraft gun and was generally operated in the dug-in position, was its considerable armour-penetration capability at long range: this meant that the T-34 and KV tanks could be engaged frontally at long range in the shorter term, and in the longer term provided the Germans with a weapon that could tackle the IS series of tanks, which appeared in 1944, at short ranges.

Such was the success of the PaK 43 that demand for this potent weapon soon outstripped supply, especially as the Krupp factories were among the German industrial targets attacked most frequently by British bombers. In fact, it was production of the carriage that fell behind that of the ordnance, and so the ordnance was adapted to a revised version of the carriage of the 105mm leFH 18 howitzer to create the 88mm PaK 43/41. The PaK 43/41 was without doubt a less elegant weapon than the PaK 43, but possessed all the original ordnance's tank-killing capabilities.

The United Kingdom used three main types of anti-tank gun in World War II, in the form of 2pdr, 6pdr and 17pdr weapons whose weight of shot is a telling indication of the thickness of protective armour that had to be penetrated during the war's six-year course.

The Ordnance, QF, 2pdr was developed in response to an official requirement issued in 1934, and entered service in 1938 as a simple yet effective weapon based on a two-wheel carriage of the split-trail type with

A fairly potent anti-aircraft gun mounting of the self-propelled type for the period in the middle of World War II, the mittlerer Zugkraftwagen 8t mit 3,7cm FlaK 36, otherwise known as the SdKfz 7/2, combined the 3.7cm FlaK 36 anti-aircraft gun with the SdKfz 7 semi-tracked vehicle to provide a good measure of road performance and cross-country capability.

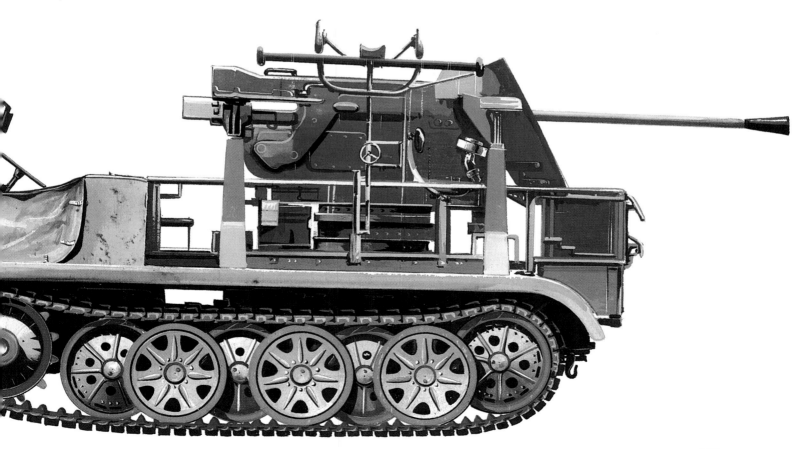

One of the most powerful tracked vehicles to see service in World War II, the SU-122 assault gun was the combination of the 121.92mm (4.8in) Field Gun Model 1931/37 (otherwise A-19) on a chassis and lower hull based on those of the KV heavy tank.

three legs and a shield. The complete equipment weighed 1,848lb (838kg), and the on-mounting elevation and traverse angles were –13 to +15 degrees and 360 degrees total respectively. The L/50 barrel had a calibre of 40mm, with no muzzle brake, and fired the 2,375lb (1,077kg) standard shot with a muzzle velocity of 2,615ft (797m) per second to penetrate 53mm (2.09in) of armour at a range of 500yds (457m) at an impact angle of 30 degrees. The weapon was very well made, but more than twice the weight of its German equivalent, which reflected a difference of tactical role envisaged by the British: the Germans planned to use their weapons offensively, in support of their own armour-led aggressive tactics, while the British planned to use their guns defensively in the prepared positions in which they would await the German attack. This was also the reason for the gun's installation on a carriage from which the two wheels could be removed, allowing the gun to settle on the ground with its tripod legs spread to provide a steady platform for fire through a traverse angle of 360 degrees. The weapon could be used in mobile warfare, either towed to a new site behind a truck or operated in the portée mode from the flatbed of a truck, but was soon rendered obsolete by the introduction of German tanks with improved armour. In the North African campaign (1940-43), the 2pdr was difficult to conceal and was soon outranged by the 50mm guns of German tanks, and it was for this reason that the 25pdr gun/howitzer was provided with anti-tank ammunition as an interim weapon pending the introduction of a more powerful specialised anti-tank gun.

The more powerful weapon was the Ordnance, QF, 6pdr that was delivered from September 1941 after a design and development process that had started in 1938. The 6pdr Mk I was essentially a development model produced only in small numbers and used mainly for training, so the first genuine production models were the 6pdr Mks II and IV that differed from each other in barrel length: the Mk II had an L/42.8 barrel while the Mk IV had an L/45 barrel, in each case without a muzzle brake. The equipment was based on a two-wheel carriage of the split-trail type with a shield, weighed 2,471lb (1,121kg), and the on-mounting elevation and traverse angles were –5 to +15 degrees and 90 degrees total respectively. The L/45 barrel had a calibre of 57mm and fired the 6.28lb (2.85kg) standard shot with a muzzle velocity of 2,700ft (823m) per second to penetrate 69mm (2.7in) of armour at a range of 1,000yds (914m) at an impact angle of 20 degrees. The anti-tank capability of the 6pdr gun was therefore considerably better than that of the 2pdr, both in terms of range and penetrable armour thickness, but the length of the equipment's development process meant that the 6pdr was obsolete within a year of its introduction. The type was also made in the USA as the 57mm Anti-Tank Gun M1.

Whereas the 2pdr and 6pdr guns were typical of British practice in being very well made weapons that were adequate for their immediate purposes, they had been designed with no real concept of the need to tackle tanks carrying considerably heavier armour than those of the current generation. The following Ordnance, QF, 17pdr was a superb weapon that was as well made as its predecessors, and was optimised for total superiority over both the current generation of tanks and those of the following generations. The weapon resulted from a March 1941 requirement for a 3in (76.2mm) anti-tank weapon, and the design and development processes of the new weapon were achieved with commendable speed so that the 17pdr entered service in August 1942 as a highly effective weapon whose capabilities were only slightly marred by the weight of its carriage, which dictated that a comparatively large crew was required for effective tactical use. The carriage was also difficult to make, and as a result the first 100 ordnances were completed before any carriages were ready for them. These ordnances were delivered to North Africa, where the obsolescence of the 6pdr was presenting major problems, and were installed on a modified version of the 25pdr gun/howitzer carriage to create an interim weapon known as the 17/25pdr. This was a moderately clumsy weapon, for the 25pdr gun/howitzer carriage could only just sustain the recoil forces generated by the 17pdr gun.

The 17pdr gun was based on a two-wheel carriage of the split-trail type with a shield, the complete equipment weighed 6,445lb (2,923kg), and the on-mounting elevation and traverse angles were –6 to +16.5 degrees and 60 degrees total respectively. The L/55.1 barrel was fitted with a double-baffle muzzle brake and fired the 17lb (7.71kg) standard shot with a muzzle velocity of 2,900ft (884m) per second to penetrate 130mm (5.12in) of armour at a range of 1,000yds at an impact angle of 30 degrees. The weapon could

Early SP Guns

THE first generations of self-propelled guns were created as expedients in the middle part of World War II, and the most important aspect of their creation was the combination of a standard piece of field artillery with a well-established medium tank chassis/hull to provide mobility for the field gun as part of the support element for armoured formations. In these circumstances a 'lash-up' design was acceptable, and this resulted in vehicles such as the American M7 and British Sexton with a simple fighting compartment able to accept the standard cradle of the selected field gun, even though this limited the on-vehicle traverse capability of the weapon and demanded a slewing of the whole vehicle to effect gross changes in bearing. This fighting compartment had to be large enough to accommodate the gun's detachment and a modest number of ready-use rounds of ammunition, and was generally designed as vertical or nearly vertical extensions of the baseline tank's upper-hull armour but without any overhead protection. Experience soon showed that the crew was inevitably vulnerable to the fragmentation effects of overhead shell bursts, and later self-propelled guns were designed with a taller fighting compartment with some measure of overhead protection.

The Sexton was a British self-propelled gun analogous to the American Howitzer Motor Carriage M7 (Priest) in that it added the 25pdr gun/howitzer to an open compartment erected on the hull and lower chassis of the Grizzly I medium tank, which was the Canadian-built version of the US M4 Sherman medium tank.

also fire a useful HE shell and was therefore effective as a dual-role anti-tank gun and field gun that remained in British service until well after the end of World War II.

The smallest of the American anti-tank guns was the 37mm Anti-Tank Gun M3, which was based on the German 37mm PaK 35/36 but with a number of important changes (including the introduction of a five-baffle muzzle brake that was later found to be unnecessary), and was mounted on the M4 series of lightweight carriage developed wholly by the Americans. The M3A1 variant that was the main production model was based on a two-wheel carriage of the split-trail type with a shield, the complete equipment weighed 912lb (414kg), and the on-mounting elevation and traverse angles were –10 to +15 degrees and 60 degrees total respectively. The L/53.5 barrel fired the 1.92lb (0.87kg) standard shot with a muzzle velocity of 2,900ft per second to penetrate 25mm (1in) of armour at a range of 1,000yds at an impact angle of 20 degrees, and could also fire an improved APC projectile to penetrate 53mm of armour at a range of 1,000yds at an impact angle of 20 degrees. Production of the M3 anti-tank gun totalled some 18,700 weapons, and although these were obsolete for use against the Germans from 1942 onwards, they were nevertheless very useful in the Pacific campaign against the Japanese until the end of World War II: the shot was capable of penetrating the armour of virtually any Japanese tank, and the weapon was also widely and successfully employed for the vital task of destroying Japanese bunkers with solid shot and repulsing Japanese massed infantry attacks with HE and canister projectiles.

Next up in size, the 57mm Anti-Tank Gun M1 was an American version of the British 6pdr. The equipment was based on a two-wheel carriage of the split-trail type with a shield and weighed 2,700lb (1,225kg), and the on-mounting elevation and traverse angles were –5 to +15 degrees and 90 degrees total respectively. The L/50 barrel had no muzzle brake and fired the 6.28lb standard shot with a muzzle velocity of 2,700ft (823m) per second to penetrate 69mm of armour at a range of 1,000yds at an impact angle of 20 degrees.

Now an obsolete type, the Creusot-Loire Mk 61 is a 105mm (4.13in) self-propelled howitzer that was designed in France during the late 1940s on the basis of the AMX-13 light tank, with its oscillating turret removed and hull rear modified into a large fixed barbette carrying the Modèle 50 howitzer in a manually operated mounting that permitted elevation in the arc between –4.5 and +66 degrees and traverse 20 degrees left and right of the centreline. The vehicle carried 56 rounds of main gun ammunition, and a local-defence capability was provided by one or two 0.3 or 0.295in (7.62 or 7.5mm) machine guns with 2,000 rounds of ammunition.

From the beginning of the 57mm Anti-Tank Gun M1 programme the Americans had realised that this could be an interim weapon at best, and by 1942 had started work on an improved weapon of indigenous design. This was the 3in (7.62mm) Anti-Tank Gun M5 that was really a judicious blend of existing components such as the barrel of the 3in Anti-Aircraft Gun M3 together with the breech mechanism, recoil system and carriage of the 105mm Howitzer M2A1. The result was a somewhat cumbersome but workable and effective weapon of which 2,500 were manufactured. The weapon was based on a two-wheel carriage of the split-trail type with a shield, the complete equipment weighed 5,850lb (2,654kg), and the on-mounting elevation and traverse angles were –5 to +30 degrees and 46 degrees total respectively. The L/50 barrel had no muzzle brake and fired the 15.43lb (7kg) standard shot with a muzzle velocity of 2,600ft (792m) per second to penetrate 98mm (3.86in) of armour at a range of 1,000yds at an impact angle of 20 degrees.

The USA made no real attempt to create and place in service any modern anti-tank guns of larger calibre, for by 1943 the US Army had decided that the anti-tank role was best fulfilled by field artillery firing heavy projectiles, and by specialised self-propelled weapons.

The smallest Soviet anti-tank gun was another copy of the German 37mm PaK 35/36, of which the Soviets bought a pilot batch before deciding on licensed manufacture for substantial numbers of a weapon known as the 37mm Anti-Tank Gun Model 1930 that differed from the German originals only in having wire-spoked wheels. Based on a two-wheel carriage of the split-trail type with a shield, the complete equipment weighed 723lb (328kg), and the on-mounting elevation and traverse angles were –8 to +25 degrees and 60 degrees total respectively. The L/45 barrel was not fitted with a muzzle brake and fired the 1.5lb standard shot with a muzzle velocity of 3,379ft (1,030m) per second to penetrate 38mm of armour at a range of 440yds at an impact angle of 30 degrees.

Like all other countries involved in the development of advanced tanks and the methods of tackling them, the USSR appreciated that the successful destruction of tanks with thicker and better disposed armour called for a

Older in concept than the Mk 61, the Creusot-Loire Mk F3 has a completely exposed mounting for its armament, which is a 155mm (6.1in) ATS gun/howitzer. This can be elevated in the arc between 0 and +67 degrees and traversed 25 degrees left and right of the centreline at lower angles of elevation, declining to 23 degrees left and right of the centreline at higher angles. The vehicle carries no ready-use ammunition; 25 rounds and the eight-man gun detachment are carried in an accompanying tracked vehicle.

189

The American M44 self-propelled equipment was of the fixed-barbette type, and its main armament was a 155mm (6.1in) M45 howitzer with 24 rounds of ready-use ammunition.

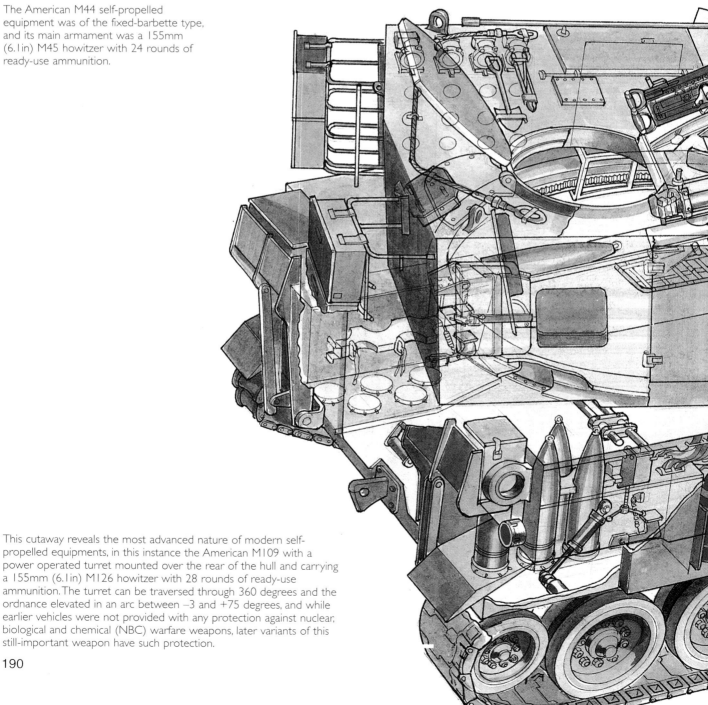

This cutaway reveals the most advanced nature of modern self-propelled equipments, in this instance the American M109 with a power operated turret mounted over the rear of the hull and carrying a 155mm (6.1in) M126 howitzer with 28 rounds of ready-use ammunition. The turret can be traversed through 360 degrees and the ordnance elevated in an arc between −3 and +75 degrees, and while earlier vehicles were not provided with any protection against nuclear, biological and chemical (NBC) warfare weapons, later variants of this still-important weapon have such protection.

two-handed approach involving the creation of anti-tank guns firing a heavier projectile at a high velocity. The first practical result of this approach was the 45mm Anti-Tank Gun Model 1932, which was in essence a scaled-up version of the ordnance of the 37mm Anti-Tank Gun Model 1930 on either of two carriage types optimised for horse and truck traction. The 45mm Anti-Tank Gun Model 1932 was based on a two-wheel carriage of the split-trail type with a shield, the complete equipment weighed 992lb (450kg) for the horse-drawn version and 1,124lb (510kg) for the truck-towed version, and the on-mounting elevation and traverse angles were –8 to +25 degrees and 60 degrees total respectively. The L/46 barrel was not fitted with a muzzle brake and fired the 3.15lb (1.43kg) standard shot with a muzzle velocity of 2,493ft (760m) per second to penetrate 38mm of armour at a range of 1,000yds at an impact angle of 30 degrees. The Model 1932 was followed by the basically similar Model 1937 that differed only in minor details and was copied by the Japanese as the 45mm Anti-Tank Gun Type 1,

This is an M109 105mm (4.13in) self-propelled howitzer of the British army. The M109A2 variant that entered service in 1979 has a turret bustle to increase the quantity of ready-use ammunition that can be carried, and other salient details of this vital Western weapon include a crew of six, weight of 55,000lb (24,948kg), length of 29ft 11in (9.12m) with the gun forward, welded aluminium armour, a powerplant of one 405hp (302kW) Detroit Diesel 8V-71T diesel engine for a maximum road speed of 35mph (56km/h) and maximum road range of 215 miles (346km), and armament of one 155mm (6.1in) M126 howitzer with 36 rounds of ammunition and one 0.5in (12.7mm) Browning machine gun with 500 rounds of ammunition.

and then by the Model 1938 with the on-mounting elevation and traverse angle altered to −10 to +10 degrees and 15 degrees total respectively, and the weight to 1,433lb (650kg). Further development of the same basic concept resulted in the 45mm Anti-Tank Gun Model 1942, which was basically the model 1937 with disc rather than spoked wheels, a lengthened barrel and a strengthened breech block. The Model 1942 was based on a two-wheel carriage of the split-trail type with a shield, the complete equipment weighed 1,257lb (570kg), and the on-mounting elevation and traverse angles were −8 to +25 degrees and 60 degrees total respectively. The L/66 barrel had no muzzle brake and fired the 3.15lb standard shot with a muzzle velocity of 2,690ft (820m) per second to penetrate 95mm (3.74in) of armour at a range of 330yds (302m).

In 1941, and just before the German invasion of their country, the Soviets introduced the 57mm Anti-Tank Gun Model 1941. This was a purpose-designed ordnance on the 76.2mm (3in) Field Gun Model 1941's two-wheel carriage of the split-trail type with a shield, the complete equipment weighed 2,480lb (1,125kg), and the on-mounting elevation and traverse angles were −10 to +18 degrees and 56 degrees total respectively. The L/73 barrel had no muzzle brake and fired the 6.94lb (3.148kg) standard shot with a muzzle velocity of 3,346ft (1,020m) per second to penetrate 140mm (5.51in) of armour at a range of 545yds. Further development resulted in the 57mm Anti-Tank Gun Model 1943, which was the same ordnance on the Model 1942's two-wheel carriage of the split-tubular trail type with a shield, the complete equipment weighed 2,535lb (1,150kg), and the on-mounting elevation and traverse angles were −5 to +25 degrees and 56 degrees total respectively.

The final Soviet anti-tank gun of World War II was the 100mm (3.94in) Anti-Tank Gun Model 1944, which was one of the most powerful weapons of its type to be developed and placed in service during the war. The ordnance was derived from that of a high-velocity naval weapon, and this was installed on a heavy carriage of the split-trail type with unusual double-tyred wheels and a shield. The complete equipment weighed 7,628lb (3,460kg), and the

The FV433 Abbot was developed by Vickers to meet a British army requirement for a light but highly mobile self-propelled howitzer. A member of the FV430 series of light armoured fighting vehicles, the FV433 uses many of the same automotive components as the FV432 armoured personnel carrier, and is armed with a 105mm (4.13in) L13A1 gun/howitzer that can be elevated in an arc between −5 and +70 degrees in a turret located over the rear of the hull and capable of traverse through 360 degrees.

on-mounting elevation and traverse angles were −5 to +45 degrees and 58 degrees total respectively. The L/59.6 barrel was fitted with a double-baffle muzzle brake and fired the 34.4lb (15.6kg) standard shot with a muzzle velocity of 2,953ft (900m) per second to penetrate 192mm (7.56in) of armour at a range of 490yds (448m).

As had been the case with field artillery weapons after World War II, the anti-tank gun entered a period of relative inactivity in terms of development and procurement, as the victorious nations were satisfied with their current equipments and saw little military advantage in adopting new equipments firing projectiles of greater weight and at higher velocity. The primary anti-tank role came to be dominated by the battle tank, in a way already foreshadowed in World War II by tanks and specialised tank destroyers, and also by the guided missile carrying a hollow-charge warhead that relies for its effect not on kinetic energy but rather on the combined chemical and physical effects of its warhead's shaping: on detonation, this vapourises a copper liner and focuses the resultant stream of violently hot gases and vaporised metal on the surface of the target armour, burning a hole through which the gas/metal stream pours to kill the crew and/or ignite the ammunition inside the tank.

This tendency toward the tank (firing a number of specialised rounds such as the HEAT type with a hollow-charge explosive filling, the HESH type with a 'pancake' of plastic explosive whose exterior detonation scales off large segments of interior armour that fly round the fighting compartment at high velocity, and the small-calibre fin-stabilised dart that penetrates the armour), the guided missile (both surface- and air-launched) and the high-velocity rocket (generally air-launched) as the primary anti-tank weapons came to assume a dominant position among the more advanced weapon-making nations in the 1950s and 1960s, although several smaller countries as well as the USSR then developed a number of large-calibre anti-tank guns that remained in service into the 1980s. Some of these weapons are detailed below by country of origin and in descending order of calibre.

The Austrian 105mm (4.13in) NORICUM ATG N 105 is a towed anti-tank

An obsolete type no longer in first-line service, the M52 was an American 105mm (4.13in) self-propelled howitzer with the M85 ordnance and 105 rounds of ammunition.

gun with an L/56.1 barrel, a split-trail carriage with two road wheels and a shield, a weight of 7,937lb (3,600kg) in travelling and firing orders, and unrevealed on-mounting elevation and traverse angles, rate of fire, range and crew. The equipment was developed initially as a mobile trials mount for NORICUM's LRN 105 long-recoil tank gun using the range of ammunition developed for the L7/M68 series of rifled tank guns, and was then evolved into a production version for countries requiring a potent anti-tank gun. Details are still sparse, but the equipment is of standard configuration with an ordnance that can be turned through 180 degrees to lie of the trail legs while being towed. The type can also fire a special NP 105 A2 armour-piercing discarding-sabot fin-stabilised (APDSFS) round whose projectile weighs 42.55lb (19.3kg) and, leaving the muzzle at a velocity of 4,872ft (1,485m) per second, can penetrate 150mm (5.91in) of armour inclined at 60 degrees at a range of 6,345yds (5,800m).

The Belgian 90mm (3.54in) MECAR KEnerga 90/46 is a towed anti-tank gun with an L/46 barrel fitted with a double-baffle muzzle brake, a split-trail carriage with two road wheels and an optional shield, a weight of 2,205lb (1,000kg), an on-mounting elevation angle of unrevealed size and an on-mounting traverse angle of 54 degrees total, a rate of fire of 10 rounds per minute (maximum) and seven rounds per minute (normal), and a crew of three or four. The equipment is a simple development of the KEnerga low recoil force rifled gun designed for use in light armoured fighting vehicles (AFVs), and its ordnance can fire nine types of fixed ammunition including APDSFS, HEAT (three varieties including one practice), HE, HESH, smoke (two varieties) and canister. The 6.02lb (2.73kg) projectile of the M603 APDSFS round leaves the muzzle at 4,692ft (1,430m) per second and can penetrate the NATO standard target armour at a range of 2,185yds (2,000m), the 9.01lb (4.085kg) projectile of the M644 HV-HEAT round leaves the muzzle at 3,346ft (1,020m) per second and can penetrate the NATO standard target armour at a range of 1,315yds (1,200m), and the

11.24lb (5.1kg) projectile of the M656 HESH round leaves the muzzle at 2,625ft (800m) per second; the M629 canister round releases 1,100 lead balls with a muzzle velocity of 2,543ft (775m) per second.

Another Belgian weapon, the 90mm Field Mount is a towed anti-tank gun with an L/32.2 barrel with no muzzle brake, has a three-leg (tripod) type of carriage with two road wheels and a shield, weighs 1,940lb (880kg), possesses on-mounting elevation and traverse angles of –10 to +12 degrees and 360 degrees total respectively, has a rate of fire of 18 rounds per minute (maximum) and 10 rounds per minute (normal), and is operated by a crew of three or four. The equipment is based on the 90mm MECAR anti-tank gun that was designed for installation in light armoured vehicles but, in this application, is fitted on a towed carriage with twin road wheels that lift to allow the folding tripod legs to be opened out for 360-degree traverse. The fixed ammunition options are HEAT-CAN-90 anti-tank with a 5.4lb (2.45kg) projectile fired at a muzzle velocity of 2,077ft (633m) per second to penetrate 375mm (14.76in) of armour at a range of 1,095yds (1,000m), HE-CAN-90 anti-personnel with an 8.8lb (4kg) projectile fired at a muzzle velocity of 1,109ft (338m) per second for a range of 3,280yds (3,000m), CNT-CAN-90 canister with an effective range of 275yds (250m), and smoke.

The Chinese 100mm (3.94in) NORINCO Anti-Tank Gun Type 86 is a towed anti-tank gun with a barrel of unrevealed length fitted with a multi-baffle muzzle brake, is carried on a split-trail carriage with two road wheels and a shield, weighs 8,069lb (3,660kg), has on-mounting elevation and traverse angles of –4 to +38 degrees and 50 degrees total respectively,

Seen here in the form of an equipment in British service, the M107 175mm (6.89in) self-propelled gun was designed for the long-range bombardment of tactically and operationally important targets deep in the enemy's rear area. The M113 gun, for which only two rounds of ready-use ammunition are carried, can deliver accurate fire to a maximum range of 35,750yds (32,690m), and the detachment and additional ammunition are carried in an accompanying tracked vehicle.

possesses a rate of fire of between eight and 10 rounds per minute, has a range of 14,930yds (13,650m), and is served by a crew of unknown number. The equipment was introduced in 1987 as a simple yet effective anti-tank gun that is apparently based on the combination of a new smooth-bore ordnance on the carriage of the Type 56 field gun. The weapon is designed primarily for the direct-fire role, but indirect-fire sights are fitted for fire to a maximum range limited by the equipment's low maximum elevation; the type can also be fitted with a night vision device. No details of the ammunition have yet been revealed, although the use of a smooth-bore barrel suggests that the primary round is an APDSFS type firing a sub-calibre dart at very high velocity.

Another Chinese equipment, the 85mm (3.35in) NORINCO Gun Type 56 is a towed field and anti-tank gun with an L/55.2 barrel fitted with a double-baffle muzzle brake, carried on a split-trail carriage with two road wheels and (on some equipments) one castor plus a shield, weighing 3,858lb (1,750kg), possessing on-mounting elevation and traverse angles of –7 to +35 degrees and 54 degrees total respectively, characterised by a rate of fire of between 15 and 20 rounds per minute, having a range of 17,115yds (15,650m), and served by a crew of between six and eight. This equipment is essentially the Soviet D-44 gun built with slight modification in China. The ordnance can fire HE, HEAT and HESH rounds, and is thus used mainly as a support and anti-tank weapon. The HEAT projectile weighs 15.43lb (7kg) and at a range of 1,060yds (970m) can penetrate 100mm (3.94in) of armour at an angle of 65 degrees.

The Czechoslovak 100mm (3.94in) M53 field and anti-tank gun is a towed equipment with an L/67.35 barrel fitted with a double-baffle muzzle brake. The gun is installed on a split-trail carriage with two road wheels and two castors plus a shield, weighs 9,436lb (4,280kg) in travelling order and 9,281lb (4,210kg) in firing position, has on-mounting elevation and traverse angles of –6 to +42 degrees and 60 degrees total respectively, possesses a

The M109G is the version of the M109 155mm (6.1in) self-propelled howitzer family for the German army, with a number of German features (including the tracks of the Leopard 1 main battle tank) and a revised breech increasing the standard range of the M126 ordnance from 16,000 to 20,230yds (14,630 to 18,500m).

rate of fire of between eight and 10 rounds per minute, has a range of 22,965yds (21,000m), and is served by a crew of six. The M53 was introduced in the early 1950s, and is a dual-purpose field and anti-tank gun firing fixed ammunition including a 35.3lb (16kg) APC-T projectile at a muzzle velocity of 3,281ft (1,000m) per second to penetrate 185mm (7.28in) of armour at a range of 1,095yds, a 27.25lb (12.36kg) HEAT-FS projectile at a muzzle velocity of 2,953ft (900m) per second to penetrate 380mm (14.96in) of armour at any range, a 12.54lb (5.69kg) HVAPDS-T projectile at a muzzle velocity of 4,642ft (1,415m) per second to penetrate 200mm (7.87in) of armour at a range of 1,095yds, and a 34.37lb (15.59kg) FRAG-HE projectile at a muzzle velocity of 2,953ft per second.

Another Czechoslovak weapon, the 85mm M52/55 85mm field and anti-tank gun is a towed equipment with an L/59.65 barrel fitted with a double-baffle muzzle brake, and its other details include a split-trail carriage with two road wheels and a shield, a weight of 4,780lb (2,168kg) in travelling order and 4,654lb (2,111kg) in firing position, on-mounting elevation and traverse angles of –6 to +38 degrees and 60 degrees total respectively, a rate of fire of 20 rounds per minute, a range of 17,675yds (16,160m), and a crew of seven. Introduced in 1952, this is a dual-purpose field and anti-tank gun, and among the fixed ammunition types available are AP-T with a 20.28lb (9.2kg) projectile fired at a muzzle velocity of 2,690ft (820m) per second to penetrate 123mm (4.84in) of armour at a range of 1,095yds, HEAT-FS, HVAP-T and HE. The M52/55 is an improved model of 1955 with the slightly greater weights.

The Swiss 90mm (3.54in) Federal Construction M57 is a towed anti-tank gun with an L/33.7 barrel fitted with a multi-baffle muzzle brake, and its other details include a split-trail carriage with two road wheels and a shield, a weight of 1,323lb (600kg) in travelling order and 1,257lb (570kg) in firing position, on-mounting elevation and traverse angles of –15 to +23 degrees and 70 degrees total up to +11 degrees elevation and 44 degrees total over 11 degrees elevation, a rate of fire of 20 rounds per minute (maximum) and six rounds per minute (normal), a range of 3,280yds overall, 985yds (900m) against a static target or 765yds (700m) against a moving target, and a crew of five. Introduced in 1958, this light anti-tank equipment fires a 5.95lb (2.7kg) HEAT projectile at a muzzle velocity of 1,969ft (600m) per second to penetrate 250mm (9.84in) of armour.

Another Swiss equipment, the 90mm Federal Construction M50 is a towed anti-tank gun with an L/32.2 barrel with no muzzle brake, and its other details include a split-trail carriage with two road wheels and a shield, a weight of 1,323lb (600kg) in travelling order and 1,226lb (556kg) in firing position, on-mounting elevation and traverse angles of –10 to +32 degrees and 66 degrees total up to +11 degrees elevation and 34 degrees total over 11 degrees elevation, a rate of fire of 20 rounds per minute (maximum) and six rounds per minute (normal), a range of 3,280yds overall, or 765yds against a static target or 545yds against a moving target, and a crew of five. Introduced in 1953, this light anti-tank equipment fires a 4.3lb (1.95kg) HEAT projectile at a muzzle velocity of 1,969ft per second to penetrate 250mm of armour.

The Soviet 100mm (3.94in) T-12 is a towed anti-tank gun with an L/84.8 barrel fitted with a 'pepperpot' muzzle brake, and its other details include a split-trail carriage with two road wheels and a shield, a weight of 6,614lb (3,000kg), on-mounting elevation and traverse angles of –10 to +20 degrees and 27 degrees total respectively, a rate of fire of 10 rounds per minute, a range of 9,295yds (8,500m), and a crew of six. Designed as successor to the 85mm D-48 anti-tank gun, the T-12 was introduced in the mid-1960s and uses fixed ammunition of two types, namely APDSFS with a 12.13lb (5.5kg)

Modern SP Guns

WHEREAS early self-propelled guns were usually based on tank chassis, modern equipments are generally based on a purpose-designed chassis carrying only comparatively light armour as the vehicle's long-range armament makes it possible to operate at a greater remove from the enemy, and the chassis generally makes extensive use of automotive components from tanks and armoured personnel carriers for improved commonality and thus a simplification of the vehicle's required logistical infrastructure. In basic design the modern SP equipment is similar to the tank with a turret capable of 360 degrees traverse, although this turret is somewhat larger and generally located farther to the rear. The additional size is required by the turret to accommodate the larger breech of the greater-calibre gun and the larger detachment needed to work the gun, although the size of the detachment can be reduced by the use of an automatic loading system that permits the equipment to maintain a higher rate of fire. Among the equipment virtually standard in modern self-propelled artillery are an NBC warfare protection package based on sealed driving and fighting compartments provided with filtered air, a land navigation system for a high degree of accuracy in spotting the equipment's position relative to its target, passive night driving gear, and an advanced fire-control system based on a digital computer to work out the solution to any fire-control problem on the basis of the vehicle's position and two-dimensional tilt, ambient air temperature, direction and speed, projectile type and ammunition charge used, and continuously updated muzzle velocity.

projectile fired at a muzzle velocity of 4,921ft (1,500m) per second to penetrate 406mm (16in) of armour at a range of 545yds, and HEAT with a 20.94lb (9.5kg) projectile fired at a muzzle velocity of 3,248ft (990m) per second to penetrate 400mm (15.75in) of armour at any range up to 1,310yds (1,200m). The T-12A is a modified version with larger wheels and a weight of 6,834lb (3,100kg).

The Soviet 100mm BS-3 is a towed field and anti-tank gun with an L/60.7 barrel fitted with a double-baffle muzzle brake, and its other details include a split-trail carriage with two twin road wheels and a shield, a weight of 8,047lb (3,650kg), on-mounting elevation and traverse angles of –5 to +45 degrees and 58 degrees total respectively, a rate of fire of between eight and 10 rounds per minute, a range of 22,965yds, and a crew of six. Introduced in 1944 as the Model 1944 (see above), this powerful weapon was later upgraded to fire more modern fixed ammunition types including a 34.4lb (15.6kg) HE-FRAG type fired at a muzzle velocity of 2,953ft (900m) per second, a 35.3lb (16kg) APC-T type fired at a muzzle velocity of 3,281ft per second to penetrate 185mm (7.28in) of armour at a range of 1,095yds, a 12.54lb (5.69kg) HVAPDS-T type fired at a muzzle velocity 4,642ft (1,415m) per second to penetrate more than 200mm (7.87in) of armour at a range of 1,095yds, and a 27.25lb (12.36kg) HEAT-FS type fired at a muzzle velocity of 2,953ft per second to penetrate 380mm (14.96in) of armour at any range up to 1,095yds. Type 59 Anti-Tank Gun is the provisional designation of the Chinese copy of the BS-3, adopted as successor to the 85mm Type 56 as an anti-tank and counter-battery weapon: the equipment's weight is estimated at 7,606lb (3,450kg), and the AP-T projectile's penetration is thought to be 157mm (6.18in) of armour at a range of 1,095yds.

The American M110 8in (203mm) self-propelled howitzer is based on the same chassis as the M107 175mm (6.89in) self-propelled gun, and can fire a 204lb (92.53kg) HE projectile with a muzzle velocity of 1,925ft (587m) per second to a maximum range of 18,400yds (16,825m). The long range of the ordnances carried by the M110 and M107 was the reason that the Americans decided that enclosed accommodation was unnecessary on the grounds that the crews would never come under fire from the enemy.

The Soviet 85mm SD-44 is a towed field and anti-tank gun with an L/53 barrel fitted with a double-baffle muzzle brake, and among its other details are a split-trail carriage with an auxiliary power unit, two road wheels and one castor plus a shield, a weight of 4,960lb (2,250kg), on-mounting elevation and traverse angles of –7 to +35 degrees and 54 degrees total respectively, a rate of fire of 15 rounds per minute (bursts) and 10 rounds per minute (sustained fire), a range of 17,115yds (15,650m), and a crew of seven. The SD-44 is essentially the D-44 divisional gun fitted with a 14hp (10.4kW) M-72 petrol-engined auxiliary power unit to provide airborne formations with a relatively powerful ordnance possessing limited self-mobility at a maximum road speed of 15.5mph (25km/h). The ordnance fires fixed ammunition, and the projectiles include a 21.2lb (9.6kg) HE-FRAG type fired at a muzzle velocity of 2,598ft (792m) per second, a 20.3lb (9.2kg) AP-T type fired at the same muzzle velocity to penetrate 125mm (4.92in) of armour at a range of 1,095yds, an 11.16lb (5.06kg) HVAP-T type fired at a muzzle velocity of 3,379ft per second to penetrate 180mm (7.09in) of armour at a range of 1,095yds, and a 16.2lb (7.34kg) HEAT-FS type fired at a muzzle velocity of 2,756ft (840m) per second to penetrate 300mm (11.8in) of armour at any range.

The Soviet 85mm D-48 is a towed anti-tank gun with an L/74 barrel fitted with a 'pepperpot' muzzle brake, and among its other details are a split-trail carriage with two road wheels and one castor plus a shield, a weight of 5,181lb (2,350kg), on-mounting elevation and traverse angles of –6 to +35 degrees and 54 degrees total respectively, a rate of fire of 15 rounds per minute (bursts) and eight rounds per minute (sustained fire), a range of 20,745yds (18,970m), and a crew of six. The D-48 was originally thought by

The FV433 is now out of first-line service, but in its time was an effective self-propelled system in which the small calibre of the ordnance was offset by its very considerable accuracy, resulting largely from Vickers' long experience with naval guns including the current 4.5in (114.3mm) weapon from which the Abbot's gun was derived.

Based on the well-proved chassis of the ZRK Krug self-propelled surface-to-air missile system with its SA-4 'Ganef' missile, the 2S3 Akatsiya is a 152mm (6in) self-propelled gun/howitzer now in Russian service. The whole equipment is very neat and possesses both an NBC protection system and passive night driving gear, but is not amphibious.

the West to be a 100mm (3.94in) weapon when introduced in the mid-1950s, and it does indeed use a 100mm type of fixed round, although necked down in this application for an 85mm (3.35in) projectile, in the form of either a 21.4lb (9.7kg) APHE type fired at a muzzle velocity of 3,281ft per second to penetrate 190mm (7.48in) of armour at a range of 1,095yds or a 20.5lb (9.3kg) HVAP type fired at a muzzle velocity of some 3,937ft (1,200m) per second to penetrate 240mm (9.45in) of armour at the same range.

Yet another Soviet type, the 57mm Ch-26 is a towed anti-tank gun with an L/71.4 barrel fitted with a double-baffle muzzle brake, and among its other details are a split-trail carriage with an auxiliary power unit and three road wheels plus a shield, a weight of 2,756lb (1,250kg), on-mounting elevation and traverse angles of –4 to +15 degrees and 56 degrees total respectively, a rate of fire of 12 rounds per minute, a range of 7,325yds (6,700m), and a crew of five. Designed for use by airborne formations, the Ch-26 remains in second-line service with a few countries, and features a 14hp (10.4kW) petrol-engined auxiliary power unit to provide a maximum road speed of 25mph (40km/h). The ordnance uses fixed ammunition whose projectiles include an 8.27lb (3.75kg) HE-FRAG type fired with a muzzle velocity of 2,280ft (695m) per second, a 6.92lb (3.14kg) AP-T type fired with a muzzle velocity of 3,215ft (980m) per second to penetrate 106mm (4.17in) of armour at a range of 545yds, and a 3.88lb (1.76kg) HVAP-T type fired at a muzzle velocity of 4,117ft (1,255m) per second to penetrate 140mm (5.51in) of armour at a range of 545yds.

The growing importance of aircraft in warfare during the 1920s and 1930s, together with their steadily improving performance, paved the way during the 1930s for the development of specialised anti-aircraft guns, which were altogether more capable than the extemporised weapons of World War I. The increasing number of roles that could be undertaken by such warplanes also demanded the creation of anti-aircraft guns dedicated to specific parts of the air-defence spectrum, ranging from small-calibre weapons capable of generating an increasingly dense 'wall of fire' to defeat low-level tactical aircraft, to medium-calibre weapons designed to tackle high-flying strategic bombers with HE-FRAG shells capable of reaching an altitude of 20,000ft (6,095m) . Yet again, it was Germany, the UK, the USA and the USSR that predominated in the development and construction of such weapons, although two neutral countries – Sweden and Switzerland – had been responsible respectively for the creation of 40mm and 20mm weapons that were widely used by most of the combatants.

Germany's smallest-calibre anti-aircraft gun was a Rheinmetall design, the 20mm Fliegerabwehrkanone (FlaK) 30 that was developed from the Solothurn S5-100 (otherwise ST-5) for a service debut in 1935. The weapon was reliable, but possessed only a modest rate of fire and was prone to jamming under certain conditions, and was built in very large numbers for use by all the German armed forces. The details of this weapon included an L/115 barrel fitted with a flash suppressor to fire a 0.2625lb (0.119kg) HE projectile with a muzzle velocity of 2,953ft (900m) per second, a two-wheel carriage with a Y-type trail fitted with a stabilising leg carrying the weapon that could be dismounted to rest on a tripod platform, a weight of 1,698lb (770kg) in travelling order and 992lb (450kg) in firing position, on-mounting elevation and traverse angles of –12 to +90 degrees and 360 degrees total respectively, a rate of fire of 280 rounds per minute (cyclic) or 120 rounds per minute (practical), an effective ceiling of 6,630ft (2,020m), and a crew of five or six.

The FlaK 30's indifferent rate of fire and tendency to jam caused considerable concern in German military circles, and the task of improving the weapon was entrusted to Mauser, which completed the task in 1940 with the creation of the 20mm FlaK 38 with a revised breech mechanism that increased the cyclic rate of fire by some 70 per cent. The details of this weapon included an L/112.6 barrel fitted with a flash suppressor to fire a 0.2625lb HE projectile with a muzzle velocity of 2,953ft per second, a weight of 1,654lb (750kg) in travelling order and 926lb (420kg) in firing position, on-mounting elevation and traverse angles of –20 to +90 degrees and 360 degrees total respectively, a rate of fire of 420 to 480 rounds per minute (cyclic) or 180 to 220 rounds per minute (practical), an effective ceiling of 6,630ft, and a crew of five or six.

A massive equipment offering excellent capabilities, the French GIAT GCT is a 155mm (6.1in) self-propelled howitzer based on the chassis of the AMX-30 main battle tank, and therefore offering full tactical compatibility with the armoured formations it was designed to support.

The odd appearance of the Bofors Bandkanon 1A, a 155mm (6.1in) self-propelled howitzer of Swedish design and construction, results from the use of a chassis based on that of the Strv 103 main battle tank surmounted by a comparatively small turret but large backward-projecting automatic loading system, which allows a high rate of fire with a 14-round ammunition clip that can be replenished in a mere two minutes.

The same 20mm calibre was retained for one of Germany's most formidable light anti-aircraft equipments, the Flakvierling 38 that was designed by Mauser as a four-barrel weapon for the defence of high-value targets. The weapon was originally developed for the German navy, with which it entered service in the late 1930s, and was then adopted by the German army and air force in 1940. So successful was the type that production was steadily increased, reaching a maximum of 410 per month during 1944. The equipment was basically four FlaK 38 barrels on a revised version of the FlaK 38's carriage, and its details included four L/112.6 barrels each fitted with a flash suppressor to fire a 0.2625lb HE projectile with a muzzle velocity of 2,953ft per second, a weight of 4,878lb (2,212kg) in travelling order and 3,338lb (1,514kg) in firing position, on-mounting elevation and traverse angles of −10 to +100 degrees and 360 degrees total respectively, a rate of fire of 1,800 rounds per minute (cyclic) or 880 rounds per minute (practical), an effective ceiling of 6,630ft, and a crew of seven.

These 20mm weapons were necessarily limited in effective ceiling and shell destructiveness, so the equipments of this calibre were complemented by 37mm weapons firing a larger and more potent shell to a greater effective ceiling. The first of these weapons was the 37mm FlaK 18 developed by Rheinmetall on the basis of the Solothurn S10-100 (otherwise ST-10). The equipment entered service in 1935 basically for ground use, with the weapon carried above a cruciform firing platform that was lowered to the ground once the four wheels had been removed, but there were a number of problems with the gun and its carriage and production was therefore ended after the delivery of only a few weapons, whose details included an L/98 barrel fitted with a flash suppressor to fire a 1.4lb (0.64kg) HE projectile with a muzzle velocity of 2,689ft (820m) per second, a weight of 8,013lb (3,634kg) in travelling order and 3,859lb (1,750kg) in firing position, on-mounting elevation and traverse angles of −8 to +85 degrees and 360 degrees total respectively, a rate of fire of 160 rounds per minute (cyclic) or 80 rounds per minute (practical), a maximum ceiling of 11,565ft (3,525m), and a crew of seven.

Early anti-aircraft guns of the mobile type, designed principally to provide a capability against airships and slow-flying bombers rather than tactical aircraft, were basically light field guns installed on the flatbeds of conventional trucks. A good example is that illustrated here, which was a British equipment using a Peerless truck carrying an 18pdr field gun with a barrel liner reducing the calibre to 3in (76.2mm) to permit the high-velocity firing of a 13pdr shell by an 18pdr cartridge.

The FlaK 18's successors were the closely related FlaK 36 and 37 equipments, which entered production in 1936 with the same ordnance as the FlaK 18, with the exception of a shortened chamber firing a projectile with one rather than two driving bands, but carried on an improved two-wheel carriage. The FlaK 37 was basically identical to the FlaK 36 except for its sight, which was a clockwork-powered Zeiss unit. The details of this weapon included an L/98 barrel fitted with a flash suppressor to fire a 1.4lb HE projectile with a muzzle velocity of 2,689ft per second, a weight of 5,292lb (2,400kg) in travelling order and 3,418lb (1,550kg) in firing position, on-mounting elevation and traverse angles of −8 to +85 degrees and 360 degrees total respectively, a rate of fire of 160 rounds per minute (cyclic) or 80 rounds per minute (practical), a maximum ceiling of 15,750ft (4,800m), and a crew of seven.

Introduced in the mid-war years as another Rheinmetall design, the 37mm FlaK 43 used basically the same barrel and exactly the same ammunition as the FlaK 36 and 37 weapons, in combination with a new gas-operated breech mechanism. The type was carried on a two-wheel carriage which was removed to allow the equipment to rest on the ground on its tripod firing platform, and the introduction of a number of manufacturing changes reduced the manhours required for the construction of each equipment from 4,320 to 1,000. The details of this weapon included an L/89.2 barrel fitted with a flash suppressor to fire a 1.4lb HE projectile with a muzzle velocity of 2,757ft (840m) per second, a weight of 2,690lb (1,220kg), on-mounting elevation and traverse angles of −7 to +90 degrees and 360 degrees total respectively, a rate of fire of 250 rounds per minute (cyclic) or 150 to 180 rounds per minute (practical), a maximum ceiling of 15,750ft, and a crew of six or seven.

The 37mm Flakzwilling 43 was a development of the FlaK 43 with two superimposed barrels for a doubling of the rate of fire. The details of this weapon included an L/89.2 barrel fitted with a flash suppressor to fire a 1.4lb HE projectile with a muzzle velocity of 2,757ft per second, a weight of 10,694lb (4,850kg) in travelling order and 5,511lb (2,500kg) in firing position, on-mounting elevation and traverse angles of −7 to +90 degrees and 360 degrees total respectively, a rate of fire of 500 rounds per minute (cyclic) or 300 to 350 rounds per minute (practical), and a maximum ceiling of 15,750ft.

The Germans also tried to develop anti-aircraft guns in 50mm calibre to fulfil the medium-altitude role, but the 50mm FlaK 41 was unsuccessful, and the 50mm FlaK 214 was about to enter service as World War II ended. The 75mm (2.95in) FlaK L/60 was a Krupp design manufactured in small quantities by Bofors in Sweden and mostly for the export market after Germany had rejected the weapon, but a few such equipments were used by the German navy for the protection of its bases in World War II.

After the initial rejection of its 75mm weapon, the Krupp design team turned its attention to an 88mm (3.465in) weapon at the beginning of a process that resulted in one of Germany's most celebrated weapons of World War II. This was the 88mm FlaK 18 that was designed for road movement on a four-wheel carriage whose axles were removed once the firing position had been reached, to permit the weapon to be emplaced on a cruciform firing platform carrying a central pedestal supporting the ordnance proper. This was an exceptional piece of work designed for decisive effect against current and all foreseeable targets. The design team decided that despite the size of the weapon and the potent shell it fired, as high a rate of fire as possible was still desirable, and for this reason the FlaK 18 was completed with a semi-automatic breech mechanism. The FlaK 18 was blooded in the Spanish Civil War, where its utility as a dual-role anti-tank and anti-aircraft weapon was realised as a result of emergency use in the anti-tank role, and the main run of these important weapons was therefore completed with a shield, a surface-to-surface sight and AP40 type anti-tank projectiles. The details of this weapon included an L/56 barrel firing a 20.34lb (9.23kg) HE projectile with a muzzle velocity of 2,689ft (820m) per second, a weight of 15,129lb (6,861kg) in travelling order, on-mounting elevation and traverse angles of –3 to +85 degrees and 360 degrees total respectively, a maximum ceiling of 26,245ft (8,000m), and a crew of 10.

The FlaK 18 was followed into production by the 88mm FlaK 36 and 37 weapons. The FlaK 36 was a development of the FlaK 18 with an improved carriage supported by double- rather than single-tyred wheels, and with a Rheinmetall-designed system of three removable barrel liners that could be changed in the field, to avoid changing the whole barrel when this became worn. The FlaK 37 was a development of the FlaK 36 with a revised data-transmission system that effectively precluded the weapon from use in the anti-tank role. In all other essential respects, the FlaK 36 and 37 were identical to the FlaK 18.

The Germans' last anti-aircraft gun of World War I was this Krupp 80mm (3.15in) weapon pedestal mounted on a four-wheel trailer for a high angle of elevation and 360 degrees traverse.

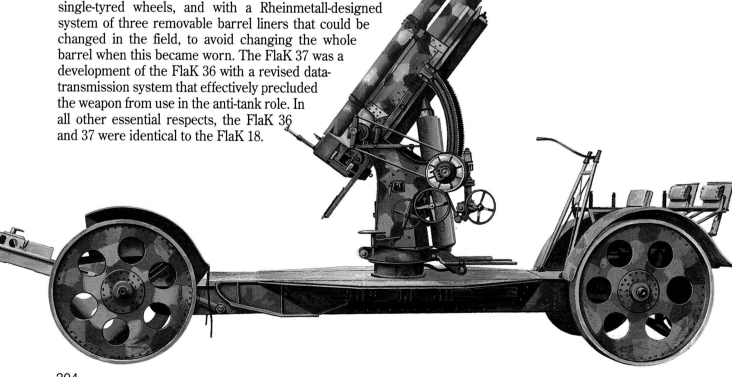

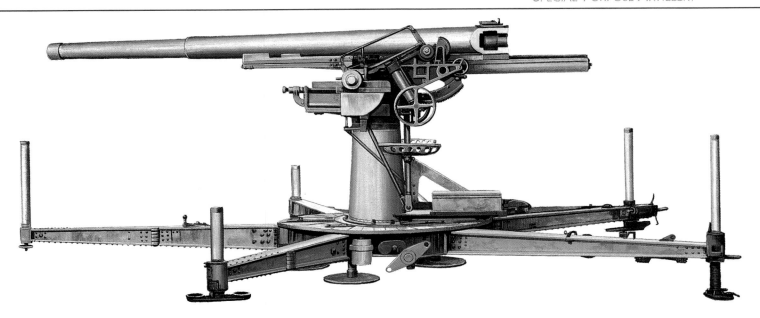

One of the most widely used of all Japanese anti-aircraft guns of World War II was the Army 75mm Mobile Field Anti-Aircraft Gun Type 88 that was introduced in 1928 and proved capable of delivering its 14.5lb (6.58kg) projectile to a maximum effective ceiling of 23,700ft (7,230m) after it had left the muzzle at a velocity of 2,360ft (720m) per second.

By the time of the outbreak of World War II, it was clear that while the first three generations of 88mm guns offered exceptional capabilities, their superiority would inevitably be eroded by the development of aircraft flying at greater speeds and higher altitudes, and in 1939 Rheinmetall was therefore instructed to start on the design and development of an improved anti-aircraft gun that retained the 88mm calibre. The first prototype weapons were completed in 1941, resulting in the designation FlaK 41, but it was 1943 before the first equipments entered full service as there were considerable problems to be overcome in the equipment's systems and its several untried features. Two of these features, incorporated specifically to provide the FlaK 41 with an anti-tank capability, were a turntable rather than pedestal carriage and a separate firing circuit for the anti-tank role. Once the teething problems had been eliminated, the FlaK 41 matured rapidly as so exceptional an anti-aircraft weapon that the type was seldom used in anything but this role. The details of this weapon included an L/74 barrel fitted to fire a 20.69lb (9.4kg) HE projectile with a muzzle velocity of 3,281ft per second, a weight of 24,784lb (11,240kg) in travelling order and 17,287lb (7,840kg) in firing position, on-mounting elevation and traverse angles of –3 to +90 degrees and 360 degrees total respectively, and a maximum ceiling of 49,215ft (15,000m).

The excellent 88mm weapons were not the last word in German anti-aircraft thinking, however, for as early as 1933 the Germans had foreseen the development of bombers and strategic reconnaissance aircraft able to fly too fast and too high for successful engagement with the 88mm weapon, and therefore ordered the start of work on a 105mm weapon. This task was entrusted to Krupp and Rheinmetall, which were each instructed to complete prototype weapons for comparative evaluation in 1935. The Rheinmetall type was deemed superior and ordered into production during 1936 as the 105mm FlaK 38. This looked as though it was merely a scaled-up 88mm weapon, but in fact there were many important changes in details such as the electrical control system, and the loading mechanism that was so effective that it was later adapted for the FlaK 41. Development changes included a major modification of the electrical control system and the introduction of a two-section barrel, and the change of the data-transmission system from that used in the 88mm FlaK 18 and 36 to that employed in the FlaK 37, and with these changes the FlaK 38 became the FlaK 39. The performance of these 105mm weapons was later overtaken by that of the

88mm FlaK 41, but production of the larger-calibre weapon was continued as production of the smaller-calibre weapon was never enough to satisfy demand. The details of this weapon included an L/63 barrel firing a 33.3lb (15.1kg) HE projectile with a muzzle velocity of 2,886ft (880m) per second, a weight of 32,193lb (14,600kg) in travelling order and 22,579lb (10,240kg) in firing position, on-mounting elevation and traverse angles of –3 to +85 degrees and 360 degrees total respectively, a maximum ceiling of 42,000ft (12,800m), and a crew of 12.

The largest calibre used by the Germans for an anti-aircraft weapon was 128mm (5.04in), and in this calibre there were two exceptional weapons, namely the FlaK 40 and the Flakzwilling 40. The FlaK 40 was ordered from Rheinmetall in 1936, and first appeared in prototype form during 1937. Only six of the type were initially produced, and in a mobile form (first in two loads and then as a single load), but from 1942 the type was built exclusively for fixed use, as the smaller and lighter 88mm FlaK 41 was generally better for the mobile role. The 128mm (5.04in) FlaK 40 was used mainly for the protection of high-value sites in Germany, and used a combination of electrical controls and electrical ramming. The details of this weapon included an L/61 barrel firing a 57.3lb (26kg) HE projectile with a muzzle velocity of 2,886ft (880m) per second, a weight of 28,660lb (13,000kg) in fixed form, on-mounting elevation and traverse angles of –3 to +88 degrees and 360 degrees total respectively, a maximum ceiling of 48,555ft (14,800m), and a crew of 10in 1936 a 150mm (5.91in) anti-aircraft gun was ordered from Krupp for installation on FlaK towers especially built around Berlin and other major German cities. The design and development of this gun was so slow that the type was cancelled, however, in favour of a twin version of the FlaK 40 with two guns side-by-side on an enlarged cradle. Comparatively few of these exceptionally powerful equipments were produced, with details that included an L/61 barrel firing a 57.3lb HE projectile with a muzzle velocity of 2,886ft per second, a weight of 59,524lb (27,000kg), on-mounting elevation and traverse angles of 0 to +88 degrees and 360 degrees total respectively, and a maximum ceiling of 48,555ft.

As with the Germans, the smallest calibre used by the British for a dedicated anti-aircraft gun was 20mm. The most common weapon in this calibre was the Polsten, whose unusual name stems from the fact that the design of the cannon originated in Poland (as a simplified version of the Swiss Oerlikon that would therefore be easier and cheaper to make) but was completed in the UK by Czechoslovak and British designers for manufacture by the Sten organisation. The result was a weapon offering

The single most important tactical anti-aircraft gun used by the Allies in World War II was the 40mm Bofors gun designed in Sweden but built under licence in the UK, the USA and in other countries. The details of this vital weapon, in its British-built Ordnance, QF, Bofors Anti-Aircraft Gun Mk I form on a four-wheel towed carriage, included an L/56 barrel, weight of 5,418lb (2,457kg), elevation in an arc between –5 and +90 degrees, traverse through 360 degrees, rate of fire of 120 rounds per minute (cyclic) or 60-90 rounds per minute (practical), and muzzle velocity of 2,800ft (854m) per second to deliver its 1.96lb (0.89kg) projectile to a maximum ceiling of 23,600ft (7,200m). The detachment numbered some five or six men including two who loaded the four-round ammunition clips into the overhead feed stay.

basically the same capabilities as the Oerlikon for a manufacturing cost of a mere £70 rather than the Swiss weapon's £320, due to the fact that the number of components had been reduced from 250 to 119 and that many of these components required considerably less or even no machining. The first such weapons were delivered in March 1944, and from that time the Polsten generally replaced the Oerlikon for land use. The type was supplied with ammunition from a 30-round box magazine inserted over the weapon, and its other details included an L/72.4 barrel firing a 0.2625lb HE projectile with a muzzle velocity of 2,725ft per second, an on-mounting traverse angle of 360 degrees total, a rate of fire of 450 rounds per minute (cyclic), a maximum ceiling of 6,630ft (2,020m), and a crew of two.

There was then a considerable gap in calibre (with the exception of a few Vickers 40mm weapons) up to the size of the 3in (76.2mm) Ordnance, QF, 3in, 20cwt, that was introduced in World War I but was built in a number of steadily improved marks for service through World War II until its retirement in 1946. This was an unexceptional weapon, and the details for the 3in Gun Mk IIIA on the Mk 1 four-wheeled carriage included an L/46.6 barrel firing a 16lb HE projectile with a muzzle velocity of 2,000ft (610m) per second, a weight of 17,584lb (7,976kg), on-mounting elevation and traverse angles of –10 to +90 degrees and 360 degrees total respectively, and a maximum ceiling of 23,500ft (7,165m).

The weapon designed to supersede the 3in weapon, although it did not achieve this objective until after World War II and was generally disliked for the fact that it was heavier and more difficult to handle than its predecessor, was the 3.7in (94mm) Ordnance, QF, 3.7in. The need for an anti-aircraft gun in this calibre had been suggested as early as 1920, but it was not until 1937 that the War Office issued the requirement for this specific weapon. A design by Vickers was approved in 1934, and the first prototype weapon was completed in April 1936. Trials revealed the satisfactory nature of the weapon, and the first production weapons were delivered in January 1938. The ordnance was a maximum yet basically straightforward unit, but the carriage was highly complex and the delivery of completed equipments was delayed by the fact that the carriages were being completed at a slower rate than the ordnances. The ordnance was eventually evolved through three marks and was of modern design with a liner that could be changed whenever it became worn, and was planned for movement on a four-wheeled carriage that was so heavy that the complete equipment was little more than semi-mobile. Other companies were brought into the programme to produce fixed mountings for the ordnance, and as a result there were the Mks I, IA, III and IIIA mobile mountings with four-wheeled carriages as well as the Mks II, IIA, IIB and IIC fixed mountings. The later ordnances were characterised by the incorporation of a power rammer and an automatic fuse setter, and other features included a data-transmission system and a predictor. The details of the Ordnance, QF, 3.7in, Mk III on Mounting Mk III included an L/50 barrel firing a 28.56lb (12.95kg) HE projectile with a muzzle velocity of 2,600ft (793m) per second, a weight of 20,541lb (9,317kg) in travelling order, on-mounting elevation and traverse angles of –5 to +80 degrees and 360 degrees total respectively, and a maximum ceiling of 32,000ft (9,755m).

The only other British anti-aircraft gun designed for land use was the 3.7in Ordnance, QF, 3.7in Mk 6, although it should be noted that two naval equipments were also adapted for land use as the 4.5in (114.3mm) Ordnance, QF, 4.5in, ANTI-AIRCRAFT, Mk II and the 5.25in (133.35mm) Ordnance, QF, 5.25in, ANTI-AIRCRAFT, Mk II. The 3.7in Mk 6 equipment resulted from an official requirement of 1940 for a gun providing a capability against bombers flying as high as 50,000ft (15,240m), and the requirement demanded that the shell reach this altitude in a time of 45 seconds (later reduced to 30 seconds as a means of simplifying the solution of the already complex fire-control problem), and that the guns be capable of firing three rounds every 20 seconds. One of the two equipments adopted to meet this requirement was the 5.25in weapon named above, and the other was a 4.5in weapon lined down to a calibre of 3.7in. The 3.7in weapon was adopted in 1943 and soon proved to be an excellent equipment that was carried on a fixed mounting that could be moved with the aid of a special transporter. The details of this weapon included an L/65 barrel firing a 28lb (12.7kg) HE projectile with a muzzle velocity of 3,470ft (1,058m) per second, on-mounting elevation and traverse angles of 0 to +80 degrees and 360 degrees total respectively, and a maximum ceiling of 59,300ft (18,075m). The equipment was fitted with an automatic fuse setter and a power rammer, and remained in service into the later part of the 1950s, when it was replaced by guided missiles.

The Americans were convinced that their superb 0.5in (12.7mm) Browning M2HB heavy machine guns had the makings of a first-class multiple mounting for the engagement of low-flying tactical aircraft, and this resulted in the creation of their smallest-calibre anti-aircraft weapon as the Multiple Cal .50 Machine-gun Carriage M51. Designed by Maxson, this was a four-wheel trainer carrying four 0.5in machine guns in mountings powered electrically by batteries carried on the trainer, which was stabilised in firing position by four jacks. The machine guns, each supplied with 200 belted rounds of ammunition, were aimed with a US Navy Mk 9 reflector sight, and could be traversed and elevated very quickly to allow the successful engagement of high-speed targets with fast crossing speeds. The weight of the entire equipment was 2,396lb (1,087kg), and the cyclic rate of fire was 2,300 rounds per minute.

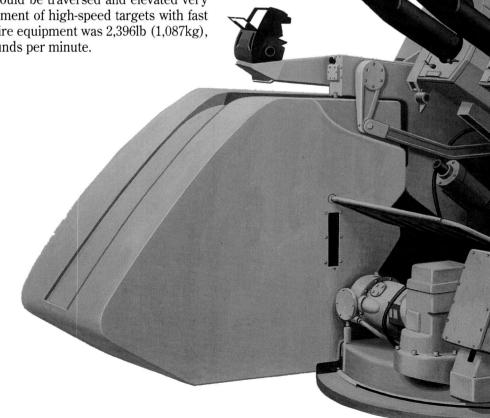

The Oerlikon GCM is typical of the modern generation of naval point-defence weapon systems for protection against low-level aircraft and missile attack. The mounting comes in three forms with open or enclosed accommodation for the single gunner, or alternatively, provision for remote control in an unmanned mounting, varying rates of traverse and elevation, and differing quantities of ammunition. Common to all is the potent armament of two 30mm KCB (originally Hispano-Suiza HS 831) cannon, firing a wide range of ammunition types at a high muzzle velocity for considerable range and accuracy

The Americans missed out the 20mm cannon for land-based applications, so their next anti-aircraft calibre was 37mm. Work on the ordnance was started in 1923 under the leadership of the celebrated John Browning, but ceased with his death in 1926 and was then resumed only in 1935 to create the 37mm Anti-aircraft Gun M1 that entered service in 1940 on the Carriage M3A1. This was a four-wheel unit whose wheels could be lifted to lower the mounting to the ground, where it was stabilised with the aid of two outrigger legs, and the ordnance could fire in single-short or automatic models using ammunition fed from the left in single rounds or from 10-round clips. Production totalled 7,278 equipments to a standard that included (in its M1A2 form on the M3A1 carriage) an L/53.7 barrel firing a 1.34lb (0.6kg) HE projectile with a muzzle velocity of 2,800ft (854m) per second, a weight of 6,124lb (2,778kg) in travelling order, on-mounting elevation and traverse angles of –5 to +90 degrees and 360 degrees total respectively, a cyclic rate of fire of 120 rounds per minute, and a maximum ceiling of 18,600ft (5,669m). The weapon was to have been replaced by the 40mm Anti-aircraft Gun M1 (the American licence-built version of the classic Swedish Bofors weapon), but supplies of this more advanced equipment never matched demand and production of the 37mm M1 was therefore continued. Experience showed that gunners tended to use tracer as a means of aiming the gun, and this expensive practice was therefore mitigated by combining the 37mm M1 gun with two 0.5in tracer-firing machine guns on the Combination Mount M54, which proved highly effective.

There was then a considerable calibre gap to the next size of American anti-aircraft gun, the 3in Anti-aircraft Gun M3 on Mount M2. This was the culmination of American use of the 3in calibre for anti-aircraft purposes from a time in World War I, and the M3 introduced a semi-automatic breech block as well as a large 'spider' firing platform stabilised by outriggers. The details of this weapon, which was obsolete by 1940 but used operationally in the Philippines during the Japanese invasion of those islands from December 1941, included an L/50 barrel firing a 12.8lb (5.8kg) HE projectile with a muzzle velocity of 2,800ft per second, a weight of 16,800lb (7,620kg) in travelling order, on-mounting elevation and traverse angles of –1 to +80 degrees and 360 degrees total respectively, and a maximum ceiling of 31,200ft (9,510m).

The successor to the 3in anti-aircraft gun in American service was the 90mm (3.54in) Anti-aircraft Gun M1 on Mount M1. Development of this weapon began in 1938, and the type was standardised for service in March 1940 as a highly effective if somewhat cumbersome weapon whose entry into service was delayed by the manufacturing complexity of the gun and the high precision of its fire-control system. The details of this weapon included an L/50 barrel firing a 23.4lb (10.6kg) HE projectile with a muzzle velocity of 2,700ft (823m) per second, a weight of 19,020lb (8,626kg) in travelling order, on-mounting elevation and traverse angles of 0 to +80 degrees and 360 degrees total respectively, and a maximum ceiling of 39,500ft (12,040m).

In July 1941 the US Army decided that its high-velocity anti-aircraft guns should also be capable of undertaking the anti-tank role in the fashion pioneered by the Germans with their 88mm weapons, and the immediate result was the Mount M2 to provide the 90mm Gun M1 with a genuinely mobile four-wheel carriage and a maximum depression angle. Design work began in September 1941 and the Mount M2 was standardised in May 1943 with a development of the 90mm Gun M1 as the Gun M2 with the M20 fuse setting and ramming system as well as a modified recoil system. Production of the 90mm Guns M1 and M2 lasted to August 1945 and totalled 7,831, and

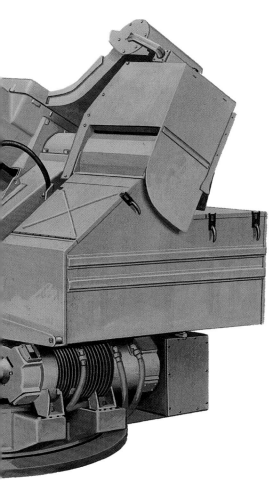

the details of the Gun M2 on mount M2 included an L/50 barrel firing a 23.4lb HE projectile with a muzzle velocity of 2,700ft per second, a weight of 32,300lb (14,651kg) in travelling order, on-mounting elevation and traverse angles of −10 to +80 degrees and 360 degrees total respectively, and a maximum ceiling of 39,500ft.

Of the American anti-aircraft guns used in World War II, that of largest calibre was the 120mm (4.72in) Anti-aircraft Gun M1 on Mount M1. The carriage had two axles with four twin-tyred wheels, and among the other features of this equipment, which was mostly retained in the USA for home defence, was two-piece ammunition loaded with the aid of a combined fuse setting and power ramming system. The details of this weapon included an L/60 barrel firing a 50lb (22.7kg) HE projectile with a muzzle velocity of 3,100ft (945m) per second, a weight of 61,500lb (27,896kg) in travelling order and 48,900lb (22,180kg) in firing position, on-mounting elevation and traverse angles of −5 to +80 degrees and 360 degrees total respectively, and a maximum ceiling of 56,000ft (17,070m).

The smallest calibre used by the Soviets for the dedicated anti-aircraft role was 25mm, and in this calibre there were three weapons, namely the 25mm Anti-Aircraft Gun Models 1939, 1940 and 1941. That made in the largest numbers, and of which the greatest amount is known, was the Model 1940 that appears to have been a development of a Bofors weapon that was carried on a carriage of four wheels that were raised as the mountings was stabilized in firing position by outriggers. The details of this weapon included an L/91.6 barrel fitted with a flash suppressor to fire an HE projectile of unrevealed weight with a muzzle velocity of 3,035ft (925m) per second, a weight of 2,370lb (1,075kg) in travelling order, on-mounting elevation and traverse angles of −10 to +85 degrees and 360 degrees total respectively, and a maximum ceiling of 15,010ft (4,575m).

Next up in calibre was the 37mm Anti-Aircraft Gun Model 1939, which appears to have been a reworking of the 40mm Bofors weapon revised to fire a clone of the 37mm Browning round from the USA. The equipment was based on a four-wheel carriage stabilized in firing position by outriggers carrying screw jacks, and among its other details was an L/74 barrel fitted with a flash suppressor to fire a 1.73lb (0.785kg) HE projectile with a muzzle velocity of 2,953ft (900m) per second, a weight of 4,630lb (2,100kg) in travelling order, on-mounting elevation and traverse angles of −5 to +85 degrees and 90 degrees total respectively, a rate of fire of 160 to 180 rounds per minute (cyclic) or 80 rounds per minute (practical), a maximum ceiling of 4,510ft (1,375m), and a crew of seven.

Complex, costly and beset by considerable teething problems, the 8.8cm FlaK 41 was the final member of Germany's 88mm (3.465in) series, and in service was a truly exceptional weapon offering magnificent anti-aircraft capability as well as a potent anti-tank facility that was seldom if ever used as the weapon was reserved for the defence of Germany's cities and industries.

Following this was the 76.2mm (3in) calibre, in which there were two equipments in the form of the Anti-Aircraft Gun Model 1931 and the Anti-Aircraft Gun Model 1938. The ordnances of the two equipments were basically similar, although a number of limited improvements was worked into that of the Model 38, so the primary differences lay in the equipments' carriages, which were a single-axle type for the Model 1931 and a two-axle type for the Model 1938. The details of the Model 1938 weapon included an L/55 barrel firing a 14.575lb (6.61kg) HE projectile with a muzzle velocity of 2,667ft (813m) per second, a weight of 9,283lb (4,210kg) in travelling order and 6,718lb (3,047kg) in firing position, on-mounting elevation and traverse angles of –3 to +82 degrees and 360 degrees total respectively, a maximum ceiling of 30,510ft (9,300m), and a crew of 11.

Another calibre used by the Soviets in the anti-aircraft role was 85mm (3.35in), and the two weapons in this calibre were the Anti-Aircraft Gun Model 1939 and Anti-Aircraft Gun 1944, alternatively known as the KS-12 and KS-18 respectively. Each of these equipments was carried on a two-axle carriage that was stabilized in firing position by four screw jacks, two of them on outrigger legs, and the details of the Model 1939 weapon included an L/55.2 barrel fitted with a multi-baffle muzzle brake to fire a 20.29lb (9.2kg) HE projectile with a muzzle velocity of 2,625ft (800m) per second, a weight of 9,305lb (4,220kg) in travelling order and 6,740lb (3,057kg) in firing position, on-mounting elevation and traverse angles of –2 to +82 degrees and 360 degrees total respectively, and a maximum ceiling of 34,450ft (10,500m). The Model 1944 was in essence an updated version of the Model 1939, and both weapons remained in service into the early 1980s.

The other two notable anti-aircraft guns used in World War II, and which also paved the way for their manufacturers' success with updated versions of these weapons as well as more advanced equipments since the end of World War II, were the 40mm Bofors gun from Sweden, and the 20mm Oerlikon cannon from Switzerland. Both weapons have been used in large numbers by a substantial number of countries, and were also made under licence by many nations for naval and land applications. The British Ordnance, QF, 40mm Bofors Mk I on Mounting Mk

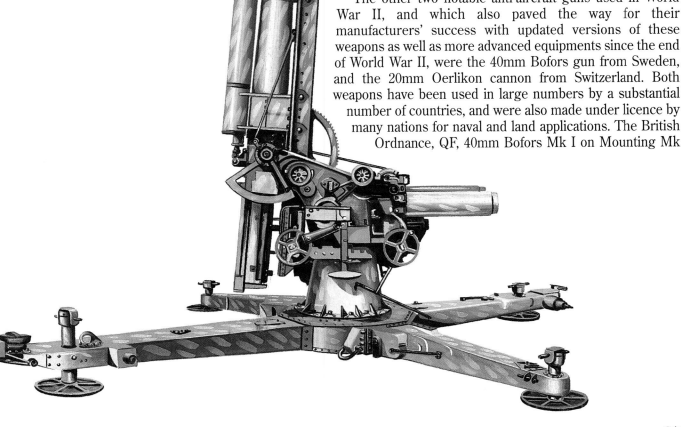

The FlaK 36 was, with the closely related FlaK 37, one of the two intermediate forms of the great family of German 88mm (3.465in) anti-aircraft guns that could also double with devastating capability in the anti-tank role.

III and Carriage Mk II, may be taken as typical of the type of Bofors guns used with such conspicuous success in World War II. The details of this weapon included an L/56 barrel fitted with a flash suppressor to fire a 1.96lb (0.89kg) HE projectile with a muzzle velocity of 2,800ft (853m) per second, a four-wheel carriage stabilised in firing position by four screw jacks (two of them on outriggers), a weight of 5,418lb (2,457kg) in travelling order, on-mounting elevation and traverse angles of –5 to +90 degrees and 360 degrees total respectively, a rate of fire of 120 rounds per minute (cyclic) or 60 to 90 rounds per minute (practical), a maximum ceiling of 23,600ft (7,195m), and a crew of five or six.

In the period after World War II, smaller-calibre anti-aircraft guns went out of favour with the exception of the 40mm Bofors weapon in its original L/56 and L/60 versions and later L/70 models, but then underwent a renaissance from the later 1950s as the medium- and high-altitude roles were assumed by guided missiles in place of the larger-calibre guns that had emerged from World War II and had been updated with a radar fire-control system. The smaller-calibre weapons were then seen to offer a capability against fixed-wing aircraft and, to an ever-increasing extent, rotary-wing machines that had come to exert a dominant effect on the land battlefield. Detailed below are some of the more important of these smaller-calibre weapons as well as a few medium-calibre weapons that were developed by the USSR and China.

The Czechoslovak 30mm M53 30mm is a twin anti-aircraft gun mounting with two L/81 barrels, a four-wheel carriage with outriggers but no shield, a weight of 4,630lb (2,100kg) in travelling order and 3,858lb (1,750kg) in firing position, on-mounting elevation and traverse angles of –10 to +85 degrees and 360 degrees total respectively, a rate of fire of 450 to 500 rounds per minute (cyclic) and 100 rounds per minute (practical) per barrel, and a horizontal range of 10,610yds (9,700m) maximum and a slant range of 3,280yds (3,000m) effective. This weapon entered service in the late 1950s, and offers considerable range advantages over Soviet towed 23mm equipments although it suffers from lack of radar fire-control, and is thus limited to clear-weather operation. Ammunition is fed by 10-round clips and the two basic ammunition types are HEI with a 0.99lb (0.45kg) projectile and AP-T with a 1.2lb (0.54kg) projectile able to pierce 55mm (2.16in) of armour at 545yds: both types are fired at a muzzle velocity of 3,281ft per second.

The French 20mm GIAT 76T2 Cerbère is a towed twin anti-aircraft gun mounting with two L/103.25 barrels, a two-wheel carriage with outriggers and a shield, a weight of 4,451lb (2,019kg) in travelling order and 3,336lb (1,513kg) in firing position, on-mounting elevation and traverse angles of –3.5 to +81.5 degrees in powered mode or –5 to +83 degrees in unpowered mode and 360 degrees total respectively, a rate of fire of 900 rounds per minute (cyclic) and 200 to 240 rounds per minute (practical) per barrel, a horizontal range of 6,560yds (6,000m) maximum and slant range of 2,185yds (2,000m) effective, and a crew of three. The equipment is a French development of the West German Rheinmetall MK 20 Rh 202 mounting with the original cannon replaced by two French GIAT M693 (F2) weapons. The type can be operated in the powered or manual modes, and there is a selectable dual-feed mechanism, ammunition supply amounting to 270 rounds per barrel. The Cerbère can be used with its on-mounting sight, or in conjunction with a radar fire-control system, or with a helmet-mounted target-indicator system.

Another French equipment, the 20mm GIAT 53T2 Tarasque is a towed twin anti-aircraft gun mounting with two L/103.25 barrels, a two-wheel carriage with outriggers and a shield, a weight of 1,852lb (840kg) in travelling order and 1,455lb (660kg) in firing position, on-mounting elevation and traverse angles of –8 to +83 degrees and 360 degrees total respectively, a rate of fire of 740 to 900 rounds per minute (cyclic) and 200 to 240 rounds per minute (practical), a horizontal range of 6,560yds maximum and slant range of 2,185yds effective, and a crew of three. Introduced in 1982, the Tarasque is a light anti-aircraft mounting (with secondary anti-AFV and anti-personnel capabilities) designed for rapid cross-country movement. The M693 (F2) weapon is hydraulically powered, and is dual-fed by belts for 100 HEI and 40 APDS rounds, the former having a muzzle velocity of 3,445ft (1,050m) per second and the latter of 4,242ft (1,293m) per second. The APDS projectile can penetrate 20mm (0.79in) of armour at a range of 1,095yds.

The German (formerly West German) 20mm Rheinmetall MK 20 Rh 202 is a towed twin anti-aircraft gun with two L/130.5 barrels, a two-wheel carriage with outriggers and a shield, a weight of 4,762lb (2,160kg) in travelling order and 3,616lb (1,640kg) in firing position, on-mounting elevation and traverse angles of –3.5 to +81.6 degrees in powered mode or –5.5 to +83.5 degrees in unpowered mode and 360 degrees total respectively, a rate of fire of 880 to 1,030 rounds per minute (cyclic) per barrel, a horizontal range of 3,280yds maximum and slant range of 2,185yds effective, and a crew of three or four. This twin-barrel light anti-aircraft equipment was produced to a West German specification, but has also been one of the most successful export weapons of its type as the designers found an excellent combination of accuracy (using a computerised optical sight), ammunition

Now obsolete as a result of its lack of armour and NBC protection, comparatively short range and limited fire-control system, the General Electric M163 was designed for battlefield protection of American mobile forces against air attack, and combined the M113 armoured personnel carrier with the M168 version of the General Electric Vulcan 20mm cannon, with a rotating assembly of six barrels to permit a rate of fire up to 3,000 rounds per minute. The type was used to devastating effect in the Vietnam War to break up infantry attacks and protect convoys against ambush.

One of the most powerful battlefield air-defence gun mountings currently in service, the Oerlikon-Bührle (now Oerlikon-Contraves) GDF combines two 35mm cannon on a powered mounting with any of several on-mounting computerised sight systems that can be cued with data from a higher-level source for earlier warning and other information.

supply and rates of traverse and elevation using an onboard power supply (a small petrol engine driving a hydraulic system). Each barrel has its own 270-round ammunition box, and there are another 10 rounds in the feed mechanism, the ammunition types being APDS-T, API-T, HEI and HEI-T fired at muzzle velocities of between 3,428 and 3,773ft (1,045 and 1,150m) per second.

The Israeli 20, 23 or 25mm RAMTA TCM Mk 3 is a towed twin anti-aircraft gun with two barrels whose length depends on the specific weapons installed, a two-wheel carriage with outriggers and a shield, a weight of 2,976lb (1,350kg) in towed configuration with 20mm Hispano-Suiza HS-404 cannon, on-mounting elevation and traverse angles of –6 to +85 in electrically powered mode or –10 to +90 degrees in manually operated mode and 360 degrees total respectively, a rate of fire of 700 rounds per minute (cyclic) and 150 rounds per minute (practical) per barrel with HS-404 cannon, a horizontal range of 6,235yds (5,700m) maximum and slant range of 1,315yds (1,200m) effective with HS-404 cannon, and a crew of three. This equipment entered service in 1984, and is essentially a product-improved TCM-20 with more modern assemblies (for greater reliability and less maintenance) plus a more advanced sight, the option of a night sight, and control by a computerised fire-control system with laser ranger. The same type of electric drive is used, and the accommodation of the weapons on special adaptors means that most types of 20, 23 and 25mm cannon can be installed. The mounting can also be fitted on the back of light armoured vehicles of the halftrack type still so favoured by the Israelis.

The Israeli 20mm RAMTA TCM-20 is a towed twin anti-aircraft gun with two barrels, a two-wheel carriage with outriggers and a shield, a weight of 2,976lb in travelling order with two loaded magazines, on-mounting elevation and traverse angles of –10 to +90 degrees and 360 degrees total respectively, a rate of fire of 700 rounds per minute (cyclic) and 150 rounds per minute (practical) per barrel, a horizontal range of 6,235yds maximum and slant range of 1,315yds effective, and a crew of three. Developed in Israel during the late 1960s, the TCM-20 is in essence an updated version of the US M55 mounting armed with two 20mm Hispano-Suiza HS-404 cannon rather than four 0.5in Browning M2HB heavy machine guns. The mounting is traversed and the weapon elevated by electric motors powered by two 12-volt batteries, the charge of the batteries being topped up by a small petrol engine. The type has built up an enviable combat record against low-flying aircraft, helicopters and light armoured vehicles, and can be installed on the back of vehicles such as the M2 and M3 halftracks. The two HS-404 cannon have been modified to use HS-804 ammunition (fed from 60-round drums) including APHE-T, APDS-T and HE-T. The type is optically controlled, but is often used with a radar warning system.

The 40mm Bofors 40L70 Type B is a towed anti-aircraft gun with an L/70 barrel, a four-wheel carriage with outriggers and a shield, a weight of 11,354lb (5,150kg) in travelling order, on-mounting elevation and traverse angles of –4 to +90 degrees and 360 degrees total respectively, a rate of fire of 240 or 300 rounds per minute (cyclic) in earlier and later models respectively, a horizontal range of 13,670yds (12,500m) maximum and slant range of 4,375yds (4,000m) effective, and a crew of four to six. The Bofors 40L70 Type A was introduced after World War II and remains one of the most powerful light weapons in the world (in both the surface-to-air and surface-to-surface roles) due to its high rate of fire (resulting from the use of an automatic breech and the ramming of each round during the run-out), good range and excellent ammunition. The Type A is the original model without on-carriage power, and weighs 10,582lb (4,800kg) in travelling order. The ammunition types are APC-T, HCHE, HE-T and PFHE fired at muzzle velocities of between 3,297 and 3,379ft (1,005 and 1,030m) per second, and the ammunition is fed in four-round clips into an optional overhead stay holding 26 rounds, and from two 48-round racks at the rear of

The ZRK Romb is a surface-to-air missile system for the short-range protection of mobile land formations, and is a self-contained equipment carried on a modified ZIL-167 6x6 truck chassis. The 'business' part of the system is carried on a turntable located on the upper decking, and comprises a single surveillance/target-acquisition radar and twin target-tracking/missile-guidance radars together with a bank of four SA-8 'Gecko' missiles delivered as certified rounds in sealed container/launchers. The system also includes an optical component (with a low-light-level TV camera) for continued capability when radar conditions have been degraded by physical conditions and/or the enemy's countermeasures.

the carriage. The Bofors 40L70 Type B is an improved model with an on-carriage power generator, but otherwise similar to the Type A and operated in local control by a gunner on the left of the ordnance. The Bofors 40L70 BOFI Fair Weather is a development of the Type B with Bofors Optronic Fire-control Instrument (BOFI) and proximity-fused ammunition. This model weighs 12,125lb (5,500kg) in travelling order, and the BOFI equipment uses a laser rangefinder, a day/night image-intensifying sight and a fire-control computer to generate aiming and firing instructions for the gunner, with early warning provided optionally by an off-carriage radar system. The Bofors 40L70 BOFI All Weather is a development of the Bofors 40L70 BOFI Fair Weather system with the addition of a pulse-Doppler radar for automatic target acquisition and tracking capability. This model has a travelling weight of 12,556lb (5,700kg). The Breda 40L70 is the Bofors 40L70 built under licence in Italy, where Breda has developed an optional automatic feeding device, which takes ammunition in groups of three from a magazine pre-loaded with 144 rounds in four-round clips. The travelling weight of the Breda equipment is 11,684lb (5,300kg) and there are other detail differences in dimensions.

The Swiss 35mm Oerlikon GDF-005 is a towed twin anti-aircraft gun with two L/90 barrels, a four-wheel carriage with outriggers and a shield, a weight of 16,975lb (7,700kg) in travelling order with ammunition, on-mounting elevation and traverse angles of –5 to +92 degrees and 360 degrees total respectively, a rate of fire of 550 rounds per minute (cyclic) per barrel, a horizontal range of 10,390yds (9,500m) maximum and slant range of 4,375yds (4,000m) effective, and a crew of three. This is the most advanced model of a family of four twin 35mm anti-aircraft gun mountings that are the heavyweight members of Oerlikon's complement of anti-aircraft cannon. The GDF-001 was introduced in the early 1960s as the 2 ZLA 353 MK, and is an exceptionally potent weapon capable of effective use in the surface-to-air and surface-to-surface roles with its HEI, HEI-T and SAPHEI-T ammunition fired at a muzzle velocity of 3,855ft (1,175m) per second from the two KDB (formerly 353 MK) cannon, which are fed automatically from two 56-round containers replenished in seven-round clips from the two 63-round reserve containers on the carriage. The mounting has three operating modes, namely remote electric control from the Super Fledermaus or Skyguard fire-control radar, local electric control with the Xaba optical sight, and local manual control with handwheels. The GDF-002 is the updated version available from 1980 with Ferranti Type GSA Mk 3 sights and digital data transmission. The type is also available with optional packages such as camouflage, automatic reloaders, a gunner's cab, integrated power source, and a Minisight Gun King incorporating a laser rangefinder. The GDF-003 is the GDF-002 equipment built with the full upgrade package. The GDF-005 is the most modern version with a Gun King optronic sight system and, as standard, all the updating features available optionally on the earlier marks.

The Swiss 25mm Oerlikon GBI-A01 is a towed anti-aircraft gun with an L/80 barrel, a two-wheel carriage with tripod legs but no shield, a weight of 1,468lb (666kg) in travelling order and 1,116lb (506kg) in firing position, on-mounting elevation and traverse angles of –10 to +70 degrees and 360 degrees total respectively, a rate of fire of 570 rounds per minute (cyclic) and 170 rounds per minute (practical), a horizontal range of 6,560yds maximum and slant range of 2,735yds effective, and a crew of three. Although designed primarily for anti-aircraft use, the manually-operated GBI-A01 mounting can be used against battlefield targets such as light AFVs, the Oerlikon KBA-C cannon being able to fire APDS-T projectiles at a muzzle velocity of 4,380ft (1,335m) per second, plus HEI, HEI-T, SAPHEI and SAPHEI-T projectiles at 3,609ft (1,100m) per second. These rounds are accommodated in two 40-round containers (one on each side of the weapon), a dual-feed mechanism allowing selection of round type.

The Swiss 20mm Oerlikon GAI-D01 is a towed twin anti-aircraft gun with two L/95.3 barrels, a two-wheel carriage with outriggers and a shield, a weight of 3,968lb (1,800kg) in travelling order and 2,932lb (1,330kg) in firing position, on-mounting elevation and traverse angles of –3 to +81 degrees in powered mode or –5 to +85 degrees in manually operated mode and 360 degrees total respectively, a rate of fire of 1,000 rounds per minute (cyclic) per barrel, a horizontal range of 6,235yds maximum and slant range of 1,640yds effective, and a crew of five. Designed in the mid-1970s as the Hispano-Suiza HS-666A and available from 1978, this equipment has successfully bridged the tactical gap between Oerlikon's single-barrel 20mm weapons and more capable equipments such as the twin-barrel 35mm GDF-002. The equipment is hydraulically powered, with reversion to manual operation in emergencies, and although intended primarily for anti-aircraft use can also be deployed for a number of battlefield roles. The two KAD-B cannon can fire AP-T, HEI, HEI-T, SAPHEI and SAPHEI-T ammunition (the first at a muzzle

The Chinese Type 59 towed anti-aircraft gun mounting is a copy of the Soviet 57mm S-60 equipment, and is wholly obsolete in the anti-aircraft role as a result of its optical sighting and poor rates of electrically powered elevation and traverse. The details of this equipment include an L/77 barrel with a muzzle brake, length of 28ft 2.65in (8.60m), weight of 10,538lb (4,780kg), elevation arc of between –5 and +87 degrees, traverse of 360 degrees, rate of fire of 100-120 rounds per minute (cyclic), muzzle velocity of 3,281ft (1,000m) per second to loft its HE projectile to a horizontal range of 13,125yds (12,000m) maximum and slant range of 6,560yds (6,000m) effective, and detachment of seven or eight.

velocity of 4,380ft (1,335m) per second, plus HEI, HEI-T, SAPHEI and SAPHEI-T projectiles at 3,609ft (1,100m) per second. These rounds are accommodated in two 40-round containers (one on each side of the weapon), a dual-feed mechanism allowing selection of round type.

The Swiss 20mm Oerlikon GAI-C04 is a towed anti-aircraft gun typical of the manufacturer's single-barrel equipments, and its details include an L/95.3 barrel, a two-wheel carriage with tripod legs but no shield, a weight of 1,299lb (589kg) in travelling order and 959lb (435kg) in firing position, on-mounting elevation and traverse angles of –7 to +83 degrees and 360 degrees total respectively, a rate of fire of 1,050 rounds per minute (cyclic), a horizontal range of 6,235yds maximum and slant range of 1,640yds effective, and a crew of three. Developed as the Hispano-Suiza HS-639-B3.1 and fitted with a KAD-B13-3 (formerly HS-820-SL7 A3-3) cannon, the baseline GAI-C01 is a manually operated equipment with weights (in travelling order and in firing position respectively, each with ammunition) of 1,177 and 816lb (534 and 370kg). The type fires the same ammunition as the GAI-D01, and is single-fed by a 75-round magazine on the right of the weapon, so limiting the type's

Above: This is the Chinese-built copy of the Soviet (now Russian) ZU-23-2 light towed anti-aircraft equipment with an armament of a side-by-side pair of 23mm cannon firing API or HEI rounds with a muzzle velocity of 3,182ft (970m) per second. The ammunition is carried in 50-round belts in boxes outside each weapon, and the equipment is designed only for clear-weather operations as it lacks anything but a simple optical sight, and its capabilities are further degraded in the anti-aircraft role by the fact that it is manually operated and therefore lacks the fast elevation and traverse rates to deal with modern high-performance aircraft.

Left: Based on the hull and automotive system of the Type 69-II main battle tank, the Chinese Type 80 self-propelled anti-aircraft gun system offers excellent mobility and good protection in its primary task of providing battlefield air defence for armoured formations but, like the Soviet (now Russian) ZSU-57-2 on which it was based, it has a distinctly limited simple optical sighting system. The turret-mounted armament comprises two 57mm Type 59 guns, each supplied with 300 rounds of 14.26lb (6.47kg) HE and 14.22lb (6.45kg) APC ammunition,.

utility in dual-role operations. The GAI-C03 was developed as the HS-639-B4.1 and is fitted with a KAD-A01 (formerly HS-820) anti-aircraft cannon. This equipment fires the same ammunition as the GAI-D01, although rounds are fed to the cannon from an overhead drum containing 50 rounds. The type has weights (in travelling order and in firing position respectively, complete with ammunition) of 1,124 and 952lb (510 and 432kg). The GAI-C04 was developed as the HS-639-B5 and is fitted with a KAD-B14 (formerly HS-820-SL7 A4) cannon. This is therefore an improved version of the GAI-C01 with a dual-feed mechanism and two 75-round magazines for greater capability in the surface-to-air and secondary surface-to-surface roles.

The Soviet 57mm S-60 is a towed anti-aircraft gun with an L/77 barrel with a 'pepperpot' muzzle brake, a four-wheel carriage with outriggers but no shield, a weight of 10,273lb (4,660kg) in travelling order and 9,921lb (4,500kg) in firing position, on-mounting elevation and traverse angles of –4 to +85 degrees and 360 degrees total respectively, a rate of fire of 110 rounds per minute (cyclic) and 70 rounds per minute (practical), a horizontal range of 13,125yds (12,000m) maximum and slant range of 4,375yds (4,000m) with on-carriage control or 6,560yds (6,000m) with off-carriage control, and a crew of seven. The S-60 was introduced in the late 1940s as a heavy tactical anti-aircraft weapon to replace the 37mm Model 1939. The equipment fires FRAG and APC ammunition (of the fixed type and fed in four-round clips) at a muzzle velocity of 3,281ft per second. Although it can be used with its on-carriage fire-control system, it is far more capable when used with 'Fire Can' or 'Flap Wheel' radar and appropriate director. Night vision sights have also been seen on the type, which can be operated manually or with servo-assistance.

The American 20mm General Electric (now Martin Marietta) M167 Vulcan is a multi-barrel towed anti-aircraft gun with an assembly of six L/76.2 barrels, a two-wheel carriage with outriggers but no shield, a weight of 3,500lb (1,588kg) in travelling order and 3,450lb (1,565kg) in firing

Known in the West as the ZSU-30-4 but in Russia as the 2S6 Tunguska, this is an extremely capable anti-aircraft system for the protection of important battlefield formations. The type is based on the fully tracked hull of the MT-S tracked command vehicle, carrying a fully traversing turret fitted with two types of armament (two 30mm cannon and eight SA-19 surface-to-air missiles) together with the advanced 'Hot Shot' fire-control system with surveillance radar, tracking radar and an optronic sight.

position, on-mounting elevation and traverse angles of –5 to +80 degrees and 360 degrees total respectively, a rate of fire selectable between 1,000 (surface-to-surface) or 3,000 (surface-to-air) rounds per minute, a horizontal range of 6,500yds (5,945m) maximum and slant range of 1,300yds (1,190m) effective, and a crew of one. The M167 is the towed version of the M163 self-propelled anti-aircraft gun, and although it features a capable fire-control system (with range-only radar and a lead-computing sight) and the formidable Vulcan six-barrel cannon plus 500 rounds of ammunition (AP and HEI fired at a muzzle velocity of 3,380ft/1,030m per second), the equipment is limited by the absence of external power and its lack of all-weather capability. The type has been improved in reliability and cross-country mobility by the addition of an extra wheel on each side.

Right: The Gepard is still one of the most powerful battlefield air defence systems available, and is a German and Swiss development with two extremely powerful 35mm cannon on the sides of a turret accommodating a highly capable radar-directed fire-control system and installed on the tracked chassis of the Leopard 1 main battle tank.

Below: The ZSU-57-2 is the Soviet original from which the Chine Type 80 was developed, and is a large and slow-traversing turret with two 57mm S-60 guns on the hull of the T-54 main battle tank.

Descended directly from the Bofors 40mm anti-aircraft guns of World War II, the Bofors 40L70 40mm gun is still an exceptional weapon for use against low-flying aircraft and lighter battlefield vehicles, as a result of its high performance with thoroughly modern ammunition and the fact that it can be fitted with an advanced sight system updatable from higher-level radars.

The Guided Missile

Throughout the greatest part of its history, right up to the period following World War II, two of the primary problems with artillery were inability to engage targets at very short range, and its relative lack of accuracy at longer ranges: these two factors combined to reduce the overall military utility of heavy artillery, and to make the destruction of long-range targets expensive in terms of the number of rounds of ammunition that had to be fired before the target had been destroyed. For these reasons, therefore, a desire was often expressed for the creation of a weapon that offered greater accuracy than artillery for the probability of the destruction of specific targets at long range.

The first practical expression of this desire was the 'locomotive' torpedo brought to a practical level by Robert Whitehead in 1868. This may truly claim to be the precursor of the modern guided missile, for it combined moderately long range and considerable destructive power in a single weapon made significantly more accurate than any of its predecessors by an onboard guidance package comprising a gyroscopic platform for course-keeping and any one of several depth-keeping systems for control of the weapon's running depth under the water. By the end of the nineteenth century, the torpedo had been brought to a high state of capability for launch firstly by surface ships and later by submarines, and then during the course of World War I by the aeroplane.

In its basic form, the torpedo had no terminal guidance system, for there were no cybernetic systems on which any real form of terminal guidance could have been based. Before it was fired, the weapon therefore relied on the insertion of the parameters of its own launch position and the expected interception point.

The same basic concept was used in the first aerial guided missile to reach the hardware stage after design as a surface-to-surface bombardment weapon. This was the Delco/Sperry Bug designed in 1917 for the US Army as a small aeroplane-type weapon that was capable of delivering a 300lb (136kg) warload over a range of some 62 miles (100km) with a fair degree of accuracy, as a result of its guidance by a Sperry system using an altimeter for longitudinal control, a primitive gyroscopic platform for lateral and directional control, and an engine revolution counter for range control. The 'missile' was a small biplane made of wood-reinforced papier maché with a card skin, and was powered by a 40hp (29.8kW) Ford petrol engine. Plans were laid for the type's mass production as a bombardment weapon for use on the Western Front, but the Armistice of November 1918 ended hostilities before the type could be placed in large-scale production.

A number of experimental types, designed to achieve the same basic function of surface-to-surface bombardment and also a limited surface-to-air capability against German airships, were built in the UK under the cover designation Aerial Target by a team under the supervision of Professor A.M. Low at the RFC Experimental Works and then the Royal Aircraft Factory at

Farnborough. These types lacked the gyroscopic control system and were therefore designed for command guidance by radio.

Germany undertook the experimental development of remotely piloted glide bombs in the course of World War I. Resulting from an initiative of Dr Wilhelm von Siemens of the Siemens-Schuckert Werke, these SSW types were tested in 1915 as glide bombs with guidance commands transmitted to the control surfaces (powered by an onboard battery), via fine copper wires that were unreeled as the weapon departed from its launch aeroplane. The concept was fully and successfully evaluated in a number of monoplane and biplane test models, but plans to use such glide bombs were overtaken by Germany's defeat.

Other such types were mooted in the 1920s and early 1930s by far-sighted designers, but foundered on a dearth of military enthusiasm for such weapons at a time of straitened finances, and on the lack of a powerplant

Based on the hull of the M113 armoured personnel carrier, the BAe Tracked Rapier is one of the world's best short-range surface-to-air missile systems, and carries eight Rapier 'hittiles' (missiles so accurate that they generally hit the target directly and therefore carry only a vestigial explosive warhead) together with the surveillance radar, optronic sight and microwave missile guidance link.

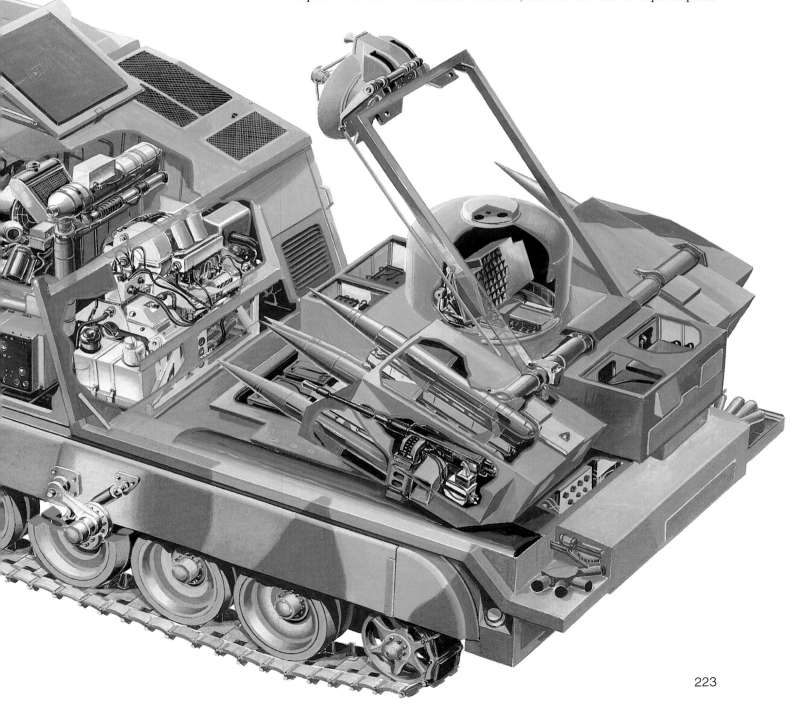

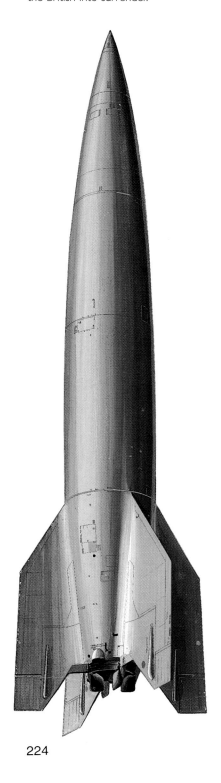

The first ballistic missile to enter service anywhere in the world, the Peenemünde A-4 is better known by its Nazi designation of V-2, and was used in moderately large numbers during the closing stage of World War II as the Germans tried to terrorise the British into surrender.

other than the piston engine whose use would result in a weapon that was not appreciably faster than current warplanes and was therefore comparatively simple to intercept and shoot down. The turning point in the concept of the guided missile, from being a feasible but not necessarily practical or desirable weapon, came in the mid-1930s with the rise to power in Germany of the Nazi party and the first development of effective reaction-type engines such as the turbojet, pulsejet and rocket motor. The German military at last began to appreciate that unmanned but guided weapons using such reaction motors offered hitherto unrealisable performance, and the leaders of the Nazi party saw the opportunity not only to redress the overall weight of the military balance in favour of Germany – which was denied the right to develop advanced weapons during the currency of the Treaty of Versailles that had signalled Germany's defeat in World War I – but also to overtake Germany's potential enemies through the mass production of weapons that resulted from the German 'genius'.

A major development effort was started in the later 1930s and during the first years of World War II, and from 1942 was progressed as a matter of high priority as Germany's conventional forces were checked for the first time in the nation's aggressive quest for territorial and political expansion, and particularly as the Allied powers began to drive the German forces back towards Germany.

The German research and development effort had strategic as well as tactical ambitions, the two strategic weapons to enter large-scale service being the Fieseler Fi 103 flying bomb or cruise missile, and the Peenemünde A-4 ballistic missile.

The first guided missile to be used operationally in large numbers, the Fi 103 was a pilotless flying bomb for the bombardment of large urban areas. Development of the weapon was authorised in June 1942, and the Fi 103 began to take shape under the leadership of Dipl.-Ing. Robert Lusser as an aeroplane-shaped weapon with a circular-section fuselage carrying, from nose to tail, the master magnetic compass, the warhead, the fuel tank, the two high-pressure air tanks used to power the control surfaces and feed the fuel to the engine, the battery, the master gyro assembly and guidance package, and the pneumatic servos controlling the elevators and rudder. The rest of the airframe comprised the flying surfaces, which included the cantilever mid-set wing and a plain tail unit whose vertical surface provided the rear support for the pulsejet engine whose forward end was carried by a pylon over the battery section.

The first unpowered test vehicle was launched from a Focke-Wulf Fw 200 Condor motherplane in December 1942, and the first powered ground launch took place later in the same month. There were a number of development problems, but the weapon was ready for use in the summer of 1944 after some 300 Fi 103s had been fired in trials. The weapon was dubbed V-1 (Vergeltungswaffe-1, or reprisal weapon-1) by the Nazi party, and the first was fired against London on 12 June 1944.

The offensive that followed saw the launch by the Luftwaffe of 8,617 standard missiles against London and other British targets in the period up to the end of August 1944, when the programme was taken over by the German army, which fired 11,988 weapons against a range of European targets in the period up to the end of March 1945. Another version of the weapon had wooden wings and a smaller warhead for longer-range attacks, and 275 of these weapons were fired by the SS against British targets between January and March 1945. Finally, the Luftwaffe fired 865 missiles from adapted Heinkel He 111 bombers between September 1944 and March 1945.

Generally known by its Nazi designation V-2 (Vergeltungswaffe-2, or reprisal weapon-2), the A-4 weapon was in every respect a prodigious

The SD-1400 X, otherwise known as the 'Fritz-X', was the first guided weapon to achieve a major success, for it was a weapon of this guided glide bomb type that was used to sink the Italian battleship *Roma* in September 1943. The weapon was basically a heavy armour-piercing bomb fitted with wings and a tail unit, the latter carrying the spoiler-type controls that were activated via a radio link from the operator in the launch aeroplane.

achievement for its period, and marked the emergence of the ballistic missile as a new type of weapon for strategic purposes. The unsuccessful first launch was attempted in June 1942, the successful second launch following in August. There were considerable development difficulties with the missile, and no fewer than 265 test launches were made before the type entered service. The weapon was based on a tapered circular-section body carrying, from top to bottom, the warhead, the guidance package of gyroscopes and integrating accelerometers, the tank for 8,311lb (3,770kg) of alcohol fuel, the tank for 10,802lb (4,900kg) of liquid oxygen oxidant, the fuel and oxidant turbopumps powered by hydrogen peroxide and calcium permanganate, and the rocket motor. Round the base of the missile was a cruciform of swept fins each carrying a control surface, and four graphite vanes were fitted in the exhaust to control the missile by vectoring the thrust of its engine before the weapon had reached a speed at which the aerodynamic control surfaces became effective. The first A-4 was fired operationally on 8 September 1944, and in a programme that lasted to 27 March 1945, a total of 3,165 A-4s was fired against British and European targets.

The Germans also expended considerable but not altogether successful effort in the creation of a number of tactical missiles of the air-to-air, surface-to-air and air-to-surface types. It was only weapons of the last category that reached operational service, and then only in limited numbers and mainly for the anti-ship role. The two most important of these weapons were the Ruhrstahl SD-1400 X and Henschel Hs 293. Otherwise known as the X-1, Fritz-X or FX-1400, the SD-1400 X was designed by Max Kramer for a first test launch in 1942, and scored its greatest success on 9 September 1943 when two such weapons hit and sank the Italian battleship *Roma* as she was steaming to Malta after the Italian armistice with the Allies: each weapon was a guided version of the SD-1400 armour-piercing bomb with an arrangement of four fixed wings on the centre of gravity and a lengthened tail section carrying an ovoid ring tail embodying spoiler controls that moved under control of the operator in the launch warplane. This weapon was fully practical in the technical and operational senses, but only about 100 of the type were used in real missions because of losses to the launch warplanes, which were heavily laden and vulnerable when flying to the target area, and then slow and vulnerable as they cruised in the target area during the attack, for which the operator used the standard Lofte 7 bombsight as the pilot flew straight and level until weapon impact. A variant with Telefunken FuG 208/238 wire command guidance did not enter service.

The Germans displayed a keen interest in the development of stand-off weapons even before the outbreak of World War II, and one of the first fruits of this enthusiasm was the Hs 293A air-to-surface missile designed under the leadership of Herbert Wagner. The core of the weapon was a standard 551lb (250kg) SC-250 bomb to which were added a mid-set wing of the constant-chord type with inset ailerons and also a cumbersome tail unit that was designed to accommodate the autopilot and guidance package (not yet available) as well as the horizontal tail surface, the deep ventral portion that stabilized the missile in the directional plane even though there was no rudder, and the large flare that facilitated optical tracking of the missile by its operator. It was in this form as a glide bomb that the weapon was first tested, but then a powerplant was added in the form of a Walter liquid-propellant rocket extended below the body of the weapon on short struts and exhausting obliquely downward and to the rear.

The first warplane selected as launch type for the Hs 293A initial production model was the Dornier Do 217E bomber, and the relevant aircraft were modified with an operator position in the starboard side of the forward crew compartment. This meant that the Hs 293A had to be released as the launch warplane paralleled the course of the target off to its right, and that the pilot had to hold a steady course as the operator kept the flare on the tail of the missile superimposed over the target image until impact. The Hs 293A was used operationally over the Mediterranean, Atlantic Ocean and North Sea (its first success was the sinking of the British sloop *Egret* on 25 August 1943 in the Bay of Biscay), and a number of the missiles were also expended in attempts to destroy the bridges being used by the Soviets to cross the Rivers Vistula and Oder in the spring of 1945.

Variants of the Hs 293 series that proceeded no further than the prototype or project stage were the Hs 293B with the Staru FuG 207/237 wire-guidance system; the Hs 293C intended to penetrate under the surface of the sea before hitting the underside of a target ship's hull; the Hs 293D with Fernseh TV guidance; the Hs 293E with spoiler controls; the Hs 293F proposed tailless model; and the He 293H with the Schmidding 109-503 or Schmidding 109-512 rocket motor for carriage by the Arado Ar 234 Blitz jet-powered bomber.

Another essentially simple but nonetheless far-sighted weapon developed in Germany during World War II, the Henschel Hs 293 was an air-to-surface missile with flying surfaces for extended range, rocket propulsion for moderately high performance, and radio for command guidance.

The type of tactical missile into which the greatest effort went was the surface-to-air type, for it was with such weapons that the Germans thought they could stem and possibly even defeat the Allied bombing effort that was destroying Germany's urban areas, communication arteries, and industrial capacity.

Although none of them entered service, the most important of these weapons were the Henschel Hs 117 Schmetterling (butterfly), Messerschmitt Enzian (gentian), Peenemünde Wasserfall (waterfall) and Rheinmetall Rheintochter (Rhine daughter). The Hs 117 was the German surface-to-air missile that came closest to operational service, and had its origins in the Hs 297 design study undertaken by Professor Wagner in 1941. The weapon was based on an aeroplane-shaped structure that was boosted by two strap-on solid-propellant rockets that fell away after exhausting their propellant, leaving the missile to fly the rest of its mission on its liquid-propellant sustainer. The operator had to have a clear line of sight to the target (although radar guidance was later incorporated into the system), and steered the missile via a radio command system. Trials began in May 1944, and full production was authorised in December 1944, the first weapon being on the verge of service when Germany surrendered in May 1945.

The Enzian was a ramp-launched surface-to-air missile based on the aerodynamics of the Me 163 Komet rocket-powered point interceptor, and was controlled by elevons responding to operator commands via a radio link. Some 38 test missiles were fired with varying degrees of success before the programme was cancelled in January 1945.

The Wasserfall was one of the most advanced surface-to-air missiles developed in Germany during World War II and was a supersonic weapon based on the aerodynamics of the A-4 (V-2) ballistic missile with a cruciform of small mid-set wings. The guidance system was notably complex and caused many problems with the development of this potentially excellent weapon, and the programme was further delayed by design modifications. The first attempt at a test launch in January 1944 ended with the explosion of the missile on its pad, but the second launch attempt was successful in the following month. Some 35 missiles had been launched in the development programme before Peenemünde was evacuated during February 1945 in the face of a Soviet advance.

The Rheintochter was an ambitious two-stage surface-to-air missile based on an extremely powerful booster stage with four swept and braced fins, and

The Soviet SS-N-6 'Serb', seen here in the course of one of the USSR's major military parades, is typical of modern strategic missile design in general and submarine-launched ballistic missile design in particular.

a less powerful sustainer stage with a cylindrical body carrying six swept wings at its rear and a cruciform of all-moving control surfaces at its nose. The first Rheintochter I missile was fired from a converted 88mm (3.465in) anti-aircraft gun mounting in August 1943, and used command-to-line-of-sight guidance. The Rheintochter I programme was abandoned in December 1944 after the firing of 82 missiles and was replaced by the Rheintochter III with laterally mounted booster rockets. This programme was abandoned after the firing of a few development missiles.

In the air-to-air category, Germany developed two missiles as the Henschel Hs 298 and Ruhrstahl X-4. The Hs 298 was the world's first air-to-air missile to reach the hardware stage before the programme was terminated in December 1944, and was an aeroplane-configured weapon with an oval-section pod-and-boom body, slightly swept wings and a tail unit with underslung endplate vertical surfaces outboard of the efflux of the rocket motor installed in the lower part of the pod to exhaust under the boom. Guidance was provided by a radio command system. The most advanced missile developed by the Germans in World War II was the Kramer-designed X-4 that was based on a circular-section body tapered fore and aft of the cruciform of swept wooden wings. Propulsion was entrusted to a liquid-propellant rocket motor exhausting through a nozzle inside the small cruciform of tail-mounted fins each carrying a control surface, and guidance was provided by commands transmitted to the missile from an

The first major type of submarine-launched ballistic missile (SLBM) developed in the USSR was the SS-N-8 'Sawfly' designed for carriage in the 'Yankee' class of submarines, which each possessed two side-by-side rows of eight missile tubes abaft the sail.

Although much discussed at the time of its first appearance in the mid-1960s, the SS-10 'Scrag' did not enter Soviet service but was important in the development of the SS-18 intercontinental ballistic missile (ICBM).

Early surface-to-air missiles, especially those intended for the high-altitude interception of strategic bombers, tended to be large and also required a significant technical infrastructure as well as major radar installations for target acquisition and tracking and then missile guidance. Typical of such missiles are two American types, the Nike Ajax (elevated) and Nike Hercules (flat).

operator in the launch aeroplane via two copper wires unwound from bobbins at the tips of two opposing wings on the missile.

The effect of these German weapons was immense, and the victorious Allies made every effort to seize German missile development centres with all their research and design data, and also to secure the services of German missile designers and engineers. The two most successful of the Allies in the garnering of this advantage were inevitably the USSR and the USA, and this gave the two countries an immense boost in the development of such weapons during the late 1940s and early 1950s. Both countries had been involved in missile development to a limited degree during World War II, but the only missile to emerge as an operational type was an American air-to-surface weapon, the ASM-N-2 Bat designed to provide the Consolidated PB4Y Privateer with a potent anti-ship capability as well as the ability to destroy point targets such as bridges. A few examples of this unpowered glide bomb type were used successfully in 1945: the weapon was based on an aeroplane-type airframe with a high-set wing and a low-set tail unit whose horizontal surface carried endplate vertical surfaces, and four slipstream-driven generators supplied electrical power for the weapon's systems and for the control package, which was based on an autopilot supplemented by Western Electric semi-active radar for the terminal phase of the flight.

Development of missiles in versatility and overall capability since the end of World War II has resulted in the guided missiles that are now widely employed in the primary surface-to-surface (land strategic, land tactical, sea strategic and sea tactical), air-to-surface (strategic and tactical), and surface-to-air roles. Below are discussed a number of the more important weapons in these categories, listed by country of origin in alphabetical order.

Designated CSS-1 in the US terminology for Chinese weapons, the Dong Feng-2 (East Wind-2) is a simple single-stage medium-range ballistic weapon that was China's first strategic missile and introduced in 1970. It is based on the technology of the Soviet SS-3 'Shyster', itself based generally on the German A-4 (V-2) of World War II. The type remains in Chinese service (some 50 such weapons), but has only very limited value with details that include a length of 74ft 9.6in (22.80m), weight of 57,319lb (26,000kg), propulsion by one liquid-propellant rocket, range of 746 miles (1,200km), CEP of 3,040yds (2,780m), warhead of one 15/20-kiloton nuclear or conventional RV in early examples or 1/3-megaton thermonuclear RV in later examples, radio-updated inertial guidance, and hot launch from a fixed pad.

The Dong Feng-3, otherwise known as the CSS-2, is another single-stage intermediate-range ballistic missile (IRBM) whose details include a length of 67ft 7in (20.60m), weight of 59,524lb (27,000kg), propulsion by one storable liquid-propellant rocket, range of 1,988 miles (3,200km), CEP of 1,520yds (1,390m), warhead of one ⅓megaton thermonuclear RV in early examples or three 100-kiloton nuclear multiple independently targeted re-entry vehicles (Mirvs) in later examples, radio-updated inertial guidance, and hot launch from a fixed pad. The DF-3 was introduced in 1971, and is based on Soviet technology using storable hypergolic propellants. Some 60 such missiles are in service, and an alternative estimate puts range at 1,680 miles (2,700km) with the megaton-class single warhead. The improved variant with Mirved warhead was first tested in 1986, and is a two-stage weapon. In 1988, China supplied some 60 modified DF-3s to Saudi Arabia, and these are of the DF-3A variant with an increased payload in the form of a large conventional warhead. The maximum payload is thought to by 4,510lb (2,045kg) of HE carried over a range of 1,680 miles.

The Dong Feng-4 (CSS-3) is a two-stage limited-range intercontinental ballistic missile (ICBM) whose details include a length of 87ft 11in (26.80m), weight of 110,229lb (50,000kg), propulsion by single storable liquid-propellant rockets in each stage, range of 4,350 miles (7,000km), CEP of 1,017yds (930m), warhead of one 2-megaton thermonuclear RV, inertial guidance, and hot launch from a silo. The DF-4 was introduced in 1978 and only a few such missiles remain in service. The type also forms the basis for the CZ-1 (Long March-1) series of satellite-launch vehicles.

The Dong Feng-5 (CSS-4) is a two-stage ICBM whose details include a length of 141ft 10.75in (43.25m), weight of 445,326lb (202,000kg) including a 3,086lb (1,400kg) payload bus, propulsion by four storable liquid-propellant rockets each delivering 154,321lb st (686.45kN) in the first stage and one storable liquid-propellant rocket in the second stage, range of 6,214 miles (10,000km), CEP of 1,017yds (930m), warhead of one 4-megaton thermonuclear RV, inertial guidance, and hot launch from a silo. The DF-5 entered limited service in 1981, and has also been developed into the CZ-2 (Long March-2) two-stage and CZ-3 (Long March-3) three-stage satellite launchers. The Dong Feng-6, also known in the West as the CSS-4, is an improved version of the DF-5 but able to carry a 5-megaton thermonuclear warhead over a range of 8,078 miles (13,000km) and believed to be the genuine production version of the type.

The Dong Feng-7 (CSS-5) is a three-stage ICBM of which very little is known other than the fact that it carries up to 10 kiloton-range Mirved warheads, has inertial guidance and is hot launched from a silo. The DF-7 is China's latest and most capable ICBM with an advanced type of warhead, and its whole launch system is based on that of the CZ-3 satellite launcher, itself derived from the DF-4 ICBM.

Carried here by a vehicle based on the hull of the PT-76 light tank, the FROG series of unguided rockets were designed to provide long-range bombardment capability with nuclear, chemical or conventional warheads.

The American MGM-31 Pershing II was an operational-level surface-to-surface missile so accurate that it could be fitted with a very small nuclear warhead, as this was more than adequate to ensure the destruction of a target after almost pinpoint arrival.

The Aérospatiale SSBS S-3D is a French two-stage IRBM whose details include a length of 45ft 3.33in (13.80m), weight of 56,878lb (25,800kg), propulsion by one SEP 902 Herisson (P16) solid-propellant rocket delivering 121,252lb st (539.35kN) for 76 seconds in the first stage and one SEP Rita II (P6) solid-propellant rocket delivering 70,547lb st (313.81kN) for 52 seconds in the second stage, range of 1,864 miles (3,000km), CEP of 908yds (830m), warhead of one 1.2-megaton thermonuclear RV with penetration aids, Sagem/EMD inertial guidance, and hot launch from a silo. Designed as a successor to the SSBS S-2 during the 1970s, the SSBS S-3D mounts a higher-performance second stage on the first stage of the S-2, and entered service in 1980 in France's 18 IRBM silos. The improved TN-61 warhead is hardened against high-altitude nuclear explosions, and carries a new generation of penetration aids. Some estimates put the range as high as 2,175 miles (3,500km), and the weapon is to be phased out of service in the late 1990s as France concentrates its nuclear deterrent capability in its missile-launching submarines.

Israel is extremely reluctant to divulge any details of the country's ballistic missile programme, and indeed the first overt public information about such developments came only in July 1986, when the USSR warned Israel against the continued development of such weapons. It is thought that the programme began in the early 1960s, resulting in the Jericho I development weapon, produced with considerable technical aid from the French and capable of a range of between 280 and 404 miles (450 and 650km) with a 1,102lb (500kg) warhead, probably of the HE type although suggestions of a nuclear type should not be discounted. After the Franco-Israeli split of 1967, the programme was advanced by Israel and, from 1977, with financial support from Iran, resulted in the Jericho IIA, otherwise known as the Shavit and the basis of a surface-to-surface missile test-fired by South Africa in 1989. The Israeli weapon is now operational, and is probably

Seen here in the course of a test launch, the MSBS M-4 is one of the French navy's more important SLBMs.

based in the Negev desert close to the Dimona facility at which Israel's nuclear weapons are manufactured. The Jericho IIA is reported to possess a range of 932 miles (1,500km) and to carry a nuclear warhead, although test flights have revealed a possible range of 510 miles (820km) with a larger 1,653lb (750kg) conventional warhead. In the late 1980s it was thought that the Israelis had an improved Jericho IIB version under development, probably to carry a heavier warload over the same basic range.

The SS-4 'Sandal' was a Soviet single-stage medium-range ballistic missile whose details included a length of 74ft 8.5in (22.77m), weight of 59,524lb (27,000kg) with a 2,976lb (1,350kg) payload bus, propulsion by one liquid-propellant rocket, range of 1,243 miles (2,000km), CEP of 2,625yds (2,400m), warhead of one 1-megaton thermonuclear or HE RV, inertial guidance, and hot launch from a pad with reload capability when fired from unhardened sites. A development of the SS-3 'Shyster', the SS-4 entered service in 1958 and was later phased out in favour of the SS-20.

The SS-11 'Sego' is a two-stage lightweight ICBM whose details include a length 65ft 7.5in (20.00m), weights of between 99,205 and 105,820lb (45,000 and 48,000kg) depending on variant with a 2,205lb (1,000kg) payload vehicle in the Models 1 and 2 or a 2,502lb (1,135kg) payload vehicle in the Model 3, propulsion by single storable liquid-propellant rockets in each stage, range of 6,214 miles (10,000km) for the Model 1, 8,080 miles (13,000km) for the Model 2 and 6,585 miles (10,600km) for the Model 3, CEP of 1,530yds (1,400m) for the Model 1 and 1,215yds (1,110m) for the Models 2 and 3, warhead of one 950-kiloton thermonuclear RV in the Model 1, one 950-kiloton thermonuclear RV with penetration aids in the Model 2 and three 100/250-kiloton thermonuclear multiple re-entry vehicles (MRVs) in the Model 3, inertial guidance, and hot launch from a hardened silo with limited reload capability. The SS-11 is a highly capable weapon introduced in 1966, and is a third-generation light ICBM built in very substantial numbers. The Model 1 was distinguished by its single RV and medium range, while the Model 2 of the late 1960s had a single RV and advanced penetration aids, and the Model 3 was an improved operational variant deployed from 1973 with longer range and three MRVs. The Model 4 was a development model of the late 1970s with three or six low-yield Mirvs.

The SS-13 'Savage' is a three-stage lightweight ICBM whose details include a length of 65ft 7.5in (20.00m), weight of 74,955lb (34,000kg) with a 1,499lb (680kg) payload vehicle, three-stage propulsion by liquid-propellant rockets, range of 4,970 miles (8,000km), CEP of 2,025yds (1,850m), warhead of one 600-kiloton nuclear RV, inertial guidance, and hot launch from a silo. Deployed from 1969, the SS-13 is a third-generation light ICBM comparable to the US Minuteman but built and deployed only in small numbers. Other estimates of the type suggest a 750-kiloton warhead carried in a 992lb (450kg) payload vehicle over a range of 6,214 miles (10,000km).

The SS-17 'Spanker' is a two-stage lightweight ICBM whose details include a length of 78ft 9in (24.00m), weight of 143,298lb (65,000kg) with a 6,041lb (2,740kg) post-boost vehicle in the Models 1 and 3 or a 6,019lb (2,730kg) vehicle in the Model 2, two-stage propulsion by storable liquid-propellant rockets, range of 6,214 miles (10,000km) in the Models 1 and 3 or 6,835 miles (11,000km) in the Model 2, CEP of 480yds (440m) in the Model 1, 465yds (425m) in the Model 2 or 385yds (350m) in the Model 3, warhead of four 750-kiloton nuclear Mirvs in the Models 1 and 3 or one 6-megaton thermonuclear RV in the Model 2, inertial guidance, and cold launch from a hardened silo offering a reload capability. The SS-17 is a fourth-generation lightweight ICBM that was introduced in 1975. In its Model 1 form, the type is comparable in performance to the SS-11, but offers the decided strategic advantage of cold launch and thus the opportunity for rapid reload of the silo. The Model 2 was introduced in 1977, and differs from the Model 1 in having a single medium-yield RV and slightly longer range. The Model 3 was introduced in the early 1980s and differs from the Model 1 in having an improved guidance system for reduced CEP: the accuracy of the type enhanced the SS-17 family's capability against US missile silos and thus made it a powerful aspect of the counterforce balance between the USA and the USSR.

The SS-18 'Satan' is a two-stage heavyweight ICBM whose details include a length of 114ft 10in (35.00m), weight of 496,032lb (225,000kg) including the post-boost vehicle that weighs 16,667lb (7,560kg) for the Model 1, 16,733lb (7,590kg) for the Models 2 and 4, and 16,534lb (7,500kg) for the Model 3, two-stage propulsion by storable liquid-propellant rockets, range of 7,455 miles (12,000km) for the Model 1, 6,835 miles (11,000km) for the Models 2 and 4, and 9,940 miles (16,000km) for the Model 3, CEP of 465yds (425m) for the Models 1 and 2, 385yds (350m) for the Model 3 and less than 285yds (260m) for the Model 5, warhead of one 27-megaton thermonuclear RV for the Model 1, eight to ten 900-kiloton thermonuclear Mirvs for the Model 2, one 20-megaton thermonuclear RV for the Model 3, ten 500-kiloton thermonuclear Mirvs for the Model 4, and ten 1-megaton thermonuclear Mirvs for the Model 5, inertial guidance, and cold launch from a hardened silo offering a reload capability. The SS-18 was introduced in 1974 in its Model 1 form, and is a fourth-generation heavyweight ICBM. The weapon is the largest missile so far deployed, and is a truly prodigious weapon with range, accuracy and warhead making it primarily effective as a counterforce weapon against missile silos and buried command/communications centres. The Model 2 followed in 1976, this variant having a computer-controlled post-boost bus with eight or 10 Mirvs. The Model 3 was introduced in 1977, and offers greater range and accuracy than the Model 1 with a slightly smaller but still enormously formidable warhead. The Model 4 was introduced in 1979, and is a derivative of the Model 2 with greater accuracy and an improved post-boost bus carrying up to 14 Mirvs (usually 10 real weapons and four decoys, plus penetration aids). The Model 5 was introduced in the mid-1980s and is still relatively unknown, but is believed to have a range of 5,592 miles (9,000km) with a post-boost bus carrying ten 750-kiloton or 1-megaton thermonuclear Mirvs.

The SS-19 'Stiletto' is a two-stage lightweight ICBM whose details include a length of 73ft 9.5in (22.50m), weight of 171,958lb (78,000kg) with a post-boost vehicle weighing 7,540lb (3,420kg) for the Model 1, 7,011lb (3,180kg) for the Model 2 and 7,518lb (3,410kg) for the Model 3, two-stage propulsion by storable liquid-propellant rockets, range of 5,965 miles (9,600km) for the Model 1 or 6,215 miles (10,000km) for the Models 2 and 3, CEP of 425yds (390m) for the Model 1, 285yds (260m) for the Model 2 and 305yds (280m) for the Model 3, warhead of six 550-kiloton nuclear Mirvs in the Models 1 and 3 or one 10-megaton thermonuclear RV in the Model 2, inertial guidance, and hot launch from a hardened silo with limited reload capability. The SS-19 was introduced in 1975 in its Model 1 form as a lightweight ICBM successor (together with the SS-17) for the SS-11. The type features the same type of advanced guidance as the SS-17 and SS-18, the onboard computer being used either to correct the course (by removing any deviations from the planned norm), or to generate a new course if this is more efficient. Like the SS-17 and SS-18, the SS-19 incorporated the range, accuracy and warhead which made it primarily a counterforce weapon against US missile silos and buried command/communications centres. Introduced in 1978, the Model 2 has a single medium-yield RV and much improved accuracy while the Model 3, introduced in 1980, reverts to a

Currently the most advanced SLBM in the world, the Lockheed UGM-133 Trident II is notable for its long range, very considerable accuracy, and ability to carry a sizeable load of warheads and penetration aids. The type is carried only by the later units of the US Navy's 'Ohio' class submarines and also by the four units of the Royal Navy's 'Vanguard' class.

Mirved payload, but with better accuracy and range than the Model 1. It is believed that surviving Model 1 and 2 weapons were retrofitted to this standard, which could have operational- as well as strategic-level taskings.

The SS-20 'Saber' was a land-mobile IRBM whose details included a length of 54ft 1in (16.49m), weight of 79,365lb (36,000kg), two-stage propulsion by solid-propellant rockets, range of 2,485 miles (4,000km) for the Models 1 and 2 or 4,600 miles (7,400km) for the Model 3, CEP of 465yds (425m), warhead of one 650-kiloton nuclear or 1.5-megaton thermonuclear RV for the Model 1, three 150-kiloton nuclear Mirvs for the Model 2 or one 50-kiloton nuclear RV for the Model 3, inertial guidance, and cold launch from a wheeled transporter/erector/launcher (TEL) with reload capability. The SS-20 was based on the upper two stages of the SS-16 lightweight ICBM and was designed to replace the SS-4 and SS-5 missile systems in the intermediate role. The SS-20 began to enter service in its Model 1 form during 1977 and was a formidable system offering the advantages of good accuracy with tactical land mobility. The warhead was believed to be a 650-kiloton type, although many reports indicate a 1.5-megaton type; this more powerful variant may have entered only limited service. The Model 2 was also introduced in 1977, and offered comparable performance but increased tactical capability through the use of a Mirved warhead. The Model 3 was an increased-range variant with a single low-yield warhead, and may not have entered service.

The SS-24 'Scalpel' is a three-stage ICBM whose details include a length of 69ft 8.5in (21.25m), weight of 220,459lb (100,000kg) with a 7,992lb (3,625kg) post-boost vehicle, three-stage propulsion by solid-propellant rockets, range of 7,455 miles (12,000km) or more, CEP of 202yds (185m), warhead of up to ten 100-kiloton nuclear Mirvs, stellar/inertial guidance, and cold launch from superhardened silos or special railcars offering a reload capability. Entering service in the mid-1980s, the SS-24 was planned as the Soviet fifth-generation counterpart to the US Peacekeeper, and has also been developed for a mobile basing system using special railcars hidden in the tunnels of those parts of the rail network without overhead wires. The type probably entered development in 1974, and suffered a comparatively high number of failures in test launches that began in 1982; the type has been operational since 1985 in its silo-based form and since 1987 in its rail-based form, mainly in northern Russia around Arhangelsk, so it must be assumed that the failings have been overcome in the production weapon, which offers a formidable combination of range, accuracy and warhead. The West believes this missile to be so accurate, that yield estimates for each of the warheads has been reduced from 350 kilotons to 100 kilotons.

Developed as the MX, the Martin LGM-118 Peacekeeper is the USA's most advanced long-range ballistic missile, and as such it is a mighty four-stage weapon designed to deliver up to 10 independently targeted and highly accurate warheads over very long ranges.

The SS-25 'Sickle' is a three-stage lightweight ICBM whose details include a length of 59ft 0.67in (18.00m), weight of 81,570lb (37,000kg) with a post-boost vehicle weight of between 1,499 and 2,205lb (680 and 1,000kg), three-stage propulsion by solid-propellant rockets, a range of 5,590 miles (9,000km) or more, CEP of between 208 and 656yds (190 and 600m), warhead of one 550-kiloton nuclear RV or three/four 150-kiloton nuclear Mirvs, stellar/inertial guidance, and cold launch from a hardened silo or wheeled TEL vehicle offering a reload capability. The SS-25 is intended as an upgraded version of the SS-13 rather than a new design, but the result is a fifth-generation road-mobile weapon with great accuracy, considerably greater throw-weight, and the offensive capability of the US Minuteman lightweight ICBM. The type has largely replaced the SS-11, and is an outgrowth of the SS-13 and SS-16 programmes, the failure of the latter adding impetus to the development of the SS-25 from the early 1970s.

The Martin Marietta LGM-25C Titan II was an American two-stage heavyweight ICBM whose details included a length of 103ft 0in (31.39m), weight of 333,000lb (151,050kg) with a post-boost vehicle weighing 8,300lb (3,765kg) or more, propulsion by two Aerojet LR87-AJ-5 storable liquid-propellant rockets each delivering 216,000lb st (960.81kN) for the first stage and one Aerojet LR91-AH-5 storable liquid-propellant rocket delivering 100,000lb st (444.82kN) for the second stage, range of 9,325 miles (15,000km), CEP of 1,425yds (1,305m), payload of one 9-megaton W53 thermonuclear warhead and penetration aids carried in a single General Electric Mk 6 RV, AC/IBM inertial guidance, and hot launch from a hardened silo. The LGM-25C Titan II was the last of the USA's heavyweight liquid-propellant ICBMs to remain in service, which finished in October 1987 after the type had been introduced in 1962 as successor to the HGM-25A Titan I. The guidance systems were extensively upgraded in 1980 and 1981 to provide effective life into the late 1980s, and the W53 warhead used the same core as the B53 free-fall thermonuclear bomb.

The Boeing LGM-30F Minuteman II is a three-stage lightweight ICBM whose details include a length of 59ft 8.5in (18.20m), approximate weight of 70,000lb (31,750kg) with the TU-120 motor or 72,810lb (33,025kg) with the TU-122 motor and including a post-boost vehicle weighing 1,610lb (730kg), propulsion by one Thiokol M55 (TU-120) or M55A1 (TU-122) solid-propellant rocket delivering 200,600 or 202,600lb st (892.31 or 901.21kN) respectively, one Aerojet SR18-AJ-1 solid-propellant rocket delivering 60,000lb st (266.89kN) for the second stage and one Hercules M57A1 solid-propellant rocket delivering 35,000lb st (155.69kN) for the third stage, range of 7,775 miles (12,510km), CEP of 400yds (365m), payload of one 1.2-megaton W56 thermonuclear warhead carried in an Avco Mk 11C Model 4 RV with Tracor Mk 1A penetration aids, Rockwell Autonetics inertial guidance, and hot launch from a hardened silo. The LGM-30F Minuteman II is a second-generation lightweight ICBM that entered service in 1966, swiftly replacing the LGM-30A and LGM-30B variants of the original

Representing the older generation of American ICBMs, the Convair Atlas was the Western world's first ICBM and its design and development was completed in the period between 1955 and 1960, when this liquid-fuelled weapon reached initial operational capability with a single re-entry vehicle carrying a thermonuclear warhead.

Designed by French and West German (now German) interests, the Euromissile HOT is a heavyweight anti-tank missile that has been developed through three variants capable of defeating thicker and better designed armour. The missile is guided by a semi-automatic command-to-line-of-sight guidance system with commands passed to the missile via a trailing wire, and all that the operator (at a ground launching station or in an armoured fighting vehicle or helicopter) has to do is keep his sight centred on the target during the missile's flight.

Minuteman I type. The Minuteman II is a simple upgrading of the LGM-30B with more advanced guidance (including an eight-target selection capability and chaff-dispensing penetration aids) and greater range.

The Boeing LGM-30G Minuteman III is a three-stage lightweight ICBM whose details include a length of 59ft 8.5in (18.20m), weight of 78,000lb (35,380kg) including the 2,400lb (1,088kg) Mk 12 or 2,535lb (1,150kg) Mk 12A post-boost vehicles, propulsion by one Thiokol M55A1 (TU-122) solid-propellant rocket delivering 202,600lb st (901.21kN) for the first stage, one Aerojet SR18-AJ-1 solid-propellant rocket delivering 60,625lb st (269.67kN) for the second stage, one Aerojet/Thiokol SR73-AJ/AG-1 solid-propellant rocket delivering 33,800lb st (150.34kN) for the third stage and one Bell Aerospace bi-propellant rocket delivering 315lb st (1.40kN) for the post-boost vehicle, range of 8,700 miles (14,000km), CEP of 300yds (275m) with the Mk 12 RV or 240yds (220m) with the Mk 12A RV, payload of three 170-kiloton W62 nuclear warheads in three General Electric Mk 12 RVs, or three 335-kiloton W78 nuclear warheads in three Mk 12A Mirvs, both types with penetration aids, Rockwell Autonetics inertial guidance, and hot launch from a hardened silo. The LGM-30G Minuteman III Model 1 lightweight ICBM was introduced in 1970 as the third-generation companion to the second-generation Minuteman II, with an improved third stage and Mirved payload, whose Mk 12 bus contains both chaff- and decoy-dispensing penetration aids. The LGM-30G Minuteman III Model 2 was introduced in 1979 as an upgraded model with the improved Mk 12A RV with higher-yield warheads and more advanced penetration aids, made possible by miniaturisation of the warheads and RV components.

The Martin Marietta LGM-118A Peacekeeper is a four-stage heavyweight ICBM whose details include a length of 70ft 10.5in (21.60m), weight of 195,000lb (88,452kg) including the 7,935lb (3,600kg) post-boost vehicle, propulsion by one Thiokol solid-propellant rocket delivering 570,000lb st (2,535.48kN) for the first stage, one Aerojet solid-propellant rocket delivering 335,000lb st (1,490.15kN) for the second stage, one Hercules solid-propellant rocket delivering 77,000lb st (342.51kN) for the third stage and one Rockwell hypergolic liquid-propellant rocket for the fourth stage, range of 8,700 miles (14,000km), CEP of between 65 and 100yds (60 and 90m), payload of ten 335-kiloton W78 thermonuclear warheads carried in 10 Avco Mk 21 (Mk 12 Modified) Mirvs in a Rockwell RS-34 bus, Rockwell Autonetics/Honeywell/Northrop inertial guidance, and cold launch from a hardened silo offering a reload capability. The LGM-118A Peacekeeper was conceived as a replacement for the LGM-25 and LGM-30 series, and as such the Peacekeeper is a fourth-generation heavyweight ICBM. The type was greatly troubled by political opposition during its relatively smooth development life, but the missile, previously known as the Advanced ICBM or MX, entered service during 1986 in upgraded Minuteman silos because political pressure prevented any of the proposed mobile basing methods. The type's accuracy makes it a potent counterforce weapon.

Although China has a small number of submarine-launched ballistic missiles (SLBMs), these are wholly indifferent weapons used mainly for development purposes. The Aérospatiale MSBS M-4 is a French three-stage SLBM whose details include a length of 36ft 3in (11.05m), weight of 77,323lb (35,073kg), propulsion by one SEP 401 (P10) solid-propellant rocket delivering 156,526lb st (696.26kN) for the first stage, one SEP 402 (P6) solid-propellant rocket delivering 66,138lb st (294.20kN) for the second stage and one SEP 403 solid-propellant rocket delivering 15,432lb st (68.45kN) for the third stage, range of 2,796 miles (4,500km) with TN-70 warheads and 3,105 miles (5,000km) or more with TN-71 warheads, CEP of 503yds (460m), warhead of six 150-kiloton TN-70 or miniaturised TN-71 thermonuclear Mirvs, Sagem/EMD inertial guidance, and launch from a submarine tube. Becoming operational in 1985, the M-4 is of a wholly new French SLBM generation designed with considerably greater weight and dimensions for significantly deeper underwater launch depth and improved range with a Mirv bus hardened against electromagnetic pulse and carrying penetration aids. Range is improved with the miniaturised TN-71 warheads, and each system is designed to cover a target area of 217.5 miles (350km) by 93.2 miles (150km). Entering service in the mid-1990s on the new SSBN *Le Triomphant*, the M-4C is an advanced development of the M-4 with longer range, anti-ABM missile features and, probably, the new TN-75 warhead.

The Aérospatiale MSBS M-20 is a two-stage SLBM whose details include a length of 34ft 1.5in (10.40m), weight of 44,213lb (20,055kg), propulsion by one SEP 904 (P10) solid-propellant rocket delivering 99,206lb st (441.29kN) for 50 seconds in the first stage and one SEP Rita 11 (P6) solid-propellant rocket delivering 70,547lb st (313.81kN) for 52 seconds in the second stage, range of 1,864 miles (3,000km), CEP of 1,017yds (930m), warhead of one 1.2-megaton TN-60 thermonuclear device in an MR-60 RV, Sagem/EMD Sagittaire inertial guidance, and launch from a submarine tube. The MSBS M-20 medium-weight SLBM entered service in 1977 as successor to the first-generation M-2, which itself entered service in 1974 as an updated version of the M-1 that was introduced in 1971. The warhead is carried in a modified Rita 11/P6 second stage and is supported by penetration aids. The TN-60 warhead is hardened against the effects of high-altitude nuclear explosions.

The SS-12 'Scaleboard' is a strategic- and operational-level ballistic missile carried on an 8x8 MAZ-543P wheeled transporter/erector/launcher (TEL) and able to deliver its 800-kiloton nuclear warhead over a range of 497 miles (800km) with a CEP of only 33yds (30m).

Two Soviet (now Russian) different approaches to the provision of air defence to ground formations is provided by the ZRK Krug two-missile and ZRK Kub three-missile launchers. The Krug system uses the SA-4 'Ganef' area-defence missile with a sustainer ramjet taking over from four drop-away solid-propellant booster rockets for the delivery of a powerful blast/fragmentation warhead over a range of 31 miles (50km) against any target except one at very low altitude, while the Kub system uses the SA-6 'Gainful' area-defence missile with integrated rocket/ramjet propulsion for the delivery of a smaller blast/fragmentation warhead over a range of 37 miles (60km) against any low- and medium-altitude target. Both missiles have high supersonic performance, and use a mix of command guidance for the mid-course phase on any flight with semi-active radar guidance for the attack phase.

The Soviet SS-N-5 'Sark' is a two-stage SLBM whose details include a 42ft 3.75in (12.90m), weight of 37,477lb (17,000kg), two-stage propulsion by solid-propellant rockets, range of 870 miles (1,400km), CEP of 3,060yds (2,800m), warhead of one 1-megaton thermonuclear RV, inertial guidance, and launch from a submarine tube. Serving in the theatre nuclear role up to the late 1980s on board 13 'Golf II' class missile submarines, the SS-N-5 missile is comparable in many respects to the original version of the US Polaris SLBM, and began to enter service in 1964 as the Soviets' first SLBM with a genuine capability for underwater launch. It is not known with certainty if the type uses solid-propellant or storable liquid-propellant rockets for a range that some sources put as high as 1,490 miles (2,400km).

The SS-N-6 'Serb' is a two-stage SLBM whose details include a length of 32ft 9.75in (10.00m), weight of 41,667lb (18,900kg) including a 1,499lb (680kg) post-boost vehicle, two-stage propulsion by storable liquid-propellant rockets, range of 1,490 miles (2,400km) for the Model 1 and 1,865 miles (3,000km) for the Models 2 and 3, CEP of 2,025yds (1,850m), warhead of one 700-kiloton nuclear RV for the Model 1, or one 650-kiloton nuclear RV for the Model 2 or two 350-kiloton nuclear MRVs for the Model 3, inertial guidance, and launch from a submarine tube. The SS-N-6 Model 1 was introduced in 1970 as a hybrid second/third-generation SLBM using technology and components derived from the SS-11. The warhead size and comparatively poor CEP dictate the weapon's targeting against area targets. Introduced in 1973, the Model 2 trades throw-weight for range, the reduction of 50 kilotons in warhead yield providing an additional 373 miles (600km) of range to provide launch submarines with a larger operating area. The Model 3 was introduced in 1974 and combines the range of the Model 2 with a double warhead configuration for maximum effect against cities and other area targets.

The SS-N-8 'Sawfly' is a two-stage SLBM whose details include a length of 42ft 3.75in (12.90m), weight of 44,974lb (20,400kg) including a 1,499lb (680kg) post-boost vehicle, two-stage propulsion by storable liquid-propellant rockets, range of 4,845 miles (7,800km) for the Model 1 and 5,655 miles (9,100km) for the Model 2, CEP of 1,540yds (1,410m) for the Model 1 and 1,695yds (1,550m) for the Model 2, warhead of one 1.2-megaton nuclear RV for the Model 1 and one or two 800-kiloton nuclear MRVs for the Model 2, stellar/inertial guidance, and launch from a submarine tube. Introduced in 1971 on board 'Delta I' class SSBNs, the SS-N-8 Model 1 is a fourth-generation SLBM with good range but only moderate CEP despite the use of two stellar fixes to update the inertial guidance. Introduced in 1977, the Model 2 is a developed version carrying the same weight of warhead over greater range.

The SS-N-17 'Snipe' is a two-stage SLBM whose details include a length of 36ft 3.5in (11.06m), an unrevealed weight including a 2,502lb (1,135kg) post-boost vehicle, two-stage propulsion by solid-propellant rockets, range of 2,425 miles (3,900km), CEP of 1,530yds (1,400m), warhead of one 500-kiloton or 1-megaton thermonuclear RV, stellar/inertial guidance, and launch from a submarine tube. Introduced in 1977 on the sole 'Yankee II' class SSBN, the SS-N-17 was the first Soviet SLBM known to have solid-propellant rockets. It is also believed that the type has post-boost propulsion for manoeuvring in space, yet the CEP is still too great for the missile's use in anything but the countervalue role.

The SS-N-18 'Stingray' is a two-stage SLBM whose details include a length of 46ft 3.25in (14.10m), weight of 55,115lb (25,000kg), two-stage propulsion by storable liquid-propellant rockets, range of 4,040 miles (6,500km) for the Models 1 and 3 or 4,970 miles (8,000km) for the Model 2, CEP of 1,540yds (1,410m) for the Models 1 and 3 or 1,695yds (1,550m) for the Model 2, warhead of three 200-kiloton nuclear Mirvs for the Model 1, one 450-kiloton nuclear RV for the Model 2 and seven 200-kiloton nuclear Mirvs for the Model 3, stellar/inertial guidance, and launch from a submarine tube. The SS-N-18 Model 1 is a fourth-generation SLBM that entered service in 1976 aboard 'Delta III' class SSBNs, and was the first Soviet SLBM with a Mirved warhead. The Model 2 was introduced in 1979 and offers greater range with a payload

The AT-I 'Snapper' was the Soviets' first-generation anti-tank missile, and was a relatively simple weapon with command-to-line-of-sight guidance using commands passed to the missile via a trailing wire link.

reduced to one RV. The Model 3 was also introduced in 1979 as successor to the Model 1 with a load of seven smaller Mirvs.

The SS-N-20 'Sturgeon' is a three-stage SLBM with a length of 49ft 2.5in (15.00m), unrevealed weight, three-stage propulsion by solid-propellant rockets, range of 5,160 miles (8,300km), CEP of 547yds (500m), warhead of between six and nine 100/200-kiloton Mirvs, stellar/inertial guidance, and launch from a submarine tube. Introduced in 1981 as the primary armament of the huge 'Typhoon' class SSBN, the SS-N-20 entered development in 1973 as a fifth-generation SLBM of good range and advanced capabilities.

The SS-N-23 'Skiff' is a two-stage SLBM whose details include a length of 44ft 7.5in (13.60m), unrevealed weight, two-stage propulsion by storable liquid-propellant rockets, range of 5,160 miles (8,300km), CEP of 612yds (560m), warhead of seven 150-kiloton nuclear Mirvs, stellar/inertial guidance, and launch from a submarine tube. Introduced in 1985 aboard the 'Delta IV' class SSBN, the SS-N-23 is a capable fifth-generation SLBM notable for its good range and low CEP. Some estimates put the number of Mirvs as high as 10, and it is possible that the type will be retrofitted in the 'Delta III' class SSBNs as replacement for the shorter-ranged SS-N-18 series.

Now used only by the UK in its UGM-27C Polaris A3TK Chevaline form, the Lockheed UGM-27A Polaris was designed in the USA as the world's first SLBM. The details of this considerably updated British two-stage SLBM include a length of 32ft 3.5in (9.84m), weight of 35,000lb (15,876kg) including a 1,500lb (680kg) post-boost vehicle, propulsion by one Aerojet A3P solid-propellant rocket delivering 80,000lb st (355.86kN) for the first stage and one Hercules solid-propellant rocket for the second stage, range of 2,950 miles (4,750km), CEP of 1,015yds (930m), payload of three 200-kiloton W58 nuclear warheads carried in three MRVs plus an unknown number of decoys and penetration aids on the basic Penetration Air Carrier (post-boost bus), General Electric/MIT/Hughes/Raytheon Mk 2 inertial guidance, and launch from a submarine tube. As noted above, this is now the only version of the Polaris SLBM left in service, the missiles having been updated in the 'Chevaline' programme of the 1970s to carry (and instead of the original three British 200-kiloton warheads) several British MRVs capable of a 45 mile (72km) lateral separation. The warheads are hardened against electromagnetic pulse and fast radiation, and the warhead bus also contains chaff penetration aids and several decoys.

The Lockheed UGM-73A Poseidon C3 is a two-stage SLBM whose details include a length of 34ft 0in (10.36m), weight of 65,000lb (29,484kg) including the 3,300lb (1,497kg) post-boost vehicle, propulsion by two Thiokol/Hercules solid-propellant rockets for the first stage and two Hercules solid-propellant rockets for the second stage, range of 2,485 miles (4,000km) with 14 Mirvs or 3,230 miles (5,200km) with 10 Mirvs, CEP of 605yds (553m), payload of ten 40/50-kiloton W68 nuclear warheads carried in 10 Mk 3 Mirvs, or 14 W76 100-kiloton nuclear warheads carried in 14 Mk 3 Mirvs, General Electric/MIT/Hughes/Raytheon Mk 4 inertial guidance, and launch from a submarine tube. Introduced in 1970 as successor to the Polaris SLBM, the Poseidon marked an eightfold increase in target-devastation capability at the same range as its predecessor, the Poseidon's real advantages being much improved CEP and a Mirved payload.

The Lockheed UGM-96A Trident I C4 is a three-stage SLBM whose details include a length of 34ft 0in (10.36m), weight of 73,000lb (33,113kg) including a powered post-boost vehicle weighing more than 3,000lb (1,361kg), propulsion by one Thiokol/Hercules solid-propellant rocket for the first stage, one Hercules solid-propellant rocket for the second stage and one UTC-CSD solid-propellant rocket for the third stage, range of 4,230

The Aérospatiale Pluton was designed for French army use in the battlefield nuclear role, and is a small inertially guided surface-to-surface weapon carried in its container/launcher on an adapted AMX-30 main battle tank chassis for the delivery of a 15-kiloton nuclear warhead.

miles (6,810km), CEP of 500yds (457m), payload of eight 100-kiloton W76 nuclear warheads carried in eight Mk 4 Mirvs, Mk 5 stellar/inertial guidance, and launch from a submarine tube. The UGM-96A Trident I C4 was introduced in 1979 as the primary armament of the 'Ohio' class SSBNs and was also carried in a number of converted 'Benjamin Franklin' and 'Lafayette' class SSBNs. The Trident I is essentially the Poseidon SLBM with a third stage for greatly increased range and a more advanced warhead based on the Mk 4 Mirv, the bus being manoeuvrable in space for maximum accuracy. The Lockheed UGM-133A Trident II D5 entered service in the late 1980s as a much improved development for use in the 'Ohio' class SSBN. The type has a length of 44ft 6.6in (13.58m), launch weight of 130,000lb (58,968kg) and a range of 7,500 miles (12,070km). The first two stages have graphite-epoxy rather than Kevlar casings but contain the same basic motors as the Trident I with a burn time of about 65 seconds each, while the third stage has a United Technologies motor with a burn time of about 40 seconds for a burn-out speed of about 13,635mph (21,943km/h). The payload comprises 10 to 15 Mk 5 RVs each with one 335-kiloton W78 warhead, and guidance is entrusted to the Mk 6 stellar-inertial system offering a CEP as low as 130yds (120m). The Royal Navy's version will probably have eight British-designed warheads in a US-provided manoeuvring bus.

Surface-to-surface missiles also include shorter-range weapons intended for the operational- and tactical-level roles. The CPMIEC Model M is typical of the Chinese concept in such weapons, and is a single-stage surface-to-surface theatre/battlefield missile with a length of 29ft 10.25in (9.10m), weight of 13,668lb (6,200kg), propulsion by one solid-propellant rocket, range of up to 373 miles (600km), an HE/fragmentation warhead, inertial guidance, and launch from a wheeled TEL vehicle. This weapon has been developed with HE/fragmentation and submunition-dispenser warheads, although a tactical nuclear warhead is also a possibility. Flight trials apparently began in 1986, with service deliveries beginning in late 1988 or early 1989. Ranges between 124 and 373 miles (200 and 600km) are possible, and the export version is designated M-9.

The Aérospatiale Pluton is a French single-stage surface-to-surface battlefield missile with a length of 25ft 0.75in (7.64m), weight of 5,342lb (2,423kg), propulsion by one SEP/SNPE/Aérospatiale dual-thrust solid-propellant rocket, range limits of 6.2 and 75 miles (10 and 120km), CEP of 360yds (330m), a 772lb (350kg) 15-kiloton nuclear or 1,102lb (500kg) 25-kiloton AN-51 nuclear warhead, SFENA strapdown inertial guidance, and launch from a box on a converted AMX-30 MBT chassis. Designed in the late 1960s, the Pluton entered French service in 1974 and is a capable battlefield weapon with fair accuracy for use primarily against operational-level targets such as transport centres and follow-on troop concentrations; the larger warhead contains the same MR50 nuclear charge as used in the CEA-developed AN-52 free-fall store carried by French strike aircraft.

The Defence Research and Development Laboratory Prithvi is an Indian single-stage surface-to-surface battlefield missile of which few details are known. The type is powered by one solid-propellant rocket, has a maximum range of 155 miles (250km) and possesses strapdown inertial guidance. First revealed late in 1988, this is a weapon of odd appearance with a comparatively short and fat body, a cruciform of low-aspect-ratio wings half-way down the body, and a cruciform of tiny rectangular fins (indexed in line with the wings) at the tail. The type can be fitted with any of several types of conventional warhead, and there are suggestions that a nuclear warhead could be retrofitted.

The Ching Feng is a Taiwanese single-stage surface-to-surface battlefield missile with a length of 22ft 11.5in (7.00m), weight of 3,086lb (1,400kg), propulsion by one solid-propellant rocket, maximum range of 75 miles (120km), HE warhead and radar-based guidance system. This 'Green Bee' missile appears to be based conceptually on the US Lance, although the fins are somewhat smaller and a radar guidance system is used. The weapon was revealed in 1981 and has since been claimed to be the precursor of a more formidable missile with a 621 mile (1,000km) range, which may explain the apparent cancellation of the programme under pressure from the USA, which feared the strategic and political implications of Taiwanese possession of a potentially nuclear-capable missile system able to reach targets on the Chinese mainland.

The FROG-3 is a Soviet (now Russian) two-stage surface-to-surface battlefield unguided rocket rather than guided missile with a length of 34ft 5.5in (10.50m), weight of 4,960lb (2,250kg), propulsion by one non-jettisonable solid-propellant booster rocket and one solid-propellant sustainer rocket, maximum range of 25 miles (40km), CEP of 435yds (400m), warhead of one interchangeable 200-kiloton nuclear or 992lb (450kg) HE type, warheads, and launch from a converted PT-76 amphibious light tank chassis. Oldest of the Free Rocket Over Ground (FROG) series still in service, the FROG-3 was introduced in 1957 and now possesses little real value as its CEP is so great. The FROG-5 is an improved two-stage surface-to-surface battlefield rocket with a length of 29ft 10.25in (9.10m), weight of 6,614lb (3,000kg), propulsion by one non-jettisonable solid-propellant booster rocket and one solid-propellant sustainer rocket, maximum range of 34 miles (55km), CEP of 435yds (400m), warhead of one interchangeable 200-kiloton nuclear and 992lb (450kg) HE type, and launch from a converted PT-76 amphibious light tank chassis. Introduced in the late 1950s or early 1960s, this is a development of the FROG-3 with a revised

Carried on a variant of the PT-76 light amphibious tank's chassis, the FROG-3 was a Soviet artillery rocket without guidance, and could deliver a 200-kiloton nuclear or alternative conventional warhead over a range of 25 miles (40km) with only limited accuracy.

propulsion system, the body of the rocket being increased in diameter to that of the FROG-3's warhead, in the process being slightly shortened. Like the FROG-3, the FROG-5 is now of little operational value. The FROG-7 is a single-stage surface-to-surface battlefield rocket with a length of 29ft 10.25in (9.10m), weight of 5,071lb (2,300kg), propulsion by one solid-propellant rocket, range limits of 6.8 and 43 miles (11 and 70km), CEP of between 490 and 765yds (450 and 700m) depending on range, warhead of one 1,213lb (550kg) 10-, 100- or 200-kiloton nuclear type, or 1,213lb (550kg) HE or 860lb (390kg) chemical type, and launch from a ZIL-135 8x8 TEL vehicle. The FROG-7A was introduced in 1965 as the last of the FROG series weapons, and is being replaced by the longer-ranged and more accurate SS-21. The FROG-7B is an improved version that is also in service with Iraq, which has developed an improved Laith model able to carry a cluster-munition warhead over a range of 55.9 miles (90km).

The SS-1C 'Scud-B' is a Soviet (now Russian) single-stage surface-to-surface battlefield missile with a length of 37ft 4.75in (11.40m), weight of 14,043lb (6,370kg), propulsion by one storable liquid-propellant rocket, range limits of 50 and 112 miles (80 and 180km) with a nuclear warhead, or 50 and 174 miles (80 and 280km) with an HE or chemical warhead, CEP of 1,015yds (930m) at maximum range and reducing with shorter range, a warhead of one 40/100-kiloton variable-yield nuclear or 4,409lb (2,000kg) HE or chemical type, inertial guidance, and launch from a MAZ-543 8x8 TEL vehicle. The SS-1A 'Scunner' was introduced in 1957 as the original operational model of this series, but is no longer in front-line service with Warsaw Pact countries. It was a considerably less capable weapon than its successors, having a weight of 9,700lb (4,400kg) and able to carry a 40-kiloton (later an HE) warhead over a range of 81 miles (130km) after launch from its TEL, a converted IS-III heavy tank chassis. The SS-1B 'Scud-A' was introduced in 1965 as an altogether more capable weapon. The SS-1C 'Scud-B' was introduced in about 1970, and this variant has a maximum range boosted to 280 miles (450km) by a better propellant load, but maximum-range CEP increases to 1,205yds (1,100m) as a consequence. With an HE rather than nuclear warhead the missile has been exported to a number of

Carried on the ZIL-135 8x8 wheeled chassis, the FROG-7 was introduced to Soviet service in 1965, and was the last of the Free Rocket Over Ground series of unguided battlefield rockets, and in this instance could carry any of three nuclear or two conventional (HE or chemical) warheads over a range of 43 miles (70km) with the indifferent accuracy typical of large rockets in this period.

The SS-1C 'Scud-B' was designed for carriage and launch from the MAZ-543 8x8 TEL vehicle, and for the time of its introduction in about 1970 was a capable battlefield missile with inertial guidance for the fairly accurate delivery of a moderately large nuclear, HE or chemical warhead over a range of 112 miles (180km) with the nuclear warhead or 174 miles (280km) with the lighter HE or chemical warheads.

Moslem countries, and of these Iraq has produced two upgraded variants, namely the Al Hussein and the Al Abas: the Al Hussein has considerably greater range than the 'Scud-B', this figure of 373 miles (600km) being achieved by reducing the warhead's explosive load to 551lb (250kg) and by a lengthening of the missile by some 4ft 3.25in (1.3m) to boost fuel load by 2,293lb (1,040kg) to just over 11,023lb (5,000kg); in the Al Abas the weight of explosive in the warhead is further reduced to 419lb (190kg), allowing a further increment in range to 534 miles (860km). These Iraqi variants have greater CEPs than the baseline Soviet missile, and have been used with chemical rather than HE warheads.

The SS-12B 'Scaleboard-B' is another Soviet (now Russian) single-stage short-range ballistic missile with a length of 40ft 7.5in (12.38m), weight of 19,841lb (9,000kg), propulsion by four solid-propellant rockets, range limits of 138 and 497 miles (220 and 800km), CEP of 33yds (30m), warhead of one 2,756lb (1,250kg) 800-kiloton nuclear type, inertial guidance with infra-red terminal homing for the very low CEP, and launch from a MAZ-543P 8x8 TEL vehicle. The SS-12A 'Scaleboard-A' was introduced in 1969 to provide the Soviet army with long-range strategic/operational capability at front (army group) level. The SS-12B 'Scaleboard-B' was originally designated SS-22 in Western terminology and subsequently redesignated SS-12M in acknowledgement of the Soviet claim that the missile was a development of the SS-12 rather than a new type. This improved SS-12 entered service in 1979, and has different ranges (138 to 547 miles; 220 to 880km) combined with reduced CEP (the original figure of 350yds/320m having been considerably reduced in recent years) and alternative 550-kiloton or 1-megaton nuclear warheads that can each be exchanged for a chemical or cluster-munition warhead.

The SS-21 'Scarab' is a Soviet (now Russian) single-stage surface-to-surface battlefield missile with a length of 30ft 10.25in (9.44m), weight of 6,614lb (3,000kg), propulsion by one solid-propellant rocket, range limits of 8.75 to 125 miles (14 to 200km), CEP of between 55 and 100yds (50 and 100m), warhead of one 10- or 100-kiloton nuclear, or 992lb (450kg) HE (unitary, anti-armour cluster, anti-personnel cluster or anti-runway) or chemical type, inertial guidance, and launch from a ZIL-5937 6x6 TEL vehicle. The SS-21 was introduced in 1976 as replacement for the FROG series, and was deployed at front (army group) level as a primary means of removing NATO defensive positions that might slow or halt the main axes of Soviet advance.

The SS-23 'Spider' is a Soviet (now Russian) single-stage short-range ballistic missile (SRBM) with a length of 24ft 8in (7.52m), weight of 10,340lb (4,690kg), propulsion by one solid-propellant rocket, range limits of 50 and 311 miles (80 and 500km), CEP of 33yds (30m), warhead of one 992lb (450kg) 100-kiloton nuclear, chemical or cluster-munition type, inertial guidance with active radar terminal homing, and launch from a MAZ-543 8x8 TEL vehicle. Introduced in 1980, this is the Soviet replacement for the 'Scud' series, and offers significantly reduced time into action as well as better range and CEP, the latter having been reduced in Western analysis to the current figure when it became apparent that the missile is a member of the Soviet 'reconnaissance strike' family with terminal guidance.

Introduced in 1976 as replacement for the FROG series of unguided battlefield rockets, the SS-21 'Scarab' is an inertially guided missile carried on the ZIL-5937 6x8 TEL vehicle that is basically similar to that of the ZRK Romb used with the SA-8 'Gecko' surface-to-air missile system. The SS-21 offers considerable accuracy to a maximum range of 125 miles (200km), and this allows effective use of conventional (chemical, unitary HE or cluster HE) warheads as an alternative to the 10- or 100- kiloton nuclear warhead.

The Douglas MGR-1B Honest John was an American single-stage surface-to-surface battlefield rocket rather than a missile, with a length of 24ft 10in (7.57m), weight of 4,710lb (2,136kg), propulsion by one solid-propellant rocket, range limits of 4.5 and 23 miles (7.2 and 37km), CEP of 910yds (830m), warhead of one 2-, 20- or 40-kiloton W31 nuclear, or 1,500lb (680kg) HE or cluster munition, or 1,243lb (564kg) chemical type, and launch from a 6x6 truck TEL vehicle. The MGR-1B was introduced in 1960 to replace the 1953-vintage MGR-1A initial version. The MGR-1B is an obsolescent system combining a powerful warhead and good cross-country mobility with the accuracy and range of tube artillery, but in the non-nuclear role it offers limited offensive capability and at considerable cost.

The Martin Marietta MGM-31B Pershing II is an American two-stage medium-range ballistic missile with a length of 34ft 5.5in (10.50m), weight of 16,000lb (7,257kg), propulsion by one Hercules XM101 solid-propellant rocket for the first stage and one Hercules solid-propellant rocket for the second stage, maximum range of 1,125 miles (1,810km), CEP of between 22 and 49yds (20 and 45m), warhead of one 650lb (295kg) 5/50-kiloton selectable-yield W85 air/surface-burst or W86 earth-penetrating nuclear type, Singer-Kearfott inertial guidance with Goodyear RADAR active radar terminal homing, and launch from an M656 truck/trailer-mounted TEL vehicle. The MGM-31A Pershing IA was introduced in 1969 as a long-range battlefield interdiction missile derived from the 1962-vintage MGM-31 Pershing I deployed on the M474 tracked launch vehicle. The Pershing IA changed to the M656 truck/trailer TEL, was 34ft 9.5in (10.60m) long, weighed 10,140lb (4,600kg), was powered by one Thiokol XM105 solid-propellant booster rocket delivering 26,750lb st (118.99kN) and one Thiokol XM106 solid-propellant sustainer rocket delivering 15,560lb st (69.21kN), and carried a 1,650lb (748kg) 60/400-kiloton variable-yield W50 air-burst nuclear warhead over a range of between 100 and 460 miles (161 and 740km) with a CEP of 400yds (365m) under the guidance of a Bendix inertial navigation system. The MGM-31B Pershing II was introduced in 1985 as a modular upgrading of the Pershing IA with far greater range and other system improvements, the most important of which was the radar area guidance (RADAG) terminal homing, which reduced the CEP to so low a figure that a much smaller warhead (W85 surface/air-burst or W86 earth-penetrator) could be carried. The range and extreme accuracy of the weapon meant that even with a small warhead the type had operational and indeed limited strategic capabilities within the European theatre. The type was phased out of service as a result of the Intermediate Nuclear Forces Treaty.

245

The Douglas MGR-1B Honest John was the standard battlefield rocket of the USA and its allies into the mid-1980s. The type was carried on a 6x6 TEL vehicle, and could deliver any of three nuclear or three conventional (chemical, unitary HE or cluster HE) warheads over a range of 23 miles (37km) with moderate accuracy.

The Vought MGM-52C Lance is an American single-stage battlefield support missile with a length of 20ft 3in (6.17m), weight of 3,373lb (1,530kg) with a nuclear warhead or 3,920lb (1,778kg) with a conventional warhead, propulsion by two Rocketdyne T22 dual-thrust storable liquid-propellant rockets, range limits of 3 and 75 miles (4.8 and 121km), CEP of 500yds (455m), warhead of one 467lb (212kg) 1-, 10- or 50-kiloton selectable-yield W70-1/2/3 nuclear or 0.5-kiloton enhanced-radiation W70-4 nuclear, or 1,000lb (454kg) M251 cluster-munition type, E-Systems/Sys-Donner/Arma simplified inertial guidance, and launch from an M752 tracked TEL vehicle. The MGM-52C was introduced in 1972 as replacement for the Sergeant and Honest John weapons. The Lance is a highly capable but obsolescent battlefield missile able to deliver an assortment of alternative warheads, including the W70-4 'neutron' type and the M251 cluster-munition type with 836 0.95lb (0.43kg) anti-personnel/anti-matériel bomblets to saturate a circle of 900yds (820m) diameter.

Anti-ship missiles fall into two basic types as surface- and air-launched weapons, the latter often being derivatives of the former without the booster rockets used to launch and accelerate the missiles.

The China Precision Machine Import and Export Corporation C-101 is very little known, although it is thought to represent another step in the Chinese evolution of air- and surface-launched anti-ship missiles derived ultimately from the Soviet P-15 (SS-N-2 'Styx') of which the Chinese received numerous examples in the late 1950s. The P-15 was developed into the Hai Ying 1 coast-launched anti-ship missile that received the combined US and NATO reporting designation CSSC-2 'Silkworm', and it is thought that the C-101 is an air-launched derivative of the HY-1 with two small ramjets for sustainer power. On release from a launch warplane, the missile falls some 195ft (60m) before the rocket booster ignites, accelerating the missile to Mach 1.8. At this point the two laterally mounted ramjets are ignited, further accelerating the weapon to Mach 2. The missile cruises at a height of 150ft (50m), and at a range of 3,280yds (3,000m) from the target it descends to sea-skimming height before impacting the target about 16.4ft (5m) above the waterline. Notable features of this weapon, known only by its Chinese export designation, are two outward-canted swept fins above the booster rocket section and two equally sized rectangular vertical surfaces, each with an inset rudder, in the dorsal and ventral position just forward of the booster rocket section.

The CPMIEC Ying Ji-1 (Eagle Strike-1) weapon is an advanced anti-ship missile about which little is known. The weapon was developed from the mid-1970s and was first publicly revealed in 1984 in its original surface-launched form, intended for use by coastal defence forces, warships and surfaced submarines with the aid of a fire-control system basically similar to that used with the Chinese HY-1 and HY-2 derivatives of the Soviet SS-N-2 'Styx'. The missile can also be launched from warplanes. The missile is based on a substantial body of cylindrical section with a tapered nosecone comprising the radome over the active radar seeker used for terminal guidance. This body is carried by a mid-set cruciform of cropped delta wings, and control is provided by a tail-mounted cruciform of smaller moving control fins, also of cropped delta configuration and indexed in line with the wings. Unlike the surface-launched versions of the weapon, which are fired with the aid of a solid-propellant booster rocket section that is discarded on burn-out, the air-launched weapon is merely released from its launch warplane (generally the Nanchang Q-5 'Fantan' attack fighter) and, once it has fallen for a set time, ignites its rocket motor for high-speed cruise at a pre-set altitude of some 82ft (25m) under control of its inertial guidance package, descending to 16.4ft (5m) for the sea-skimming terminal phase of the attack under active radar control. The YJ-1 was probably entering Chinese service only in the mid-1990s, and although the weapon is also offered on the export market, there have been no known sales of this C-801 version. First reported in 1988, the YJ-2 is a longer-range development of the YJ-1 with the body lengthened for the incorporation of a small turbofan engine, aspirated via a ventral inlet, in place of the YJ-1's rocket motor. The revised missile weighs 1,576lb (715kg) and is thought to possess a range of 74.6 miles (120km). The current status of this improved YJ-2 weapon is not clear, but the type has been offered on the export market with the revised designation C-802.

The standard French anti-ship missile is the Aérospatiale Exocet. Second only to the McDonnell Douglas Harpoon as the most widely produced anti-ship missile of Western origins, the Exocet was designed from 1967 originally as the MM.38 ship-launched missile which entered service in 1975. Since that date the missile has been developed in several forms and has seen extensive operational use, notably in the Falklands War (1982) and

The Aérospatiale Exocet is the Western world's second most important anti-ship missile after the McDonnell Douglas Harpoon series, and is a potent weapon with an advanced warhead whose destructive effect is enhanced by the detonation of any residual fuel. The type has been produced in several forms for ship-, air- and submarine-launched use, and illustrated here is the baseline MM.38 ship-launched weapon (bottom) and MM.40 improved ship-launched weapon (inset). In the MM.40 version the use of a lighter container/launcher allows the weapon to be carried on smaller vessels despite the greater weight of the missile, which is fitted with a longer and heavier rocket-motor section for a range of 43.5 (70km) rather than 28 miles (45km).

247

The AM.39 (inboard) is the standard air-launched version of the Aérospatiale Exocet anti-ship missile, and has been used with considerable success in two wars.

in the Iraqi-Iranian Gulf War (1980-88). Development of the AM.38 as the Exocet's air-launched version began in 1975, and the first round was test-fired in December 1976 to allow service entry in 1977. This initial AM.38 was a limited-production helicopter-launched version of the MM.38 using SNPE Epervier booster and SNPE Eole V sustainer rocket motors with concentric nozzles. A delay of one second was built into the booster rocket's ignition sequence to avoid damage to the launch platform. Entering service in 1979, the AM.39 is the full-production version of the MM.38 optimised for air launch with a revised propulsion arrangement in a shorter body, thus reducing weight but increasing range. The basic configuration of the Exocet is of the 'classic' air-launched anti-ship missile type, with a cylindrical body terminating at its forward end in an ogivally tapered nose that constitutes the radome over the antenna for the active radar, a mid-set cruciform of cropped delta wings, and a tail-mounted cruciform of smaller control fins indexed in line with the wings. The missile is launched toward the target on range and bearing data provided by the launch warplane's sensors and fire-control system, and after the two-second acceleration phase by the Condor booster rocket, the Hélios sustainer rocket fires for 150 seconds as the missile cruises at low altitude until some 6.2 miles (10km) from the target's anticipated position, when the monopulse active seeker head is turned on, the target acquired and the terminal phase initiated at one of three heights preselected at launch (on the basis of anticipated sea state in the target area). Residual fuel adds considerably to the effects of the warhead detonation, which has in itself proved somewhat troublesome and unreliable. Late-production rounds have the Super ADAC frequency-agile homing radar with digital signal processing, which offers the considerable tactical advantage of improved resistance to electronic countermeasures (ECM) as well as the ability to discriminate between real targets and features such as decoys and coastal features. This improvement package also adds an upgraded inertial platform allowing the missile to fly at a height of between 6.6 and 9.8ft (2 and 3m) and also to make pre-programmed manoeuvres.

The MBB Kormoran 1 entered West German naval service as the primary anti-ship weapon of Lockheed F-104G Starfighters operated by the Marineflieger, and is now used on the Panavia Tornado IDS warplanes operated by the same service and by the Italian air force. The origins of the missile can be traced to 1962, when the West German defence ministry contracted with Bölkow K.G. for a study designed to highlight the capabilities and limitations of current air-to-surface missiles, and a similar study was undertaken in France by Nord-Aviation, which was largely responsible for the AS.33 missile that had been designed to a Franco-West German requirement. In 1967, MBB was contracted to produce a production-standard version of the AS.33 as the AS.34 that later received the

German name Kormoran. The new weapon was tested in 1974, and in 1976 MBB received an initial contract for 350 Kormoran anti-ship missiles, in a programme that saw delivery of the last missiles in 1983. The Kormoran is of classic air-launched anti-ship missile and also of typical Nord missile configuration. The weapon is based on a cylindrical body of considerable diameter and terminating at its forward end in the ogival radome over the antenna for the terminal guidance package's active radar. The body carries two sets of flying surfaces in the forms of a mid-set cruciform of swept delta wings with cropped tips, and a smaller cruciform of tail-mounted control fins indexed in line with the wings. After launch from its parent warplane, the missile is accelerated by the 1-second thrust of its two booster rocket motors, and then cruises under the 100-second thrust of its sustainer rocket motor at a height of 100ft (30m) to the approximate location of the target, where it descends to wave-top height for the pre-set active or passive radar attack. The warhead is a particularly impressive feature of the missile, being designed to penetrate up to 3.54in (90mm) of metal before the 16 radially disposed charges detonate to pierce the ship's bottom, decks and internal bulkheads.

The Kormoran 2 is an improved model weighing 1,389lb (630kg) and fitted with a new Thomson-CSF solid-state radar seeker. The weapon has the same airframe as the Kormoran 1, but replacement of the earlier weapon's analogue electronics by more advanced and less bulky digital electronics provides the additional volume for a larger 485lb (220kg) semi-armour-piercing blast/fragmentation warhead of greater penetration capability. The digital electronics also improve hit probability, increase the guidance package's resistance to countermeasures, enhance reliability, and simplify launch procedures. The Kormoran 2 also has an uprated powerplant for higher speed and modestly improved range. Development of the Kormoran 2 started in 1983, and a small series of successful test launches was completed in October 1990. The German navy has a requirement for between 175 and 210 examples of the new missile type, but the collapse of the USSR as an effective threat to western Europe in the late 1980s has meant a postponement if not cancellation of any production order.

The Israel Aircraft Industries Gabriel Mk IIIA/S is the air-launched version of the ship-launched Gabriel Mk III anti-ship missile, itself derived from the earlier Gabriel Mks I and II. The Gabriel Mk I was developed in the 1960s as a surface-launched missile with a range of 13.05 miles (21km) and

The McDonnell Douglas Harpoon is a comparatively small anti-ship missile that can be fired from air, surface and submarine platforms. The type has a powerful warhead and an advanced guidance package that has been considerably improved in successive variants of the missile, and secures a considerable range from the use of a sustainer turbojet for the main part of the flight after the missile has been launched, as in this RGM-84 shipborne model, by a solid-propellant rocket-motor section that is then jettisoned.

optimised for deployment on fast attack craft, while the Gabriel Mk II introduced a longer body for more fuel as a means of boosting range to 22.4 miles (36km). The ship-launched Gabriel Mk III introduced a frequency-agile active radar seeker, although the optical and semi-active radar homing systems of the Gabriel Mks I and II can also be used to provide greater tactical flexibility and continued operability in the face of enemy ECM. The Gabriel Mk III can thus have three guidance modes, namely fire-and-forget, fire-and-update via a data link from a targeting helicopter, and fire-and-command using the launch vessel's radar for better targeting data. The missile cruises at 330ft (100m) and then descends to 66ft (20m) for its approach to the target, the attack phase being flown at a pre-set height of 4.9, 8.25 or 13.1ft (1.5, 2.5 or 4m) depending on the anticipated sea state in the target area. The Gabriel Mk IIIA/S has a slightly longer body, reduced-span wings and lighter weight, which all contribute to higher speed but shorter range. The missile has three operating modes: range-and-bearing launch using radar-derived data, range-and-bearing launch using manually entered data, and bearing-only launch. In its basic layout the Gabriel is of typical anti-ship missile configuration, with a cylindrical body terminating forward in the ogival nosecone that constitutes the radome for the active radar guidance's antenna, a mid-set cruciform of fixed wings, and a tail-mounted cruciform of moving control fins indexed in line with the wings.

The Gabriel Mk IIIA/S ER is an extended-range version with a longer sustainer rocket that increases maximum range to 37.3 miles (60km), which is similar to that of the ship-launched Gabriel Mk III variant. Both the Gabriel Mk IIIA/S and Mk IIIA/S ER have the same guidance options as the basic Gabriel Mk III. The Gabriel Mk IVLR is an updated version developed during the early 1990s for a service debut in the middle of the decade. Although it is clearly related to the Gabriel Mk III, the Gabriel Mk IV is a somewhat larger and more massive weapon with turbojet sustainer propulsion for longer range and with a more potent warhead. The Gabriel Mk IV weighs 2,116lb (960kg) with its 529lb (240kg) proximity- and impact-fused semi-armour-piercing blast/fragmentation warhead, and its

One of the most important missiles used by the Israeli navy, and also by the South African and Taiwanese navies, is the Gabriel anti-ship missile developed by Israel Military Industries. This has been developed and produced for shipborne and air-launched use in several forms, that illustrated here being an example of the Gabriel I baseline shipborne weapon with the option of several guidance modes to enhance its versatility and resistance to enemy countermeasures.

The first anti-ship missile to enter Western service, the Norwegian-designed Kongsberg Penguin is still a capable weapon in its later forms, including this air-launched version that can be programmed to fly a dog-leg approach to the target area under the control of an inertial system before making its attack under control of a passive infra-red system.

propulsion arrangement uses a solid-propellant rocket for the boost phase and a small turbojet for the sustain phase of the mission, which can extend to a range of 124 miles (200km). The Gabriel Mk IV has the same basic configuration as the Gabriel Mk III with the exception of its wings, which are changed in shape from trapezoidal to swept with cropped tips. The missile has the same guidance options and attack modes as the Gabriel Mk III.

A Norwegian weapon, the Kongsberg Penguin was the Western world's first anti-ship missile, the original Penguin Mk I having been conceived in the early 1960s for a service debut in 1972 as part of Norway's scheme of coastal defence against maritime invasion. This initial model was optimised for good performance in the country's particular coastal waters after launch from fast attack craft and other small naval platforms. The result is a missile with IR terminal homing, treated as a certified round of ammunition, and launched upon information supplied by the launch platform's sensors and fire-control system; this ship-launched version has a two-stage rocket, and height control by an interesting pulsed-laser altimeter. The missile's launch weight is 750lb (340kg) including the powerful warhead essentially identical with the Martin Marietta AGM-12B Bullpup air-to-surface missile, and its performance figures include a range of 12.4 miles (20km). The missiles still in service have been upgraded to Penguin Mk I Mod 7 standard with the seeker of the Penguin Mk II Mod 3. The Penguin Mk II is an improved Mk I with range boosted to 18.6 miles (30km). The type entered service in the early 1980s, and surviving rounds have been upgraded to Penguin Mk II Mod 5 standard with enhanced seeker performance. The basic type has been further developed for helicopter launch as the Penguin Mk II Mod 7 (US designation AGM-119B for use by helicopters such as the Kaman SH-2F Seasprite and Sikorsky SH-60B Seahawk) with a weight of 849lb (385kg). This variant includes a number of Penguin Mk III improvements (notably in the seeker and signal processor), and has a new two-stage rocket motor and fully digital electronics, unlike the earlier Mk II variants, which have analogue electronics. Production of the weapon is undertaken in the USA by Grumman, and the type entered American helicopter-launched service during 1992, although production is thought to have totalled only 82 missiles.

The Penguin Mk III is an air-launched development (also capable of ship launch) intended primarily for use on the Royal Norwegian air force's Lockheed Martin F-16 Fighting Falcon multi-role fighter. The variant, which possesses the alternative designation AGM-119A in the US system, has a longer body, shorter-span wings, a single-stage rocket motor and a radar altimeter. The Penguin Mk III is a highly capable weapon programmed to fly a circuitous approach to the target via one or more waypoints after launch on the basis of radar information from the launch warplane, or through visual sighting with data entered into the missile via the pilot's HUD or optical sight. As with the earlier versions of the missile, the use of IR terminal homing (activated only when the missile has reached the target's anticipated position) gives the target vessel virtually no warning of the missile's imminent arrival, so reducing the time available for countermeasures.

Better known by its combined US and NATO reporting designation AS-2 'Kipper', the K-10 was introduced as the primary Soviet anti-ship weapon of the Tupolev Tu-16 'Badger-C', (one or two such missiles carried semi-recessed under the fuselage) but was also capable of undertaking attacks on large land targets. The K-10 homed on objectives with a large radar signature and, because of its size and lack of electronic sophistication, was completely obsolete by the time of its withdrawal from service in favour of the AS-5 'Kelt'. The type was launched by its parent warplane at a speed of about Mach 0.8 at an altitude of 36,090ft (11,000m), and then accelerated to a high-altitude cruising speed of between Mach 1.4 and Mach 1.5 before descending toward the anticipated target position at about Mach 1.2. The cruise phase of the flight was undertaken under command of an autopilot, which could be overridden and/or updated by data-linked commands from a mid-course guidance aeroplane of the fixed- or rotary-wing type, and then homed on information provided by its onboard active radar seeker. As it was optimised for attacks on targets presenting a large radar signature, this massive missile had as its primary objectives high-value targets such as aircraft carriers. It is worth noting that range estimates for the missile vary considerably from a minimum of 134 miles (215km) to a maximum of 348 miles (560km), although it is likely that the comparative inaccuracy of the guidance system and the desire to maximise the warhead probably dictated a comparatively small fuel capacity and shorter range.

The BAe Sea Eagle is an advanced anti-ship missile used only in its air-launched form. The type has a notably powerful warhead and an advanced guidance package, and achieves long range by the use of a turbojet rather than rocket motor, which allows the whole of the fuel volume to be occupied by liquid fuel (the necessary oxidant being supplied from the air drawn through a ventral inlet) rather than by fuel and oxidant as is necessary for a rocket motor.

The primary British anti-ship missile, the BAe Sea Eagle was designed from 1976 as the P3T, and the structural and aerodynamic basis of the missile was found in the BAe/Matra Martel missile in service with the British and French air forces and the type to be replaced by the new weapon in the anti-ship role. The origins of the type can be found in the Ministry of Defence's 1973 Air Staff Target 1226, which demanded a weapon possessing considerably greater range than the AJ.168 version of the Martel. The P3T was therefore designed with an air-breathing powerplant in the form of a turbojet aspirated through a ventral inlet whose front was sealed from the airflow by a fairing discarded only after the missile's release from its launch warplane. The missile is otherwise of 'classic' air-launched anti-ship missile configuration, with a cylindrical body terminating forward in the ogival radome for the antenna of the active radar terminal guidance package, a mid-set cruciform of cropped delta wings, and a close-coupled cruciform of cropped delta control fins mounted near the tail and indexed in line with the wings. The Sea Eagle has a thoroughly modern guidance system, and data on the target's position, bearing, course and speed are loaded into this just before the Sea Eagle is launched. After release and engine ignition, the missile accelerates to Mach 0.85 and descends to sea-skimming height under control of its inertial guidance package with height data provided by a radar altimeter: the low-altitude cruise reduces the chances of the missile being spotted by electromagnetic or visual means. The active radar terminal guidance package is activated at a distance of 11 miles (18km) from the target, and the missile then completes its attack. The weapon is controlled via an advanced digital computer, and this allows varying attack heights, the flying of random evasive manoeuvres in the closing stages of the attack, final attack from any bearing, the detection and ignoring of decoys and countermeasures, and on longer-range missions a short climb, when about 18.6 miles (30km) from the target's anticipated position, for use of the active radar to fix the missile's position relative to the target before a descent once again to sea-skimming height. The missile is notable for its good speed and range, and was planned mainly for warplane launch platforms such as the BAe Sea Harrier which can carry two missiles, and also the BAe Buccaneer and Panavia Tornado which can each carry four missiles.

The standard American anti-ship missile is the McDonnell Douglas Harpoon. This is the Western world's most important anti-ship missile, and was conceived in the late 1960s as a capable but comparatively cheap weapon in which reliability rather than outright performance was emphasised in all respects but electronic capability and range. In this last capacity, the use of a turbojet (aspirated via a ventral NACA inlet between the two lower wings) rather than a rocket in the sustainer role pays handsome dividends. In June 1971, McDonnell Douglas received a Department of Defense contract for the full-scale development of this weapon as an air-launched missile, to be carried by the full spectrum of US tactical warplanes for the destruction of surfaced submarines, destroyers, frigates and fast attack craft. It was soon decided that this AGM-84 weapon would be complemented by a ship-launched RGM-84 version, and in 1973 the programme was further enhanced by the addition of the UGM-84 member of the family as an encapsulated version for launch from submerged submarines.

Seven fully guided test launches were completed in June 1974, and the success of this effort was followed by authorisation of pilot production in July 1974 and the start of the US Navy's technical evaluation in October 1974. All three initial variants of the Harpoon missile entered service in 1977 as the AGM-84A air-launched, RGM-84A ship-launched and UGM-84A submarine-launched weapons, the last two having a jettisonable Aerojet booster rocket. The Harpoon is of the standard air-launched anti-ship missile layout, with a cylindrical body terminating forward in the pointed radome over the antenna for the terminal guidance package's active radar, a mid-set cruciform of trapezoidal wings, and a tail-mounted cruciform of swept control fins indexed in line with the wings. Being designed for high-speed air-launch, the AGM-84A requires no booster. This baseline missile can be fired in two modes. The range and bearing launch (RBL) mode allows the late activation of the active radar as a means of reducing the chances of the missile being detected through its own emissions, and in this mode the radar is set for large, medium or small acquisition windows that fix the distance from the anticipated target position at which the radar is activated, although the smaller the acquisition window the more accurate the initial target data must be. The other launch mode is the bearing only launch (BOL), used when the precise location of the target is not available at missile launch time. In this mode the missile is fired on the target's bearing from the launch warplane and the radar is activated comparatively early in the flight to search through 90 degrees (45 degrees left and right of the centreline) in azimuth mode. If no target is found after the low-level approach, the missile undertakes a pre-programmed search pattern and, should this not find a target, the missile self-destructs. Target acquisition is followed in the Block 1A missiles of the initial production batch, typified by a range of 57.6 miles (92.7km), by a steep pop-up climb at a distance of some 2,000yds (1,830m) from the target, and then a terminal dive onto the target's more vulnerable upper surfaces.

The AGM-84B Harpoon was introduced in 1982 as the Block 1B missile that flies a sea-skimming attack, has improved resistance to ECM, and possesses a larger and more devastating warhead. The AGM-84C Harpoon was introduced in 1985 as the Block 1C missile that incorporates the pop-up/terminal dive and sea-skimming flight profile capabilities of the AGM-84A and AGM-84B respectively, together with the latter's larger warhead. The weapon also features an increase in range to more than 121 miles (195km) as a result of its greater fuel capacity and a change from JP-5 to JP-10 fuel, has an improved seeker, and greater computer memory for variable flight profiles including an indirect approach to the target.

The AGM-84D missile would have been a Block 1D development of the Block 1C standard with an advanced version of the current seeker package upgraded with a global positioning system (GPS) receiver, range increased still further to 150 miles (241km) by the carriage of more fuel in a longer body, and the ability to undertake more complex search patterns as well as a dog-leg approach to the target via three waypoints before selection of the more appropriate of the two alternative attack modes, but was cancelled.

Starting trials in 1988 and entering accelerated service during 1990 in time for the UN-led war to free Kuwait from Iraqi occupation, the AGM-84E stand-off land attack missile (SLAM) was developed as a company-funded derivative of the Harpoon for carriage by US Navy and US Marine Corps Northrop Grumman A-6 Intruder and McDonnell Douglas F/A-18 Hornet warplanes. The weapon combines the airframe, powerplant and warhead of the Harpoon with the imaging IR terminal guidance unit of the Hughes AGM-65D Maverick ASM, the data link of the Hughes/Martin Marietta AGM-62 'Walleye' glide bomb, and a GPS receiver, to create a missile that is longer and heavier than the basic Harpoon models. The SLAM provides a stand-off capability against high-value targets such as power stations, harbour equipment and bridges, using inertial guidance for the mid-course phase of the flight before the missile is aligned precisely at the target through the GPS link, allowing the operator to acquire the target up to 10,000yds (9,145m) distant from the missile, lock onto the image and depart the scene as the missile completes its attack. Further development of the SLAM concept could result from McDonnell Douglas's stand-off land attack missile – expanded response (SLAM-ER) proposal that will be evaluated in hardware form towards the end of the present decade with an improved and larger

Seen under this Saab 39 Gripen of the Swedish air force are three important types of air-launched missile, namely the AIM-9 Sidewinder air-to-air missile (wingtip rails), AGM-65 Maverick air-to-surface missile (outboard underwing hardpoints) and Rbs 15 anti-ship missile (inboard underwing hardpoints).

750lb (340kg) warhead, modified wings, and an automated mission-planning capability to improve range to 75 miles (121km).

Air-to-surface missiles fall into two basic categories, as strategic weapons and tactical weapons. The strategic weapons are generally known as cruise missiles. The main French weapon in this category, which is produced by only a very few nations, is the Aérospatiale ASMP (Air-Sol Moyenne Portée, or air-to-surface medium-range missile). Designed from 1978, the ASMP is an air-launched cruise missile now optimised for carriage by the Dassault Mirage IVP bomber (after conversion from Mirage IVA standard), the Dassault Mirage 2000N low-altitude strike warplane and the Dassault Super Etendard carrierborne strike fighter. The ASMP entered service in 1986, and provides the French air forces with a stand-off nuclear capability against large targets such as railway yards, major bridges, and command and communication centres. The type can fly a high-altitude profile ending with a steep supersonic dive, or alternatively a low-altitude profile of shorter range.

The designation AS-15 'Kent' is the US/NATO reporting designation for a cruise missile believed to have the Russian designators Kh-55, Kh-65 and/or RKV-500, and the weapon is the air-launched version of the standard Soviet (now Russian) cruise missile. The missile was developed from the late 1970s in response to the American development of small cruise missiles with folding flying surfaces for minimal containerised storage or aircraft carriage requirements, and with a small turbofan powerplant for maximum range. The weapon is currently operated by the Tupolev Tu-95 'Bear-H' subsonic bomber (six AS-15A 'Kent' missiles in the Tu-95MS-6 on an internal rotary launcher and 16 AS-15A missiles on the Tu-95MS-16 in the form of six missiles internally on a rotary launcher and 10 externally on five two-round pylons) and by the Tupolev Tu-160 'Blackjack' supersonic variable-geometry bomber (12 AS-15B missiles carried internally on two six-round rotary launchers). The AS-15B differs from the AS-15A in its greater diameter, although the significance of this increased fuselage volume has not been discovered. The weapon compares favourably with the USAF's Boeing AGM-86B type, but differs from the American weapon in having land- and sea-based counterparts in the forms of the SS-C-4 and SS-N-21 'Sampson'.

The origins of the cruise missile in Western service can be traced to a time in the early 1950s, when there were serious concerns in Western military circles about the continued viability of the free-fall bomber as the primary weapon for the projection of strategic air power, because the deep penetration of Soviet airspace to drop such nuclear weapons on primary targets left such bombers increasingly vulnerable to interception and destruction. The interception capabilities of turbojet-powered fighters such as the MiG-15 'Fagot' were amply revealed in the Korean War (1950-53), and the transonic performance of such warplanes would soon be exceeded by that of the supersonic fighters that the USSR was known to be developing. The current and foreseeable state of the technological art offered no complete solution to this problem facing the Western powers, and the USA in particular, but the USAF felt that emerging warhead, propulsion and guidance technologies offered the possibility of a partial solution. This partial solution was a large air-to-surface missile carrying a nuclear warhead, guided by an inertial navigation system, and powered by a liquid-propellant rocket motor for supersonic performance and moderately long range.

The USA appreciated that the rocket technology of the day would not provide the range to allow such a missile to be launched from points outside Soviet airspace, but felt that it would offer the type of stand-off launch range that would make it possible for launch warplanes to avoid the heaviest concentrations of Soviet defensive weapons. The first US weapon in this category was the Bell GAM-63 Rascal that saw limited service between 1957 and 1959 with a version of the Boeing B-47 Stratojet medium strategic bomber as its launcher: this DB-47E version carried one 13,500lb (6,124kg) Rascal on a hardpoint on the lower starboard side of the fuselage. The Rascal could carry any of three types of warhead (two of them nuclear), was powered by a liquid-propellant rocket motor for a speed of Mach 1.6 and a range of 75 miles (120km), and used inertial navigation for a CEP in the order of 500yds (457m). The Rascal was a worthy initial effort, but it was appreciated that the type's size and weight reduced range to a wholly indifferent figure.

Even before the Rascal entered service, however, the USAF had decided that a major effort was required to give its Boeing B-52 Stratofortress the ability to penetrate Soviet air defences. This resulted in two parallel programmes: Weapon System 131B was planned as a supersonic missile carrying a thermonuclear warhead, and Weapon System 132B as a supersonic missile carrying an ECM payload. The latter requirement was soon dropped, and after intense industrial competition, the development contract for WS-131B was awarded to the Missile Development Division of North American Aviation in August 1957.

The division was short of work, for its incredible SM-64 Navajo strategic missile had recently been cancelled. The SM-64 was designed to provide the USAF with a missile carrying a large thermonuclear warhead over intercontinental ranges, and had been developed to the point of production as a supersonic cruise missile lifted piggyback fashion by a rocket booster before igniting its own ramjet sustainers for wingborne flight at Mach 3 over a range of 6,333 miles (10,192km.) North American decided that the aerodynamics of the Navajo, or more specifically its X-10 test vehicle, were ideal for the required air-launched cruise missile, and the new type was therefore planned with a very slender fuselage carrying all-moving delta canard foreplane halves for longitudinal control, a rear-mounted delta wing with ailerons for lateral control, and a swept vertical tail surface with an inset rudder for directional control. The powerplant was one Pratt & Whitney J52 turbojet: this was mounted in a nacelle below the fuselage immediately under the rear-mounted wing, and had variable inlet and nozzle systems matching the handling of the non-afterburning engine to flight at up to Mach 2.1 at heights between sea level and 55,000ft (16,765m). Guidance was entrusted to a North American Autonetics inertial system that was primed right up to the point of missile release by the launch warplane's systems, updated by a Kollsman KS-120 astro-tracker located in the missile launch pylon.

The missile was originally designated B-77, but this was changed to GAM-77 and it was with this designation that the first powered test was undertaken in April 1959. The GAM-77 Hound Dog achieved initial

The most important of the USA's early cruise missiles was the North American AGM-28 Hound Dog, which was a nuclear-armed and turbojet-powered winged weapon of which two could be carried by the Boeing B-52 Stratofortress heavy bomber on special underwing pylons (seen attached to the two right-hand weapons ready for rapid connection to the bomber). The range of these inertially guided weapons meant that the bomber no longer had to overfly its target and thereby undergo the threat posed by the target's anti-aircraft guns and surface-to-air missile defences.

operational capability in 1961 on the two underwing pylons of the B-52G Stratofortress, and in 1962 was redesignated as the AGM-28A Hound Dog. Originally designated GAM-77A, the AGM-28B Hound Dog was an improved missile with a number of guidance system refinements as well as the KS-140 astro-tracker in the launch pylon. Production of the Hound Dog lasted to 1963 and encompassed the delivery of 593 missiles.

The launch crew could programme high- or low-altitude flight profiles, including dog-legs and evasive manoeuvres, right up to the point of missile release, whereupon the Hound Dog became entirely autonomous and therefore unjammable. Experiments were undertaken with Hound Dogs converted with anti-radar and terrain comparison or terrain contour matching (TERCOM) guidance, but neither of these types entered operational service before the AGM-28 was withdrawn from service in 1976.

The Boeing AGM-86B entered service in 1981 as one of the USAF's most important weapons. The weapon was originally schemed as the subsonic cruise army decoy (SCAD) to supersede the McDonnell Douglas ADM-20 Quail decoy missile, but was then developed as the long-range complement to the short-range Boeing AGM-69 SRAM, with which it enjoys full launcher compatibility. The warplane for which the new long-range missile was designed was the Rockwell B-1A supersonic bomber and missile launcher, and in its original AGM-86A version the missile was sized in fuselage length to the weapons bay of this important warplane. The B-1A was then cancelled, and the AGM-86A was redesigned as the AGM-86B with a longer fuselage and a wing of reduced sweep, as the primary launch platform was now envisaged as the already venerable Boeing B-52 Stratofortress. The primary launch platform for the weapon in the 1990s is the B-1B Lancer, a radically revised development of the B-1A, that can carry up to 22 such missiles (eight on an internally carried rotary launcher and 14 under the wings), and this penetration bomber is due to be supplemented by the Northrop Grumman B-2A Spirit bomber capable of carrying up to 16 such missiles on two eight-round rotary launchers carried internally, although the preferred cruise missile for this more advanced delivery system is the General Dynamics AGM-129.

Although a total of 4,348 AGM-86Bs was planned, only 1,715 were built between 1982 and 1986, to allow the diversion of funding to the improved

AGM-129 that offered greater capabilities at a time when the Soviets were strengthening their capabilities against air-launched cruise missiles during the mid- and late 1980s. From 1985, in-service rounds were retrofitted with an ECM package to improve their capabilities against such Soviet defences. Designed from 1986 but first revealed in 1991 after its use in the Gulf War, the AGM-86C is the conventionally armed version of the AGM-86B with a 1,000lb (454kg) blast/fragmentation warhead. The greater size of this warhead dictates a reduction in fuel capacity, and hence a reduction in range, but the addition of a GPS receiver considerably enhances terminal accuracy over the already excellent figure for the AGM-86B variant.

It has been suggested that from 1992 the number of AGM-86B missiles in first-line service has been reduced, and that many of these weapons have been revised to the conventionally armed role or the air-launched decoy role with ECM equipment, chaff and IR flares. It has further been suggested that many of the weapons remaining in the nuclear-armed role have been adapted with a bulbous nose containing shielding against electromagnetic pulse effects, and painted with a radar-absorbent coating to reduce their electromagnetic signature.

It is also worth noting that there is a ship- and submarine-launched counterpart to the AGM-86. This General Dynamics BGM-109 Tomahawk was also proposed in air-launched variants and, perhaps most importantly of all, was placed in ground-launched service until withdrawn in the later 1980s as a result of treaty restrictions. The BGM-109 has inertial guidance for the mid-course phase of its flight and either TERCOM or some other guidance package for the terminal phase, and entered service in 1983.

The variants of this important operational- and tactical-level weapon are discussed below in alphabetical order of their variants. The BGM-109A naval variant is also known as the tactical land attack missile – nuclear (TLAM-N), and is a ship- and submarine-launched encapsulated version with the selectable-yield 200-kiloton W80 Model 0 warhead, a range of 1,555 miles (2,500km) and a CEP of 305yds (280m) with inertial and TERCOM guidance.

The BGM-109B Tomahawk is also known as the tactical anti-ship missile (TASM), is designed for ship and submarine launch, and carries a 1,000lb (454kg) HE warhead (derived from that of the AGM-12 Bullpup ASM) over a range of 282 miles (454km). The variant's terminal guidance is provided by an active radar seeker derived from that of the McDonnell Douglas RGM-84A Harpoon anti-ship missile, and this commands the missile into a pop-up/dive attack to strike the target on its vulnerable upper surfaces.

The BGM-109C is also known as the tactical land attack missile – conventional (TLAM-C) and is essentially the airframe of the BGM-109A with the warhead of the BGM-109B and DSW-15(V) DSMAC terminal guidance for great accuracy over a range of 921 miles (1,482km).

The BGM-109D was the variant of the ground-launched Tomahawk cruise missile with Block III

The Martin ASM-N-7 and GAM-83 (from 1962 AGM-12) Bullpup series was the most important air-to-surface missile available to the US Air Force and US Navy in the late 1950s and early 1960s. Seen here are four of the most important members of the family: clockwise from the slim missile (right front) these are the ATM-12A training missile, the AGM-12B, the AGM-12D and the AGM-12C.

improvements and a submunition-dispensing warhead. The type was powered by a version of the F402 turbofan offering 19 per cent greater thrust at 2 per cent less fuel consumption, and other improvements included the Mk IIA version of the DSMAC guidance package.

The BGM-109G Tomahawk was known as the ground-launched cruise missile (GLCM) and was the strategic version of the series deployed extensively in Europe in the theatre-level nuclear role. The weapon was carried in a high-mobility four-round TEL vehicle designed for rapid deployment (in times of crisis and war) away from Soviet-targeted base areas. A group of four TELs was supported by two wheeled launch control centres to provide launch and targeting data, and to provide the crews with nuclear, biological and chemical (NBC) protection.

The AGM-109H Tomahawk was the proposed medium-range air-launched airfield attack cruise missile for the USAF with the Teledyne Continental J402-CA-401 engine and a conventional warhead with tactical submunition payload. The AGM-109K Tomahawk was the proposed medium-range air-launched land attack and sea lane control cruise missile for the USAF with the J402-CA-401 engine and the WDU-25A/B conventional warhead. The AGM-109L Tomahawk was the proposed medium-range air-launched land/sea attack cruise missile for the US Navy

with the J402-CA-401 engine and the WDU-7B conventional warhead.

The General Dynamics AGM-129A is an important weapon that entered service in 1991, but very little is known of its highly classified development. The programme to develop this successor to the Boeing AGM-86B air-launched cruise missile was launched in 1977 with the object of improving performance in several crucial fields. Low observability was required for an increased capability to penetrate into airspace protected by advanced air defences, and led to the development and introduction of 'stealth' technology. Improved propulsion was demanded through the installation of an engine offering greater power at lower specific fuel consumption for the greater range that would allow the missile to circumnavigate the most heavily defended areas of Soviet (now Russian) airspace. Greater survivability was desired for better operational capability, and was provided through the incorporation of the most advanced electronic and IR countermeasures. Finally, enhanced targeting flexibility and terminal accuracy were important improvements that were generated by use of the latest computer hardware and software.

The fact that development of the AGM had been awarded to General Dynamics was announced in 1983 when full-scale development began, and the type was designed for use on the Boeing B-52 Stratofortress, with the Rockwell B-1B Lancer and Northrop Grumman B-2A Spirit bombers later becoming operational with the type. Key features are longer range than the AGM-86B combined with a high measure of 'stealth' technology (especially in terms of IR emission) to reduce the missile's observability. The type has a flattened fuselage shape with a pointed

259

wedge nose and a flat wedge tail section, and the folding aerodynamic surfaces comprise forward-swept wings on the central part of the fuselage and at the tail a combination of an unswept tailplane and a swept ventral fin, all of the tail surfaces being of the 'slab' or all-moving type. The whole design, probably making extensive use of composite materials, was optimised for low observability, and the same can be said of the powerplant, which has a low thermal signature and is aspirated via a flush ventral inlet and exhausts through a two-dimensional slot beneath the missile's upswept tail. The missile's low detectability by radar is ensured by the careful design of the nose and upper surfaces, reflecting the fact that the most likely detectors will be those above and ahead of the missile: the nose accommodates on its undersurface the conformal antenna for the laser radar associated with the primary guidance system, while the inlet, exhaust and rudder are all shielded by the missile's afterbody. Production of 1,461 such missiles was planned but, reflecting the effective collapse of the USSR in the late 1980s, the programme was terminated in 1993 after the delivery of just 460 missiles.

Under development in the mid-1990s for possible production by Hughes (originally General Dynamics) and McDonnell Douglas, which was qualified as second-source manufacturer during 1987, the AGM-129B is a derivative of the AGM-129A with a conventional warhead or, according to some sources, provision for the carriage of advanced submunitions.

The Hughes AIM-4 Falcon was the world's first fully guided air-to-air (AAM) to enter operational service, an event that took place in 1956. The origins of this weapon can be traced to 1947, when the USAF demanded the creation of a sophisticated combination of radar fire-control system and

The single most important designer and manufacturer of air-launched missiles in the USA is Hughes, and among this company's series of such weapons are the BGM-71 TOW surface- and helicopter-launched anti-tank missile (foreground) and (background left to right) the AIM-47A Super Falcon air-to-air missile, the AIM-4F Falcon air-to-air missile, the AIM-26A Super Falcon, the AGM-65 Maverick air-to-surface missile, the AIM-4D Falcon air-to-air missile, and the AIM-54A Phoenix air-to-air missile.

guided missile for installation in the high-performance manned interceptors that the service considered to be the only satisfactory weapon for the defence of the continental USA against the possible depredations of bombers carrying free-fall nuclear bombs. The resulting competition drew responses from most American electronics and aircraft manufacturers, but all of these were surprised when the decisions for the fire-control and missile systems were made in favour of Hughes Aircraft, a newcomer in this highly advanced field.

The first fire-control system to emerge from Hughes' victory in the design competition was the E-9 installed in the Northrop F-89H Scorpion all-weather fighter, and this was followed by the MG-10 for the Convair F-102 Delta Dagger supersonic interceptor, the MG-13 for the McDonnell F-101 Voodoo supersonic interceptor, and the MA-1 for the Convair F-106 Delta Dart Mach 2 interceptor. All these systems were designed for use with a single AAM type, which resulted from Project 'Dragonfly' and was ordered in 1947 as the XF-98 in the fighter category, before becoming the GAR-1 Falcon in the new guided missile system during 1950, and finally the AIM-4 Falcon in the 1962 rationalisation of the designation systems.

The missile established a basic configuration that has been typical of Hughes missiles since that time: a cylindrical body of comparatively great diameter with a hemispherical nose and a large proportion of composites (in this instance glassfibre-reinforced plastics), and a cruciform of low-aspect-ratio delta flying surfaces each trailed by a rectangular elevon for aerodynamic control of the missile's flight. In the GAR-1, the nose was fitted with four receiver antennae (shaped like small fins and spaced at 90 degrees to each other) giving proportional navigation capability to the semi-active radar guidance system, and propulsion was entrusted to a single-charge rocket motor that boosted the missile at about 50 g until motor burn-out. The GAR-1 reached full service in 1956 on the F-89H/J (three missiles in each of the two wing-tip pods) and F-102A (six missiles in the lower-fuselage weapon bay).

Introduced after the GAR-2 (from 1962 AIM-4B) and known until 1962 as the GAR-1D, this model had control surfaces of greater area moved farther to the rear of the missile's centre of gravity, and a result was enhanced manoeuvrability. The same type of semi-active radar guidance was employed in this model.

Introduced late in 1956 as the second operational Falcon model, the AIM-4B was known until 1962 as the GAR-2 and introduced IR guidance with its seeker in a glazed nose. Known until 1962 as the GAR-2A, the AIM-4C was the second IR-guided version to enter service, and was in essence an improved GAR-2 with an upgraded seeker able to lock onto its target against a wider range of background temperatures.

Ordered as the GAR-2B but entering service in 1963 as the AIM-4D after the tri-service rationalisation of US designation systems, this was the last production version of the Falcon, produced to the extent of more than 12,000 weapons in the form of 4,000 new-build weapons and more than 8,000 remanufactured from surplus AIM-4A and AIM-4C missiles. The type was carried mainly by the F-106A Delta Dart, and was the only Falcon variant optimised for the air-combat role. A hybrid model, the AIM-4D combined the small airframe of the early Falcon models with the more powerful rocket motor and advanced IR seeker of the larger AIM-4G Falcon to create a comparatively short-ranged but very fast missile that otherwise differed from the AIM-4C only in its maximum speed of Mach 4.

Known as the GAR-3 when it entered service in 1958 and built to the extent of just 300 missiles, the AIM-4E Super Falcon was a special high-performance variant of the basic Falcon family, optimised for compatibility with the F-106A Delta Dart with a larger airframe supporting a longer-burning rocket motor, a cruciform wing arrangement with long root fillets, a more powerful warhead, and an improved semi-active radar homing system using an antenna under a pointed radome. In respect of its dimensions, weight and performance, the AIM-4E was basically similar to the AIM-4F. Introduced in 1959 as the GAR-3A, the AIM-4F Super Falcon was a much-improved model matched to the F-106A Delta Dart interceptor and based on the airframe introduced in the GAR-3A but fitted with a two-stage rocket motor and an improved guidance package offering greater accuracy and improved ECM capability. Also introduced in 1959 with the initial designation GAR-4A, the AIM-4G Super Falcon was a version of the AIM-4F with IR guidance capable of locking onto smaller targets at longer ranges. The last development of the Falcon series was the XAIM-4H, evolved between 1969 and the programme's termination in 1971 with an active laser fuse system, and the last of the Falcon series in operational service were the models in Swedish and Swiss service up to the early 1990s.

In 1946 the US Navy's Bureau of Aeronautics was convinced that the guided AAM was the way forward in fighter armament, and contracted with Sperry Gyroscope for initial conceptual work within the context of Project 'Hot Shot'. By 1951, Sperry had made sufficient progress for the US Navy to contract for full engineering development of the AAM-N-2 Sparrow I (redesignated as the AIM-7A in 1962). The Sparrow I made its first flight in 1953, based on a long and slender body with a pointed nose carrying the 52lb (23.6kg) proximity-fused blast/fragmentation warhead, an Aerojet solid-propellant rocket motor, and flying surfaces that included a cruciform of moving wings located on the body's mid-point and, indexed in line with these wings, a cruciform of fixed fins at the tail. This model used radar beam-riding guidance with flush dipole antennae round the body to detect the missile's position in the beam stretching from the launch fighter to the target, and thus provided the data with which the guidance system could keep the missile centred in the beam by movement of the control wings.

The AAM-N-2 reached initial operational capability in July 1956, and about 2,000 such missiles were produced for fighters such as the Douglas F3D-2M Skyknight, McDonnell F3H-2M Demon and Vought F7U-3M Cutlass, each of which could carry four missiles under their wings. In 1955, Douglas was developing for the US Navy the F5D-1 Skylancer as a Mach 2 interceptor with the Westinghouse Aero X-24A target-acquisition and fire-control radar, and decided that a much-improved version of the Sparrow would make ideal armament for this advanced type. In that year, therefore, the company received a US Navy contract for the AAM-N-3 Sparrow II AAM to arm the Skylancer. Douglas concentrated on aerodynamic and structural development of the missile on the basis of the Sparrow I, and contracted parallel development of the all-important missile guidance package to Bendix-Pacific. The logical choice of guidance type would have been semi-active radar homing, but the design team opted instead to design and develop a far more ambitious active radar guidance, despite the considerable problems posed by the missile's diameter of only 8in (0.203m). The body was given greater volume, especially in its forward portion, and the flying surfaces were given square-cut tips. About 100 missiles, which received the retrospective designation AIM-7B Sparrow II in 1962, were produced for test and development work, but in 1956 the US Navy cancelled both the Skylancer and the Sparrow II as more advanced fighter/missile combinations were imminent.

When production of the Sparrow I ended in 1956, Raytheon took over the Naval Reserve Plant at Bristol, Tennessee, previously operated by the

Farragut Division of Sperry Gyroscope. Here the new prime contractor set about the creation of the Sparrow III as a derivative of the Sparrow II with semi-active radar guidance. The body was of precision-cast light alloy and accommodated, from nose to tail, the guidance package based on the novel continuous-wave semi-active radar homing system, the autopilot and the motors for the cruciform arrangement of moving control wings, the blast/fragmentation warhead behind the wings, and the Aerojet rocket motor whose solid propellant was not cast integrally with the case. This created the AAM-N-6 Sparrow III that entered service during 1958 on the F3H-3M Demon and became the AIM-7C in 1962. This initial Sparrow III had the same dimensions as its later derivatives, but weighed 380lb (172.4kg) and was capable of reaching a range of 25 miles (40km). The missile was designed for the medium-range engagement of non-manoeuvring targets.

Initially accepted for service with the US Navy as the AAM-N-6A Sparrow III and with the USAF as the AIM-101 Sparrow III before both models received the revised designation AIM-7D in 1962, this was an improved version of the AAM-N-6 with a Thiokol (Reaction Motors) pre-packaged liquid-propellant rocket motor that raised weight to 440lb (200kg).

Introduced in 1962 as the AAM-N-6B Sparrow III, the AIM-7E was the first member of the Sparrow family to enter large-scale production: 25,000 missiles were built, and the variant remains in limited service with several important fighter types. The type is powered by a Rocketdyne Mk 38 Model 2 (later Aerojet Mk 52) single-stage rocket motor for a burn-out speed of Mach 3.7 and range of 28 miles (44km), and weighs 452lb (205kg) with its revised 66lb (29.9kg) continuous rod blast/fragmentation warhead whose casing breaks into some 2,600 fragments on detonation. The weapon uses Raytheon continuous-wave semi-active radar guidance matched to a number of radars such as the Rockwell R21G/H (Aeritalia F-104S), APQ-72, APQ-100, APQ-109, APQ-120 and APG-59 (F-4 Phantom II) and AWG-9 (Grumman F-14 Tomcat). This variant was also built in Japan by Mitsubishi as the AIM-7EJ Sparrow III and in Italy by Selenia, and a limited-production

The latest Hughes air-to-air missile is the AIM-120 advanced medium-range air-to-air missile (AMRAAM), which was designed to provide the same range and lethality as the AIM-7 Sparrow air-to-air missile, with semi-active radar guidance in a package of little more than the size of the AIM-9 Sidewinder short-range air-to-air missile, together with advanced features such as a combination of inertial and active radar guidance for the mid-course and terminal phases of the flight respectively.

shorter-range and more manoeuvrable version was produced in the USA as the AIM-7E2 Sparrow III.

This last version was developed in response to a requirement that became apparent in the Vietnam War, in which US fighters were seldom able to use the long-range AIM-7E because of the political ban on firing missiles against aircraft that had not been identified visually; on the few occasions when pilots were able to fire their early-generation Sparrow IIIs, they found these initial models to be virtually useless against manoeuvring targets at shorter ranges. The AIM-7E2 was therefore developed with a reduced minimum range and enhanced manoeuvrability, the latter being provided by higher-powered hydraulic controls for its cruciform of moving wings; the opportunity was also taken to provide aerodynamic surfaces that could be plugged in rather than attached with the aid of special tools. The definitive version still in limited and declining service is the AIM-7E3 Sparrow III, which is a conversion of the AIM-7E2 with improved reliability and greater target-sensing capability. Further refined models, thought to remain in only very limited service up to the early 1990s, were the AIM-7E4 Sparrow III and AIM-7E6 Sparrow III.

The AIM-7F Sparrow III is a redesigned version for use on the McDonnell Douglas F-15 Eagle and now carried also by the McDonnell Douglas F/A-18 Hornet. The variant was introduced in 1977, and was built by Raytheon with the Pomona Division of General Dynamics (now Hughes Missile Systems) brought into the programme as the second-source manufacturer. Whereas the AIM-7E has the forward part of its body filled with guidance equipment (homing head and autopilot) and the rear part aft of the wings occupied by a comparatively small warhead and a short rocket motor, the AIM-7F uses the advantages of more compact solid-state electronics to reduce guidance package volume by some 40 per cent, allowing a larger warhead to be incorporated in the space vacated in front of the wings, and a longer motor to be used in the whole of the portion aft of the wings. The variant therefore has a much larger engagement envelope through the adoption of solid-state electronics and a Mk 58 or Mk 65 dual-thrust rocket motor for a range of 62 miles (100km). The AIM-7F is dimensionally identical with the AIM-7E, but weighs 503lb (228kg) and has

Built in larger numbers than any other missile and over a longer production period, the AIM-9 Sidewinder is still the most important short-range air-to-air missile in the inventory of the USA and its allies. The type was initially limited to basic pursuit-course engagements at very short ranges and under ideal optical conditions, but has since been developed into a considerably more versatile weapon with an all-aspect engagement capability together with longer range and considerable dogfighting agility for the tackling of manoeuvring targets.

an 88lb (39.9kg) Mk 71 continuous rod blast/fragmentation warhead. The use of continuous-wave and pulse-Doppler guidance with a conical-scan slotted antenna considerably enhances 'look-down/shoot-down' capability, even at the longer ranges possible with the variant, and the AIM-7F also possesses superior ECM resistance.

Introduced in 1982 as an interim type pending availability of the Hughes AIM-120 advanced medium-range AAM (AMRAAM), the AIM-7M Sparrow III has a new digital monopulse seeker that was selected in preference to a General Dynamics seeker developed initially for the Standard 2 naval SAM. The chosen seeker offers performance comparable with the Marconi unit in the British Sky Flash derivative, especially in the longer-range look-down/shoot-down mode. The variant also offers other electronic and engineering improvements to bring down production cost while enhancing reliability and performance at low altitude and in ECM environments.

Developed in the late 1980s by Raytheon, the AIM-7P Sparrow III is the latest evolution of the basic Sparrow III AAM. Few details of the programme have been released, but it is known that the development is centred on electronic rather than aerodynamic or powerplant features, and is based on improved guidance electronics, a new fuse, an onboard computer using very high speed integrated circuit (VHSIC) technology for twice the data capacity and handling speed of the current model, and the ability to receive mid-course guidance updates from the launch warplane. The AIM-7P entered service in 1992, and possesses the same dimensions, weights and performance as the AIM-7M.

In 1991 a contract was issued to Iriss (a joint-venture company created by Raytheon and General Dynamics) for the development of an IR seeker suitable for installation in the Sparrow III AAM and the RIM-67A Standard 2 SAM, providing these two weapons with a passive homing system as an alternative to their semi-active radar homing system. The practical result of this programme is the AIM-7R Sparrow III, which has, on the tip of its semi-active radar antenna's radome, an IR seeker derived from that of the AIM-9 Sidewinder. This additional seeker unit is cooled by compressed gas carried in the body of the missile. On launch, the missile activates the IR seeker to undertake its standard search routine: if the IR seeker acquires and locks onto a target, the rest of the engagement is flown with IR guidance; if the IR seeker fails to acquire or lock onto a target, or if target lock is subsequently lost, the semi-active radar guidance package is activated and assumes the primary guidance role unless the reactivated IR seeker again acquires the target. The AIM-7R is scheduled to enter service later in the current decade, and possesses the same dimensions, weights and performance as the AIM-7M.

The short-range partner to the medium-range AIM-7 Sparrow has been the AIM-9 Sidewinder, a truly remarkable weapon designed under the aegis of the US Navy and built to the extent of 200,000 or more examples in a programme that is still witnessing the active development of this seminally important type. Convinced that one of the keys to air-combat success with jet-powered fighters would be the replacement of the four standard 20mm cannon by the fully guided missile, the US Navy decided in the late 1940s to set in hand, at one of its own establishments, the creation of a simple AAM. The establishment selected was the Naval Ordnance Test Station (later Naval Weapons Center) at China Lake, California, and in 1949 work started on a novel weapon that would be cheap to make, simple to use but wholly effective in operation.

The success of the NOTS team is attested by the fact that its missile is still in development well as production and service, and has been built in larger numbers than any other AAM in history, with the possible exception of the R-3 (AA-2 'Atoll'), a Soviet weapon that was developed from the American weapon. The NOTS team decided to base its design on a body fabricated from aluminium tubing with a diameter of only 5in (0.127m), and carrying a passive seeker working on IR principles. NOTS developed the basic concept for this IR seeker despite the difficulties of installing vacuum-tube electronics in so slender a body, and in 1951 Philco (later Philco-Ford) was awarded the contract to develop this basic research into a practical seeker unit for the missile's production models. From front to rear, the missile carried the seeker head and associated guidance package, the cruciform of moving control fins, the annular blast/fragmentation warhead, the solid-propellant rocket motor and, round the motor's exhaust, a cruciform of fixed fins indexed in line with the control fins. The tip of each fixed fin's trailing edge carried a slipstream-driven 'rolleron' whose gyroscopic action helped to stabilize the missile in flight.

The missile's powerplant was designed by the Naval Propellant Plant but built for production weapons by Hercules, Hunter-Douglas and Norris-Thermador: this unit boosted the missile to Mach 2.5 in its burn time of 2.2 seconds. The seeker was based on an uncooled lead sulphide sensor with a target-acquisition angle of 25 degrees, a seeker field of vision of 4 degrees and a tracking rate of 11 degrees per second, and trials (from the first fully guided test firing in September 1953) confirmed that the seeker and guidance package could indeed produce a 70 per cent single-shot kill probability. The trials also confirmed, however, that this percentage could only be achieved in a high-altitude pursuit engagement in good optical conditions, and that the percentage fell dramatically at lower altitudes, in poor optical conditions (including cloud and rain), and whenever the seeker was offered the chance to lock onto tempting alternative targets such as the sun, bright sky or even reflections in lakes and rivers. Even so, the Sidewinder was clearly a usable weapon by the standards of the day, and it was obvious that the basic concept had only just started to explore the capabilities inherent in the new technology embodied in its seeker. The utility of the Sidewinder was increased by its light weight, basic simplicity (it was claimed that the weapon carried less than 25 moving parts) and independence from any targeting system other than the pilot's eyes. This meant that virtually any fighter capable of lifting the weapon as an external load could be equipped with the Sidewinder.

All the pilot had to do was acquire a target optically, fly straight towards it until his fighter was within launch range, activate the missile, listen in his headset as the low-pitched growl of the seeker rose to a high-pitched whine indicating that the target had been acquired by the seeker and locked into the missile's seeker/guidance system, and then launched the weapon. The missile was thus a fire-and-forget weapon, and this had the important tactical advantage of permitting the pilot to turn his fighter away from the target as soon as a missile had been launched.

Designed for the abortive General Dynamics F-111B swing-wing naval fighter, the Hughes AIM-54 Phoenix long-range AAM was brought to fruition (together with its associated Hughes AWG-9 pulse-Doppler radar fire-control system) in the Grumman F-14 Tomcat fleet-defence fighter. In 1957 the US Navy had issued a request for proposals for a new fighter/missile combination that would provide its carrier battle groups with the aerial means to carry "the entire burden of effecting the interception" of inbound hostile warplanes at long range from their American targets. The warplane designed to meet this need was the Douglas F6D Missileer, which was planned as a completely subsonic launch platform for six long-range AAMs. The sole function of the Missileer was to patrol at an altitude of

Seen here in prototype form, the Hughes AIM-54 is the Western world's longest-ranged air-to-air missile, and is a truly formidable weapon providing the Northrop Grumman F-14 Tomcat carrierborne fighters of the US Navy with the ability to deal with nuclear-armed aircraft and even missiles at significant range from the carrier battle group under threat.

35,000ft (10,670m) and at a radius of 150 miles (241km) from its parent carrier, and use its powerful Westinghouse APQ-81 track-while-scan radar to detect and track hostile warplanes at the maximum possible range, and then launch the requisite number of AAMs to home on the targets using their own active radar guidance.

The missile selected for development was the Grumman/Bendix AAM-N-10 Eagle, at that time the largest AAM planned anywhere in the world. The missile was based on a two-stage layout at a maximum weight of 1,284lb (582kg) and an overall length of 16ft 1.5in (4.91m), and was designed to cruise at Mach 4 over a maximum range of 127 miles (204km).

There was considerable political antipathy to a 'fighter' as slow as the Missileer, however, and the fact that the warplane was a launch platform rather than a fighter was not allowed to intervene in the December 1960 decision to cancel the Missileer. The Eagle programme was allowed to continued for a short while to provide technical data for the new missile that was now needed, and which would be carried by the F-111B selected in place of the Missileer. The new AAM was required to match the AWG-9 pulse-Doppler radar and associated fire-control system (derived from the ASQ-18 system of the Lockheed YF-12A experimental fighter), which was intended to detect targets under look-down conditions at a range of more than 150 miles (241 km). Another AAM of the period was the Hughes GAR-9 (AIM-47A from 1962), designed as a radical development of the Falcon series to arm the USAF's North American F-108 Rapier Mach 3 interceptor: this warplane was cancelled, but the GAR-9 was carried on an experimental basis by the YF-12A.

Hughes began work on its AAM-N-11 naval missile contender in 1960, and was able to draw on data from the AAM-N-10 and GAR-9 programmes.

The design team decided to retain the classic aerodynamics of Hughes' earlier AAMs: a substantial body therefore carried on its rear portion a cruciform of low-aspect-ratio delta wings trailed by rectangular control surfaces indexed in line with the wings. The considerable body diameter allowed the use of a wide planar-array radar antenna behind the nose radome, and also provided volume for the missile's other primary components which were, from front to rear, the electronics (radar, guidance package and radar proximity fuse system), the large warhead, the solid-propellant rocket and, round this motor's nozzle, the autopilot and hydraulically powered actuators for the control surfaces.

By then redesignated AIM-54 Phoenix, the missile made its first test flight in 1965 and soon proved itself to possess exceptional capabilities. The standard flight profile flown by the Phoenix starts with a post-launch climb to a peak altitude of 81,400ft (24,810m), where the missile cruises under control of the onboard autopilot with guidance of the semi-active type using reflections from the target of the radar in the launch warplane's AWG-9 system. This high-altitude cruise maximises range by reducing drag and providing the rocket motor with optimum operating conditions, and as the missile finally dives down to the attack the energy potential of the cruise altitude is converted into kinetic energy for greater manoeuvrability in the terminal phase of the flight. The missile's radar switches to the active mode for the final 20,000yds (18,290m) of the attack, the availability of three fusing modes offering maximum target-destruction capability.

The Phoenix entered service in 1974 as the AIM-54A, and notable features of the missile and fire-control combination include exceptional range, and the ability to engage six targets simultaneously (using a time-share system so that the AWG-9 can control the missiles, which can lose touch with the radar for 14 seconds before failing to re-acquire the designated target) regardless of weather conditions and target aspect. Production continued up to 1980, by which time some 2,566 AIM-54A and AIM-54B rounds had been made.

The AIM-54B Phoenix version entered production in late 1977, and is in essence a product-improved AIM-54A with sheet-metal rather than honeycomb aerodynamic surfaces, non-liquid hydraulic and thermal-conditioning systems, and a degree of simplified engineering to ease production.

Developed from 1977 and introduced to production and service in 1982 and 1985 respectively, the AIM-54C Phoenix is a considerably improved missile with digital rather than analogue electronics, a new Nortronics strapdown inertial reference unit, solid-state radar, eight internal rather than four semi-external radar proximity fuse antennae, and more-capable electronic counter-countermeasures (ECCM). This variant weighs 1,008lb (457kg), and its other data include a speed of Mach 5 and a ceiling of more than 100,000ft (30,490m). As with the AIM-54A, legend range has been considerably exceeded in service, especially when the F-14 launch warplane is supported by a Grumman E-2C Hawkeye airborne early warning and control system platform.

Developed under the designation AIM-54C (Sealed), the AIM-54C+ Phoenix is the definitive AIM-54 variant for the F-14D variant of the Tomcat fighter. The new model has a self-contained closed-cycle cooling system (to obviate some of the aerodynamic restrictions imposed on earlier variants by

The AIM-7 Sparrow air-to-air missile was the most important of the American-designed missiles used between the 1960s and mid-1980s for the medium-range role, and was designed to provide fighters such as the McDonnell Douglas F-4 Phantom with the ability to tackle targets under beyond visual range (BVR) conditions. These are examples of the AIM-7F variant.

aerodynamic heating) and improved ECCM capability. Production of the AIM-54C ended in 1993 after the delivery of some 2,000 missiles.

Currently one of the most important American air-launched weapons, the Hughes AIM-120 AMRAAM resulted from the US forces' appreciation by the mid-1970s that the Raytheon AIM-7F Sparrow III medium-range AAM was obsolescent in its intended role of BVR (beyond visual range) engagements of high-value targets. As the two primary warplane-operating services, the USAF and US Navy decided that it made technical as well as financial sense to combine their needs into a requirement for a single type that was interchangeable not only with the Sparrow III but also with the smaller and lighter Ford/Raytheon AIM-9 Sidewinder. The requirement called for an advanced weapon providing considerably higher performance and lethality than any conceivable Sparrow III development, within the context of an aerodynamic and structural package that was also to be cheaper, more reliable, smaller and lighter than the Sparrow III.

Although the new missile was required to replace the Sparrow III on existing fighters, it was also planned with later warplanes in mind. These fighters would be fitted with advanced pulse-Doppler radar equipments using prtogrammeable signal processors for the type of beam sharpening that can provide active but accurate target detection at long range, and also with IR sensors for passive but less accurate target detection at slightly shorter ranges. This opened the way for the AAM to be launched at the upper end of the medium-range bracket without any lock onto the target.

The engagement sequence therefore calls for the pilot of the launch warplane to acquire and track the target, an onboard computer meanwhile calculating the launch acceptability zones and displaying this information to the pilot. The pilot then decides to launch a missile, and inertial reference data on the launch warplane and the target are then loaded into the missile's computer to provide initial navigation information. Once it has been fired, the missile flies the mid-course phase of its flight under control of its strapdown INS, using both the guidance laws stored in its own computer and reference data supplied from the launch warplane's computer to fly the missile to the three-dimensional point previously calculated to put the missile in active seeker range of its target. During this phase of the missile's flight, the pilot of the launch warplane continues to track the target until the moment the missile's active seeker is activated, and he is then free to break away. Once its active seeker has been turned on, the missile acquires and tracks the target, the onboard computer controlling the terminal phase of the flight. As the missile acquires its target with its own active seeker (which also has a 'home-on-jam' mode), only in the last stage of its high-speed flight, the target thus receives minimal warning of the impending attack and has very little time to counter its attacker.

Five industrial groupings competed for the AMRAAM's development contract, but by February 1979 these had been reduced to two, and in late 1981 Hughes was selected as winner over Raytheon. Hughes was contracted to build 94 test missiles with options for another 924 initial-production weapons at the beginning of a programme planned to total at least 20,000 missiles produced by Hughes and a second-source manufacturer, as which Raytheon was later selected. The programme was seen as complementary to that being considered for an advanced short-range air-to-air missile (ASRAAM) to succeed the Ford AIM-9 Sidewinder. Both efforts were understood to have NATO applications, and during August 1980 the UK, USA and West Germany signed a memorandum of understanding for the USA to develop the AMRAAM while the two European countries concentrated on the collaborative development of the ASRAAM. The whole AMRAAM project, which envisaged a missile with size and weight little more than that of the Sidewinder, and with capabilities and performance better than those of the larger Sparrow, was bedevilled during its development period by technical problems, slipping schedules, cost overruns and political antipathy, while pilot production missiles revealed an unacceptably low level of reliability and maintainability.

Thus it was only in 1992 that the AIM-120A finally entered full-scale production within the context of a programme that envisaged the delivery of 13,000 or more missiles for the USAF and US Navy, which accepted the type in 1991 and 1993 respectively.

The missile deviates from the basic configuration used in all previous missiles from the Hughes stable, for it resembles the Sparrow III in its layout: a slender body carries the radar and associated guidance system in its forward portion, the central and rear portions are occupied by the warhead and rocket motor, and the flying surfaces comprise a mid-set cruciform of fixed delta wings and, indexed in line with these surfaces, a cruciform of cropped delta moving tail fins.

With most of its technical problems solved, the AMRAAM offers far greater lethality than even the AIM-7M/P/R variants of the Sparrow III, and among its other advantages are increased speed and range, reduced smoke emission, superior guidance and ECCM capabilities, a more potent warhead with a more effective fusing system, and the ability to be installed on hardpoints previously capable of accepting only the lightweight Sidewinder. US production of the AIM-120A ended in December 1994 after delivery of some 4,000 such missiles.

Entering production in 1994, the AIM-120B AMRAAM is a development of the AIM-120A with a more advanced active radar guidance package incorporating a reprogrammeable signal processor that considerably enhances the missile's tactical versatility. Designed from 1993 and due to enter service in 1997, the AIM-120C AMRAAM further-enhanced missile is the result of Phase 1 of the AMRAAM P3I (Pre-Planned Product Improvement) programme, and its two major differences from the AIM-120A/B are flying surfaces of reduced span to allow internal carriage by the Lockheed Martin/Boeing F-22 Rapier advanced tactical fighter, and an ECCM subsystem that can be reprogrammed for greater operational flexibility in the face of any evolving threat. The Phase 2 development is later expected to add an aimable warhead, an improved fuse, and an updated safety and arming unit, while the Phase 3 development planned for the longer term could include propulsion by a rocket/ramjet unit installed in a body of composite construction for greater speed and range.

The United States also leads the field in SAMs, and a brief survey of some of that country's most important weapons indicates the 'current state of the art' in shoulder-launched short-range and land-mobile medium-range weapons, with a British

The FIM-43 Redeye was the world's first operational shoulder-launched surface-to-air missile. It is therefore of seminal importance in the development of weapons to provide infantry units with a measure of organic capability against attack aircraft of both the fixed- and rotary-wing types. As might be expected of a first-generation weapon of this type, the weapon was decidedly limited in capability; being limited to pursuit-course interceptions, to engage targets only after they that delivered their ordnance and were departing the scene.

system serving as a good example of the type of battlefield weapon currently in service for tasks such as defence against attack helicopters.

When it entered service in 1964, the General Dynamics FIM-43 Redeye provided the US forces with a new breed of air-defence weapon, as it was the world's first man-portable SAM system to reach operational status, and the Redeye was produced in substantial numbers. Yet it was clear from the type's infancy in service that the weapon possessed severe tactical limitations: the operating frequency of its IR seeker was matched to hot metal (in fact the temperature of a typical jetpipe), and its performance in speed and range was low. This meant that the Redeye was limited to the pursuit-course engagement of warplanes that had already delivered their weapons, while the missile's indifferent flight performance meant that successful interception of all but slow and non-manoeuvring targets was very unlikely. Throughout the 1960s, General Dynamics' Pomona Division worked closely with the US Army and US Marine Corps in formulating the tactical and technical specification for a 'Redeye II' missile system, and then in evolving the technologies required for this considerably improved weapon. Naturally enough, the requirement was centred on a radically improved seeker unit offering a virtually total all-aspect engagement capability, and on a superior rocket motor for considerably enhanced performance so that pursuit-course engagements of high-performance warplanes could be undertaken.

By the early 1970s it was believed that the technology had matured adequately for development of the 'Redeye II' to begin. By this time the missile was sufficiently different from the original Redeye and received a wholly different designation, and when General Dynamics was awarded a full engineering development contract in July 1972, the missile became the FIM-92 Stinger. The primary design features of the Stinger were the new Atlantic Research dual-thrust rocket motor, using advanced propellants to ensure performance levels appreciably higher than those of the Redeye despite the Stinger's greater weight, and the considerably more capable IR seeker, with a frequency matched to that of the exhaust plume rather than hot metal. This latter feature offered a significantly expanded acquisition envelope, the only genuinely 'dead' spot being the head-on angle. Other major and important improvements over the Redeye were the incorporation of an integral identification friend or foe (IFF) system (to allow launch before positive visual identification of high-performance targets) and greater resistance to countermeasures of the electronic and IR varieties.

The Stinger emerged as a slim weapon based on a cylindrical body with an untapered nose section and tapered tail section. The former has a hemispherical nose transparency over the seeker, followed by the fuse system, guidance and control electronics (from which the cruciform of rectangular control surfaces springs out as the missile leaves its launch tube), and warhead that terminates in the rocket nozzle and modestly swept cruciform of fixed fins indexed in line with the control surfaces.

Like the Redeye, the Stinger is delivered as a certified round of ammunition in its own container/launcher. This allows the missile to be transported in a manner least likely to result in physical damage, and keeps the weapon under optimum humidity conditions to prevent electronic damage. The missile is further protected by use of a carrying container for the complete system (containerised missile, gripstock assembly, IFF unit, and battery/coolant unit). In action the containerised missile, the firing unit/gripstock, IFF subsystem and battery/coolant unit have merely to be joined together in a process that completes all the electrical connections required. The operator then acquires his target visually in the system's open sight, which projects upwards and to the left from the gripstock to a point in front of the operator's right eye, and interrogates it with his belt-mounted IFF subsystem (claimed to be the smallest such unit in the world) whose antennae are plate-like units to the right of the gripstock.

If an unacceptable IFF response is received, the operator then activates the Stinger system: the battery powers the gyro and electronics, and the coolant chills the seeker to produce the greatest possible temperature differential. On receiving an aural system that the Stinger's seeker has locked onto the target, the operator uses his trigger to fire the missile. The booster stage pops the missile out of the launcher tube, and the sustainer ignites only when the missile has coasted far enough ahead of the operator to avoid any possibility of the sustainer burning him. Thereafter the engagement is automatic, the missile's guidance electronics using proportional navigation laws to home on the target, special circuitry modifying the steering command to make the missile hit the aircraft rather than its exhaust plume. The operator discards the spent container and fits a fresh round.

The Stinger was first test-fired in 1974. Early trials confirmed that the missile possessed the required performance, but that the seeker unit left much to be required in accuracy and reliability. Initial attempts to rectify these limitations were generally unsuccessful, a fact highlighted by the US Army's urgent contract with Ford Aerospace for an Alternate Stinger with laser beam-riding guidance: the laser was built into the launcher unit, requiring the operator to keep his sight on the target until the missile impacted.

In August 1976 an Alternate Stinger successfully engaged a supersonic target, but by this time progress was finally being made with the IR Stinger, allowing production to begin in the late 1970s. The weapon was finally introduced in 1981 as the FIM-92A Stinger, and has proved generally successful. The missile and launcher weigh 30lb (13.6kg), or 33.3lb (15.1kg) with the IFF system and battery. The early problems have been fully overcome, and the Stinger has been widely accepted.

Experience soon showed, however, that the Stinger has the same vulnerability as the Redeye to IR countermeasures (IRCM). This led to the development from 1977 of the more advanced FIM-92B Stinger-POST, which is currently in production, and features a passive optical scanning technique (POST) seeker with cells sensitive to UV as well as IR radiation: this image-scan optical processing system (in place of the Stinger's reticle and discrete components) uses a microprocessor to compare the two types of return and thus provides better discrimination between the target and decoys, and also between the target and the ground in low-altitude engagements. The basic shoulder-launched Stinger provides the USA and its allies with a capable man-portable SAM whose main tactical limitations are both to deal with targets at medium altitudes and an inability to engage targets flying lower than the launcher. The latter translates into the impossibility of hilltop Stinger positions to fire down onto fixed- and rotary-wing warplanes operating in valleys.

One of the most important land-mobile SAMs yet to have appeared, the BAe Rapier was conceived in the early 1960s as a point-defence weapon to provide battlefield formations with the capability of destroying all types of attack warplanes (in the performance bracket from hovering helicopters to terrain-following supersonic fixed-wing machines) at ranges greater than those of the attackers' stand-off weapons. The origins of the programme lay with an army requirement for a point-defence missile, originally to have been the PT428. By 1962 it was clear that this would be too expensive a

Successor to the Redeye, the FIM-92 Stinger is an altogether more capable surface-to-air missile of the man-portable type, and included in its capabilities are the ability to engage oncoming aircraft. This gives the infantryman a chance to destroy an attacking warplane before it had dropped its weapons.

system, however, so the army decided to adopt the Mauler being developed for the US Army by the Pomona Division of Convair. However, this system was plagued by development problems and would also be very expensive, so in 1963 the army decided once more on a British system.

The Guided Weapons Division of the British Aircraft Corporation (later British Aerospace Dynamics Group and now the British Aerospace Army Weapons Division) had been working on a private-venture system called Sightline since 1961, and this formed the basis for the ET316 proposal of September 1964. The resultant development programme was a model of its kind, and key features of the missile were supersonic performance combined with great accuracy: the former was designed to maximise the missile's kinetic energy and reduce the time available for the target to implement any sort of countermeasures, and the latter to make possible the carriage of a very small warhead. This is of the semi-armour-piercing type that achieves its destructive effect by actual penetration of the target before detonation in the confined and vulnerable spaces inside the target structure.

Although severe doubts were expressed in some quarters about the tactical utility of a weapon with so small a warhead containing only 1.1lb (0.5kg) of explosive, the Rapier's warhead has proved more than adequate in service. Indeed, so great is the missile's accuracy that the general term 'hittile' was coined for the Rapier: the degree of accuracy is attested by the fact that in one test firing the missile pierced a towed target only 7.5in (0.19m) in diameter. Another advantage is the elimination of a costly proximity fuse, allowing the missile to be used against very-low-level targets without fear of the premature detonation that can be induced in proximity fuses by ground returns. This latter capability has been proved by test firings against ground targets to meet US Army requirements: an Alvis Saracen armoured personnel carrier was hit in the turret, the following explosion blew off the turret and otherwise devastated the vehicle.

Thus the BAC decision was for a smaller, lighter and cheaper weapon than the contemporary generation of larger missiles possessing comparable performance, and this has been a useful asset in the Rapier's undoubted commercial success. Test firings began in 1965 (the year in which the US Mauler system was cancelled) and were almost universally successful. Production contracts for the British army and RAF Regiment were issued in 1968, and the Rapier Mk 1 entered service in 1971 for an initial operational capability in 1973. Since that time the missile has been built in large numbers and has been integrated into a number of increasingly sophisticated overall systems. The Rapier has been blooded in combat, and during the Falklands War of 1982 was credited with the confirmed destruction of 14 Argentine warplanes and with the probable destruction of another six. The Rapier system has demonstrated an average single-shot kill probability of more than 70 per cent, this percentage rising markedly in salvo engagements of a single target.

In configuration the Rapier adheres to the basic design philosophy of BAe surface-launched missiles: the body is cylindrical (with a slim tapered nose) and carries on the mid-body section a cruciform of low-aspect-ratio delta wings and at the tail a cruciform of high-aspect-ratio control fins, which are indexed in line with the wings and activated by powerful gas generators for rapid and accurate control response at low level: throughout its life the Rapier has provided constant proof of its agility to pull high-g turns at all ranges against manoeuvring and fast-crossing targets.

The basic Rapier system introduced in 1971 is the Towed Rapier, and this comprises the four-round launcher plus surveillance radar and associated Cossor IFF subsystem on a two-wheel trailer for towing by any light cross-

country vehicle such as a Land Rover, the Barr & Stroud optical tracker, a secondary sight, a tactical control unit and a generator (all carried by the towing vehicle), and nine reload missiles carried in a second vehicle. The towing vehicle carries the basic crew of two, while the second vehicle accommodates three personnel. It requires three people to deploy the Towed Rapier system (a task taking about 15 minutes and requiring the interconnection by cable of the various components spread out within a circle with a diameter of 100ft/30.5m) and two people to reload missiles. Although one person can then operate the system in simple conditions, it is more common for the operator to be supported by a tactical controller when there is a mix of friendly and hostile warplanes in the area, or in conditions of severe ECM. Once in position, the Rapier fire unit (launcher) is levelled on four jacks and its wheels are removed, while the operator sets the parameters of the 'taboo' facility which prevents the firing of a missile on bearings and elevations obstructed by physical items such as buildings, hills or woods. The operator can also use an engagement zone selector to create closed arcs of fire: warplanes appearing in any of these arcs are signalled by a visual signal rather than the standard aural warning, and while no target can be engaged in such a preselected closed arc, a target engaged outside such an arc can be followed into it by an intercepting missile. The four ready-use missiles carried on the fire unit's towing vehicle are removed from their containers, in which they are treated as no-maintenance rounds of ammunition, and loaded onto the launcher's four rails, which can be elevated through an arc of 65 degrees (between –5 degrees and +60 degrees) and are disposed as a vertical pair on each side of the central pedestal, which can be traversed through 360 degrees.

Once the system is in position and the missiles have been loaded onto their rails, the Racal-Decca surveillance radar is switched on. This is mounted in the large cylindrical pedestal of the fire unit, and its antenna completes one turn every second, ensuring surveillance through 360 degrees out to a range of 13,000yds (11,885m). The radar is a coherent pulse-Doppler equipment and can detect warplanes between ground level and 10,000ft (3,050m). If a possible target is detected, the system automatically IFFs it before alerting the operator: if the echo proves to be friendly, the preliminary data are wiped out and the radar goes back to its search; but if the echo proves to be hostile, the radar and fire unit's onboard computer begin the solution of the resultant fire-control problem while alerting the operator with an aural signal and slewing the launcher and the operator's optical tracker to the correct bearing. The operator then acquires and tracks the target using a small control column, whose movements are outputted from the tracker to the fire unit. The operator is automatically informed when the target is within the system's launch parameters, and then fires a missile. The reaction time can be as little as six seconds from target detection to missile launch, which offers very useful advantages in the engagement of fast-moving targets that may pop up from behind masking terrain quite close to their intended targets. After launch the missile is rapidly gathered, the fire unit having been aligned automatically so that the missile flies into the tracker's line of sight immediately after launch. The operator uses his joystick control to keep the tracker's binocular sight fixed firmly on the target, and a TV missile tracker boresighted to the optical tracker watches the flares on the missile's tail: any angular deviations are measured, and the system's computer automatically generates the signals necessary to bring the missile back into the centre of the tracker's line of sight, and to keep it there until impact with the target. These control signals are transmitted to the missile via a Racal-Decca microwave link whose antenna is mounted on the front of the cylindrical housing for the surveillance radar.

Reaction time for a second launch against the same target, or for another target within the operator's field of vision, can be as short as three seconds after the impact of the first missile, and when all four missiles have been expended, the two-man reload crew can load another four missiles on the fire unit's rails in 2½ minutes. Its overall capabilities combine with its rapid reloading facility to give the Towed Rapier system considerable tactical importance.

Another useful feature of the Towed Rapier has been its basic design on a modular basis, and this has proved particularly advantageous in the updating of the system. Since the type entered service, such updates have been undertaken on a constant basis to keep the weapon fully abreast of developments. From the beginning of the Towed Rapier's service life, reliability in the order of 90 per cent has been the norm, and this figure has been improved usefully by the introduction of built-In test equipment and a degree of redundancy. Apart from improving reliability, these two features have a beneficial battlefield function in improving survivability and speeding the repair process for damaged equipments.

The Rapier system has also been installed in a tracked chassis for improved operational compatibility with mobile forces, and has been considerably upgraded in the basic missile as well as in the system's ancillary systems.

The Raytheon MIM-104 Patriot is a highly capable air-defence weapon designed to supplement the Raytheon MIM-23B Improved HAWK and to replace the Western Electric MIM-14B/C Nike Hercules missiles in the medium-range roles. It had become clear to the US Army as early as 1960 that the combination of the scarcely-mobile Nike Hercules and cumbersome HAWK systems would be inadequate to provide US Army combat formations with any real measure of area air-defence capability in the type of mobile warfare anticipated for the 1970s and later. From 1961, therefore, the service instituted a feasibility study under the designation FABMDS (Field Army Ballistic Missile Defence System), and this led to the AADS-70 (Army Air Defense System for the 1970s) requirement.

The basic design parameters had been settled by 1965, and the US Army Missile Command then began to undertake the hardware validation phase of the weapon, at that time designated SAM-D. By August of the same year the requirement for the missile had been finalised, calling for capability under the most adverse weather, geographic, climatic and electronic conditions against warplane targets at all altitudes, and also against SRBMs. The service's request for proposals was issued in April 1966 and elicited responses from Hughes, Raytheon and RCA, and in May 1967 Raytheon received contractual authorisation to proceed as prime contractor for the SAM-D programme. The main subcontractors were Hazeltine (IFF system), Martin Marietta (missile airframe and launcher) and Thiokol (rocket motor).

The original concept had envisaged the complete system embarked on just two M548 tracked carriers (one with the missile launcher and the other with the radar) for a high degree of battlefield mobility, but by the second half of the 1970s this had declined to a firing battery of three truck units and eight truck-towed launcher stations: the basic firing unit had thus not only increased in overall size, but had declined in mobility. It can be argued, however, that the capabilities of the Patriot system are so great that it need not keep up with the forward elements involved in a mobile campaign. For tactical operations, four or six batteries constitute a Patriot battalion, which therefore has 32 or 48 Patriot launchers as the standard battery; eight firing trailers together with the associated MPQ-53 multi-function radar. The battalion therefore has a theoretical maximum complement of 128 or 192 Patriot missiles excluding reloads, which are allocated at the rate of six per M901 firing trailer.

The missile was first test-fired in 1970 with fully guided test firings following in 1975, and is superficially an unremarkable vehicle in aerodynamic and structural terms. The body is a comparatively wide-diameter cylinder with an ogival nosecone and a rear-mounted cruciform of modestly swept control fins. Under the nosecone is the antenna for the command mid-course and semi-active radar terminal guidance systems, trailed by the control electronics, the warhead and associated fuse system, the advanced rocket motor of which no details have been released, and the high-powered actuator system for the fins, which are claimed to give this body-lift missile a degree of agility unmatched by any manned warplane.

The missile is delivered as a complete round inside a sealed transportation container that doubles as the launcher. The sealed-in missile is certified for a shelf life of five years, and a special vehicle is used to fit the four containers onto the M901 launcher. This is carried on an M860 two-axle semi-trailer towed by a 5-ton M818 6x6 tractor. The M860 is disconnected from its tractor and then levelled on four jacks before the beginning of an engagement, and has its own 20 hp (14.91kW) diesel generator for electrical power. The missile containers fit into a special frame that is traversed and elevated under command of the battery's fire-control system, the orders being relayed by secure radio data-link. The M901 launcher can be traversed through 360 degrees, but is locked in position before an engagement as the launcher does not follow the target. The firing trailer has its missile canisters at the fixed launch elevation angle of +30 degrees.

Normally four or five (but up to eight) launchers are controlled from the MSQ-104 Engagement Control Centre (ECC), giving a total of between 16 and 32 missiles (excluding reloads) per battery. Apart from the launcher reload vehicle, this is the only manned equipment in the battery, is carried in a 5.6-ton shelter on the back of an M814 6x6 truck, and accommodates the system's two operators, the digital weapon-control computer and two tactical display consoles, with power provided by the associated MQJ-20 6x6 powerplant truck, which supplies both the ECC and MPQ-53 radar from two 200hp (149kW) turbine-driven generators. The ECC's 24-bit high-speed digital computer is extremely capable, and is a software-controlled unit with twin (optionally triple) computer/memory subunits fully capable of exercising tactical control over a whole interception sequence from radar scheduling to intercept assessment via weapon assignment, missile launch, hardware monitoring and the full spectrum of fault detection, location and

isolation. The computer provides the essential man/machine interfaces via the tactical display consoles.

The system allows several operating modes, ranging from fully automatic down to computer-aided manual interceptions, and fire-control data are supplied automatically to the relevant launcher unit via the battery's secure data-link network. The advanced software developed for the ECC's computer falls into three main groups: operational readiness, real-time control of the fire unit, and fault detection analysis. The first group brings the complete outfit to a state of readiness by loading all appropriate data into the fire-control computer and radar computers, and by the collection and storage of firing position data (antenna orientation, radar coverage limitations, blind spots and horizon contours). The second group includes functions such as control of the radar (in search, target tracking, IFF interrogation, missile acquisition and tracking, and transmission of missile-guidance commands in the mid-course and terminal phases of the flight); selection and processing of information for the operators, and implementation of operator commands; selection of missile launcher, and transmission of the appropriate laying and launch commands; communication via digital data-link with higher-level command sources as well as neighbouring Patriot batteries; and monitoring of battery status. This programme group also carries out threat evaluation and threat prioritisation, allowing anything from fully automatic to manual engagement depending on the engagement mode in operation.

The real core of the system, however, is the Raytheon MPQ-53 radar, and the significance of this equipment is attested by the fact that its manufacturer was selected as prime contractor in preference to the missile maker. Whereas the Nike Hercules and HAWK systems require four separate radar types (some of them in multiples so that one equipment can be allocated to each launcher), the Patriot system has only a single radar. This multi-function equipment provides the whole battery with surveillance, target acquisition, tracking, ranging and range rate, as well as missile tracking, command guidance and target illumination facilities: this is made possible by the advanced nature of the complete equipment, which uses computer control for the enormously complex time-sharing system that makes the system operate effectively. The radar operates with its planar antenna locked at an angle of +67.5 degrees to the horizontal. Like the launcher, the radar is installed on an M860 two-axle semi-trailer, which is unhitched from its tractor and levelled with jacks before being brought into operation. The primary elements are a shelter accommodating the bulk of the equipment's electronics, and a large planar antenna unit accommodating the separate phased-array elements for target acquisition and tracking, and missile tracking (5,161 elements in the main 8ft/2.44m main antenna). The array is also the location for the supplementary arrays associated with track-via-missile system (251 elements), and with the Hazeltine TPX-46(V)7 IFF system.

The programme was characterised by a number of innovative technologies that inevitably caused delays before they could be brought to fruition. The programme also proved considerably more expensive than first envisaged, and this resulted in the US Army's decision to stretch out the development phase as a means of reducing yearly research and development costs. In the event, full-scale engineering development did not begin until 1972, and in 1974 the stretch in the development phase was used to validate the system's unique track-via-missile (TVM) guidance method: even as the radar tracks the target and missile, the missile's own two-way data link provides the fire-control computer with up-to-the-second data about the missile's position and performance, optimising the computer's ability to shape the Patriot's trajectory for maximum range and accuracy before the activation of the missile's semi-active terminal guidance. In 1975 a series of 14 test firings yielded 12 complete successes and one partial success, resulting in a 1976 decision to press ahead with development at an accelerated rate. Further delay resulted from the 1977 decision to replace the missile's onboard analogue computer system with a new digital unit, but this delay was vindicated in 1984 by four successes in four test launches against targets operating with assorted ECM.

The Patriot is launched through the frangible cover of its container, the Thiokol rocket motor providing extremely potent acceleration and a very high maximum speed. A large proportion of the missile's weight is attributable to the solid propellants for this motor, the object being to provide high speed over long range as a means of destroying the target beyond the range of its stand-off weapons and of reducing the time available to the target for the implementation of countermeasures. The spent container is removed by the reload vehicle and a fresh round installed on the launcher. The first Patriot units were formed in 1984, and the missile became operational in 1986. Despite the length of its development programme, the Patriot is still at the very forefront of surface-to-air missile technology and capability, due largely to its excellent radar and flight performance.

Raytheon is continuing to develop the system, the prime objects being improved capability against targets using advanced ECM, tactical ballistic missiles, cruise missiles and other targets with low radar signatures. The use of software-controlled computer systems gives the Patriot great flexibility, and in 1986 a Patriot was directed with the aid of special software to the interception of a Vought MGM-52 Lance ballistic missile at a height of 26,000ft (7,925m) some 14,250yds (13,030m) down-range of the Patriot's launch position. The first firing of a Patriot Anti-Tactical Missile was undertaken in 1987, the missile successfully intercepting another Patriot, which was used because its performance and radar signature approximate those of the latest generation of tactical ballistic missiles fielded by the USSR. In 1988 the US Army completed a patriot anti-tactical ballistic missile capability 1 (PAC-1) programme to update the software of operational Patriots and to allow interception of ballistic missiles such as the SS-21 'Scarab' and SS-1 'Scud' battlefield missiles. The programme improved the search-and-track algorithms in the radar computer software to give the Patriot system the ability to intercept an incoming missile and knock it off course, but probably without destroying its warhead.

Further development was concentrated in the short term on the PAC-2 programme for a new warhead/fuse combination together with improved missile guidance algorithms. These provide a higher level of accuracy and lethality, including the ability to intercept an incoming missile at speeds between Mach 6 and Mach 8 with sufficient accuracy to destroy the missile's warhead section.

All Patriots delivered since 1989 have been of the PAC-2 type, and the basic anti-missile capabilities of the Patriot for the interception of short-range ballistic missiles were confirmed in the 1991 Gulf War. During this campaign, Patriot missiles successfully intercepted a number of 'Scud' missiles fired by the Iraqis at targets in Israel and Saudi Arabia, although the Patriot's lack of ceiling and a devastating warhead meant that large portions of the 'Scud' missiles continued on ballistic trajectories to cause some measure of damage.

Part of the MIM-104 Patriot's capabilities stem from its track-via-missile system, in which target data from the missile's active radar terminal guidance package are downloaded to the launcher system and its fire-control computer for the generation of a continuously computed intercept course whose details are data-linked to the missile as a means of shaping the trajectory, and therefore securing the double objectives of maximising range and securing an interception as far distant as possible from the warplane's objective.

The Euromissile Roland SAM system is used by a
number of NATO countries.

Glossary

ACTIVE HOMING   type of homing based on the use of an on-board target detection system using an emitter

APPLIQUÉ   type of armour that is added for extra protection over the baseline armour, and often spaced slightly from the baseline armour

BARBETTE   raised and fixed part of the superstructure carrying the fighting compartment or, in heavy tanks of the 1930s, a turret designed to fire over a smaller turret located forward of it

BATTERY   group of four or six guns (with command post, communications etc) calibrated to fire as a single weapon

BEAM riding guidance   type of guidance in which the weapon rides along the path of a beam (radar or laser) extending to the target from the launcher or other designation site

BOMB   type of shell fired by a mortar

BOMBLET   type of submunition carried by a shell or missile for the creation of a scattering effect

BREECH   rear end of barrel into which the propellant and projectile are loaded, now universally by an opening breech mechanism providing direct access to this section of the weapon

BUSTLE   overhanging rear part of the turret helping to balance the weight of the gun and generally containing radio equipment or, in later tanks, main gun ammunition and/or an automatic loader

CALIBRE   diameter of bore, and also used to express the length of the barrel in terms of L/x where the Length is expressed in multiples of the calibre (L/45, for example, describes a barrel 45 times the length of its calibre)

CARRIAGE   the wheels, axle(s), trail(s), recoil gear etc on which the barrel is mounted

CARTRIDGE   made-up charge(s) of propellant containing in bags or in a fixed metal cartridge case attached to the rear of the projectile

CEP   the Circular Error Probable is the measure of accuracy of any weapon, and is the radius of the circle into which 50% of the weapons fired are statistically likely to land

COMMAND GUIDANCE   type of guidance in which the missile is guided to the moment of impact by commands generated manually, semi-automatically or automatically at the launcher

CUPOLA raised one- or two-man position providing improved fields of vision

DETACHMENT crew of a gun

DIRECT FIRE the type of artillery fire in which the target is visible from the gun position

DISCARDING SABOT phrase used for the type of very high velocity projectile that is fired from a barrel of greater calibre than the projectile itself, the greater cross section of the barrel permitting increased propulsive affect to be applied to the projectile, which it blocked out to the calibre of the barrel by sabots that drop away as the projectile emerges from the muzzle

ELEVATION angular movement of barrel in the vertical plane to vary trajectory and thus range

EQUIPMENT word used for the whole of an artillery piece including the gun, carriage, sights, stores etc

FASCINE bundle of chain-wrapped wooden rods (or other contrivance of the same basic shape) for release into a trench or other such obstacle to fill it and so create a pathway

FIXED AMMUNITION type of ammunition in which the projectile is attached at the front of a metal case containing the propellant to speed the loading of quick-firing guns

FRAGMENTATION the breaking up of the wall of a shell to provide fragments or splinters travelling outward from the point of detonation and lethal velocity

FUSE device fitted to a shell or other explosive device to initiate the detonation of the explosive filling at the desired moment (before impact, on impact or after impact)

GLACIS downward-sloping plate of frontal armour

GUN higher-velocity weapon firing its projectile with a relatively flat trajectory

HEAT HE Anti-Tank warhead of the hollow-charge principle

HESH HE Squash Head warhead designed to spread on impact before detonation, when a sock wave is sent through the target armour to blow off lethal fragments of plate from the inside of the armour

HOLLOW CHARGE   warhead with a charge of explosive round a shaped liner, the detonation resulting in a stream of vapourised gas and metal that strikes the target armour at very high velocity and extremely high temperature to burn a hole through it

HOWITZER   lower-velocity weapon firing its projectile with a relatively high trajectory to plunge onto the target

INDIRECT FIRE   the type of artillery fire in which the target is not visible from the gun position

INERTIAL GUIDANCE   type of computer-based guidance based on accelerometers to detect any deviations from the planned trajectory

MANTLET   piece of armour protecting the open space where the main gun emerges from the turret

MONOCOQUE   type of structure in which the 'single shell' skin bears the primary structural loads, thereby removing the need for a conventional chassis

MORTAR   piece of ordnance usually mounted on a baseplate and based on a smooth-bore barrel, and generally using muzzle-loaded ammunition for high-angle fire

MUZZLE BRAKE   arrangement of baffles of similar traps at the muzzle to catch some of the propellant gases and thus reduce the recoil force

MUZZLE VELOCITY   the velocity at which a projectile leaves the muzzle of the gun

OPTRONIC HOMING   type of homing based on the use of an image of the target locked into the guidance package and sought in the view provided by the weapon's TV or imaging infra-red sensor

PASSIVE HOMING   type of homing based on the use of an on-board target detection system not using an emitter

RE-ENTRANT   spot in which armour panels slope inward to create a dangerous shot trap

SEMI-ACTIVE HOMING   type of homing based on the use of an on-board target detection system of the passive type to home on the energy of an active emitter and then reflected by the target

SHELL projectile containing explosive and therefore combining chemical with kinetic energies for its effect

SHOT solid projectile containing no explosive and securing its effect by kinetic energy alone

SKIRT ARMOUR thin plate armour for the protection of the upper and central parts of the tracks and the tank's running gear

SPALL splinters knocked off the interior of the armour by the impact of a bullet, shell or shot on the outside

SPLASH fragment of bullet entering the interior of the tank after being semi-liquefied by its impact with the rim of the opening

SPONSON position on the side of a tank for the accommodation of a gun and/or a machine-gun

TRACK SHOE individual plate connected by a hinged attachment to its neighbours to create the tank track

TRAIL long member by which the gun carriage is towed and, in firing position, in lowered to the ground to improve the weapon's stability

TRAVERSE angular movement of the barrel or complete piece of artillery in the horizontal plane

TURRET revolving unit carrying the tank's main armament, fighting crew and often part of the secondary armament in the form of a co-axial machine-gun and/or an overhead machine-gun

Index